Landscapes & Cycles

An Environmentalist's Journey to Climate Skepticism

Landscapes & Cycles

An Environmentalist's Journey to Climate Skepticism

Jim Steele

ISBN: 1490 390189
ISBN-13: 978-1490 390185

DEDICATION

To the Sierra Nevada wilderness, where one always feels humbled by its
magnificence without ever feeling small.

And to all my students. You taught me more about life than you will ever know.

CONTENTS

ACKNOWLEDGMENTS

Cover photograph Sierra Buttes, Sierra Co. by Darby Hayes

Illustrations by Mike Shepard

Editorial assistance from Don Weldon, Mary Claire Neumann, and Katy German

I greatly appreciate the discussions and helpful comments from Dr. James Kelley, Dr. Paul Opler, Kristen DeAndreis, Bob DeAndreis, Patty Harmon, Jared Steele, Paul Jones and Ginger Vagenas.

landscapesandcycles@earthlink.net

Foreword

These days there seems to be an underlying assumption about climate—that it should not change, and if it does, something unnatural must be going on. To those of us who have devoted our lives to the study of the Earth Sciences, this is a curious notion indeed. We have to wonder where it came from. Nearly everything we know about the history of the planet is based on the fact that climate changes. Biological evolution and adaptation is driven by changes in the environment. If the entire geological record represented a history of unchanging climate, it would be impossible to interpret.

Climate change is a complex and highly nuanced phenomenon, but the subject has been hijacked by politicians and media pundits and represented as a simple response to a single variable—carbon dioxide. Please believe me when I say that, based upon a lifetime of work in the Earth Sciences, "Nothing in Nature is that simple."

In this book, Jim Steele addresses a number of these complexities. As a biologist, he is able to also address the subtleties of biological responses to climate change. The Earth's biosphere has experienced several mass extinction events in the geological past, at least one of which was caused by a catastrophic extraterrestrial event. Had we been around 65 million years ago when the Chicxulub asteroid hit the Yucatán peninsula and wiped out the dinosaurs, we might have been excused for saying, "The sky is falling!" Today's news is filled with so much hyperbole and alarmism that it is little wonder that people are misinformed and anxious.

Reading Jim Steele's book should help put the important scientific facts in perspective and relieve the anxiety. Jim explains the extent of our scientific understanding carefully and in a way that most readers can easily understand. The book is a thoughtful presentation of the state of our knowledge based upon measurements made on the phenomena themselves, rather than on computer models of those phenomena. It provides a reasoned interpretation of the nature of the climate change that is actually occurring and how it is affecting the biosphere. It is a welcome contribution because instead of focusing on nebulous global average measurements, it grounds our understanding of climate change in the all-important context of the local environment. As Jim points out, "Although it is wise to think globally, all wildlife reacts locally."

San Francisco State University, where Jim Steele and I worked together, is an extremely diverse urban university. Many of our students come from backgrounds where there may not be many or any local role models in the sciences. We need to show them not only what science is, but that there are people—just like them—who are successfully pursuing careers in our disciplines. In fields which involve the study of the physical and biological environments of our planet, this means introducing these students to natural environmental systems. The first step is to take them out of their urban surroundings and into the field. San Francisco State University operates a science field campus in the Sierra Nevada which is a perfect setting for this sort of introduction. When we started, the facilities were badly distressed and the academic programs in need of significant improvement.

Jim Steele and I set about to correct these deficiencies because we both believe deeply in the importance of field campus experiences as a fundamental component of education in the field disciplines: geology, ecology, etc. Students must have the experience of going into the field and observing the real world directly, not as represented in a laboratory reconstruction or a computer model. Working in the field teaches us several important lessons immediately, such as the fact that we cannot control *any* of the important variables which drive the phenomenon of interest, that a short-time series of data are nearly always badly misleading and therefore almost completely useless, and that the way the important variables interact is often subtle and extremely difficult to understand.

We also learn that most well-thought-out and carefully designed field studies often fail to produce the desired results, and that only years of experience produce the kind of intuitive sense which is essential to understanding these complex natural systems. There is a saying in geology, that the best geologists are the ones who have seen the most rocks. Certainly the analogous rule for the ocean is that the best oceanographers are those who have spent the most time at sea, and for ecologists those who have examined the largest number of ecosystems.

Jim Steele and I worked closely together for many years to build a field campus which best provided the initial field experience to students, so that they could begin to appreciate how difficult it is to simply *obtain* good field data, much less to interpret and understand it. At the same time, it is important for students to understand that it is within their grasp. I always tell my students, "The most important thing to understand about science is that it is done by people—just like you." Scientists as a group are not particularly brilliant or clever or insightful people. But we are people who collectively believe in a simple principle: That if you study a phenomenon long enough and carefully enough, you can figure it out. Obviously the "long enough and carefully enough" part is the difficult and challenging aspect, but if you are willing to work hard enough and long enough and carefully enough, you can understand the phenomenon. And when you do, it so exhilarating that it keeps you going through the next series of long and difficult studies. I have watched Jim Steele for years as he has worked out the subtle changes in the Sierra Nevada ecosystems and can testify that he is a living example of how this process works.

Finally, there is the matter of philosophical and political perception of the nature of science and our approach to understanding natural phenomena. Science is based on measurement, on the careful collection of data, and upon its unbiased analysis. It does not include advocacy for or promotion of any philosophical or political position or opinion. Scientists may, of course, adopt and espouse such positions, but when they do, they are not practicing science; they are engaged in marketing. It is common to hear lay people ask scientists questions such as: "Do you believe in evolution?" or "Do you believe in global warming?" These are not questions to which there is any *scientific* response. Belief systems provide responses to these questions, but science cannot.

It is therefore fundamentally inappropriate to attack scientists who refuse to adopt one or another philosophical or political position as being anti-environmental or anti-intellectual or, especially, anti-science. Those who take the oft-heard position, "The science is settled, it's time for action" reveal their fundamental misunderstanding of the very nature of science, for in science we never claim to have completed our understanding and that it is always provisional. We need only compare our current, albeit quite incomplete understanding of the nature of our planet's natural systems, with the 19th century conceit which held that all the important scientific questions had been answered and that all that remained was to fill in a few remaining details. The worst possible action for any scientist would be to simply accept a prevailing political position as the final word on any scientific issue. We are taught throughout our careers to be skeptical and to question the prevailing paradigms in our disciplines. We can be quite sure that, however generally and passionately they are held, they are almost certainly incorrect or incomplete. It is well to remember Bertrand Russell's admonition, "Even when all the experts agree, they may well be mistaken." All that being said, scientific understanding is still by far the best way to understand our world and the behavior of its systems.

This book by Jim Steele will help the reader understand how climate change works. It is based on a lifetime spent educating students from elementary school through the university level about our natural systems, how they work, how sensitive or robust they are to change, and most importantly, how that change is realized locally. It is also based on a lifetime of work in habitat restoration, including working with regulatory and community groups as well as scientific experts. It is locally that students and others interested in the effects of climate change can both understand and respond. Changing the global carbon dioxide content of the atmosphere is beyond the individual abilities of most people concerned about the effects of climate change. Addressing land use changes, or ground and surface water consumption is not. This book will help readers understand the issues and choose an individual course of action in which they can be effective.

Dr. James Kelley

Dean of the College of Science and Engineering, San Francisco State University 1975-2001; President, California Academy of Sciences, 1981-1993.

1

My Journey's First Steps

"It is wiser to find out than suppose."

Mark Twain

"It is inconceivable that policymakers will be willing to make billion-and trillion-dollar decisions for adaptation to the projected regional climate change based on models that do not even describe and simulate the processes that are the building blocks of climate variability." [973]

Dr. Jagadish Shukla President, Institute of Global Environment and Society

It is always unsettling whenever our best intentions are misinterpreted. After dedicating 25 years of my life to improving the environment I had simply argued that landscape changes, not climate change, had a far greater impact on California's wildlife. I was puzzled that a few individuals who I would otherwise consider my allies could demonize such a viewpoint, but I now understand the problem. They saw climate change through the lens of a globally averaged statistic. I view climate change as the combination of local and global factors, and believe we can only understand climate variability from a local perspective.

Although it is wise to think globally, all wildlife reacts locally. Always. Understanding local microclimates is our key to protecting our environment. In the late 1990's, I was compelled to understand why a community of birds in California's Sierra Nevada suffered a population crash. Since the early 90's, while serving as the director of San Francisco State University's Sierra Nevada Field Campus, I had been contracted by the US Forest Service to study the bird communities in high mountain meadows in the Tahoe National Forest. In 1998 I witnessed a sudden collapse of the bird populations in one of those meadows, but detecting the cause of that collapse was far from straightforward.

As in climate science, ecological studies are plagued by a multitude of puzzling environmental elements that contribute to the problem, and the impact of each element is not readily teased apart. We had to separate climate effects from land use effects from biological effects. Was the population collapse caused by conditions on this breeding ground, or on their wintering grounds hundreds of miles to the south? Or was it due to conditions present in migration points between their breeding and wintering grounds? Not all species declined as dramatically as others. Was it due to the ongoing cattle and sheep grazing or because of changes in the meadow's stream flow? The population declines were most dramatic in the hottest months of July and August. So could the birds be victims of heat stress related to global warming generated by rising levels of carbon dioxide (CO_2)?

For my first theory, I suspected global warming was the most likely killer. I confess it was an overly simplistic correlation: the bird populations had changed and so had climate. Such a crude correlation however is often the starting point for scientific investigation. But correlations only suggest possibilities. Some correlations are meaningful while most are mere illusions. The real research requires a clear understanding of the mechanisms of change.

A flood of recent papers in both the popular media and prominent scientific journals had statistically linked rising CO_2 levels with other wildlife declines. Moreover, Edith's checkerspot butterfly and the small rabbit-like pika had become icons of purported global-warming-caused tragedies rivaled only by concerns for penguins and polar bears. I had observed both "threatened" species near our research station, so I feared that climate change had brought a "silent spring" to our meadows.

Pika, courtesy of Connie Millar

NASA's Dr. James Hansen is sometimes referred to as the father of modern global warming theory. It was his global models[2] and his 1988 congressional testimony that fanned the flames of concern about global warming. His global models had predicted a steady rise in the average global temperature that he attributed to rising CO_2 levels. His prediction of a 0.9°F rise from 1950 to the end of the 1990s coincided with the observed warming trend, and his views enlisted a growing legion of supporters.

Hansen also believed that an average increase of just 0.9°F could cause ecological catastrophes by altering species' "climate envelope". The climate envelope defines the maximum and minimum temperatures tolerated by a species, and Hansen warned that rising *maximum* temperatures would be deadly for creatures living on the edge of their envelope. He wrote "Negative impacts of greenhouse warming on the biosphere are undoubtedly greatest in regions where species are close to *maximum temperature* tolerance limits (emphasis added)."[2] He calculated that as CO_2 concentrations rose, warmer maximum temperatures would rapidly shift northward by 50 to 75 kilometers per decade. If plants and animals did not migrate fast enough, he warned that they would suffer from heat stress and ultimately face extinction. Thus any northward migration, or migration to higher elevations, was uncritically seen as fulfillment of this scientific apocalyptic prophesy.

In a 2006, Hansen's warnings were increasingly alarming. Expressing heightened catastrophic concerns, he wrote if CO_2 continued to be produced from a "business as usual" scenario, it would result in a 5.4°F rise in global temperature over the 21st century that would eliminate approximately 60% of species on the planet.[4] To support this heightened fear, he referenced a similar analysis by biologist Dr. C.D. Thomas who predicted that by 2050, 15 to 37% of the earth's species would be headed toward inevitable extinction.[5]

Understandably these horrifying predictions caught the world's attention. These weren't end of the world predictions commonly uttered by bedraggled doomsday cult leaders, but fears of established scientists and their predictions evoked a worldwide sense of dread. Nonetheless to my great surprise and great relief, when I examined 100 years of local climate observations throughout California, I found they contradicted the global models. Global warming was not global and the local perspective suggested wildlife was not being harmed by climate change.

Local Contradictions

"Maximum temperatures have not increased in "eastern Canada, the southern United States, portions of eastern Europe, southern China, and parts of southern South America." [7]38

Dr. David Easterling, National Climatic Data Center

"Like other parts of the world, Canada has not become hotter (no increase in higher quantiles of maximum temperature), but has become less cold".[11]

Dr. Xuebin Zhang, Meteorological Service of Canada

Here is a closer look at the local climate data. It tells a very different story than the global average (see Figure 1). The Tahoe City weather station is a member of the United States Historical Climate Network (USHCN), which contributes to the calculation of the global average temperature. Tahoe City is located on the north shore of Lake Tahoe, about 48 miles east from the meadow where our bird populations had collapsed. Like much of the United States, the average temperature for Tahoe City has never significantly exceeded the 1930s and 40s. *However, an average temperature, either global or local, is not very useful to a biologist.*

Far more important are the changes in maximum and minimum temperatures, which determine the boundaries of a species' climate envelope. If the envelope's maximum temperature is surpassed as Hansen predicted, then the organism suffers heat stress. To avoid heat stress, organisms must move to cooler microclimates, change their midday behavior, migrate to higher elevations, or migrate further north. *However local maximum temperatures had decreased significantly since the 1930s* (see Figure 1, upper panel). There had been an insignificant warming trend since 1950, but in the context of the past 100 years that change was trivial.

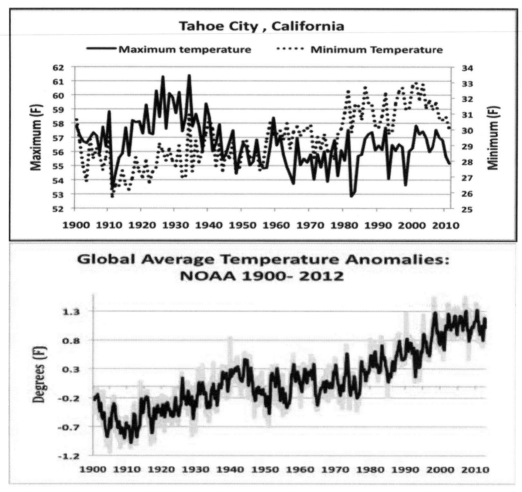

Figure 1 Comparison of Tahoe City Maximum and Minimum temperatures from USHCN versus Global Average temperature from NOAA

Surprisingly Tahoe City's maximum temperatures were no higher than the 1900s. Many other surrounding USHCN weather stations such as Lake Spaulding and Yosemite National Park exhibited the same pattern. In fact, elsewhere climate scientists had observed much of the world is not getting hotter, just less cold.[11]

Factors such as urbanization, rising greenhouse gases or changes in cloud cover can raise minimum temperatures. An increase in clouds can lower the maximum temperature and raise the minimum but in sunny California summer clouds were not a factor. Whatever the reason for the rising minimum temperature, a rising minimum alleviates any cold stress. If you have ever been camping, you likely experienced the cold stress of the predawn minimum temperatures. Although I doubt that temperature trends in a tourist town like Tahoe City accurately represented the micro-climate of our wilderness meadows, most USHCN weather stations throughout the Sierra Nevada indicated that *the climate envelope was converging towards a temperature optimum by lessening both heat and cold stress*. In contrast to predictions of accelerating heat stress by "CO_2 advocates" like Dr. Hansen, the past 60 years of climate change in California should have benefited wildlife. That was an eye-opener.

Eventually we determined that a deterioration of the local watershed had caused the bird population decline. A railroad track built 100 years earlier during a period of heavy railroad logging had disrupted the meadow's stream flow. This caused the stream to become trapped in an ever-deepening channel that increasingly drained the meadow's subsurface reservoir of water. As the meadow dried, desert sagebrush steadily invaded. Raging stream flows during the last El Niño accelerated the erosion and the deepening of the channel caused the water table to finally drop below the reach of the willows' roots, shortening their growing season and killing their upper branches. This resulted in fewer seeds and insects for the birds, who were then forced to find food elsewhere. A meadow once vibrant with a symphony of song became eerily quiet.

To remedy the situation, we formed a partnership with the US Forest Service, the Environmental Protection Agency, and a local restoration organization, the Plumas Corporation, to restore the watershed. In essence the project was an experiment costing several hundred thousand dollars. If our diagnosis was correct, the bird populations would rapidly recover. To our delight, most species immediately rebounded with greater numbers than we had previously documented. It was gratifying to witness. As the willows grew more lush and more songs filled the air, I felt great pride in being a better steward of the environment. Instead of my initial despair that we were victims of a global catastrophe, I was inspired by knowing the problem was local and readily remedied.

Whether or not climate change is natural or human-caused, the watershed restoration made the local environment more resilient to all climate extremes. California's climate is intimately linked to natural cycles of El Niños and La Niñas. El Niños bring floods to the Sierra Nevada while La Niñas bring droughts. Droughts recently induced high temperatures in much of the United States, but even during that severe dryness our restored meadows remained wetter throughout the entire summer; wetter than I had ever observed before. Instead of wildlife fleeing the drying meadow, they now sought refuge in it.

Many people mistakenly believe limiting CO_2 concentrations will control the devastating cycles of El Niño's floods and La Niña's droughts. However global climate models have shown El Niño cycles are natural and independent of CO_2 concentrations. Other researchers have shown El Niño cycles responded "opposite to what is expected" from rising greenhouse gases.[119] If we have no control over an El Niño cycle, then our most valuable course of action would be to ensure the resiliency of the environment. Restoring watersheds is a crucial step in that process, but we have been distracted by the emphasis on rising CO_2 and I am increasingly concerned that a focus on our carbon footprint is diverting funding from vital habitat restoration. (The mechanisms driving the El Niño cycle and its global impact are discussed in Chapter 9.)

Separating the Foxes from the Tiger

"Convenient assumptions should not be turned prematurely into 'facts,' nor uncertainties and ambiguities suppressed." … *"Anyone can write a model: the challenge is to demonstrate its accuracy and precision... Otherwise, the scientific debate is controlled by the most articulate, colorful, or adamant players."* [486]

Dr. Carl Wunsch, Massachusetts Institute of Technology

"Never Stop Questioning"

Albert Einstein

I participated in several professional discussions in which biologists immediately assumed global warming was the ultimate cause of changes in local wildlife. This was somewhat expected because people, myself included, readily adopt the prevailing bias. However, uncritical assumptions usually generate dangerous diagnoses. Let me illustrate. Recently a good friend fell while hiking in the Sierra Nevada. Due to persistent nagging pain she had x-rays taken to see if she had cracked her ribs. There was no sign of a fracture, but the radiograph detected a dark spot on her lungs. Her doctor feared cancer and performed three biopsies. One was inconclusive but the other two suggested cancer. A panel of cancer experts reviewed the results and all agreed. It was a cancer that had progressed to a life-threatening stage. The precautionary principle dictated immediate removal of half of the affected lung. The life-and-death choice was clear-cut and she agreed to immediate surgery. Afterwards the doctors examined the excised fragment more carefully. To their great embarrassment, they discovered the dark spot had been caused by a fungal infection, an infection curable by medication.

She is a wonderfully upbeat person and despite losing half of one of her lungs, she held no ill will and did not blame the doctors. She understood that even under such highly controlled conditions, and despite the best of intentions, confounding factors could lead to a dreadful misdiagnosis. Several conditions can cause a "dark spot" on a lung x-ray and induce abnormal growths. However because cancer is far more common, it generated a bias that misguided the doctors' interpretation. They had failed to ask what other confounding factors could create similar symptoms, and then test for those possibilities. Such failure is why we teach all science majors to always consider multiple hypotheses.

Sloppy science caused by a prevailing bias and a failure to test alternatives has been the subject of much discussion within the medical research community. In a recent paper, "Why Most Published Research Findings Are False,"[58] Stanford University epidemiologist John Ioannidis determined that "for most study designs and settings, it is more likely for a research claim to be false than true. Moreover, *for many current scientific fields, claimed research findings may often be simply accurate measures of the prevailing bias* (emphasis added)." Ioannidis' paper was highlighted with other similar findings in a New Yorker article, "The Truth Wears Off," by Jonah Lehrer. It is available online and well worth the read. The article echoes the eternal truism, "Our beliefs are a form of blindness."

A scientist's opinion is often confused with a scientific finding. Until a conclusion has been tested and cross-examined, it is just an educated guess, not science. Science is a process. Without rigorous cross-examination, false data readily infiltrates the scientific literature. For example, during surgery, the misapplication of anesthesia can be deadly. We therefore expect all research related to anesthesia to be intensely scrutinized. However, Japanese anesthesiologist Yoshitaka Fujii fabricated data in a whopping 172 peer-reviewed papers starting in 1993.[897] When false data can be continuously published in peer-reviewed journals for 10 to 20 years, it is a worrisome sign of failed cross-examination, muted debate, and a broken process. It is estimated that well over 30% of all published studies have never been tested, yet those same publications may be cited as scientific gospel. The resulting cycle of misinformation usually requires a tragic contradiction before the truth is revealed.

Hypothesis testing drives western science. A good scientific hypothesis is simply a cohesive story that transforms a ball of confusing evidence into an easily grasped scenario. A hypothesis provides a set of likely outcomes that allows others to test its validity and make predictions. However the mere creation of a hypothesis has the unintended consequence of creating powerful illusions that prejudice our interpretations. And any hypothesis that appeals to our prejudices readily possesses our minds. As illustrated in an ancient Chinese allegory, a persuasive hypothesis blinds us to our own power.

The Fox Borrows the Tiger's Power

One day a hungry Tiger captures a Fox. Desperately trying to avoid his impending doom, the Fox warns the Tiger that harming him would be a horrible mistake and then tells a story of the gods who had sent the fox to rule over all the other animals. The gods would surely punish the Tiger if the Fox was ever harmed.

The Tiger with a skeptical snicker demands, "Why should I believe such a story from a puny fox?"
So the Fox describes an experiment to prove his power. "Walk behind me," suggests the Fox, "As I lead you through the forest, observe for yourself how all the animals fear me."
So together they walked. Whenever the forest creatures spied the approaching Tiger, they quickly scattered and hid.
"You see how they run from me!" proclaimed the Fox, "They all know how powerful I am!"
And with such "proof" from this experiment, the Tiger was blinded to his own power and freed the Fox.

In scientific jargon, the fox and tiger are confounding factors. The fox's prediction became the prevailing bias, which resulted in a false positive that even the Tiger embraced. For this reason Nobel-prize-winning physicist Richard Feynman warned, "The first principle is that you must not fool yourself, and you are the easiest person to fool." Since the beginning of the Scientific Revolution, Galileo warned, "the same experiment which at first glance seemed to show one thing, when more carefully examined, assures us of the contrary."[950] Einstein wrote, "No amount of experimentation can ever prove me right; a single experiment can prove me wrong." In other words, fifty studies that confirm the fox's prediction, even with 99.9% statistical confidence, are worthless unless the studies separate the foxes from the tiger. It is that one observation that separates the fox from the Tiger that is most revealing. Climate change is highly complex and I was intrigued that local climates behaved so differently than the global average.

Separating Local and Global Change

"No single location follows the global average" [886]

Intergovernmental Panel on Climate Change, The Physical Science Basis, 2007

"influences on climate are the emission of greenhouse gases and changes in land use, such as urbanization and agriculture. But it has been difficult to separate these two influences because both tend to increase the daily mean surface temperature" [19]

Dr. Eugenia Kalnay, University of Maryland

Solar activity, warm and cold ocean cycles, and changes in greenhouse gases affect climate on a global level. Unprecedented population growth, extensive landscape changes and spreading urbanization have a more powerful effect on local climate. The challenge is to determine the relative contributions of each. For global factors the next two decades will be telling. During the 20th century high solar activity and warm ocean cycles "walked together" with rising greenhouse gases as the average temperature warmed. Now solar activity is waning and oceans are cycling to their cool phases. The warming effect of CO_2 is now "walking alone." This will allow scientists to more readily separate global climate factors in the coming decades.

Dr. James Hansen acknowledges "*The five-year running mean of global temperature has been flat for the past decade.*" [531] This current lull in the warming trend has evoked growing skepticism. Is the lull signaling a reversal in global warming, or just a pause in predicted warming? If CO_2 is the most powerful driver of climate change, the global average temperature should continue to rise and we should experience warmer winters during the next two decades. If ocean cycles and the sun dominate, we should expect the global average to start to decline bringing colder winters and increasing snowfall.

To create a greater sense of urgency, advocates have attempted to link changes in wildlife populations to rising CO_2 even though landscape changes, habitat loss and overhunting cause most wildlife declines. CO_2 has been so demonized and so politicized, the global warming hypothesis has created a blinding bias that is misguiding our perceptions of local environmental problems. As a result when I told friends that the crash in bird populations in our Sierra Nevada meadow had nothing to do with climate change and everything to do with an abused watershed, my conclusions were greeted with mixed reactions. While most celebrated our successful restoration, a few accused me of letting global warming off the hook. When I responded that there was no warming in the Sierra Nevada (see Figure 1), I was called a denier and accused of helping Big Oil. I encouraged them to look at the USHCN temperature data for themselves, but until this day they have refused to even look.

Such a stunning refusal reminded me of Galileo's lament. People who clung to the earth-centered model of the universe had refused to look through a telescope and test Galileo's conclusions. It wasn't a matter of religion. The Jesuit scientists were eager for a closer look at the heavens and they quickly supported Galileo's views. It was the entrenched Dominican scientists who refused to look. Their combined religious and scientific authority was based on the old views of Aristotle, and Galileo was undermining their authority. The easiest way to short circuit the scientific process was to stop observing and suppress questioning. In utter disbelief, Galileo wrote to Johannes Kepler that the most learned "steadfastly refused to cast a glance through the telescope. What shall we make of this? Shall we laugh, or shall we cry?"[949]

I felt I had stepped back in time. Just as the intelligentsia refused to look through the telescope to see how Venus contradicted the earth-centered view, people refused to look at local climate contradictions. When the prevailing bias is challenged, people still react as Galileo had observed, "*whatever is brought forward against their fixed idea, however ingenious and conclusive, they receive it with disdain or with hot rage--if indeed it does not make them ill.*"[950]

People on both sides of the climate debate will protect their "fixed ideas" and given the current political polarization and the climate of fear, I understand their reactions. But we need to at least look at all the evidence. Top-down global climate models have repeatedly failed to explain regional climate change.[976] If we want to be better stewards of the environment, restricting our understanding to the view point of global models will only misguide our conservation efforts. We must understand the local contradictions.

Tornados: Think Globally or Locally?

"Our understanding of the complex climate system is hampered by myriad uncertainties, ignorance, and cognitive biases." "The IPCC's consensus approach enforces overconfidence, marginalization of skeptical arguments, and belief polarization." [969]

Dr. Judith Curry, Georgia Institute of Technology

"most tornadoes occur in the afternoon and evening hours, with a minimum frequency around dawn"

NOAA National Climatic Data Center

After the May 2013 tragedy in Moore, Oklahoma I was horrified to read several comments on the Internet, which in effect gloated that conservative "deniers" got what they deserved. Politicians also piled on. Senator Sheldon Whitehouse used the tragedy to attack Republicans, saying, "the damage that your polluters and deniers are doing doesn't just hit Oklahoma and Alabama and Texas. It hits Rhode Island with floods and storms. It hits Oregon with acidified seas, it hits Montana with dying forests." If only Senator Whitehouse had looked at the local data, he may have realized some skeptics are guided by real life experiences. Most tornados happen at midday when maximum temperatures amplify rising air currents. However Oklahoma has not been overheating; the average maximum temperature has remained lower than the first half of the twentieth century (Figure A).[*]

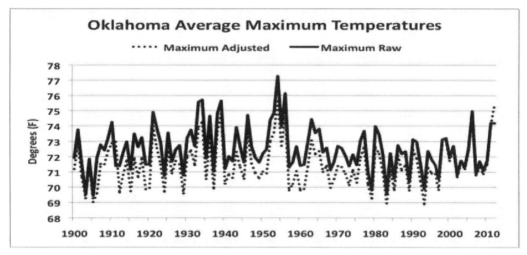

Figure A. Average Maximum Temperatures for 14 northern Oklahoma USHCN weather stations 1900 to 2012

The politicization of the climate debate has created this tragic divisiveness that has blinded us to the distinctions between global and local climate change. Extreme weather events like tornados are driven by local and regional climate, not global climate. Yet to defend the global perspective, Dr. Kevin Trenberth (head of the National Center for Atmospheric Research) has relentlessly argued that rising CO_2 is increasing all extreme weather. He has published, "Framing the way to relate climate extremes to climate change,"[210] and after every major tragedy and in every interview Trenberth repeats his mantra: rising CO_2 causes a "warmer and wetter" world and that increases the likelihood of extreme weather.[549,957] But Oklahoma wasn't warmer or wetter. Tornados are formed by sharp contrasts between cold and warm air as well as contrasts between moist and dry air and Trenberth's tornado commentary reveals more about his bias than it does about tornado formation.

The United States is not particularly warmer or wetter than elsewhere. In fact the western Great Plains was called the Great American Desert in the 19th century. The Great Plains is also nicknamed tornado alley. *Seventy-five percent of all tornados occur in the United States.* The north-south alignment of the Rocky Mountains and the Appalachians transforms the Great Plains into a conduit for cold dry arctic air that

---

[*] The 14 USHCN stations used to compute average were Bartlesville, Buffalo, Cherokee, Claremore, Enid, Guthrie, Jefferson, Meeker, Miami, Mutual, Okeene, Paul's Valley, Pawhuska, and Perry.

can push southward unobstructed while simultaneously warm moist air from the Gulf of Mexico is drawn northward by the advancing summer sun. Tornado formation requires a trigger mechanism that can lift warm moist air from the surface into cold dry air above. An approaching "cold front" is typically the crucial element that rapidly lifts moist Gulf air.

Great Plains' weather forecasters are ever vigilant for advancing cold fronts, because cold fronts are the most reliable predictors of the thunderstorms that may evolve into tornados. In the cartoon (Figure B), an advancing cold front on the left plows into the warm air and lifts it to create clouds, and thunderstorms. The adjacent satellite picture taken over Moore, Oklahoma reveals the same sharp contrast between dry cold air to the left (where clouds are lacking) versus moist warm air to the right. Cloud formation is most intense at the "front" of the advancing cold air. Although the prevailing bias of climate change has focused on only contributions from global warming, it is the collision with contrasting cold air that triggers the extreme weather.

Cold Front

Satellite picture over Moore, Oklahoma May 20, 2013. Credit NOAA

Figure B Left: Cartoon of an advancing cold front. Right Satellite picture of the front over Moore OK, May 20, 201

Cold waves are governed by how rapidly cold arctic air can penetrate into warmer lands. Dry, snow-free land surfaces heat quickly and those heated surfaces warm and neutralize any advancing cold front. Ultimately it diminishes the clash between contrasting air temperatures. In contrast, frozen snow-covered surfaces maintain the colder temperatures of the invading arctic air. Just weeks before the tornado, the Great Plains experienced record breaking low temperatures and late snowfall that enabled a deeper southward penetration of cold Canadian air and set the stage for a bigger battle of contrasts. As we might predict, extreme tornados are historically more frequent during colder years (see Figure C). We could reasonably ask if stronger tornados indicate cooler temperatures.

Cold fronts induce thunderstorms but for a thunderstorm to evolve into a tornado, the rising warm air must also be lifted into an overlying layer of cold dry air. Because moist air holds latent heat and holds its heat longer, rising moist air cools much more slowly than dry air. As the moisture condenses it releases latent heat that accelerates the moist air's ascent. The resulting high-speed winds spawn more severe thunderstorms and increase the likelihood of a tornado. What causes the final rotation needed to turn a thunderstorm into a tornado is still a bit of a mystery, but local "jet streaks", high winds generated from temperature contrasts between land surfaces, have been suggested as contributors.

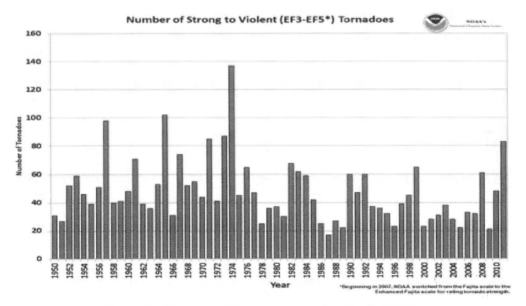

Figure C. 60 year trend in extreme tornados. Credit NOAA

The worst tornado outbreak in recorded history occurred April 3, 1974 but occurred further east.[34] *Again an advancing cold front provided the lifting power to spawn 148 identified tornados over a period of 16 hours, and at one time 15 tornados were on the ground simultaneously.* There were six F5 tornadoes that had paths of over 30 miles and two exceeded 100 miles. In contrast the Moore OK tornado had a 17-mile path. The 1974 outbreak occurred further east in Ohio, largely because the El Niño cycles also affect the location of tornados. During El Niño-neutral years, the jet stream is more likely to blow across the southern Rockies, as was the case in 2013. However during La Niña years, the jet stream is pushed further northward and then loops southward bringing cold dry air to the eastern side of the Great Plains. It was a La Niña year that altered the jet stream and drove the deadly 1974 tornados further east.

Blaming Rising Carbon Dioxide

"For many current scientific fields, claimed research findings may often be simply accurate measures of the prevailing bias." [58]

Dr. John Ioannidis, Stanford University

In a *Scientific American* interview the day following the tornado's devastation, Dr. Trenberth was asked about the contribution of climate change. He again implicated rising CO_2 by stating, "Warmer and moister conditions are the key for unstable air."[957] Not once did Trenberth mention the contributions from the cold front, or mention the below average local temperatures or the late snow cover. Acknowledging that tornados are a common "weather phenomenon", he claimed climate change was the "straw that breaks the camel's back." He suggested climate change had directly contributed only "5 to 10 percent of the weather instability," but caused "up to 33 percent effect in terms of damage". That untestable statistic was then widely disseminated by the media.

Not only were Oklahoma's maximum temperatures cooler for the past 50 years, it was drier during the last decade. Oklahoma's rainfall is largely controlled by natural ocean cycles in the Pacific and the Atlantic (see Chapter 9).[73] The current cycle of more La Niñas produced the drought in 2011 and the lack of moisture from the Gulf of Mexico was the immediate cause of the 2012 drought and experts for the National Oceanic and Atmospheric Administration (NOAA) concluded that drought was caused by natural factors.[904] So where is Oklahoma's wetter and warmer world that Trenberth proclaimed had caused "33% of the damage"?

Such contradictions between local climate and global warming theory demonstrate the need for more respectful debates to separate the local and global viewpoints. Government sponsored debates between climate scientists who are skeptics and advocates would be a healing first step. Unfortunately those debates have been exceedingly rare and most people have never witnessed such a debate. Perhaps not coincidentally, Dr Trenberth has also led the charge to suppress public debates. In his illusively titled speech *Communicating Climate Science,* Trenberth labeled skeptics as deniers and advised against any debates warning, "a debate actually gives alternative views credibility." The published version of that speech ended with a cartoon branding skeptics as the "biggest threat to the planet".[478] I suspect Senator Whitehouse was victimized by Trenberth's overzealous advocacy of a global perspective that ran contrary to local reality.

Although debating alternative views is the very heart and soul of the scientific process, Trenberth's colleagues have circled the wagons and refused public debate. He prefers to issue an unsupported "papal bull" that blames one third of the tornado damage on rising CO_2. I suspect Senator Whitehouse never looked at Oklahoma's local climate. If he had, perhaps a call for more polite discussion would have replaced his hurtful fury. What shall we make of this political atmosphere when people refuse to look at local climate change? Shall we laugh, or shall we cry?

Endangered Species: Think Globally or Locally?

"It is the regional responses, not a global average, that produce drought, floods, and other societally important climate impacts." [464]

Dr. Rezaul Mahmood. Kentucky Climate Center

"For those regions that have undergone intensive human landscape change, or would undergo intensive change in the future, we conclude that the failure to factor in this forcing risks a misalignment of investment in climate mitigation and adaptation." [462]

Dr. Roger Pielke Sr., University of Colorado

Climate scientist Dr. Roger Pielke, Sr. has championed the crucial need to include a local climate perspective. He and several climate scientists have published numerous studies demonstrating the powerful effects of local landscape changes on climate.[42,464] He had been one of the expert reviewers for the Intergovernmental Panel on Climate Change (IPCC) but resigned because the IPCC persistently trivialized the local perspective in order to promote the effects of rising CO_2.

Dr. Pielke has also expressed grave concerns about the ease with which journals now publish any study that simply speculates on a connection to global climate change writing, "What the current publication process has evolved into, at the detriment of proper scientific investigation, are the publication of untested (and often untestable) hypotheses." "When I served as Chief Editor of the *Monthly Weather Reviews* (1981-1985), the Co-Chief Editor of the *Journal of Atmospheric Sciences* (1996-2000), and as Editor-in-Chief of the *US National Science Report to the IUGG for the American Geophysical Union* (1993-1996), such papers would never have been accepted."[978]

This book echoes his concerns. Leading scientific journals have published research blaming rising CO_2 for several local wildlife extinctions, even though local temperatures never warmed or were never examined. For example in Chapter two, all experts had agreed that southern California's increasing urban sprawl and extensive agriculture was endangering the Edith's checkerspot butterfly. But without ever examining the local temperatures Camille Parmesan blamed global warming. The two competing diagnoses called for two very different remedies. To save the butterfly from extinction conservationists argued for habitat protection, while Parmesan argued to limit our carbon footprint. Her erroneous conclusion was quickly embraced not because it helped save the butterflies, but because it supported the global perspective and served as an illusory example of the catastrophic consequences of a one degree rise in global temperature.[59] Furthermore she guarded her faulty interpretation by short-circuiting the scientific process and refusing to publish her methods or share her data.

In numerous other wildlife studies, crucial local factors have been repeatedly overlooked in a similar attempt to "prove global warming". Researchers blamed a decline in a single colony of Emperor penguins in the 1970s on global warming. Yet there has been absolutely no local warming. Nonetheless climate scientists created a model suggesting Antarctica's Emperors are on the precipice of collapse, when in reality there are more penguins and more Antarctic sea ice now than has ever been observed before (see Chapter 4).

In Chapter six, I report how a superb study saved endangered butterfly species from extinction in England. Yet as butterflies recovered and expanded, the good news was hijacked and portrayed as an example of climate change disruption and forced migration. In Chapter eight, you will read about conservationists who were frantically mobilizing to save several species of frogs from a wave of extinction caused by an introduced fungus. Yet they were attacked in prestigious journals for giving "false hope" because they did not blame global warming. In Chapters 11, 12, 13 and 14, advocates have suggested those species are on verge of extinction when in fact their populations are at all time highs and should be icons of conservation success.

In Chapter ten, the researcher omitted all new observations of pika found at elevations lower than previously recorded, and then concluded global warming was driving pika up the mountainside and over the climate cliff of extinction. In Chapter 14, we see that despite the Inuit's steadfast claims that now is "the time of the most polar bears," researchers misinterpreted natural cycles, used inappropriate statistics and failed to publish contradictory data in order to usurp the Inuit's hard-fought right for self determination.

The causes of local climate change are still debated but global models have provided very little insight. Dr. Hans von Storch is a prominent climate scientists and a lead author for the Intergovernmental Panel on Climate Change. He was interviewed in June 2013 and asked about the failure of global models to predict the current lull in the global warming trend. Dr. von Storch replied, "*If things continue as they have been, in five years, at the latest, we will need to acknowledge that something is fundamentally wrong with our climate models. A 20-year pause in global warming does not occur in a single modeled scenario. But even today, we are finding it very difficult to reconcile actual temperature trends with our expectations.*"[997]

"There are two conceivable explanations — and neither is very pleasant for us. *The first possibility is that less global warming is occurring than expected because greenhouse gases, especially CO2, have less of an effect than we have assumed.* This wouldn't mean that there is no man-made greenhouse effect, but simply that our effect on climate events is not as great as we have believed. The other possibility is that, in our simulations, *we have underestimated how much the climate fluctuates owing to natural causes.*" (*Landscapes and Cycles* explores those natural causes in Chapters 5, 7, 9 & 11.)

Dr. Jagadish Shukla warned, "the current climate models have such large errors in simulating the statistics of regional (climate) that we are not ready to provide policymakers a robust scientific basis for "action" at regional scale."[973] But the failure of global climate models doesn't mean there is no need to act. Climate change, whether natural or human-caused, demands we ensure a more resilient environment that can moderate against all extremes whether we face global warming or global cooling. As this book will demonstrate, controlling our carbon footprint will never solve the most pressing environmental problems of habitat loss and watershed degradation. Those problems will only be solved locally and to that end I pledge 10% of all book profits to the Sierra County and Feather River Land Trusts that are dedicated to preserving natural habitat, to the Plumas Corp that is dedicated to watershed restoration, and to the Sierra Nevada Field Campus that is dedicated to environmental education.

2

Landscape Change Not Climate Change

Parmesan's Butterfly Effect

"[A]lthough we now know that the butterfly likely disappeared from Orange County thirty years ago, it was rediscovered in Riverside County in the early 1990s, and in San Diego County at several formerly occupied sites soon after." [61]

Dr. Travis Longcore, The Urban Wildlands Group

"[T]he lack of warming for maximum temperatures throughout California is found only since 1970, and it is suggested that an increase in precipitation (and thus cloudiness) over California in the last 35 years has masked warming." [891]

Dr. Eugene Cordero, San Jose State University

The pioneers of chaos theory coined the term "butterfly effect" to suggest that a hurricane's formation could be affected by such unpredictable influences as the flap of a distant butterfly's wings that changed the winds' direction weeks before. Ironically, it was Dr. Camille Parmesan's 1996 seminal butterfly paper titled "Species and Climate Range"[59] that became the model for future peer-reviewed papers that blamed climate change for species extinctions. Despite the lack of any local warming,[891] she argued global warming had caused the extermination of several colonies of the Edith's checkerspot butterfly, and implied the survivors were fleeing northward and upward to cooler refuges. "Species and Climate Range" was not some obscure study by an inconsequential author, suitable for use as a straw man. Nearly 500 papers have cited her study, and Parmesan is considered one of the leading figures in climate-change research. She has co-authored some of the most influential and highly cited papers in the field. As of 2009, Parmesan ranked as the second-most cited author in papers devoted expressly to global warming and climate change.[454]

Her work rallied advocates of Dr. Jim Hansen's catastrophic predictions that global warming was already forcing ecological collapse. Featured on the Union of Concerned Scientists' website, Parmesan echoed Hansen's fears. "The latest research shows clearly that we face the threat of mass extinctions in coming years," she says. "My hope is that we will be able to reduce emissions enough so that assisted colonization efforts can be successful, because at the higher ranges of scientists' projections of warming trends, frankly, we're sunk." For promoting global warming theory, she subsequently earned an invitation to speak at the White House and became one of just four biologists to partake in third global climate assessment by the United Nations' Nobel-Prize-winning Intergovernmental Panel on Climate Change (IPCC).

As Einstein said, "A question that sometimes drives me hazy: am I or are the others crazy?" Such fanfare drove me hazy. Parmesan's conclusions not only contradicted the butterfly's well-established biology, but there never was any real migration northward or upward. She blamed "global" warming even though local maximum temperatures had cooled.[891] Although butterfly experts and scientists dedicated to saving the butterfly from extinction had pointed to habitat destruction as the culprit and sought habitat restoration, Parmesan argued for reduced carbon emissions. In addition, she now seeks funding to support an ecologist's worst nightmare, assisted colonization, even though introducing species into new habitat brings disease and disrupts the established balance. Parmesan envisions herself shuttling animals northwards and upwards so they can escape the rising tide of warmth produced by models.

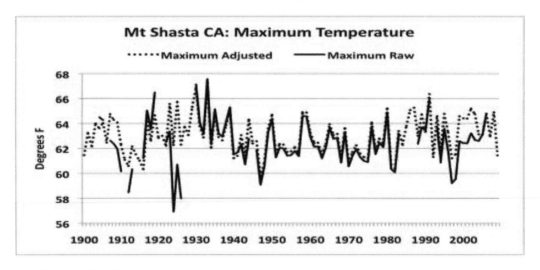

To her credit, Parmesan diligently spent four years of extensive and laborious fieldwork revisiting locations where the butterfly had been observed earlier in the century. After verifying that more populations had gone extinct in the southern extremes and at the lowest elevations of the butterfly's range, Parmesan enthusiastically claimed her results were consistent with global warming theory. In 2010 Parmesan summarized her work: "it was a bloody obvious change. These butterflies were shifting their entire range over the past century northward and upward, which is the simplest possible link you could have with warming. I was expecting some incredibly subtle, sophisticated response to warming, if at all. What I got was 80% of the populations in Mexico and the Southern California populations were extinct, even though their habitats still looked perfectly fine."[454] Despite her public statements, Parmesan always knew the butterflies had never migrated further north or to higher elevations.

Although Hansen had predicted that the increasing maximum temperatures would push animals northward and upward, Parmesan failed to mention that most of California's maximum temperatures had never exceeded the highs of the 1940s. In fact her paper never analyzed local temperatures at all. Parmesan simply relied on the prevailing global warming bias. Parmesan was speaking globally, but the butterflies always act locally. Ask any university ecology professor. They would not hesitate to harshly criticize an undergraduate term paper that used a "global average" to explain a local event. Nevertheless Parmesan's unsupported claim was published in one of the most prestigious scientific journals with one of the highest rejection rates, *Nature*.

Parmesan also failed to address the fact that higher temperatures enhanced the butterfly's survival. Warm microclimates are critical for survival. Caterpillars living in cooler microclimates develop more slowly, while those actively basking in the direct sunlight digest their food more quickly and grow more robustly.

Since the 1950s, Stanford University's Paul Ehrlich and his colleagues had made detailed observations throughout the checkerspot's habitat on the Jasper Ridge Preserve. In addition to local air temperatures, they also measured the varied microclimates at the tops of mounds and bottoms of gullies, under bushes and on bare ground. They even measured the caterpillar's inner body temperature. They found noontime surface temperatures on south-facing slopes can exceed air temperatures by 36-54°F during the growing season, whereas flat areas exceed air temperatures by 9-21°F. In contrast, surface temperatures on north-facing slopes were often below average air temperature. Within a slope there could be as much as a 27°F difference between the warmest and coolest spots. They also determined that the caterpillars must raise their body temperature an additional 18-21°F above ambient air temperatures and to raise their body temperature caterpillars shuffled across the hillsides seeking life-giving hotspots.[62,63,65] Any global warming, natural or anthropogenic, should have been a benefactor, not an executioner.

Years before Parmesan's study, conservationists had already sounded the extinction alarm. Butterfly populations had diminished so quickly that the checkerspot's apparent fate was compared to the rapid ruination of the extinct passenger pigeon. Scientists working to prevent extinction had warned that the suburban sprawl from Los Angeles to San Diego had devoured the butterfly's critical habitat and extirpated most populations.[60,61]

How did Parmesan deal with those contradictory factors? Instead of a more detailed study, she simply argued, "the predicted effects of climate change will come, not from attempts to analyze all possible confounding variables in single studies such as this one, but from replication of this type of study." In essence, by arguing that confounding factors were no longer important, she suggested we throw out the foundation of good scientific analyses. To demonstrate the negative impacts of climate change, all anyone needed to do was demonstrate that populations were dwindling in the south more than in the north, or dwindling more at lower elevations than at higher elevations. Implausibly, the prestigious journal *Nature* supported this "new science."

In contrast, conservationists were not looking to prove or disprove global warming theory, but working to save the Edith's checkerspot from extinction. Their success necessitated understanding all the contributing local factors, and they never wavered in their indictment of land use changes. When the checkerspot's southern California Quino subspecies was finally listed as endangered, conservation scientists wrote, "The basis for the listing was habitat loss, degradation, and fragmentation, recognizing additional negative effects from fire management practice. All factors are the results of intensive human economic development of ever diminishing resources."[60]

Parmesan's had also failed to detail the timeframe of those local extinctions. As a result, advocates mistakenly portrayed her study as proof that the rising level of CO_2 was causing a rising tide of extinctions. But that was a myth. The conservationists' detailed studies had reported that most extinctions observed in southern California had already transpired by the 1970s, before any purported CO_2 warming had developed. More importantly the butterflies were now recovering. In 2003 researchers wrote, "although we now know that the butterfly likely disappeared from Orange County thirty years ago, it was rediscovered in Riverside County in the early 1990s, and in San Diego County at several formerly occupied sites soon after."[61] So if the agent of death had been global warming, why were those populations now recovering as temperatures rose from the cooler 1970s?

Furthermore, extinctions were not limited to the southern end of the butterfly's range. Throughout Vancouver, Canada, rapid urban development entirely extirpated the Canadian subspecies (the Taylor checkerspot) from Canada. However because there was a greater preponderance of extinctions in southern California, the "average statistical center" for the species migrated northward. There was never any evidence of any real migration. There was never an apocalyptic flight to cooler lands. Parmesan's claim was a statistical fairy tale.

Defying the Experts

"Our observation that human impacts [land use] were almost always involved in local extirpations in southern California (even for those areas that may seem to still have "suitable habitat"), the role of global warming as the proximate cause of extinction must be carefully evaluated" [60]

Dr. Rudi Mattoni, University of California Los Angeles

The evidence against a CO_2 connection was overwhelming. But I was no butterfly expert. Needing a reality check, I talked with my friend Dr. Paul Opler, one of North America's top butterfly experts. If you have ever spent any time with Paul, you quickly realize that no one has a greater love for butterflies. If there was the smallest threat, he would be the first to speak out. In 1974, he was hired as the first invertebrate specialist for the United States Federal Endangered Species program. Virtually every butterfly species now listed as endangered was listed under his watch. He has authored several books on butterflies and most recently co-authored the exquisite "Moths of North America". In 2012 he was made an honorary life member of the Lepidopterists' Society†; to quote the society's article in his honor, Paul has made "innumerable contributions on threatened and endangered insects: recovery plans, status reports, and various symposia over his tenure in Washington."

To my great good fortune, he agreed to teach a course, "Butterflies of the Sierra Nevada" (which he still teaches), for my environmental education program at the field campus each year. I expressed my doubts about the legitimacy of Parmesan's claims and my bewilderment at all the media hype, and I asked if he had seen any evidence to support her global warming claims.

He carefully stated that from all the data he had perused, he had seen absolutely no evidence that any butterflies had ever moved northwards, nor had they been pushed to higher elevations. He too couldn't understand the public fanfare given the

---

† Lepidopterists study moths and butterflies

Parmesan papers. He echoed my thoughts that "only her statistical averages moved, not the butterflies". He also informed me the butterfly had been discovered further south in Baja, Mexico. Opler never published his disagreements with Parmesan in a scientific journal. But due to his expertise, Opler had been invited by the Fish and Wildlife Service to comment on the proposed recovery plans for the subspecies in southern California:

> The lengthy space given to Camille Parmesan's study and the suggestion that newly found colonies are the result of global warming is highly speculative. Her study did not find new northern, or higher populations of the species. *Her results were a statistical artifact of the purported loss of low-lying southern populations* (emphasis added). Her surveys that showed the absence of butterflies in some population areas could have been carried out in relatively bad years when the species was present only as diapausing‡ larval clusters.

> The speculations about various percentages of butterflies going extinct is highly speculative. Local populations may be extirpated, but virtually all of these species have undergone more extreme climate change during post-glacial xerothermal§ epochs. Although I have no doubt that global warming exists and that it may affect insects' distributions, much of the biological evidence is not sound. Much of this discussion of global warming and its application to Euphydryas editha could have been easily omitted without any affect on the proposal and could have saved the taxpayers considerable money in personnel time and printing costs.

Opler was not the only expert to dissent. Other scientists, armed with detailed studies aimed at insuring the butterfly's recovery and survival, also disagreed. "Our observation that human impacts were almost always involved in local extirpations in southern California (even for those areas that may seem to still have "suitable habitat"), the role of global warming as the proximate cause of extinction must be carefully evaluated. We suspect that warming is perhaps an exacerbating factor, but that increased extinction rates in southern California are primarily caused by more direct anthropogenic forces."[60]

Encouraged that my skepticism was justified, I decided to replicate Parmesan's landmark study myself but with an eye on the contributing land use factors. At the time, I was surprised that such a highly publicized paper had never been fully replicated. However the enormous time involved in such ecological studies deters repeat studies. But I had retired, had time, and biology was still in my blood. However when I looked for the methods section and the list of locations and extinctions, there was none. Her study had been published as a correspondence, and

---

‡ Diapause is a period of dormancy similar to hibernation.

§ The xerothermal epochs refers to the Holocene Optimum period between 9000 and 5000 years ago when temperatures averaged 3 to 6°F warmer than today's climate, and the earth began to dry, turning the Green Sahara into a desert, and drying the inland seas of North America

in *Nature*, a correspondence doesn't require a methods section that allows for independent verification. That also explained how her paper survived a gauntlet of disagreement by leading experts. A correspondence is not typically peer reviewed. It is published simply based on the advocacy of *Nature's* editors.

Withholding the Evidence

"We are trying to prove ourselves wrong as quickly as possible, because only in that way can we find progress."

Dr. Richard Feynman, Nobel Prize in Physics

I emailed Dr. Parmesan and asked for the locations of her research sites. After months without reply, I called. Caught off guard, she initially refused to share any data, but after more discussion she finally offered the possibility of collaboration. She said she needed to hang up but promised to send some data. More than three years later, I am still waiting. So much for Feynman's good scientist "trying to prove ourselves wrong as quickly as possible."

Her husband eventually responded to a follow-up email I sent a year later in which I expressed my frustration with their failure to allow independent verification. Her husband, Dr. Michael Singer, is also a checkerspot expert who had shared in her research. He confessed that my friendship with Paul Opler had been an issue due to Opler's disapproving comments to the Fish and Wildlife Service. Singer sent me Opler's comments and his rebuttal to Opler's criticisms. Oddly enough, Singer confirmed every criticism. There never had been any evidence of an actual migration northward or upward as predicted by global warming. And the butterflies were recovering.

Singer wrote, "Her study did not find new northern, or higher populations of the species…There are no 'new' northern populations in Parmesan's study. *The study consisted entirely of re-examining populations known from past records and assessing which of them was currently extant or extinct. No 'new' populations were sought or found* (emphasis added)." Apparently Singer had never read his wife's published claims about "bloody obvious northward and upward range shifts" or the opening paragraph of her seminal paper, "I report here the first study to provide evidence of the predicted range shift." For over a decade she had perpetuated the myth of butterflies fleeing global warming in comments to the media. In later publications she even specified the distances that they had migrated. This mythical portrayal of butterflies fleeing global warming has dominated the imagination of CO_2 advocates, and it has been repeated over and over again.

There was another illusion. Her statistical story was built on absent populations during a small snapshot in time. As Dr. Ehrlich warns, "Snapshots of the histories of single populations over brief periods repeatedly have proven to give at best a partial, and at worst an erroneous, impression of the factors controlling the distribution and abundance of plants and animals."[65] If CO_2 was truly causing extinctions, then the test of time predicted that number of extinctions would continue to increase. Instead the butterflies have been recovering but unlike the trumpeting of her dooms day scenario, there have been no press releases to celebrate the good news.

Dr. Singer's email continued, "But I do remember writing to you to say that E. editha has been increasing through the 2000s and that many of the populations that Camille and I recorded as extinct in the 1990s have been recolonized. For example, populations at Walker Pass, California, Hot Springs, Sonora Junction, Bircham Flat Road, Ebbett's Pass, Saddlebag Reservoir (SW corner), Tahoe Meadows, Yucca Point and Tamarack Ridge were, I think, all extinct in her data and extant at our most recent visits. On the other hand, we have observed no recent Sierra extinctions, with the possible exception of Tuolumne Meadows. So, any new census of Sierra Nevada populations would show a reduced correlation between elevation and population status, perhaps no longer a significant correlation." So why haven't they published this good news of the recovery? This illustrates a glaring problem of limiting debate to peer-reviewed journals. Contradicting evidence is simply not published.

Bad Science, Bad Solutions

"But I do remember writing to you to say that E. editha has been increasing through the 2000s and that many of the populations that Camille and I recorded as extinct in the 1990s have been recolonized."

Dr. Michael Singer, University of Texas

While the efforts of conservationist who actually saved the butterfly in southern California languished in obscurity, Parmesan became the darling of global warming advocates. Despite the fact that her 1996 claims have been refuted from every corner of research (including her own), the myth of butterflies fleeing northward and upwards continues to survive. In the wake of her misdiagnosis, the worst possible solutions are now advocated.

Parmesan has harnessed her political fame to fundraise for "assisted migration". She wants to move animals northward and upward to new habitats. Although assisted migration has historically devastated local ecosystems with disease and invasive species, Parmesan wants to unleash this Pandora's box of environmental calamities. Animals are not migrating as fast as her statistical story requires, so she wants to create a Noah's Ark. She wants to relocate populations based on struggling climate models that have failed to simulate California's climate trends.[1] More likely she will deliver a Trojan Horse filled with biological unknowns that will emerge to plunder the landscape. In addition to assisted migration, other researchers are pursuing a host of bizarre "climate engineering" solutions such as purposefully injecting aerosols into the stratosphere to block the sun or cutting trees and sinking them in the ocean to sequester carbon.

In 2009 *Scientific American* (a subsidiary journal of *Nature* since 2008) published "Can 'Assisted Migration' Save Species from Global Warming?" The subtitle read "As the world warms up, some species cannot move to cooler climes in time to survive. Camille Parmesan thinks humans should help even if it means creating invasive species." Sidestepping evidence that 1) most extinctions happened by the 1970s, 2) populations have been rebounding for over a decade, and 3) California's maximum temperatures had cooled, *Scientific American* perpetuated her myth. "Scientists already knew that human development and climate were driving down its populations, but Parmesan's systematic science startled everyone: three fourths of the populations at the lowest latitudes had become extinct, whereas only 20 percent of those in Canada had disappeared. Populations at higher altitudes were only one third as likely to go extinct as those at lower, warmer heights."

As Robert Louis Stevenson warned, "The truth that is suppressed by friends is the readiest weapon of the enemy." Conservative critic Rush Limbaugh was quick to capitalize on the lack of scientific rigor in Parmesan's paper and mocked its conclusions. Parmesan's paper and those that followed have done more to undermine the public's trust in legitimate conservation efforts, while doing nothing to protect the checkerspot or any other threatened species. Good conservation requires the support of all the people. Like all science, conservation must examine all contributing factors and demands an honest and transparent process with full public disclosure. The case of Global Warming vs. the Edith's checkerspot has failed on all accounts.

Altered Landscapes Endangered the Checkerspot

"The basis for the listing was habitat loss, degradation, and fragmentation, recognizing additional negative effects from fire management practice. All factors are the results of intensive human economic development of ever diminishing resources." [60]

Dr. Rudi Mattoni, University of California Los Angeles

Controlled experiments in a greenhouse environment unequivocally demonstrated that the Edith's checkerspot caterpillars have enhanced survival under elevated temperatures, but only if drying soils do not cause their food plants to wilt prematurely.[66] However California's growing human population and changing landscape altered the traditional ecology of the checkerspot's food plants and pushed the plants to more rapidly drying soils.

Along the more coastal regions of western North America, from Baja California to

Vancouver, British Columbia, the primary food plant for the checkerspot's caterpillars is an annual plant species, *Plantago erecta*. At one time, plantago was also a major food crop for humans. Archaeological sites reveal that Native Americans stored extensive piles of plantago seeds. Ecologists also refer to this plantago species as a "fire follower", and California's Native Americans seized upon that readily apparent characteristic. To increase the plant's abundance, Native Americans frequently set fires to keep the grasslands open. Fire farming cleared away unwanted competitors and released nutrients back to the soil, thus enhancing the growing conditions for their more preferred plants.

Much of the California's "natural" landscape has been sculpted by such early human intervention. The pure groves of fire-tolerant black oaks throughout the Sierra Nevada stand as ghostly remnants of a time when Native Americans periodically set fires to increase acorn production. For the plantago along California's coast, fire farming ensured access to deeper and better soils, and that meant a longer growing season with copious seed production. That longer growing season was also necessary for the checkerspot to complete its life cycle, but the arrival of Europeans dramatically altered those ancient agricultural practices. Their preferred crops did not rely on fires and to protect property, fires were suppressed.

Analysis of fire scars and tree rings indicate that the frequency of fires have been reduced by 75% in most places. This modern regime of fire suppression challenged the fire-adapted giant sequoias whose seedlings require sunny open spaces. Without natural fires to open the canopy, sequoias were no longer reproducing because invading shade-tolerant species like White Fir were not periodically burnt away. In Sequoia and Kings Canyon National Park, managers periodically set controlled burns to preserve the very trees for which the national park is named.

Similarly in the Great Lakes region, the Jack Pine was adapted to frequent fires caused by periodic droughts. However fire suppression and logging reduced the extent of the pine's range to less than seven square miles. Because of their dependence on Jack Pines, Kirtland's Warbler plummeted to less than 500 individuals by 1970. Prescribed burns and staggered logging have enabled the warbler's rapid recovery.

European settlers also introduced a multitude of invasive plant species that outcompeted California's native plants. The increasing shade from those invasives overshadowed the checkerspot's food plants and reduced the caterpillars' premium sunbathing hot spots. The rapid browning of the California hills soon after the winter rains stop is only a recent phenomenon, caused by the domination of invasive short-lived annual grasses that relentlessly replaced the native perennial plants. Moreover, modern agriculture increasingly claimed the best soils for crops that now help feed the world. The combination of fire suppression, invasive species, and modern agriculture reduced the plantago's overall abundance.

Nonetheless, plantago still survives quite well on more marginal soils. Throughout California, abundant earthquake faults generated chemically-challenging and rapidly-draining serpentine soils. These soils often served as refuges for plantago. Plantago adapted to those marginal soils by relying on a shorter growing season, and it remains abundant throughout California. However a shorter growing season was a disaster for the butterfly. The shorter growing season meant warmth and fast growth was even more critical than ever for caterpillar development. The lack of warmth is why researchers like Dr. Ehrlich watched populations of checkerspot go extinct during cool rainy years.[64,65] At Jasper Ridge, Ehrlich had observed a population go extinct in 1964, recolonize in 1966 and go extinct again in 1974.

Trees like the sequoia are perennials that persist without producing seeds each year. In contrast, annual plants like plantago die each year. Annual species only survive into the following year by producing seeds from which sprouts the next generation. Thus annuals are acutely sensitive to weather conditions. Whenever conditions become unfavorable, annuals stop growing and quickly set seed. Furthermore the seeds of annuals themselves are also very sensitive to unfavorable weather and may remain dormant for years awaiting better conditions. In deeper soils that held the moisture longer, plantago enjoyed a longer growing season and that provided the checkerspot with adequate time to develop. However, on marginal soils that drained quickly, plantago was forced to set seed much sooner and that limited caterpillars' development.

After hatching, the caterpillars have very little time to grow before California's summer drought begins to wilt their food plants. If the caterpillars grow large enough before the leaves wilt, they successfully enter diapause. On the west coast, diapausing caterpillars emerge around February when the winter rains bring a new flush of growth. The caterpillars must then complete their growth and metamorphose into adults who immediately lay their eggs. The eggs quickly hatch and the caterpillars must then grow to the required size by mid-May. If they reach that critical size they enter diapause. If not they die. And it is warm temperatures that determine if they live or die.

Researchers observed that when caterpillars shuffled from cool to warm slopes they could complete their life cycle up to two weeks sooner, even though travelling time deducted days from their feeding time.[62] Absurdly, although these caterpillars sought out local hot spots that were 20°F hotter than the local air temperatures, Parmesan argued that the 1.4°F global warming trend over the last century had extirpated the species.

Although a hot year favored the caterpillar's growth, it accelerated the drying of the soils causing plantago to set seed and wilt much sooner. This was bad for the butterflies but cool wet years were equally problematic. The cool temperatures during the heavy rains inhibited the caterpillar's growth. If the soils held the extra moisture, plantago could extend its growing season and the butterfly would still benefit. In quickly draining soils, however, plantago still set seed very early. Deprived of warmth by the heavy rains, and a longer growing season due to rapidly draining soils, young caterpillars frequently failed to achieve the required size to survive the winter. In Parmesan's defense, the butterflies often died but the food plant remained. This deceived Parmesan into assuming that if plantago was present but the butterflies were not, then land use was not a factor.[68] However by shady subtraction she then assumed the problem must be CO_2.

The checkerspot exists in what biologists refer to as a metapopulation. Metapopulations consist of a constellation of smaller distinct satellite populations that "blink on and off". At any given point in time, the weather will extirpate (make locally extinct) a population. Some populations blink off when it is too dry, while right next door a population may blink off when it is too wet. When local conditions are poor, satellite populations on marginal habitat are often extirpated. However in the "just-right" habitat, the butterflies can complete their life cycle every year. Ehrlich called the populations living in the just-right places "reservoir populations".[65]

During optimal weather, the butterfly population explodes and individuals wing their way across the landscape, recolonizing satellite habitat that had blinked off. Unfortunately it was the just-right places that had been increasingly lost due to California's human population boom. Periodic boom and bust cycles of butterflies on marginal habitat are expected. But extinctions in reservoir populations were rare. Critical habitat with deep soils had sustained the reservoir populations for millennia throughout major climate changes and megadroughts. However with the recent loss of that critical habitat, every weather event was a potential tragedy.[60,61,64,65]

There is no mystery why conservationists prescribe habitat protection to preserve this species. The bigger mystery is why CO_2 advocates continue to blame global warming.

3

Why Average Isn't Good Enough

The Limits of Global Models

"Neither the nature of climate trends in California nor their causes are well understood." [1]
Dr. Phillip Duffy, Lawrence Livermore National Laboratory

"That climate should be the function of a single parameter (like CO$_2$) has always seemed implausible. Yet an obsessive focus on such an obvious oversimplification has likely set back progress by decades." [937]
Dr. Richard Lindzen, Massachusetts Institute of Technology

Despite their inability to replicate the effects of landscape change and bizarre conclusions that suggest deforestation cools the planet, top-down global models provide an important perspective that cannot be analyzed from a local standpoint. The climate outside the tropics depends on heat and moisture exported from the tropics. The tropics are the only regions where at least once a year the sun shines directly overhead. As a result, the tropics absorb the bulk of incoming solar energy.

Outside the tropics the slanting rays of the sun add decreasing amounts of heat as we move towards the poles. Yet the temperatures outside the tropics are far warmer than we would estimate if we only considered heating by the sun. The discrepancy is caused by ocean currents such as the Gulf Stream in the Atlantic and the Kuroshio Current in the Pacific that constantly carry heat from the tropics towards the poles. In addition, heat and moisture evaporated from tropical waters are carried pole-ward by "atmospheric rivers."[176] As a result, temperatures are cooler than expected in the tropics and warmer than expected outside the tropics. Any changes in the redistribution of tropical heat have profound consequences for regional climates.

Only a global perspective can capture the redistribution of heat from the equator to the poles, but due to the enormous amount of computing power required to simulate global climates, global models cannot afford to accurately represent smaller details. Coastline irregularities and small mountain ranges are not accurately represented. Global models also fail to simulate the redistribution of heat from the north Atlantic into the Arctic Ocean,[974] and the redistribution of heat and moisture worldwide every 3 to 7 years by El Niño events.[976] As a result of these systematic deficiencies, global models are essentially useless for predicting local climate change.

Even when global models are scaled to focus on smaller regions such as California, they still fail to recreate the local climate. In 2006, modelers lamented, "Neither the nature of climate trends in California nor their causes are well understood."[1] These climate scientists attributed their difficulties to "the complex effects of multiple climate forcings*. The state's natural climate is diverse, highly variable, and strongly influenced by the El Niño-Southern Oscillation (ENSO) phenomenon. Humans are perturbing this complex climate system through urbanization, irrigation, and the emission of multiple types of aerosols and greenhouse gases. Despite better-than-average observational coverage, *scientists are only beginning to understand the manifestations of these forcings in California's temperature record* (emphasis added)."[1] (ENSO is discussed in more detail in Chapter 9.) If climate scientists are stymied by California's climate, our understanding of other regions can be no better.

Temperature Chimeras

"the significant human development of the surface may be responsible for the rising Minimum temperature while having little impact on Maximum temperature in East Africa." [966]

Dr. John Christy, Earth System Science Center, University of Alabama, Huntsville.

"It is unlikely that one or a few weather stations are representative of regional climate trends, and equally unlikely that regionally projected climate change from coarse-scale general circulation models will accurately portray trends at sub-regional scales." [462]

Dr. Roger Pielke Sr., University of Colorado

In order to estimate how the sun or greenhouse gases affect global climate, researchers devised a measurement called the global average temperature. Thousands of measurements from varying local microclimates from around the world are blended by a computer model that estimates each measurement's relative importance and then produces a global average. Despite its political significance, the global average temperature is useless for conservation efforts.

---

* In Climate-speak, a forcing is any change that alters the balance between incoming and outgoing energy.

California's wildlife is not affected by an average that includes heat trapped deep inside an urban heat island, or elevated temperatures caused by persistent drought on distant continents. The global average includes warming caused by deforestation and desertification of grasslands, as well as ancient heat ventilated from ice-free waters into the frigid Arctic air. For practical purposes, researchers argue *"it is the regional responses, not a global average, that produce drought, floods, and other societally important climate impacts."*[464]

The average is a chimera. The Chimera was a monster from Greek mythology. Etruscan sculptures portrayed the Chimera as a fire-breathing fusion of a lion, serpent and goat to create one unfathomable beast. Geneticists similarly call any organism composed of cells with different genomes a chimera. For example, two fertilized eggs that would normally develop into non-identical twins can fuse to make a single individual. The heart contains the genes from one twin, while the brain develops from the genes of the other. Researchers recently developed human-sheep chimeras, human genes forming some organs and 15% of the sheep's blood. The concept of the global average temperature is likewise a scientific chimera of unrelated temperatures.

Many scientists have questioned the value of a global average temperature.[29,41,96] Dr. Craig Bohren derided, "I consider the concept of a global mean (average) temperature to be somewhat dubious, and I say so in my recent book *Fundamentals of Atmospheric Radiation*. A single number cannot adequately capture climate change. *This number, as I see it, is aimed mostly at politicians and journalists* (emphasis added)."[89] Massachusetts Institute of Technology's Dr. Richard Lindzen calls it an obvious oversimplification that has set back climate science progress and *"misses some crucial aspects of the physics* (emphasis added)".[937]

To construct a globally averaged land temperature, researchers begin by averaging the maximum and minimum temperatures at a local weather station. However because those two measures represent very different dynamics, the daily average is also a chimera. Similar to Tahoe City (see Figure 1, page 4), the maximum and minimum temperatures from Yosemite Park Headquarters (see Figure 2 upper panel) demonstrate paradoxical trends. The maximum is measured when the heat of the midday sun causes rising convection currents to vigorously mix the air column. Except during heat waves (see Chapter 7), the maximum temperature measures a well-mixed atmosphere that extends upwards for several miles.

In contrast, heat held by the earth's surface largely determines the minimum temperature. Minimum temperatures are measured just before dawn when the air is still and mixing is infrequent. The minimum will be colder in small depressions where pools of cold nighttime air collect, whereas the minimum is warmer on nearby flat or sloping surfaces. In addition, various surfaces hold heat differently, causing each surface to cool at varied rates independently of any greenhouse effect. Moist soils hold the heat longer than dry soils. Road pavement retains the heat more than most other surfaces and barren ground is heated more than vegetated surfaces. Deforestation, agriculture, and urbanization have altered the earth's surface so dramatically that many researchers believe the minimum average temperature is inappropriate for determining climate change and only the maximum average temperature should be used.[88]

The factors causing the observed differences are still debated. However, no matter what the cause of these diverging trends, California's local climates cannot be overheating. Any added heat represented by the rising minimum is not stored; if it were, maximum temperatures would also rise. Alternatively the diverging trends could mean less heat is being added during the day. Wherever the minimum rises more than the maximum, constructing an average creates a false illusion of overheating. The average also blinds us to natural climate variations and important climate questions. What natural factors are powerful enough to cool the region despite rising CO_2? If CO_2 caused three decades of rising minimum temperatures, why has Yosemite's minimum been cooling for the past 15 years? (See Figure 2)?

California's average temperature is represented by 54 USHCN weather stations, each representing one region of the state's climate. The question that then arises is 'how well do the temperatures at any given station, such as Yosemite's park headquarters, represent its entire region?' For example, the waste heat generated from the tremendous volume of tourists or from the ranger's residence undoubtedly contributes to temperatures surrounding the headquarters, but those factors have little impact in the hinterlands. Furthermore within the limited confines of the park, the microclimates vary tremendously amongst mountaintops, valleys, wetlands, rocky outcrops, dense forest, etc. Does this one USHCN station truly measure all the heat affecting all of Yosemite's microclimates?

A recent study determined Yosemite's varied landscapes respond in very contrary ways. A 10-year period of weakening westerly winds caused three very different climate trends in nearby locations. One section of Yosemite National Park cooled by 1.1°F. However temperatures rose by 0.72°F in an adjacent section, while in a third location temperatures did not change at all.[873] Depending on the location of a weather station, it will produce very different trends. For a biologist, even the average temperature measured at park headquarters can be a misleading estimate of climate change in a nearby meadow.

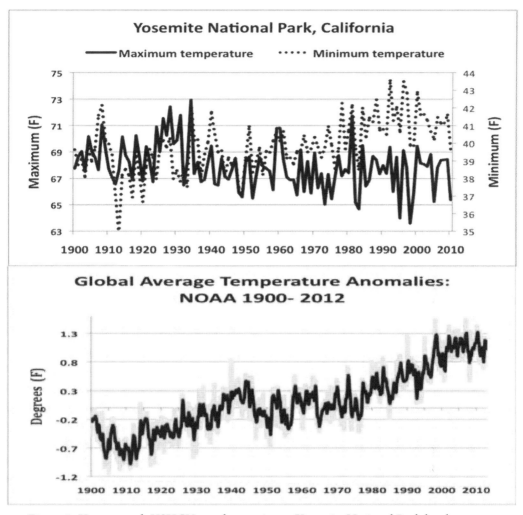

Figure 2 Upper panel: USHCN weather station at Yosemite National Park headquarters. Lower panel: Global Average Temperature Anomalies. Credit NOAA

To improve our regional climate models, hundreds of researchers are diligently investigating how other factors have contributed to climate change. Although the consensus agrees CO_2 slows down escaping infrared heat waves, CO_2's affect on local climate remains shrouded in uncertainty. To reduce that uncertainty, scientists are analyzing the contributions from urbanization, land cultivation, deforestation, etc.

Does Deforestation Really Cool the Planet?

"Will afforestation in temperate zones warm the Earth?' The answer will vary depending on the model used." [963]

Dr. David South, Auburn University

As the human population swelled to over seven billion people, we have altered the global landscape at unparalleled rates. To feed ourselves we have converted 11% of the earth's land surface to croplands. Over 20% of the earth is grassland and savannahs that are now threatened by desertification due to overgrazing and other abuses. We have lost 50% of our wetlands. Tropical rainforests have been lost at worrisome rates, and the spread of global urbanization is unprecedented. Our weather stations measure the air temperature 6 feet above the earth's surface, but *it is the air's contact with the earth's surfaces that drives air temperature.*

Global models struggle to estimate the climatic effects of local landscape changes. Different surfaces create vastly different temperatures and we know this intuitively and scientifically. Simply walk barefoot on a hot summer's day and enjoy the cool grass beneath your feet. Then step onto the pavement. The heat of the burning pavement is shocking. Higher surface temperatures always produce higher air temperatures,[15,463,] so by comparing satellite measurements of maximum surface temperatures, we can evaluate how landscape changes have impacted local climate.[468]

Direct satellite observations show forests have a cooling effect.[463] The canopies of the world's forests averaged no higher than 86°F, and in the shade beneath the canopy, temperatures are much lower. Grassland temperatures are much higher, ranging from 95 to 122°F, while the average temperatures of barren ground and deserts can reach 140°F.[15] The most persistently high surface temperatures in satellite history have been observed in Iran's Lut Desert, frequently reaching 154.4°F. Because barren ground heats so intensely, natives of America's southwestern deserts have used the high surface heat to bake their tortilla-like flat breads by spreading them over the rocks heated only by the sun. Before the satellite era, the highest North American ground temperature ever recorded nearly reached the boiling point. On July 15, 1972 the barren surfaces of Death Valley measured 201°F.

Wherever a forest is converted to a grassland, or a grassland to desert, or barren ground is created, it raises maximum surface temperatures by 10 to 40°F. Hotter land surfaces not only heat the air more severely during the day; hotter surfaces also emit much more infrared radiation at night. Even if concentrations of CO_2 or water vapor remained unchanged, the infrared radiation from warmer surfaces would add to the greenhouse effect. Although still debated, studies focused on landscape change now suggest trends in surface temperatures across the U.S. and the world have played an approximately equal or greater role in warming trends over the latter half of the 20th century.[8,9,19,20,41,50,466]

Studies measuring the direct effects of deforestation have concluded deforestation warms local and regional climates by drying the ground.[464,469,475,952,955] Deforestation has been shown to intensify and prolong droughts.[468,469] Scientists have also calculated that the recent loss of forests has contributed 15 to 30% of the increased CO_2. So land managers around the world are preparing to implement reforestation schemes to benefit both wildlife and climate. Nonetheless, some climate models argue against reforestation.

Although we instinctually seek a shady tree on a hot day, and intuitively understand the forest's cooling effect, global climate models argue that planting more trees will warm the planet.[470,471] They argue that bare ground and snow cover reflects more light but trees prevent that reflection. Therefore they believe trees raise the average temperature. Published in the Proceedings of the National Academy of Sciences of the United States of America, one study concluded, "We find that global-scale deforestation has a net cooling influence on Earth's climate."[470] To suggest that planting more trees will increase global warming, and denuding the planet will cool the climate is absolutely bizarre. I suggest the modelers visit the nearest desert for a reality check. In fact researchers now report that a misplaced emphasis on the reflection of light is the main reason why models have increasingly disagreed with actual temperature observations. [953]

The focus on rising CO_2 has additional negative consequences for our forests. It is estimated that swathes of tropical forest equal to the size of Panama are deforested each year. Ironically, part of that deforestation has been promoted in the name of minimizing our carbon footprints. The frenzied demand for immediate action against the global average temperature has spurred the razing of natural habitat in order to grow subsidized corn and sugarcane for biofuels. Putting aside the debate regarding biofuel's trivial effect on the net production of CO_2 and its disruption of food prices, from a conservation point of view this is a horrendous step backwards.

If we truly want to protect biodiversity, it would be much wiser to take energy from below the earth's surface, instead of scraping away more wild lands in order to farm biofuels. Yet in an article for the Huffington Post titled "Biofuel Could Eat Brazil's Savannas & Deforest the Amazon," Chris McGowan wrote that to exploit the government's subsidized gold rush in biofuels, "AOL founder Steve Case, film producer Steven Bing, supermarket magnate Ron Burkle, global financier George Soros, and other well-known investors could end up playing leading roles in Brazilian deforestation."[959] Maybe Soros believes he is cooling the planet.

A reliance on biofuels has other hidden costs. For example, after thousands of years of deforestation, the United Kingdom is now one of the few countries where forests have recently expanded thanks to conservation efforts. However, the government is now promoting biofuels by subsidizing wood-burning power plants. The UK's meager forest cannot supply enough wood fuel, so they import timber from California. The UK is also ignoring the lessons learned from Haiti and the

Dominican Republic where biofuels' negative impacts are clearly evident. When Columbus first discovered Haiti, he wrote of extensive forests with green trees full of fruit. Sugar plantations soon began replacing those forests and because Haitians depend on wood charcoal for fuel, they have continued to denude their forests at an accelerating pace. NASA satellite pictures easily detect a clear demarcation between Haiti's denuded landscape and the adjacent Dominican Republic where people use fossil fuels instead of trees.

Urbanization's Powerful Impacts

"The contribution of urbanization and other land uses to overall regional warming is determined to be 24.22%." [964]

Dr. Xuchao Yang, China Meteorological Administration

"Warming over barren areas is larger than most other land types. Urban areas show a large warming second only to barren areas." [43]

Dr. Young-Kwon Lim, Florida State University

Theoretically a blanket of CO_2 uniformly slows the cooling process throughout the day and night, everywhere in the world. However in many places maximum temperatures are cooling while minimum temperatures are rising. Globally, the average minimum temperatures rose two to three times faster than the average maximum temperatures.[10] This was not anticipated by the earlier climate models driven by CO_2. Even after fine-tuning, CO_2 driven models do not fully recreate the different behaviors of these temperatures.[22] Changes in cloud cover and landscape are known to affect these temperatures differently, but are difficult to model. However there is one consistent pattern. Weather stations near cities and airports consistently exhibited higher minimum temperatures than nearby rural areas.[476]

Dr. Thomas Karl, who now serves as the director of the NOAA's National Climatic Data Center, compared the temperatures in rural towns consisting of fewer than 2,000 people with more populated cities and towns. After accounting for changes in elevation and latitude, he reported that when populations reached 50,000 people, the average temperature was 0.43°F higher. Although the change in maximum temperatures was trivial, the minimum temperature was 0.86°F higher and the sole cause of the rising average. As populations increased, so did minimum temperatures. A town of two million people experienced a whopping increase of 4.5°F in the minimum causing a 2.25°F average increase.[52] Because a uniform blanket of CO_2 affected these cities and towns equally, the jump in temperatures must be due to urbanization effects.

Although urban heat islands are undeniable, many CO_2 advocates argue that growing urbanization has not contributed to recent climate trends because both urban and rural communities have experienced similar warming trends. However, those studies failed to account for the fact that small population increases in rural areas also generate extremely high rates of warming. For example, in 1967 Columbia, Maryland was a newly established, planned community designed to end racial and social segregation. Climate researchers following the city's development found that over a period of just three years, a heat island of up to 8.1°F appeared as the land filled with 10,000 residents.[17] Although Columbia would be classified as a rural town, that small population raised temperatures five times greater than a century's worth of global warming. If we extrapolated that trend as so many climate studies do, growing populations in rural areas would cause a whopping warming trend of 26°F per decade.

California climatologist James Goodridge also found that the size of a county's population impacted temperature trends. The average rate of 20th century warming for weather stations located in a county that exceeded one million people was 3.14°F per century, which is twice the rate of the global average. In contrast, the average warming rate for stations situated in a county with less than 100,000 people was a paltry 0.04°F per century.[18] The warming rate of sparsely populated counties was 35 times less than the global average. Since all counties were equally affected by increasing CO_2 levels, population and landscape changes better explain these vastly different trends. Have the warming effects of urbanization impacted the average more than rising greenhouse gases? Because current global climate models do not adequately account for landscape changes, scientists warn that failure to do so will have profound consequences on future policies.[462,463]

Global urbanization has contributed to higher minimum temperatures worldwide. In 1993, Karl reported that in over half of North America "the *rise of the minimum temperature has occurred at a rate three times that of the maximum temperature during the period 1951-90* (1.5°F versus 0.5°F) (emphasis added)."[10] Many skeptics became concerned that urbanization had affected weather stations directly, so meteorologist Anthony Watts organized a grassroots volunteer effort to photograph the surface conditions of every USHCN weather station. His results were published in the 2011 peer-reviewed paper, "Analysis of the impacts of station exposure on the U.S. Historical Climatology Network temperatures and temperature trends,"[26] and can be viewed on the website SurfaceStations.org.

In accord with Karl's urbanization studies, poorly sited weather stations located too close to buildings or sitting on pavement had led "to an overestimate of minimum temperature trends and an underestimate of maximum temperature trends". Well-sited weather stations were situated on grassy fields with greater separation from buildings and other sources of human-produced heat. Those well-sited stations did not show contradictory trends between maximum and minimum temperatures.

I first stumbled onto Watts' surface station efforts when investigating climate factors that controlled the upslope migration of birds in the Sierra Nevada. To understand the population declines in our high-elevation meadows, I surveyed birds at several low-elevation breeding sites and examined the climate data from foothill weather stations. Marysville, CA was one of those stations, but its steeper warming trend contrasted with other stations' data.

I later found a picture of the Marysville's weather station at SurfaceStations.org website. The Marysville weather station was Watts' poster child for a bad USHCN site; he compared it to the less-disturbed surface conditions at a neighboring weather station in Orland, CA. The Marysville station was located on an asphalt parking lot just a few feet from air conditioning exhaust fans. The proximity to buildings also altered the winds, and added heat radiating from the walls. Clearly these urbanization effects would distort Maryville's climate trends.

CO_2 advocates downplay the urbanization of weather stations arguing they only represent a small fraction of the earth's land surface and therefore urbanization contributes very little to the overall warming. That is true, however all the weather stations used to calculate the global average are located near some form of human disturbance. There is only one way to determine temperature trends in undisturbed natural areas. Tree rings are widely used by scientists as an indicator of temperatures in the wild where instrumental data is unavailable. Thus by comparing temperatures determined from trees in remote locations, we can disentangle some distortions caused by increasing urbanization.

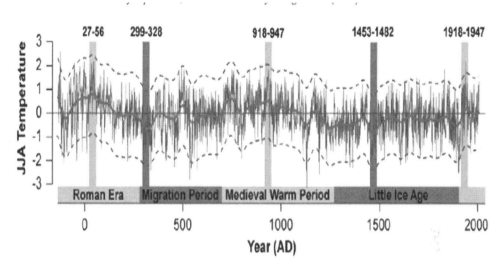

Figure 3. 2000 year summer temperature reconstruction of northern Scandinavia. Warmest 30-year periods are highlighted in by light gray bars (i.e. 27-56, or 1918-1947) and coldest 30-year periods are highlighted by dark gray bars (i.e. 1453-1482) Reprinted from Global and Planetary Change, vol. 88-89, Esper, J. et al, Variability and extremes of northern Scandinavian summer temperatures over the past two millennia, 2012, with permission from Elsevier.[705]

Not surprisingly, tree ring temperatures reveal much different trends than urbanized instrumental data. Most tree-ring studies reveal *lower* temperatures than the current instrumental data. A 2007 paper by 10 leading tree-ring scientists reported, "No current tree ring based reconstruction of extratropical Northern Hemisphere temperatures that extends into the 1990s captures the full range of late 20th century warming observed in the instrumental record."[714]

Because tree ring temperatures disagree with a sharply rising instrumental average, climate scientists dubbed it the "divergence problem."[79] However when studies compared tree ring temperatures with maximum temperatures there was no disagreement.[720,721] A collaboration of German, Swiss, and Finnish scientists found the average instrumental temperatures at remote rural stations in northern Scandinavia, also agreed with tree ring temperatures.[705] As illustrated in Figure 3, the 20th century trend for both the instrumental average temperature and tree rings in Scandinavia is strikingly similar to maximum temperature trends of the Sierra Nevada with peak temperatures in the 1940s. (Tree rings and the divergence problem are discussed further in Chapter 15.)

Ocean Cycles & the Global Average

"The IPCC has not paid enough attention to natural variability, on several time scales, especially El Niños and La Niñas, the Pacific Ocean phenomena that are not yet captured by climate models, and the longer term Pacific Decadal Oscillation (PDO) and Atlantic Multidecadal Oscillation (AMO) which have cycle lengths of about 60 years." [938]

Dr. Kevin Trenberth, National Center for Atmospheric Research

"The huge warming of the Arctic that started in the early 1920s and lasted for almost two decades is one of the most spectacular climate events of the twentieth century." [412]

Dr. Lennart Bengtsson, Max Planck Institute for Meteorology

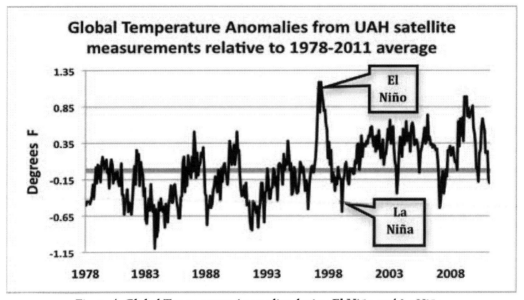

Figure 4. Global Temperature Anomalies during El Niño and La Niña .

Oceans store an awesome amount of heat; the mere top 10 feet of the world's oceans hold more heat than our entire atmosphere. For that reason, more than any other factor, the El Niño-Southern Oscillation (ENSO) dominates the global average. During a La Niña, the ocean absorbs heat and the trade winds confine heated tropical waters in a gigantic warm pool on the western side of the Pacific. During an El Niño, the warm pool is unleashed and warm waters sweep eastward across the Pacific. As warm waters spread across the surface, stored heat is ventilated and water vapor is pumped into the atmosphere[899] increasing the greenhouse effect.

During the 1997 El Niño, global average temperatures rose by 1.6°F. As soon as the ocean returned to the more normal conditions of a cool La Niña, temperatures dropped by 1.6°F (see Figure 4). That's a temperature change greater than a whole century of global warming.

In 1997, biologists studying abrupt changes in salmon populations uncovered a natural phenomenon that drives climate change and restructures ocean ecosystems and named it the Pacific Decadal Oscillation (PDO).[414] (see Chapter 11) Although technically the PDO describes cycles during which half of the Pacific Ocean's surface warms while the other half cools, it is useful to think of the PDO as a cycle between periods of more persistent El Niños versus more La Niñas. During the PDO's cool phase the Pacific Ocean undergoes an approximate 20-year period of more frequent La Niñas during which the Pacific absorbs more heat. In contrast, the PDO warm phase is a 20-year period of more frequent El Niños that ventilate stored heat. The cycles of heat absorption and ventilation are a major reason why the global average temperature does not always correlate with the strength of the sun or rising CO_2 concentrations.

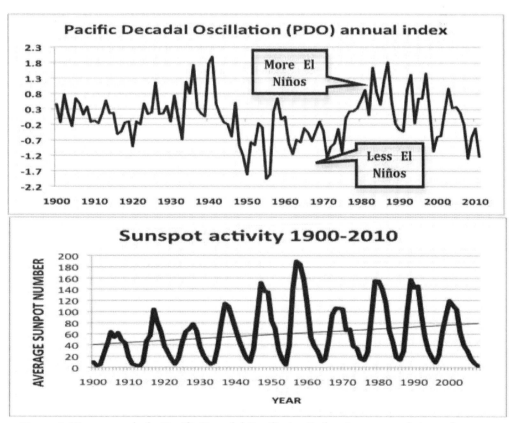

Figure 5. Upper panel: the Pacific Decadal Oscillation Index. Lower panel: Annual sunspot activity.

There were two PDO warm phases this century. The first began in the 1920s and lasted until about 1946. Climate scientists note coincidentally the "huge warming of the Arctic that started in the early 1920s and lasted for almost two decades is one of the most spectacular climate events of the twentieth century."[412] During that time, the Arctic rapidly warmed, reaching temperatures that were not equaled until about 2005. The second warm phase occurred between 1976 and 1999, and coincided with the most recent two decades of rapid warming.

In contrast, after the PDO entered its cool phase in 1999, global temperatures stopped rising despite all-time high levels of CO_2. Similarly during the PDO's previous cool phase between 1946 and 1976, temperatures cooled despite historic solar activity that was likely greater than any other time in the last one thousand years.[934] (Figure 5) Because heat is absorbed or ventilated during each phase, the PDO has become a pivotal focal point in the climate debate; the next warm phase will be enlightening.

Many skeptics argue that most of the warming during the last two decades had been caused when frequent El Niños ventilated solar-heated waters stored during the PDO's previous cool phase. Nature is now testing their argument. After wavering for a few years, the PDO entered its cool phase around 2003, but unlike the last heat-absorbing phase, solar activity has dropped to its lowest levels since 1900, and several astrophysicists suspect we are approaching a solar minimum similar to those that occurred during the Little Ice Age. If high solar activity has been the ocean's main heating source, then the next PDO warm phase will have less heat to ventilate and temperatures will be cooler than in the 1980s and 90s. This sun-PDO model predicts a trend towards cooler winters and more snow. Russian astrophysicists are not quite so cautious and they predict this cycle of low solar activity will launch a new Little Ice Age[†] within the next 30 years.[940]

Global warming advocates believe that the oceans have warmed primarily due to rising levels of CO_2. Based on that assumption Dr. James Hansen predicted a super El Niño in 2006 that would exceed the one in 1997, but that prediction failed.[202] Dr. Kevin Trenberth also believes rising CO_2 was the main cause of warmer oceans. Up to 2003, temperature measurements of the oceans' upper 900 feet have shown definite warming, but since then there has been no warming, and in fact there has been a slight cooling paralleling the recent decline in solar activity.[483] To explain the lack of recent warming, Trenberth believes the current cool phase of the PDO is absorbing the "missing heat" and storing it several thousand feet below the surface.[909] He intimates that during the next PDO warm phase, that stored heat will be ventilated by subsequent El Niños, causing temperatures to soar much higher than in the 1990s.

Counterintuitively, heat is carried to relatively shallow depths (see Chapter 5). But theory and past observations have shown that most of the warming and cooling of

---

[†] Little Ice Age was a abnormally cold period with widespread advancing glaciers spanning the 14th to 19th centuries.

the oceans typically happens within a few hundred feet of the surface.[919] Any mechanism that could cause widespread warming at the great depths suggested by Trenberth is strictly speculative and reliable data for those lower depths are quite scarce before 2003. Due to the lack of measurements, it will require at least another decade of observation before we understand how heat is transported to such depths if in fact that is the case.

Climate scientists like Dr. Roger Pielke, Sr. cautions that if heat can be so readily stored at great depths, then "we have a large gap in our understanding of the climate system."[938] It also means the global average is an unreliable measure of the heat stored on earth. Whether or not the PDO and other ocean cycles can explain the lack of recent warming, there is a growing awareness of the power of these 20 to 60-year cycles to affect climate change. Hardcore CO_2 advocates like Trenberth now acknowledge, "the IPCC has not paid enough attention to natural variability".[938]

The Great Adjustment Controversy

"results cast some doubts in the use of homogenization procedures and tend to indicate that the global temperature increase during the last century is between 0.4°C and 0.7°C, where these two values are the estimates derived from raw and adjusted data, respectively." [727]

Dr. E. Steirou, National Technical University of Athens, Greece

"a trend-type change in climate data series should only be adjusted if there is sufficient evidence showing that it is related to a change at the observing station, such as a change in the exposure or location of the station, or in its instrumentation or observing procedures." [35]

Dr. Xiaolan Wang, Meteorological Service of Canada

The global average suffers from another chimeric creation. Temperatures used to construct the average are not the originally observed temperatures. All the data has been adjusted. In the good old days, weather stations such as the one in Orland, CA (pictured on p. 40) would have been a perfect candidate to serve as a reference station. It was well sited, away from pavement and buildings, and its location and thermometers had not changed throughout its history. Climate scientists use reference stations to evaluate artificial human disturbances that might alter a temperature trend. For example, if a weather station is relocated, the new microclimate can create a different trend. If there was an unusual jump in temperature after the relocation, but no such jump at the neighboring reference station, scientists conclude that the relocation altered the trend.

Whenever there was a documented change in the instruments or the station's location, climate scientists rightfully adjusted the data if it resulted in a telltale "change-point". Unfortunately after all the documented quality control adjustments had been made, the trends and change-points of neighboring stations still varied widely. Although different locations create a variety of climate trends as demonstrated in Yosemite (otherwise why adjust the data for a relocated station?), scientists were looking for a homogeneous, statistically significant global trend. Local variability defies such a trend, but some feared there must be other unseen and undocumented changes distorting the data. However their new adjustments raised suspicions both inside and outside the scientific community.

After homogenizing the data, Orland's pre-1950 temperatures, that had originally captured the warm phase of the PDO, were lowered to create a steeper rising trend similar to Marysville's. In contrast, despite overwhelming urbanization, Marysville's data only experienced trivial adjustments (see Figure 6). This made absolutely no sense and similar adjustments to worldwide raw data soon ignited suspicions of a climate conspiracy among skeptics. I in no way suspect a deliberate conspiracy. For example, the raw data from Tahoe City's maximum were adjusted slightly lower. However, I do believe an inappropriate, one-size-fits-all statistical approach was misapplied and obscured other powerful climate factors such as the PDO.

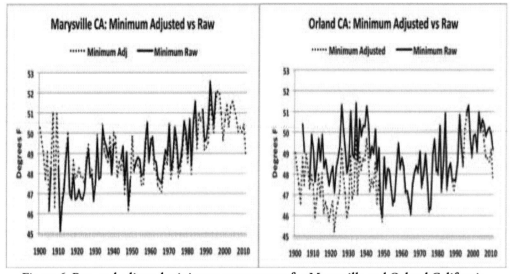

Figure 6. Raw and adjusted minimum temperature for Marysville and Orland California.

Climate scientists cloistered in their offices on the other side of the continent have absolutely no way of knowing to what degree urbanization or other landscape factors have distorted each weather station's data. So they developed a statistical method that compared trends amongst several neighboring stations, many of which had lower quality control than the USHCN stations.[74] Their methods boil down to what I term the "blind majority rules" method. The most commonly shared trend among neighboring stations became the computer's reference, and temperatures from deviant stations were then blended to create a "chimeric climate smoothie."

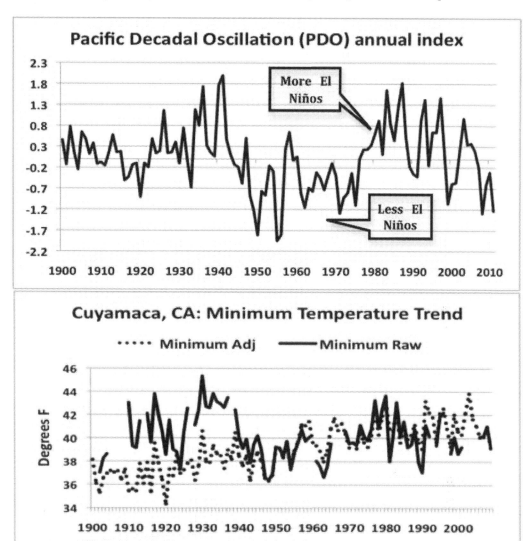

Figure 7. Upper panel PDO Index. Lower Panel Cuyamaca CA raw versus adjusted minimum temperatures.

Because the computers had been programmed to seek unusual "change-points" as a sign of undocumented modifications, natural cyclical change-points looked like deviations relative to steadily rising trends from increasing urbanization. The Pacific Decadal Oscillation caused natural change-points around 1946 and 1976. The rural station of Orland was minimally affected by urbanization, and thus more sensitive to the rise and fall of the PDO. Similarly, the raw data for other well-sited rural stations like the Cuyamaca in southern California also exhibited cyclical temperatures predicted by the PDO (see Figure 7, lower panel).

Marysville however was overwhelmed by California's growing urbanization and

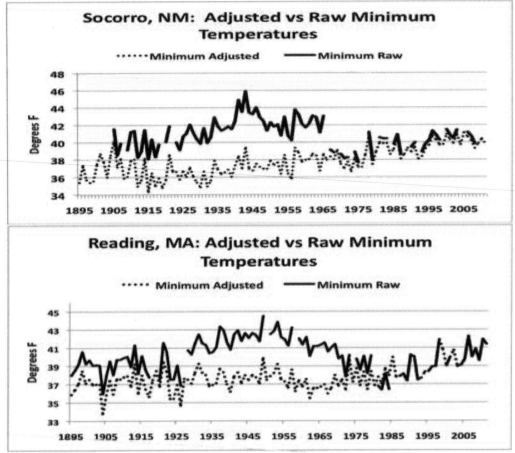

Figure 8. Original raw temperatures versus adjusted after homogenization for Socorro New Mexico and Reading Massachusetts.

exhibited a steady rising trend. Ironically, a computer program seeking any and all change-points dramatically adjusted the natural variations of rural stations to conform to the steady trend of urbanized stations. Around the country, very similar adjustments lowered the peak warming in the original data as shown for Reading, MA or Socorro, NM (see Figure 8). Paradoxically, an attempt to clean the data had allowed the effects of urbanization to infiltrate well-sited rural stations that were most sensitive to natural climate change.

Those homogenization adjustments now alter our perceptions, and affect our interpretations of climate change. Cyclical temperature trends were unwittingly transformed into rapidly rising warming trends, suggesting a climate on CO_2 steroids. The unadjusted average for the United States (see Figure 9) suggests the climate is more sensitive to cycles of the PDO, in contrast to the adjusted temperatures that suggests the climate is more sensitive to a steady rise in CO_2 levels.

Many climate scientists opposed those undocumented adjustments: "If the ultimate goal of the change point detection is to form homogeneous climate data series by correcting biases, a trend-type change in *climate data series should only be adjusted if there is sufficient evidence* showing that it is related to a change at the observing station, such as a change in the exposure or location of the station, or in its instrumentation or observing procedures (emphasis added)."[35] Others scientists reported that their analysis "cast some doubts in the use of homogenization procedures." *They found that the unadjusted rise in the 20th century's global temperature was just 0.7°F compared an adjusted rise of 1.3°F.*[727] The causes of climate change take on a much different focus when non-homogenized data are used, as seen in Figure 9.

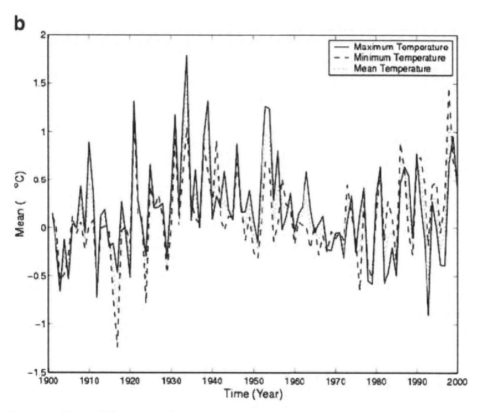

Figure 9. From: "The twentieth century contiguous US temperature changes indicated by daily data and higher statistical moments" 2011.[12]

For scientists examining the effect of local microclimates on the ecology of local wildlife, or for scientists examining trends in weather variability, homogenized data obliterates local variations. So those studies must use unhomogenized data that has only been corrected for documented changes, such as data from the US National Climatic Data Center's Global Daily Climatology Network (see Figure 9). In contrast to predictions that the rising global average would cause wilder weather, climate scientists found weather variability in the United States had decreased, and found more extremes of cold.[12]

That unadjusted data shows no signs of catastrophic global warming, and the original temperature data agrees with most tree-ring studies. All told, no American has experienced a decade of temperatures exceeding the 1930s. Advocates acknowledge this contradiction, but argue that the United States only represents 2% of the earth. Despite record breaking "average temperature" during the USA's 2012 drought, no state endured a record breaking maximum temperature. By turning a blind eye to these contradictions, they fail to ask the right questions. Why has rising CO_2 failed to raise American temperatures above the previous natural cycle? Is the climate less sensitive to CO_2? Or do more powerful cooling factors exist that overwhelm CO_2's effect?

Again, I urge every reader to visit the US Historical Climate Network website[‡] and compare the maximum and minimum temperature trends, and the raw and adjusted versions, to see how the homogenization adjustments altered the original data near your home and throughout the United States. Record breaking temperatures will vary depending on which data sets (original or crispy) are used. You will understand why scientists have debated those adjustments and why skeptics distrust these climate chimeras. It is a slippery slope when we begin rewriting climate history.

[‡] Google: USHCN interactive maps, or go to http://cdiac.ornl.gov/epubs/ndp/ushcn/ushcn_map_interface.html

4

The Emperor Penguin Has No Clothes

"If anything is clear, it is the unusual nature of this event, having never been seen before nor observed since among any other vertebrates anywhere in the Antarctic." [253]

Dr. David Ainley, Penguin Science

Fig. 10 Emperor Penguins.
Photo freely available via Wikimedia Commons.
http://www.flickr.com/photos/ianduffy/4322964957/

The Endangered Species Act (ESA) is an invaluable tool for saving species from extinction. Due to overhunting, the populations of numerous species had plummeted to precariously low numbers. However, a combination of more efficient food production and prudent hunting regulations has saved many species from imminent extinction. Many have now rebounded to historical highs. Whales, walrus, fur seals, and polar bears are all conservation success stories because of prudent hunting regulations. With the politicization of global warming however, gross exaggerations regarding the impact of recent climate change have been fabricated so that the ESA can be used as a legal tool to fight global warming. The unintended consequence has been a flood of irresponsible science that has created a dangerous political backlash that

51

threatens to undermine prudent regulations, specifically the ESA.

For example, from 2004 to 2009 when the Emperor penguin population was estimated at approximately 220,000 individuals,[912] the International Union for Conservation of Nature (IUCN) considered this a healthy number and listed the Emperor as a species of "Least Concern." Recent satellite surveys determined that by 2012, the population was even healthier, with nearly 600,000 individuals.[480,479] Instead of celebrating this success story, CO_2 advocates dredged up old data from a single colony that had suddenly declined during the 1970s to create a model demonstrating that rising CO_2 will cause the Emperors to soon go extinct. Although that colony has been stable and slightly increasing since the 1980s, and despite knowing that, overall, the 2012 data showed nearly three times more penguins than previously estimated, the IUCN raised widespread suspicions when they changed the Emperors status from "Least Concern" to "Near Threatened."

The model's deadly virtual reality was immediately trumpeted around the world. A 2009 *New Scientist* article warned, "Melting ice could push penguins to extinction...Emperor penguins are likely to be melted out of house and home by climate change, according to a new study...It doesn't look good. The models predict that, unless fossil fuels are phased out, there is more than a one-in-three chance that 95% of the Adélie Land colony of eastern Antarctica – *the best studied emperor penguin colony – will be gone by 2100* (emphasis added)."[256] The headlines in the *ScienceDaily* posed this question: "Emperor Penguins March Toward Extinction?"[254] And the BBC joined in: "Emperor penguins, whose long treks across Antarctic ice to mate have been immortalized by Hollywood, are heading towards extinction, scientists say."[257]

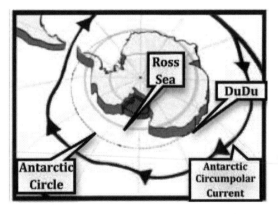

The population on which the extinction predictions were modeled is the same penguin colony that later starred in the superb documentary "March of the Penguins." The colony is located near the Antarctic Circle on the far side of the continent, opposite the Antarctic Peninsula, in an area under French jurisdiction called Adélie Land. On a series of small islands called the Pointe Geologie archipelago, just a few hundred meters from the Emperor's breeding ice, is the French research station, Dumont D'Urville, or as the locals like to say, DuDu. In making "March of the Penguins", the cinematographers framed every scene so that the viewers are never aware of the numerous buildings that sit close to the penguin colony. When the icebreaker delivers supplies each summer, it anchors in the open waters that just months earlier had served as a frozen penguin nursery.

The unusual proximity of the colony to the research station has allowed scientists to monitor this population longer than any other. Coincidentally, DuDu's penguin expert, Dr. Christophe Barbraud, whose papers initially claimed that the Emperor Penguins were decimated by climate change, was also the scientific advisor for "March of the Penguins" documentary. However the research station's proximity also subjected the Emperors to unprecedented human disturbance. In addition to disruptive survey methods, DuDu was at the center of heavy international criticism from conservationists when the French dynamited local islands to build an airstrip during the breeding season of the Adelie penguin, displacing ten percent of the penguins in the process.

The experts still debate the Emperors' mysterious 1970s disappearance. The sudden loss of half of the adults was so bizarre that penguin experts wrote, "If anything is clear, it is the unusual nature of this event, having never been seen before nor observed since among any other vertebrates anywhere in the Antarctic."[253] Although many lines of evidence point to preventable human interference, the prevailing global warming bias fueled an extinction model that arbitrarily blamed rising CO_2 levels. The model is more complex but this simplified model clearly states its logic.[260,275]

Simplified model: More CO_2 = more warmth = less sea ice = dead penguins

---

However, all observations contradicted their model. Indeed there has been more CO_2, but the local temperatures have not warmed (see Figure 11). In contrast to the models' predictions, Antarctic sea ice has been expanding (see Figure 12) and the kind of ice that the penguins breed on, fast-ice, is getting thicker.[262] Furthermore most studies show less ice benefits the penguins.[269] Finally, *there were never any dead penguins*. The adults just never returned.

Whether CO_2 levels played a role or not, any model designed with calculations that equate rising CO_2 to lost ice to dead penguins will inevitably kill all penguins in the model's virtual reality. Accordingly, the modelers predicted that DuDu's Emperors would inevitably plummet from about 6,000 to just 400 breeding pairs by the year 2100, with at least a 36% chance of extinction.[260,275]

I polled several groups of students, asking them what was the biggest threat to penguin species. Many had no idea. However the others had been grossly misled and unanimously indicted global warming and shrinking sea ice. In reality, of the approximately 17 penguin species worldwide, only the Emperor and the Adelie penguins (see Chapter 12) are tied to Antarctic sea ice, and both their populations are at all-time highs. In contrast, the most endangered penguins are the ice-avoiding species, and the biggest threats to those species have been human disturbance and the assisted colonization of invasive species.

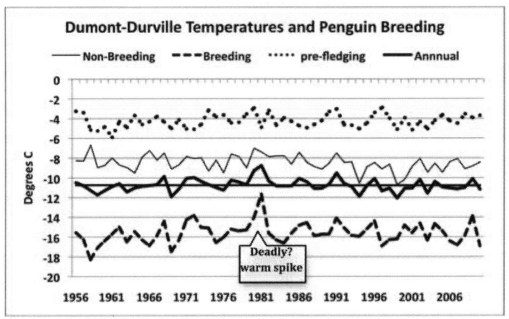

Figure 11. Temperature trends during critical periods of Emperor life cycle. Data courtesy the British Antarctic Survey.

Over the course of millennia, penguins—vulnerable, flightless birds—have survived because they've evolved on islands free of land predators. The Galapagos Penguin lives at the equator and thrives in the cold upwelling waters typical during normal La Niña years. It is the most threatened penguin and listed as critically endangered. Humans had introduced cats to the islands, and at some breeding sites cats have claimed as much as 49% of Galapagos adults.[258] Furthermore, cats introduced toxoplasma parasites against which the penguins had never built an immunological defense.[259] Similarly the African, the Humboldt, the Erect-crested, and the Yellow-eyed penguins are all endangered due to insults that include egg and guano collecting, tourists trampling nest burrows, introduced rats, ferrets and stoats, and oil spills. Most students did not even know there were penguins on the Galapagos. In contrast to these real environmental problems, students were only worried about Antarctica's healthy species because global-warming advocates have repeated deadly scenarios of CO_2 climate change.

A Deadly Warm Spike?

"the adults died en masse"

Shaye Wolf , Center for Biological Diversity

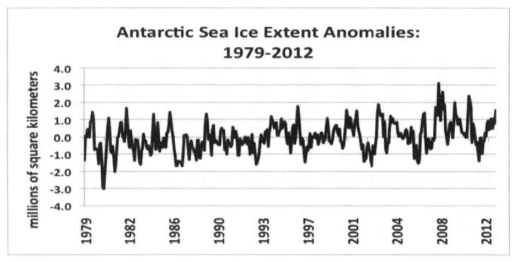

Figure 12. Increasing Antarctic Sea Ice Extent. Data courtesy of Cryosphere Today University of Illinois.

The ballyhooed extinction model was based on Dr. Barbraud's earlier work that suggested the disappearance of half of the Emperors in the 1970s was due to a warm spike and a temporary reduction in sea ice extent.[261] However, the logic of blaming sea ice extent completely contradicts the penguin's biology. It is well established that sea ice extent has absolutely no impact on the breeding Emperors. *In contrast, the most up-to-date research has verified that Emperors benefit most with more open water nearer their colony.*[269]

During my 25 years of studying birds, I had developed a fascination with Emperor penguins. I confess, my original interest in Emperor penguins was never driven by a concern for climate change, nor predictions of their pending extinction. I simply wanted to understand why the male of a nonhuman species accepted such a brutal co-parenting arrangement, which resulted in higher death rates for males. Were the males brave and selfless, or were they duped and awestruck by some crass sexual desire? Their unusual co-parenting scheme however, as beautifully portrayed in the "March of the Penguins", unfolds as a miraculous example of life adapting to the earth's harshest climate. And it was precisely the rigorous demands of this co-parenting scheme that made Barbraud's global warming and sea-ice extent argument so absurd.

As the sun fades with the passing March equinox, Emperors shuffle and belly-slide for distances of 20 kilometers or more over the sea ice. Inching along at top speeds of two to three km/hour, the trip takes several days. The male is driven by anticipation of a brief sexual encounter on the ice with a female he has likely just met. By the time the egg arrives, both he and the female will have fasted for about two months. Then, audaciously, the female persuades her new mate to care for the egg for an additional two months. After handing off the egg, (or more accurately footing off) the female departs to gorge on krill, fish, and squid in ocean waters that are 30–60°F warmer than the air temperatures her mate must endure.

Temporarily abandoned, the male carefully balances the entrusted egg on his feet while huddled with hundreds to thousands of jostling and braying brethren. For the next two months, he stalwartly incubates the egg in near-complete darkness, braced against bouts of sustained hurricane-force winds and temperatures that plummet as low as -58°F. He balances an instinctual blind faith that his new mate will return against his gnawing starvation. There is always the chance a leopard seal or shifting ice will prevent her return. Should he stay or should he go? At the risk of anthropomorphizing, such a grueling wait must evoke every possible separation anxiety. Perhaps marred by this deep psychological conflict, the males rarely mate with the same female ever again. Nonetheless, the following year he marches landward seeking new a mate and once again he will be left out in the cold.

The Emperor penguins are the largest of all penguins. They can store fat more rapidly than other penguin species, and with more fat they can withstand longer periods of food deprivation. (The ability to rapidly store fat and then judiciously consume it is the key to survival for species in the freezing polar regions) Being the largest, Emperors also conserve body heat more economically, and the larger males more so than females. Due to the female's smaller size, and her depleted energy store from egg-laying, the male is indeed the best candidate to endure an additional two months of fasting during the egg-incubation shift. The males' huddling behavior helps to successfully fend off the biting winds. Males continuously jostle for the warmth near the inner circle and a napping male may find himself on the unprotected, frozen periphery of the scrum. Very small colonies are at a disadvantage, lacking the aggregate body mass to generate a warmer microclimate. The key to the Emperor's survival however is their ability to find open water in the dead of winter so they can feed.

Although there was a brief and unusual warming spike during the 1980s breeding season (Figure 11), by any measure of logic, this brief warm spike would have eased their battle with the deadly cold. Temperatures were still far colder than all other seasons. However, to support their lawsuit, Shaye Wolf from the Center for Biological Diversity (CBD) wrote that the population had "plummeted by more than 50% in the late 1970s during a warm period with little sea ice cover, when adults died en masse. Because the sea ice continues to disintegrate, and the prolonged blizzards cause ongoing chick mortality, the colony has yet to recover."[911]

But CBD's claims are pure sensationalism and inaccurate. To blame "little sea ice cover" is absurdly meaningless. Furthermore *the penguins never died "en masse"*. The population declined over several years and the biggest drop in numbers occurred before the warm spike. There were never any dead bodies or evidence of starving penguins. In fact there was high breeding success during most years, and starving penguins do not have high breeding success. The adult penguins simply never returned to DuDu. Before the politics of global warming resurrected this incident, the French researchers in the 1980s suspected penguins had moved away or suffered from a heavy winter.[913,914]

The Critical Importance of Open Water

"Successful penguin breeding seasons in 1993, 1998 and 1999 coincided with lower-than-average fast ice extents and persistently short distances to nearest open water." [269]

Dr. Robert Massom, Antarctic Climate and Ecosystems Cooperative Research Centre

Although there are great benefits to the Emperors' extra bulk, it has some considerable downsides. It has bequeathed them with such terrestrial clumsiness, Emperors are confined to very low-lying flat surfaces, which are a rare feature on the Antarctic coast. Wherever the multitude of glaciers meet the coastline, Emperors face towering, insurmountable ice shelves. Elsewhere, ancient ice sheets have carved prohibitively steep shorelines. So Emperors are typically forced to nest on the ocean's smooth <u>fast-ice</u>. In modern times, Emperors have found only three small land patches on the entire rugged coastline that are suitably flat for breeding, and one was recently abandoned. All other colonies breed on flat fast-ice.

Fast-ice is sea ice that is *fastened* to the coast, or to islands, or to grounded icebergs. Except for occasional disturbances from shifting icebergs, fast-ice remains in place all winter. In contrast, pack-ice is free-floating and shifts with the winds. The winds that blow from the continent separate the pack-ice from the fast-ice, creating areas of open water called "leads" or "polynya" (pronounced *puh-lin-yuh*). When water freezes, it releases latent heat that temporarily maintains the open waters. As winds remove ice and water from the upper surface, warmer water also upwells from below. As long as the winds keep removing newly formed pack ice away from the coast, the combination of warmer ocean waters and the constant release of latent heat preserves vast stretches of open waters.[268] However, if the winds shift, the pack-ice can be blown against the coast and close the open waters. The fate of the penguins is blowing in the wind.

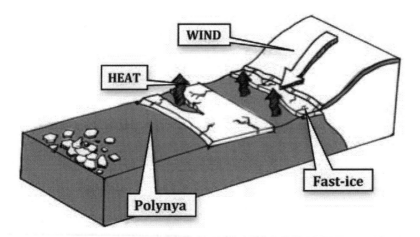

The Emperor's larger size also demands a lengthy nine-month breeding period, forcing them to breed through the winter. So they seek stable fast-ice that is first to form and last to melt. As soon as the fast-ice begins to solidify in late March, the Emperors begin their shoreward journey. But as the cold season progresses, both fast-ice and pack-ice continue to expand seaward. By the time the egg finally arrives in early winter, the colony is no longer just 20 kilometers from open water. The fast-ice now extends 60 to 100 km[§§] from shore, while the edge of the sea ice may be 200 to 400 km away. If an exhausted female was forced to waddle to the edge of the pack ice, she would most assuredly die. It is access to the open waters of polynyas (areas with 25% or more open water in an ocean otherwise completely covered with pack ice) and leads at the edge of the fast-ice, (or any opening in the ice) which permits successful breeding and survival.

Predictable winds funneled through ancient glacial valleys conspire with stored ocean heat to sustain open polynya all winter, and literally provide room to breathe for whales, seals and penguins. "Leads" are similar to polynya, but are typically narrower

---

[§§] 100 km is the equivalent of clambering from Boston to Providence, Rhode Island, or from San Francisco to San Jose, California.

and less reliable. To guarantee access to open water, most Emperor and Adelie penguin colonies are located near large, reliable polynya.[268] The Ross Sea polynya is the world's largest, nearly the size of California. This humungous body of open water not only sustains more air breathers during the winter, but allows more photosynthesis when the sun returns. The resulting robust food chain makes the Ross Sea a wildlife hot spot.

David Ainley and the scientists at Penguinscience.com are urging governments to make the Ross Sea a World Heritage Site, and I encourage you to support their efforts. The Ross Sea is home to 38% of the world's population of Adelie penguins; 26% of the world's population of Emperor penguins; more than 30% of the world's population of Antarctic petrels; and about 21% of world's population of Antarctic Minke whales.

The relatively shorter treks to nearby polynya or leads still inflict considerable hardships. For example, after footing off their eggs to their mates, satellite-tracked females took eight days to find open water that was just 100 kilometers away. It was not a nonstop march, and they needed to occasionally huddle together to minimize heat loss. They then spent "50-60 days at sea foraging, and took another 4 days to return across the fast-ice to the colony."[265] If forced to travel much greater distances to the edge of the pack ice, the consequences would be deadly. That's why pack-ice extent is simply not a factor in the Penguins' survival. If it ever were, less pack-ice would always be beneficial. Using the distance to the pack-ice edge to model penguin extinction is an abuse of a meaningless statistic that was opportunistically used to fit global warming theory. *It is the distance to the nearest open water that is critical for survival.*

The edge of the fast ice is under constant assault from colliding pack ice and weakened by upward surges of stored heat from the ocean depths. Although studies have determined the fast-ice has thickened over recent decades,[262] the winds and currents cause the extent of the fast-ice edge to vary. By comparing satellite pictures of the ice around DuDu, researchers determined the greatest breeding success, higher than 75%, occurred in 1998 and 1999 when areas of open water were within 60 km of the colony. In contrast, in 1996 and 1997, open water was more than 100 km from the colony, and breeding success plummeted to below 15%. A few satellite photographs from August 1963 have revealed that open waters were closer to the DuDu's colony than has ever been observed. That year the Emperor's breeding success was greater than 80% and the population hovered at its all-time high.[269]

DuDu's Emperor's ancestors had wisely founded a colony at one of Antarctica's premiere "just right" breeding places. Reliable, smooth fast-ice is protected from marauding icebergs by islands, ice tongues, and a myriad of grounded glaciers. Dependable ocean access was ensured by an open lead at the edge of the fast-ice just 100 km from the colony, and the Mertz Glacier Polynya to the east. And ocean currents, funneled upward through ancient troughs scoured in the sea floor, promoted occasional break-outs that brought open waters closer to the colony and enabled breeding bonanzas.

Yet with absolutely no evidence to support their speculation that climate change had killed the missing Emperors, Barbraud and his colleagues suggested that perhaps a few years of low pack-ice extent had somehow limited the Emperors' summer food supply and starved the adults. However, the adults had easily survived the winter with high breeding success. The plankton blooms during the following summer would surely multiply the available food supply. Summer starvation was highly unlikely.

There had been some evidence from the Antarctic Peninsula that sea ice affects the abundance of krill. Krill are shrimp-like creatures, and are the main link in the Antarctic food chain. However based on the abundance of other krill eaters there was no lack of food. DuDu's Adelie penguins feed on krill during the summer, and Adelie numbers were expanding. Humpback and Blue whales are massive krill eaters. Just a few decades earlier these whales were absent off the coast. Recently, Humpback whales near DuDu have increased by "an astounding 12%–13%" per year. Blue whale numbers were similarly increasing although more slowly.[279] These whales were staging a swift comeback thanks to hunting restrictions; however, such a rapid resurgence would be impossible without ample krill. There appeared to be plenty of food for all and Barbraud was grasping at CO_2 straws.

The Case For Direct Human Disturbance

"our understanding of the effects of climate change on marine ecosystems based on flipper-band data should be reconsidered." [277]

Dr. Clair Saraux, 2011

Perhaps it was simply the prevailing bias that prompted DuDu scientists to blame global warming for the missing adult Emperor penguins. Or perhaps they were trying to deflect the growing criticism that their own hands were to blame. By 1984, deaths caused by attached flipper bands were a growing concern. [270,271,272,273] Researchers at DuDu had attached flipper bands to Emperors during the years 1967 to 1980, [261] and it was precisely during this period that the Emperor population steadily plummeted to half of their pre-banding abundance. After banding ceased in 1980, survival estimates rapidly increased. Keep in mind that survival estimates do not necessarily mean the missing penguins died. Survival estimates merely calculate the percentage of banded birds that failed to return in following years and are then presumed to have died. Just as likely, the penguins may have lost their bands or migrated elsewhere to avoid having their breeding period so rudely interrupted. If the banded penguins had indeed died, there was no evidence of starvation.

In contrast, several lines of evidence made death-by-flipper-band more likely. After breeding, all birds must molt their feathers. In so doing, the skin around their feathers engorges with blood. Sadly, if flipper bands are attached too tightly, the bands restrict blood flow like a tourniquet and cause the penguins' flippers to atrophy. Studies of other penguin species estimated that flipper bands could lower survivorship by up to 13% a year. [270]

Another study noted increased drag while swimming and greater wear of the flippers, while others have observed lowered hunting efficiency that required more time to forage for food. The most recent study reports, "responses of flipper-banded penguins to climate variability differ from those of non-banded birds," and "*our understanding of the effects of climate change on marine ecosystems based on flipper-band data should be reconsidered.*" [277] I am not against the judicious use of flipper bands per se. I used leg bands for 20 years to track bird populations and careful banding provided invaluable information that helped us restore mountain meadows. However, the use of flippers bands has had deadly consequences, and researchers are now investigating much safer alternatives.

When DuDu's flipper banding ended in 1980, coincidentally the Emperors' survival rate immediately rebounded. Survival rates remained high for the next four years despite extreme shifts in weather and sea-ice extent. However, survival rates suddenly plummeted once again in 1985, despite an above-normal pack-ice extent. [261] Coincidentally, that is when the French began building an airstrip at DuDu, and to that end they had dynamited and joined three small islands. I have no way of knowing how the airstrip directly affected the Emperors who would have been completing their breeding when construction commenced. But it is easy to imagine that the shockwaves from those blasts permeated the waters. Such a powerful assault on their ears would certainly discourage a few Emperors from returning the following year.

In contrast to the Emperors, Adelie penguins arrive at DuDu after the snow and ice have melted, and they breed during the summer. Yet a similar population change accompanied the flipper banding of this species. Despite the ardent protests by Greenpeace activists and a host of conservationists, airstrip construction destroyed about 3000 Adelie penguin nests. The Adelie Penguins have yet to repopulate these islands, even after a marauding iceberg later demolished the airstrip.

Responding to protests against the destruction of the Adelie's nesting islands, DuDu researchers again employed flipper bands to evaluate the Adelies' response to the airstrip construction. They banded over 1000 Adelie penguins in 1989, another 930 in 1990, and less than 100 more by 1992. Perhaps coincidentally, the population of Adelie penguins immediately crashed during that time. And perhaps coincidentally, when the banding ceased the populations immediately recovered. After 1992, Adelie penguins proceeded to double their numbers in spite of global warming. However DuDu's Emperor population has yet to fully recover.

It is likely that atrophied flippers from tight bands cannot fully explain the 50% drop in the Emperor's abundance. However, interrupting the Emperor's pair-bonding to capture and wrestle each penguin and attach a flipper band is a significant disruption. Placing a band on an Emperor is no easy task. Emperors try to conserve energy in order to survive their winter fast, and tussles with researchers consumed precious energy. Furthermore, huddling was disrupted when researchers drove the penguins in single files in order to systematically read the bands. It is highly likely the Emperors chose to avoid these alien disturbances and sought more secluded breeding spots in Antarctica's "suburbs". Although penguins are loyal to a breeding site, penguins will relocate as needed; the suspected Emperor exodus is supported by a recent satellite survey.[274]

Because Emperors breed during the harshest of winters, most colonies are very difficult to access, and even large colonies can escape detection. However, satellites can now survey the entire continent by searching the white snow and ice for the telltale tarnish from piles of penguin poo. Satellite imagery has detected 10 previously unknown colonies, and one new colony was located very close to DuDu near the Mertz Glacier Polynya. There is ample reason to believe this new colony includes DuDu refugees and scientists are now doing genetic testing to determine if the two colonies are closely related.

The satellite data provided extremely good news for penguin lovers. *Compared to previously known estimates, that survey nearly tripled the number of known Emperor penguins.*[479,480] This larger population enumeration doesn't necessarily mean the number of penguins is rapidly increasing due to global warming. It only means more penguins have been detected. There is no way to know how many truly existed before these more comprehensive surveys were possible. However, a larger population does make the species less vulnerable to natural episodic calamities, which means the Emperors are less vulnerable as a species.

Emperors have evolved the flexibility to cope with changes in their food supply by hunting krill, fish, or squid, but they have not evolved coping mechanisms to remedy atrophied flippers due to improper banding. Nor are breeding Emperors predisposed to acquiesce to disturbances by unwelcomed humans. In addition, penguin populations have not evolved immune systems to deal with exposure to novel diseases. Antarctica's isolation has protected Emperors from invading diseases for millennia, but humans have now assisted the migration of a suite of illnesses into Antarctica. Studies show Emperors now have antibodies for fowl cholera and the infectious bursal disease virus. Paramyxoviruses were isolated from Adelie penguins at DuDu and one nearby station, but no others. Furthermore the waters around DuDu contain unusually high bacteria counts due to the research station's effluent. There have been a few noted Adelie penguin die-offs around other research stations at Signy Island and Casey Station where viral agents have been suspected, but necropsies were never done. At Mawson Station, well-fed Adelie penguin chicks were suddenly unable to walk, and 65% of the chicks soon died.[280] *These diseases were likely introduced by human tourists and researchers.*

The Power of Global Warming Bias

"In religion and politics people's beliefs and convictions are in almost every case gotten at second-hand, and without examination, from authorities who have not themselves examined the questions at issue but have taken them at second-hand from others."

Mark Twain

Not only has the CO_2 bias misdirected conservation concerns, it has hijacked the objectivity of good scientists. For example, I have always admired the work of penguin expert Dr. David Ainley. He has dedicated his life to studying and preserving wildlife. He has published numerous papers and wrote the book on Adelie penguins. Although Ainley adamantly disagrees with Barbraud's suggestion that Emperor penguins had starved to death during the 1970s decline, he believed global warming had prevented the Emperor's recovery. He suspected CO_2-warming was causing thinner fast-ice that allowed for premature ice breakouts that could potentially wash the chicks out to sea[278] Although those proposed breakouts were consistent with global warming concerns, at DuDu they were a myth. Ainley had been deceived by one careless and nebulous sentence by Barbraud, who had simply written, "Complete or extensive breeding failures in some years resulted from early break-out of the sea-ice holding up the colony, **or** from prolonged blizzards during the early chick-rearing period".[261]

After an extensive search of the scientific literature, other than a few collisions from marauding icebergs, there was absolutely no evidence of any such deadly breakouts. However if Ainley had observed chicks being washed out to sea, I believed I could trust his observations. So I emailed him and after several friendly exchanges, it became clear that his belief in catastrophic ice breakouts had been based solely on Barbraud's reference, not due to observation. Echoing Galileo's concerns century's ago, Mark Twain wrote, "In religion and politics people's beliefs and convictions are in almost every case gotten at second-hand, and without examination, from authorities who have not themselves examined the questions at issue but have taken them at second-hand from others." Scientists are not immune to such second-hand folly.

Twain also wrote, "It is wiser to find out than to suppose," so following that advice, I emailed Barbraud and asked for the dates during which he had observed "early break-out of sea-ice holding up the colony". As it turns out, I was not the only one having difficulty finding evidence for such catastrophic events. Dr Barbraud replied, "We are currently doing analyses to investigate the relationships between meteorological factors and breeding success in this species, including dates of sea ice break out, *which are relatively difficult to find for the moment!*" So why did he ever make the claim of "premature breakouts" in the first place? It should make us all stop and consider how easily blind suppositions become edified in the scientific literature and in models.

From our email discussions, I felt a kindred spirit with Ainley. We share a great desire to understand and communicate the wonders of nature. And again I urge you to support his efforts to make the Ross Sea a World Heritage site. However it is clear that the bias of global warming had compromised his scientific objectivity.

I apologize for any embarrassment that my statements may bring, but I feel it demonstrates a critical point. *Whether we are skeptics or advocates, we are all blinded by our beliefs.* Ainley's website provided student activities for the classroom. One lesson presented the graph in Figure 13, (his Fig. 5) showing the mysterious decline of the Emperor Penguins at DuDu and a *fictitious* temperature trend. Students are then prompted, "Look at the Figure which shows the population trend of Emperors at Pt

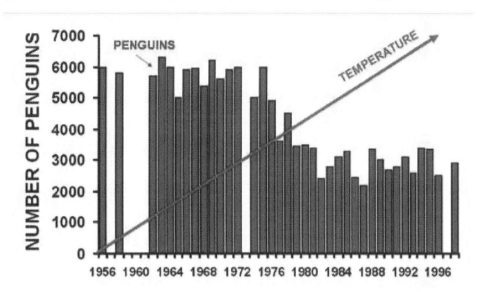

Figure 13. Graph from PenguinScience showing imagined relationship between penguins and temperature

Geologie and the temperature. Make a statement about the future of this colony if the temperature trend continues."

Then in the teacher notes for those who missed the obvious implications, the answer is provided. *"If the temperature trends continue at Pt Geologie, the Emperor penguins will not be able to raise their chicks and the colony will continue to decline."* However the students were never told that temperature trend never existed. It was absolute fiction. I emailed David and asked how he justified such a false representation. He apologized and promised to fix it saying, "My intent with the graph was to refer to the temperature trend, a period when temperature was increasing. Sorry about that." I have superimposed Ainley's rising temperature arrow on the real DuDu temperatures in Figure 14.

I have no doubt Ainley's global warming concerns are sincere and driven by an undying, selfless passion to preserve Antarctica's wildlife. His earlier work had connected penguin success and failures with climate change driven by natural cycles and shifting winds, and those connections are all well supported by observation. Yet he was a victim of the prevailing global warming bias.

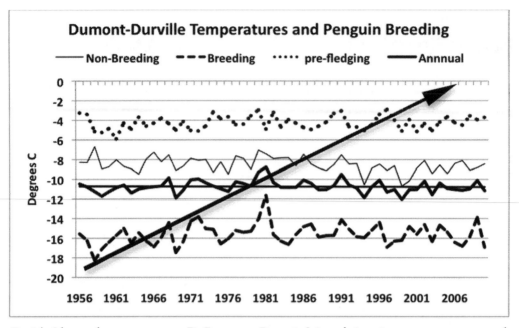

Fig 14. Observed temperatures at DuDu versus PenguinScience's imaginary temperature trend (Thick arrow)

So I would like to suggest a more valuable activity, not only for teachers and students, but scientists and lay people, skeptics and advocates alike. Compare the real temperatures at DuDu with the fabricated big black temperature arrow that suggested rising CO_2 and global warming had killed the Emperors. Then ask yourselves, "Why would an expert, whose work is so admirable in so many ways, fabricate a false warming trend?"

The real lesson here is that people from all walks of life, even dedicated scientists, will be blinded by their beliefs. Only respectful debate from a diverse audience can save us from our own illusions. It is why the rallying cry of my generation's fight for social justice was always "Question authority!" Yet in a widespread attempt to stop meaningful debate, those who still question are condemned as deniers.

5

All Temperatures Are Not Created Equal

"Temperature, by itself, is an incomplete characterization of surface air heat content" [965]

Dr. Roger Pielke, Sr. University of Colorado

"the trend in global surface temperatures has been nearly flat since the late 1990s despite continuing increases in the forcing due to the sum of the well-mixed greenhouse gases." [455]

Dr. Susan Solomon, National Oceanic and Atmospheric Administration (NOAA)

The global average temperature is a poor indicator of how much heat has been *added* to Earth's climate system. Without adding any additional heat, temperatures will rise whenever stored heat ventilates from the oceans. In the Arctic, as in the Antarctic, stronger winds expand the open water of coastal polynya (see Chapter 4), even when temperatures are 20° below freezing. More open water allows more heat to ventilate, and as new ice forms, more latent heat is released, causing temperatures to rise. Similarly ventilated heat during the 1997-98 El Niño caused the average global temperature to rise 1.6°F as the oceans cooled. Again, just the top 10 feet of the world's oceans contain more heat than the entire atmosphere, and winds typically ventilate the ocean's top 100—300 feet.

In addition, the El Niño cycles cause alternating periods of droughts and floods (see Chapter 9). Without adding any additional heat, temperatures will rise wherever there is a loss of soil moisture. During a drought, the lost heat capacity of the soil can raise air temperatures to record-breaking highs even during periods of global cooling. The world's record for the hottest temperature was set in Death Valley on July 10, 1913 (see Chapter 7). Conversely, even when the sun adds heat, temperatures may not change at all because that heat is absorbed by the oceans or by wetter soils.

El Niños also release water vapor, which increases both the heat capacity of the atmosphere and the greenhouse effect.[899] Fewer El Niños in the past 10 years and less water vapor have been associated with the recent lack of warming.[898] NOAA scientists have observed that a decrease in the water vapor in the stratosphere is allowing more heat to escape back to space. Scientists calculated declining stratospheric water vapor "acted to slow the rate of increase in global surface temperature over 2000–2009 by about 25%."[481] Conversely, the cycle of more frequent El Niños and the added water vapor suggests El Niños could account for 25% of global warming.

Without accounting for the heat capacity of the air and soil, it is absolutely impossible to estimate how much heat any given temperature represents. *It takes 1000 times more units of heat to raise the temperature of a bucket of water by 1° than it does to raise a bucket of air by 1°.* Averaging dry temperatures with moist tempreatues creates a chimeric measurement that tells us precious little about how much heat has been added by greenhouse gases.

At the risk of being silly, a simple thought experiment provides a visceral example of why all temperatures are not created equal. But a word of warning: Unless you hope to grab a starring role in a movie sequel to "Jackass", this experiment is just a thought experiment. Imagine turning your oven on to 212°F (100°C). On the stovetop, you also bring a pot of water to boil. Since water boils at 212°F (100°C), both the air in the oven and the boiling water have reached equal temperatures. Imagine placing your hand in the oven and counting. You could count to one hundred without breaking a sweat.

For the second part, I again stress the thought-only part of this experiment. Imagine placing your hand in the boiling water and counting. In reality, you wouldn't get the first number out of your mouth before screaming in pain! Despite registering the exact same temperatures, you were burnt by the water's "hidden" heat.

In addition to water's heat capacity, water absorbs and releases heat as it changes between solid ice, liquid water, and water vapor. For example, liquid water at 32°F contains 80 times more heat than ice at 32°F. Because the observable temperature does not change, the heat required to melt the ice is called "*latent heat* of melting." When water freezes, it releases latent heat; that heat is the main mechanism that promotes the open waters of polynya. Conversely, in order for ice or snow to melt, it absorbs heat without raising air temperatures. The local highlanders of the Sierra Nevada know that a heavy winter snowpack will always bring cooler summer temperatures, because much of the summer heat melts the snow without raising air temperatures.

In addition, the snowpack stores water, which then moistens the soil during the summer drought. When water changes from a liquid to a vapor, it must absorb 600 times more heat before any additional heat will raise the temperature. Moist habitats are always cooler than adjacent dry habitats. For example, ride a bike at night. Without seeing anything, you can feel the coolness in the air whenever you approach a stream. Climate models struggle to simulate California's temperature trends[1] in part because changes in rainfall, snowfall, soil moisture, lost wetlands, and irrigation can have a far greater impact on local temperatures than rising CO_2 levels. To add to their difficulties, global climate models still struggle to simulate El Niño cycles[228] and California's precipitation patterns are determined by El Niño.

Lost Wetlands Raise Temperatures

"The results continue to show a positive feedback in which land degradation in drylands increases local temperatures and potential evapotranspiration levels thereby exacerbating the degradation of the landscape."[20]

Dr. Robert Balling, Arizona State University

On a global level, researchers have concluded that changes in surface moisture that accompany landscape changes give rise to changes in climate that may be equal to the theoretical changes caused by rising CO_2.[6] Partially due to lost wetlands and degraded watersheds, many scientists argue land use is playing a measurable and significant role in ongoing climate change through a "set of mechanisms independent of greenhouse gas emissions."[19,50,466]

A rise in a region's maximum temperature may be a much stronger indication that we have degraded the local environment than it is an indication of our carbon footprint. For example, studies of temperatures in Arizona and Mexico have shown that lost vegetation from severe overgrazing and other careless practices had caused the soil surface to dry. This drying process increased temperatures by as much as 7°F compared to adjacent lands that had not been so mistreated.[20]

When a stream is trapped in a deep channel, the amount of erosion caused by the passage of the water increases with every passing year. The loss of subsurface water in our Sierra Nevada meadows began over a century ago. Hydrologists tell me nearly every stream in the United States has been similarly degraded to some extent, and studies have demonstrated that stream channel erosion radically alters the microclimate. Temperature differences of up to 36°F have been measured between habitats kept wet by a perennial stream versus adjacent upland habitat where soils were no longer moistened by the stream.[71]

Additionally, channelized streams and degraded watersheds more readily shunt water from the land to the oceans. A 2007 study published in the Proceedings of the National Academy of Sciences reported, "On average, land-use change has increased global runoff by 0.08 mm/year and accounts for ~50% of the reconstructed global runoff trend over the last century. Therefore, we emphasize the importance of land-cover change in forecasting future freshwater availability and climate."[72] If humans truly want to help the environment, help wildlife, and improve local climate, restoring watersheds and natural stream flow will provide far greater benefits than trying to control CO_2 levels.

California and the world have already lost 50% of their natural wetlands, which significantly affects local climate change.[76] When we were restoring the Carman Valley watershed, I became acutely aware of how the lost wetlands in California and Nevada affected temperature trends. The weather stations at Tahoe City (page 4), and Battle Mountain, Nevada are about 200 miles apart. Although weather varies, the climate trends at both stations were broadly similar. Both registered similar 2-4°F cooling trends in maximum temperature since the 1930s. However, the neighboring Winnemucca, Nevada weather station exhibited the exact opposite, a steep rising trend (see Figure 15).

The weather station at Winnemucca is located just 50 miles west of Battle Mountain and about 150 miles east of Tahoe City. The two Nevada sites have virtually identical elevations and experienced the same CO_2 effects. Yet since 1905 the Winnemucca station displayed a steep 6-7°F warming trend. Such a remarkable contrast in temperature trends can only be due to changes in local factors. And the lower heat capacity due to lost wetlands is the most compelling and comprehensive explanation.

Lake Winnemucca was one of three major remnants of ancient Lake Lahontan that once covered most of Nevada about 10,000 years ago. Since that time the earth has entered a long-term drying cycle. Although Lake Winnemucca withstood the drying trend of the past ten millennia, it could not survive mankind's transformation of the Great Basin. The Derby Dam was the first project of the National Reclamation Act of 1902, which funded irrigation projects throughout the arid western United States. In 1903 the dam was built on the Truckee River, and began diverting waters that had normally flowed from Lake Tahoe into Pyramid Lake and then continued eastward into Lake Winnemucca. By the late 1930s Lake Winnemucca went dry. Accordingly, while Battle Mountain cooled, Winnemucca experienced a warming trend that paralleled the drying of the lake. As might be expected after the lake was lost, the trend in maximum temperatures at both stations have been similar for the past 40 years.

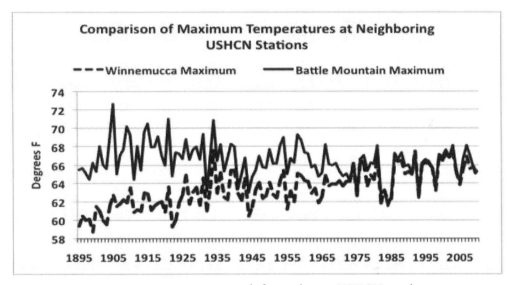

Figure 15. Opposite temperature trends from adjacent USHCN weather stations

The physics of lost heat capacity predicts a warming trend for maximum temperatures, but a cooling trend for minimum temperatures. Climate scientists call this the "hot days/cool nights phenomenon" observed during droughts[34] and observed in climate models when soil moisture changes.[27] As anyone who has camped in the desert realizes, dry land heats more quickly in the day, and it cools more rapidly at night. When the lake was still present, heat stored during the day was slowly released at night. The lake also increased atmospheric moisture that trapped heat waves and slowed the cooling process. After the wetlands had been lost, basic physics tells us that minimum temperatures would drop lower. Indeed that was exactly what we see in the raw data (although the Pacific Decadal Oscillation also played a role). Although the original data captures the expected cooling, the current practice of homogenizing climate data adjusted minimum temperatures again resulting in an incongruous warming trend.

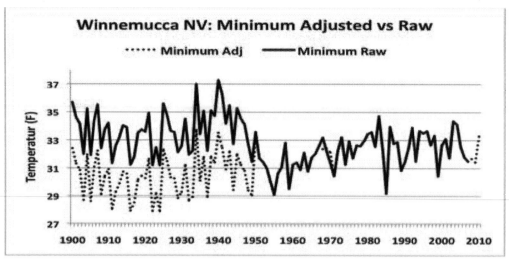

Figure 16. Comparison of Raw versus adjusted minimum temperatures at Winnemucca, NV.

Heating The Everglades

"summertime maximum temperatures increased and convective rainfall decreased when natural vegetation was replaced with current land cover."[51]

Dr. Curtis Marshall, Colorado State University

The effect of lost wetlands on temperature and local climate can be seen on much larger scales. The Everglades ranks as one of my top three all-time favorite parks. A bike ride through Shark Valley is always a must. There is something unspeakably awesome about coasting by hundreds of alligators basking just a few feet away, alongside sunning Anhingas and wading roseate spoonbills and white ibises. Alarmingly, as humans drained the swamps, they noticed dwindling wildlife as well as reduced rainfall and higher temperatures. While most of the southeastern United States (Mississippi, Alabama, Georgia, South Carolina, and northern Florida) has experienced a cooling trend since 1900,[3] only southern Florida has abruptly warmed.[74]

The Everglades determines much of the region's rain cycle. Moisture evaporates from the swamps and is carried northward as clouds, where it then falls as rain, feeding the Kissimmee River and Lake Okeechobee. Waters then recycle back to the Everglades via rivers and streams. Draining the swamps breaks the cycle. Nonetheless, since the 1890s people have been draining the swamps for agricultural and residential use. The heavy rains from the hurricane of 1926 triggered a chain of events that would soon wreak havoc on the Everglades' ecosystem for decades to come. The hurricane wrought massive flooding that breeched the early-generation levees that surrounded

Lake Okeechobee and hundreds of new residents in reclaimed swamplands drowned. In response, the Army Corps of Engineers walled off Lake Okeechobee with the massive Herbert Hoover Dike, interrupting southern Florida's natural water cycle. In addition, the Central and Southern Florida Flood Control Project set about building levees and channelizing streams in order to control future floods. As a result, the Everglades continued to dry, and by the 1970s it was clear that the Everglades' ecosystem was in serious peril.

As the Everglades Park was increasingly drained, people also observed a coincidental decrease in rainfall. Regional climate models mapped rainfall in 1900 across simulated natural landscape and compared that with rainfall across the altered landscapes of 1973 and 1993. In agreement with observations, their models showed that the lost wetlands caused a decrease in rainfall by 9% in 1973 and 11% in 1993.[75] Southern Florida's contrasting rise in temperature coincides neatly with the draining of its swamps and decreased rainfall.[951] It is highly unlikely that CO_2 warmed only southern Florida but not the rest of the southeastern USA.

Fortunately, although Florida's water issues are still very contentious, there has been increasing bipartisan support to preserve the Everglades, and conservation efforts are now striving to restore the natural hydrology. The Everglades' wildlife will certainly benefit as wetland restoration will buffer the region from all climate change. However, wetland restoration may not offset the growing threats from the assisted colonization. Invasive species like the introduced walking catfish or the Burmese pythons are altering the native ecosystem.

Raising Temperatures from Below

"There are, however, arguments in support of an important role for oceanic heat in shaping the Arctic pack ice. They are often keyed to the presence of warm intermediate-depth (150–900 m) water of Atlantic origin" [252]

Dr. Igor Polyakov, University of Alaska, Fairbanks.

"Until concentrations of Green House Gases reach higher values, climate signals from natural variability may be comparable in magnitude to those from external forcing [i.e. CO_2]." [643]

Dr. Vladamir Kattsov, Voeikov Main Geophysical Observatory

In the polar regions, rising temperatures are often caused by stored heat escaping from the ocean below. Counterintuitively, warmer air temperatures in polar regions often indicate heat ventilated from a cooling ocean. There is so much heat stored between the 100 and 1000 foot depths of the Arctic Ocean, scientists estimate it could easily melt all the Arctic's winter sea ice several times over.[485,656] Although temperatures around the South Pole are predictably the coldest in the southern hemisphere, temperatures around the North Pole are higher than temperatures over

Siberian and Canadian landmasses due to heat emanating from the ocean. Accordingly Inuit hunters prefer to build a winter igloo over the ice in order to capture the escaping heat.

Although intuitively we would expect warm water to float to the surface, warm salty water formed in the tropics is transported to the Arctic where it sinks below the surface and is stored at significant depths. Decades later the winds can bring that heat to the surface. Prominent climate scientists studying the Arctic wrote, "One could ask, did the warming air temperatures act to thin and decrease the area of sea ice, *or did the thinner and less expansive area of sea ice allow more heat to flux from the ocean to warm the atmosphere?*"[536] In other words, it is extremely difficult to determine directly if warmer air temperatures caused less ice, or if less ice caused warmer temperatures. But there is a plethora of evidence to suggest a great proportion of the warming comes from below.

Just before the loss of Arctic sea ice began, researchers measuring air temperatures over the ice-covered Arctic Ocean in the 1980s and 90s reported, "we do not observe the large surface warming trends predicted by models; indeed, *we detect significant surface cooling trends* over the western Arctic Ocean during winter and autumn. This discrepancy suggests that present climate models do not adequately incorporate the physical processes that affect the polar regions (emphasis added)."[538]

A few years later, climate scientists observed that an atmospheric cycle called the Arctic Oscillation had caused a major shift in the winds. They reported a strengthening of the surface winds from the interior of Eurasia, the coldest region of the Northern Hemisphere.[536] During the dead of a brutal winter, those winds expanded the polynya (see Chapter 4) along the Eurasian coast, while simultaneously pushing thicker ice from the Arctic Ocean out into the North Atlantic. Climate scientists concluded "it can be inferred that at least part of the warming that has been observed is due to the *heat released during the increased production of new ice*, and the *increased flux of heat to the atmosphere through the larger area of thin ice* (emphasis added)."

The initial loss of Arctic sea ice was not caused by air temperatures heated above the melting point by rising CO_2. Below-freeezing winds had removed thick ice trapped inside the Arctic, resulting in more open water.[535,536] The removal of the insulating ice cover suddenly allowed the winds to mix the Arctic Ocean to far greater depths, and that brought more warm water to the surface. The wind-blown loss of thick ice resulted in more extensive areas of thinner first-year ice. As in the Antarctic, first-year ice melts rapidly each summer, but rapid melting is not an indication of warmer air temperatures. For example new, thinner ice was blown into Alaskan coastal waters during the 2002 and 2003 summers "where extensive melting was observed, even though temperatures were locally colder than normal"[535]

The notion of "lurking hot water" below the frigid Arctic seems to defy our intuitive understanding. However, whether or not a substance sinks or floats is determined by its density. Cold air is denser than warm air, so warm air rises and cold air sinks. Likewise warmer fresh water will rise and colder fresh water will sink. Salt water adds another complication to the equation. When the sun evaporates water from the surface of the tropical oceans, the salt is left behind and becomes increasingly concentrated. The increasing salinity makes the water so dense that warm salty water can then sink below cold water that is less salty.

Figure 17. Fresh water

A simple experiment demonstrates how changes in saltiness cause heated water to sink or float. Begin by placing an egg in a glass of fresh water and watch it sink (sometimes an old, air-filled egg will float). The egg sinks because the fluids inside the egg are denser than the surrounding freshwater. The egg is denser because it contains more dissolved salts and nutrients. (see Figure 17)

By adding enough salt (see Figure 18), the water in the glass becomes denser than the egg, so the egg "magically" floats to the surface as the denser salty water claims the bottom of the glass. (Non-iodized salt dissolves better, otherwise you may need to add quite a bit of salt to carry out this experiment.) Likewise because fresh water is less dense, it also floats on top of denser salt water.

Figure 18. Salty water

Now imagine that the floating egg represents a mass of warm, salty water from the Gulf Stream. You can imitate the insulating effects of fresh melt water or rainwater by gently pouring a thin layer of fresh water into the glass. The fresh water will sit on the surface above the saltier water and cause the egg to sink below the freshwater boundary (see Figure 19). Throughout the world's oceans, masses of warmer salty water lurk beneath cooler surfaces. When storms or events such as an El Niño bring this warmer water to the surface, air temperatures rise as the heat is ventilated.

You can simulate how the winds can bring that warmer water to the surface by blowing on the freshwater to mix the upper layer with the saltier

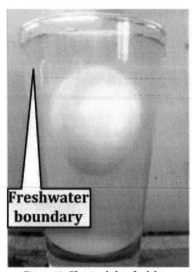

Figure 19. Floating below fresh layer

water below. At first, the egg (representing stored heat) may sink even lower as the fresh water layer merely dilutes the uppermost layer of salt water. However after the sustained turbulence from a breath, the upper layer will become salty enough to allow the egg to once again float on the surface. It is a combination of latent heat released from the freezing of new ice and the heat brought to the surface by the winds that maintains the open waters of polynyas.[666]

In both the Antarctic and Arctic, surface waters are always colder and fresher than the water below. When oceans freeze, the water freezes but the salt doesn't. Instead, that salt concentrates into a cold dense brine that sinks to the very bottom of the ocean. Satellite images have traced a flow of cold brine first formed along the coast of Antarctica as it moves along the bottom of the sea floor up to the middle of the Atlantic.

When the winter sea ice melts each summer, it produces a layer of fresher water that floats on the surface. However unlike the Antarctic that is isolated by the world's most powerful current (see Chapter 12), warm and salty waters heated in the tropics, can readily enter the Arctic Ocean via the Gulf Stream or Bering Strait. Those heated waters sink below the fresher surface layer. The freshwater creates a boundary layer that insulates warmer saltier water from the sea ice above. Scientists can trace the paths of intruding "Atlantic Water" and "Pacific Water" and have documented that Atlantic Water takes an approximate 14-year journey around the Arctic ocean. That heat is typically ventilated in polynya or when currents force the water onto shallow coastal shelves.[252]

The melting of sea ice by heat stored below the ocean's surface is most easily seen from satellite pictures (see Figure 20). Arctic ice reaches its maximum extent in March. Freezing air temperatures south of the Arctic Circle still keep the Hudson Bay and Bering Sea frozen. However, intrusions of warm Atlantic water have melted sea ice deep inside the Arctic Circle despite the freezing air temperatures. A weather cycle known as the North Atlantic Oscillation changes the winds and alters the flow of intruding Atlantic Water which has its greatest impact on sea ice in the Barents Sea. During the past two decades scientists have observed an increase in the volume of warm water penetrating more deeply inside the Arctic Circle, which preconditioned the polar ice cap for a greater loss of summer ice.[485]

Similarly during the warm phase of the Pacific Decadal Oscillation (PDO) (see

Chapter 11), winds pump more warm water through the Bering Strait, but due to the narrowness of the strait, less Pacific Water enters the Arctic Ocean.[546] During the PDO's warm phase, Bering Sea ice rapidly retreated, and scientists predicted that retreat would intensify.[555] However when the PDO cycled to its cold phase, Bering Sea ice expanded and reached record extents in 2012. Others who have tracked the inflow of warm Pacific Water into the Arctic Ocean observed that even after the inflow decreased, there was still an increase in the melting of summer sea ice because winds continued to raise the warm water from below.[484]

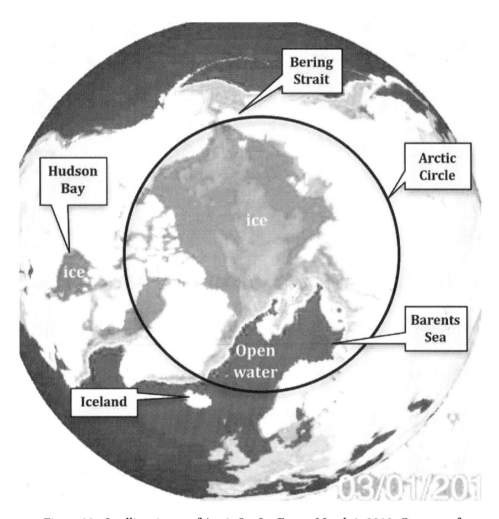

Figure 20. Satellite picture of Arctic Sea Ice Extent March 1, 2012. Courtesy of Cyrosphere Today, University of Illinois.

Because the oceans contain virtually all of the earth's stored heat, and have such a tremendous impact on polar sea ice, many climate scientists argue that only changes in the oceans' heat content can truly track climate change. Unfortunately, there are no long-term reliable measurements: any estimates of temperatures in the upper 900 feet before 1980 are highly uncertain, and any estimates of temperatures at lower depths are only reliable since 2003. Since the early 2000s a worldwide system known as Argo has dispatched over 3200 floating weather stations across the "seven seas". Each float remains at a depth of 3000 feet for nine days. On the tenth day it sinks to a depth of 6000 feet and begins a slow ascent to the surface, measuring temperatures and salinity along the way. At the surface, the data is retrieved via satellite, and the float then descends back to a depth of 3000 feet to begin another cycle.

The Argo data reveals dynamic changes in the ocean's heat content. As of 2012, a consensus analysis of the oceans' upper 900 feet determined that ocean heat "increased from 1984 to 1992 followed by a short cooling episode in 1992/93, and then increased from 1994 to 2003/2004, *followed by flattening or a decrease.*"[483] Since 2003 the cooling has been observed in the surface of tropical oceans and the southern hemisphere oceans.[90]

The lack of ocean warming for over a decade is seen as proof by most skeptics that CO_2's affect on climate is trivial. A decade of cooling has also raised concerns about the accuracy of models that calculate changes in global sea level. On the other hand advocates like Kevin Trenberth suggest CO_2-heated water is carried several thousand feet below the surface, and his models have calculated a slight warming at great depths. However, he concedes that how heated water is transported to great depths remains a mystery, and suggests the winds. If his speculations are true, the warmer water must be dense enough to sink to that level, raising the question of how that heat can resurface. The climate debate is faced with a growing sea of unknowns.

6

Deceptive Extremes

Saving the Large Blue Butterfly

"National extinction rates of temperate butterflies and other arthropods have recently exceeded those of terrestrial vertebrates and vascular plants, and population extinctions have frequently occurred on nature reserves where species' resources remained abundant." [281]

Dr. Jeremy Thomas, University of Oxford

Good stewards of the environment are compelled to engage in good science. In 1980, butterfly experts in the United Kingdom predicted that both the Silver-spotted Skipper and the Large Blue butterfly were doomed to extinction. The widespread Silver-spotted Skipper was gradually restricted to just 46 locations. The more rare Large Blue had been declining from over 90 estimated colonies supporting tens of thousands in the 1800s to just two colonies and about 325 individuals by 1972. The question that had continuously eluded conservationists was why? Disturbed by repeated failures to correctly identify the causes of the decline, Dr. Jeremy Thomas embarked upon extensive research that ultimately unraveled the mystery. It is a model of superb scientific research and demonstrates why good environmental stewards must employ carefully detailed studies. For those of you who enjoy bizarre nature stories, the life of the Large Blue is a fascinating tale of deception and betrayal in which plump, seemingly helpless caterpillars turn the tables on voracious ants. And oddly enough, despite global warming, the Large Blue went extinct in England because its microclimate had cooled.

In earlier attempts to stave off the Large Blue's extirpation, UK conservationists had protected nine areas in order to minimize any human impact on the remaining populations. However this habitat protection uncharacteristically failed to slow the species' decline, so conservationists inferred that the most likely culprits must be unscrupulous butterfly collectors who were trying to cash in on the value of its increasing rarity. So conservationists hurriedly erected protective fences, only to watch hopelessly as the last population continued to decline. Ironically, the fence itself, not greedy collectors, was the final nail in the Large Blue's coffin.[281]

Europe's Large Blue belongs to a group of butterflies whose survival has been eternally entwined with the fate of local ants. In a process that sounds lifted from a Disney or Pixar screenplay, Large Blue caterpillars summon ant bodyguards with special calls and scents. The discovery of talking caterpillars is a fascinating story in itself, but the story gets better. Upon arriving, the summoned ants are fed with a sugary reward oozed from special pores in the caterpillar's bodies. The caterpillars also exude intoxicating chemicals that make their new ant bodyguards more aggressive against other less friendly ant species. (Search YouTube for "ant caterpillar mutualism" for a 2-minute real-life video)

One species of the Blues not only beckons the ants to come to its protection, but then seduces the ants to carry it into the ant colony. Once inside, the caterpillar then mimics the sounds of the queen ant, demanding to be fed in royal ant fashion. This is not quite the royal treatment imagined by humans: the caterpillar's instinctual impersonation induces the worker ants to approach and regurgitate their stomach contents, upon which the caterpillar gratefully dines.

The Large Blue's relationship with ants has an added twist more reminiscent of a grade B movie depicting the horrors of adopting a mysterious orphan. After hatching, Large Blue caterpillars feed on their

host plant just as all other caterpillars do. And like other species of Blues, they soon drop to the ground to summon and then mesmerize a local ant species. Because the ants' worm-like larvae resemble the size and shape of the early stage of these caterpillars, the intoxicating charade is sufficiently convincing, and the ants quickly carry the caterpillar into their nest.

Once the caterpillar is safely nestled into the ant's nursery, the hideous betrayal commences. One by one the ungrateful adoptee devours the ant's larvae. The Large Blue's very existence has evolved to become completely dependent on eating "baby ants." And only this one species of ant will do. Ironically, these butterflies often cause the extirpation of the adopting ant colony, which in turn limits the butterfly's population.

Earlier conservation solutions had been simply based on the prevailing biases that failed to prevent extinction. Thomas lamented, "every hypothesis [collectors, insecticides, fragmentation, inbreeding, climate, pollution] on which the conservation measures of the previous 50 years had been based was untenable." [281]

To be kind to those earlier researchers, the critical changes in the Large Blue's protected habitat were barely perceptible. These changes created a baffling illusion that something was oozing across the boundaries of their protected conservation areas and decimating the species. So blaming collectors, pollution, climate change, or disease made sense simply because those phenomena readily cross artificial boundaries. But further observations never supported these suspicions. To unravel the Large Blue's extinction mystery, Jeremy Thomas painstakingly identified and measured every possible confounding factor that might affect not only the butterfly directly, but also its host plants and the host ants. In addition to general weather variables, he tallied the various local ant species, measured temperatures above and below ground, differences in turf height, plant species composition, and the amounts of bare ground available.

It was laborious and detailed work, but exactly what good science dictates. Why the real agent of extinction had gone unnoticed finally became clear. Thomas discovered that just a few millimeters of change in the height of the grass, during the spring and autumn, could lead to the butterflies' local extinction. The species of ants that the Large Blue plundered requires a very short grass habitat, which allowed the sun to warm the soil and their underground colony. When the grass grew from 1 to 2 centimeters, the temperatures just below the surface in the ants' brood chamber dropped by 3–5°F. When the turf exceeded 3 cm, the microclimate below the grass cooled enough that competing ant species overran the Large Blue's host ants. Three centimeters is less than your little finger, so such a small change in the height of the grass was understandably overlooked.

Over the years, as more efficient animal husbandry reduced sheep and cattle grazing, pastures were increasingly abandoned. Biologists assumed that as more pastures returned to their natural state, wildlife biodiversity and abundance would also increase. That assumption is often true, but without human management, not only did the grass grow taller, but shady trees and shrubs soon invaded. The increasing shade was killing not only the Large Blue but was also endangering a diverse array of the United Kingdom's other warmth-requiring butterflies like the Silver-spotted Skipper.

In addition to reduced grazing, earlier attempts to control UK rabbit populations added to the demise of these warmth-loving butterflies. Rabbits are not native to the British Isles, or to Australia, but had been introduced long ago as a source of meat. As growing populations of escaped rabbits competed for grasslands with the sheep and cattle (also nonnative), people attempted various forms of pest control. In Australia, humans erected the "great rabbit fence" to separate western and eastern Australia. Eventually, they turned to germ warfare, employing a newly discovered myxomatosis virus, which decimated the Australian rabbit population. In France a bacteriologist introduced the disease to rid his estate of rabbits. It then quickly spread, killing 90% of France's native rabbit population. The virus then spread, either naturally or intentionally, into Great Britain. By the mid 1950s it had devastated the rabbit populations there.[284] With fewer cattle, fewer sheep, and fewer rabbits grazing, the grasslands became increasingly overgrown, and warmth-loving butterflies became increasingly scarce. Not realizing the importance of grazers, the well-intentioned conservationists who had erected the protective fence unwittingly destroyed that which they sought to protect.

Once informed by the detailed work of Jeremy Thomas and his colleagues, by 1980 conservationists had begun efforts to successfully reintroduce the extinct Large Blue. Government subsidies and environmental schemes were enacted to encourage grazing, while conservationists mowed abandoned pastures to the optimum turf height. Individuals from Large Blue populations that still survived in Sweden were shuttled to England's "terra nova" for a second chance. Under careful management, the reintroduced Large Blue is slowly rebounding.

But why should people need to intervene so directly and so intensively? Why couldn't the Large Blue and other butterflies just exist "naturally"? Another ironic twist to this story is that humans actively created much of England's grasslands, starting between four and six thousand years ago when new colonists introduced farming and grazing to England. To feed their sheep and cattle, early Britons increasingly cut down the natural forests that had once covered most of Great Britain. These human-generated grasslands were then maintained by grazing sheep and cattle that ate the sprouts of any trees that dared to recolonize. Similarly, the Victorians set fires to clear much of Scotland's forest to encourage heather for grouse hunting. Much of Great Britain's "natural" habitat is actually the product of millennia of human design. To maintain human-made biodiversity requires human stewardship.

Metamorphosing Success into Alarm

"We search for a climate fingerprint in the overall patterns, rather than critiquing each study individually"[133]

Dr. Camille Parmesan, University of Texas

While serving on the Intergovernmental Panel on Climate Change (IPCC), Dr. Camille Parmesan (whose work was introduced in Chapter 2) issued the paper "A Globally Coherent Fingerprint of Climate Change Impacts Across Natural Systems."[133] In contrast to Jeremy Thomas's detailed investigations, Parmesan again advocated that biologists should ignore local details. She wrote, "Here we present quantitative estimates of the global biological impacts of climate change. We search for a climate fingerprint in the overall patterns, rather than critiquing each study individually."[133] However, critiquing individual studies is always the essential first step. Otherwise the overall pattern will be distilled from faulty information. And in order to support her supposed pattern of global warming disruption, she omitted crucial contradictory details.

Parmesan tactfully offered lip service to altered landscapes, but stated that her "probabilistic model" accurately separated the effects of land use from climate change. To demonstrate her model's power, she wrote, "Consider the case of the silver-spotted skipper butterfly (*Hesperia comma*) that has expanded its distribution close to its northern boundary in England over the past 20 years. *Possible ecological explanations for this expansion are regional warming and changes in land use.* Comparing the magnitudes and directions of these two factors suggests that climate change is more likely than land-use change to be the cause of expansion." That was a very odd claim.

This was the very same Silver-spotted Skipper that Jeremy Thomas' detailed studies and subsequent conservation prescriptions had saved from extinction along with the Large Blue. Parmesan was hijacking a conservation success story to spin a tale of climate disruption. Her "proof" that climate change was driving the Silver-spotted Skipper northward came from the work of her old friend C.D. Thomas, known for predicting that rising CO_2 levels had committed 60% of the world's species to extinction.[5] Using a mesmerizing statistical model, C.D. Thomas argued that because the Silver-spotted Skipper "needs warmth," only global warming could account for its recent colonization of a few cooler north-facing slopes of England's southern hills.

The Skipper is indeed fond of hotter south-facing slopes. However, the butterfly had historically inhabited cooler northern slopes if those slopes had been grazed. Like the Large Blue, the Skipper had disappeared from both cool north-facing slopes and warm south-facing slopes whenever the turf grew too high.[283,458] C.D. Thomas' model was statistically significant only if he ignored recent conservation efforts to promote warmer, short-turf habitat. At the end of his paper, relegated to his methods sections, he quietly stated, "we assumed that grazing patterns were the same in 1982 as in 2000."[877] Parmesan and C.D. were guilty of grave sins of omission.

I emailed Dr. Jeremy Thomas regarding the study by C.D. Thomas and asked, "I assume due to earlier collaboration, you are aware of the habitat his study referenced? If so, is his implied assumption of no changes to turf height valid?" He replied, "No, it's not valid. *There was a massive change in turf height and vegetation structure* …between 1980 and the 1990s onwards for 2 reasons. (emphasis added)" First, since the 1986 paper, several of the key surviving sites were grazed more appropriately by conservationists and most of them, and many neighbors, are today in "agri-environmental schemes" to maintain optimum grass heights. Second, from 1990 onwards the rabbits had gradually returned and did the same job on several abandoned former sites.

Although he did not have local climate data for the Silver-spotted Skipper's recovery, Jeremy Thomas suggested that at least two thirds of the Skippers' recovery and their subsequent recolonization had resulted from both the increased grazing and the rabbits' recovery. He was willing to attribute as much as a third of the butterflies' recovery to climate warming between the 1970s and the present.

If, for argument's sake, we accept that one-third of the recovery was due solely to CO_2 warming and ignore published arguments that the warming in England was caused by the warm mode of the North Atlantic Oscillation,[457] habitat improvements still account for two-thirds of the skippers' expansion. Furthermore, the Silver-spotted Skipper had yet to expand further northward than its previous 1920s boundary. Yet that was Parmesan's best example of a fingerprint of global warming disruption! It was bad science, but the consensus flocked to it in agreement.

To date more than 3500 papers have referenced her paper as evidence of climate disruption. It is a consensus built on misleading results that hijacked conservation efforts. In contrast, Jeremy Thomas' successful preservation of two species on the brink of extinction had unequivocally demonstrated that the long-term changes were due to the quality of the caterpillar's habitat. Although weather change causes short-term fluctuations in butterfly populations, a change in habitat quality affects populations 100 times more powerfully than weather.[901] But such successful conservation efforts do not get funded in the same way as global warming horror stories do, and Jeremy Thomas' "Evidence Based Conservation of Butterflies" has been cited by just 14 scientists.

Parmesan's IPCC paper also claimed that thousands of other species similarly suffered at the hands of CO_2-caused global warming. The purported plight of penguins, frogs, and the pika are considered in depth in other chapters. Several species of butterflies that she suggested are being forced northward have been retracting south since the 1950s at their northern boundaries in Finland.[875] Nearly every change in a species range or abundance is more convincingly explained—or outright contradicted—by land use considerations, natural cycles, and more long-term data. Of all her papers that ignore landscape changes Parmesan's paper, "Impacts of Extreme Weather and Climate on Terrestrial Biota" is the most egregious.[876] Her conclusions are based on deceptive half-truths and grave sins of omission, yet it mesmerized the nation's top climate scientists, who rapidly adopted her as blindly as the ants adopted a Large Blue.

An Illusion of Extreme Climate Disruption

"While clearing larvae were starving in response to destruction of their hosts, survival in the outcrop was higher than previously recorded: an estimated 80% of larval groups survived." [879]

C. D. Thomas, University of Leeds, United Kingdom

In "Impacts of Extreme Weather and Climate on Terrestrial Biota," Parmesan, Terry Root, and Michael Willig wrote, "Here, evidence is brought forward that extreme weather events can be implicated as mechanistic drivers of broad ecological responses to climatic trends. They are, therefore, essential to include in predictive biological models, such as doubled CO_2 scenarios."[876] To demonstrate the destructive power of extreme weather, Parmesan and company detailed the sequence of events that caused an extinction of a Sierra Nevada population of Edith's checkerspot. However unlike Parmesan's 1996 paper, it was no longer global warming at low elevations that caused the population's extinction. She now blamed climate change for unusually cold weather at higher elevations. The authors wrote:

> "Twenty years of studies at one site in the Sierra Nevada of California have implicated three extreme weather events in carving a pathway to extinction of a whole set of E. editha populations at 2400 m.

> "The first catastrophe occurred in 1989 when low winter snowpack led to an early and unusually synchronous adult emergence in April (as compared to the usual June flight). So early, in fact, that flowers were not yet in bloom and most adults died from starvation. Just one year later another relatively light snowpack again caused adults to emerge early. Adult butterflies, adapted to summertime conditions of warmth and sun, suffered many deaths during a "normal" May snow-storm. Each of these events decreased the population size by an order of magnitude…

"The finale came but 2 years later in 1992 when (unusually low) temperatures of -5° C on June 16, without the insulating snowfall, killed an estimated 97% of the Collinsia (host) plants....The butterflies had already finished flying and left behind young caterpillars that were not killed directly but starved in the absence of hosts. As of the latest census (1999), these sites remained extinct."

Parmesan and her colleagues argued that CO_2 warming had triggered cold events, which disrupted the "synchrony" between the weather, the butterflies and their food plants. Unlike Jeremy Thomas who was seeking to save an endangered species, Camille Parmesan was not interested in the details required for successful conservation. She was looking to support her global warming theory, "searching for a climate fingerprint rather than critiquing each study". And she knowingly omitted contradictory details and failed to mention that the other half of the population had prospered during those same events.

I say that she knowingly omitted the details because her future husband, Mike Singer, and C.D. Thomas wrote the research papers[286,287] from which Parmesan manufactured her extreme weather story; when written, Parmesan served as their field assistant. Although weather is involved in each and every wildlife boom or bust, her reported extinctions had everything to do with how land use had changed the butterflies' "microclimates".

Parmesan directed the reader's attention to just one of two neighboring populations. Both populations were literally within a stone's throw of each other. Normally they would be considered two halves of the same population equally affected by global warming. Yet only one half went extinct while simultaneously the other "natural" half survived. In fact by all accounts, the natural half didn't just survive the "extreme weather", it thrived.

In the early 1960s, only the "natural" half ever existed. As far as we know, it had always inhabited the rocky outcrops where the Sierra Nevada's thin, glaciated soils prevented dense forest growth and permitted sufficient sunny patches for the caterpillars to warm their bodies. In contrast, the extinct population had just recently colonized habitat created in the 1960s after the US Forest Service had expanded logging into higher elevations. The logging opened the canopy to the warmth of the sun and created new microclimates.

Parmesan's extinction story was a very selective retelling of the referenced study, "Catastrophic Extinction of Population Sources in a Butterfly Metapopulation"[878] and a second companion paper.[879] The caterpillars of the surviving natural population had fed mostly on a hardy perennial plant, which easily survives the Sierra Nevada's erratic weather. The half-population that went extinct uncharacteristically fed on a fragile annual species *Collinsia torreyi* that typically invades logged areas. The checkerspot in the Sierra Nevada rarely laid its eggs on *Collinsia*, because normally it was not a reliable food source.

But recent logging near their natural habitat changed all that. Not only did logging open the forest floor to more sunlight, it also exposed deeper soils that had been enriched from the logging debris and burn-piles. That human disturbance created the just-right conditions for the annual *Collinsia* to survive for much longer periods. Serendipitously it also created a novel butterfly-plant synchrony. The longer-lived and more abundant *Collinsia* could now sustain the full development of hungry caterpillars.

With the life cycles of *Collinsia* and the checkerspot temporarily in synchrony, *Collinsia* suddenly became a valuable food resource. The butterflies from the outcrops opportunistically colonized the logged area and created the new second population. However this serendipitous food supply had simply prompted a boom and bust, not unlike the nearby ghost towns during the Sierra Nevada gold rush days.

While Parmesan indicted climate change in "the grand finale" during which frost killed 99.9% of the annual *Collinsia*, she omitted the crucial detail that the frost had little effect on the perennial food plants that sustained the natural population. Parmesan also omitted that *she had observed survival for the natural population "was higher than previously recorded, an estimated 80% of larval groups survived".*[878,879]

The deadly logged landscape had altered the microclimate and thus the timing of the caterpillars' emergence from diapause.[***] In the Sierra Nevada, the checkerspot caterpillars diapause throughout the winter, snuggled safely under the soil and surface debris. Over the millennia, the caterpillar has evolved an instinctual sensitivity to the critical weather cues that triggered the safest time to emerge from the subsurface retreat. However, logging had opened the forest canopy, changing the pattern of snowfall accumulation, snow melt and forest-floor vegetation. Just as one centimeter of taller grass had cooled the subsurface for the Large Blue's ant hosts, the recently logged forest floor was also heated differently. That sent the wrong signal to the diapausing caterpillars. Extreme weather affects the region equally; however, it is the different microclimates that determine how the animals respond.

Parmesan never told her readers that the natural population thrived or that the natural population maintained their synchrony with both the weather and their food plants. By constructing only half of the details, and with the apparent blessings of Dr. C.D. Thomas and her husband Dr. Singer, Parmesan metamorphosed a story of nature's adaptability and resilience into another story of climate catastrophe. Such blatant sins of omission are a very serious offense, and this "scientific" paper should be retracted. The peer review process failed to detect an obvious distortion of the truth that was readily noticed by anyone who read the original study. To date, a modest 243 papers have cited this paper as evidence of catastrophic climate change caused by extreme weather. However when leading climate scientists uncritically embraced her story, it was referenced by thousands more.

Climate Scientists Embrace the Myth

"overall in the United States there is a slight downward trend in the number of these extremes despite an overall warming in the mean temperature, but with cooling in the southeastern United States" [3]

"The number of deaths related to tornadoes, hurricanes, and severe storms have either decreased or remained unchanged over the past 20 years." [3]

Dr. David Easterling, National Oceanic and Atmospheric Administration

D.R. Easterling from the National Oceanic and Atmospheric Administration (NOAA), Thomas Karl, now the director of National Climatic Data Center and G.A. Meehl, the Senior Scientist at the National Center for Atmospheric Research immediately invited Parmesan to coauthor a new paper titled "Climate Extremes: Observations, Modeling, and Impacts"[3] which they quickly published just months after Parmesans' extreme weather paper was published. Although Easterling had just published nearly identical information a few months earlier,[893] they now attached Parmesan's deceptive tale to claim *"a growing body of evidence linking climatic and*

[***] Diapause is a period of inactivity and reduced metabolism similar to hibernation.

biological changes suggests systematic global increases in both the frequency and impact of extreme weather and climate events." (They also highlighted another paper suggesting extreme climate change had caused "40% of the 50 local amphibian species have become extinct since 1983." That fallacy is exposed in Chapter 8.)

Easterling and company are also advocates looking to support CO_2-caused warming. Easterling wrote, "if there are indeed identifiable trends in extreme climatic events it would add to the body of evidence that there is a discernible human affect on the climate." In truth, they admittedly had very little evidence of any deadly extremes. Apparently feeling a need to promote a greater sense of urgency, Easterling, Meehl, and Karl uncritically embraced any research that linked rising CO_2 levels with extreme climate events and biological tragedy. Although I have no basis of knowing what indeed motivated them, if they had read the original research, they would never have had adopted Parmesan as a coauthor. Alternative explanations for embracing a deceptive extinction story are less savory and less believable.

To raise our concerns about climate extremes, the first few paragraphs of Easterling's paper listed the death and destruction caused by recent hurricanes and asked if the extreme events were natural or caused by humans. However he then reported that through the 1990s damage from extreme events had actually declined reporting, "*The number of deaths related to tornadoes, hurricanes, and severe storms have either decreased or remained unchanged over the past 20 years.*"[3]

Heat stress was also declining; they reported that the number of days with extreme temperatures over 90.5°F and over the 90th percentile threshold peaked during the droughts of the 1930s and 1950s. They concluded, "Thus, *overall in the United States there is a slight downward trend in the number of these extremes* despite an overall warming in the mean temperature, but with cooling in the southeastern United States_(emphasis added)."[3] In an earlier paper he also reported that maximums had not increased in Russia and China.[893]

So they emphasized the rise in minimum temperatures to demonstrate "extreme weather". However an increase in frost-free days reduces cold stress and does not catalyze great public concern for climate change. An increase in minimum temperature means we use less energy to heat our homes. Similar to the Sierra Nevada, temperatures were trending towards an optimum. And as discussed in Chapter 3, urbanization and the increased water vapor from frequent El Niños impact minimum temperatures as much, if not more, than rising greenhouse gases.

They also reported, "Examination of drought over the 20th century in the United States shows considerable variability, the droughts of the 1930s and 1950s dominating any long-term trend. Recent investigation of longer term U.S. Great Plains drought variability over the past 2000 years with the use of paleo-climatic data suggests that *no droughts as intense as those of the 1930s have occurred since the 1700s. However, before the 16th century some droughts appear to have occurred that were of greater spatial and temporal intensity than any of the 20th-century U.S. droughts.*"[3] They also reported that some countries had experienced wetter years and others drier, but those differences can be explained by El Niño (see Chapter 9) and the Pacific Decadal Oscillation. Wherever more rain occurred they registered more "rainfall extremes."

Finally Easterling lamented, "lack of long-term climate data suitable for analysis of extremes is the single biggest obstacle to quantifying whether extreme events have changed over the 20th century."[3] And he confessed that great caution needs to be taken when comparing extreme weather events warning, "investigators have often used quite different criteria to define an extreme climate event. This lack of consensus on the definition of extreme events, coupled with other problems, such as a lack of suitable homogeneous data for many parts of the world, likely means that it will be difficult, *if not impossible, to say that extreme events in general have changed in the observed record* (emphasis added)."[3] Ironically this paper marked the beginning of an era in which every weather event would be translated into "unprecedented extremes" and again the butterfly effect was instrumental.

With scant evidence that climate change had caused any increase in extreme weather they wrote, "Several apparently gradual biological changes are linked to responses to extreme weather and climate events." While admitting earlier studies provided "little analyses of more detailed linkages," they repeated Parmesan's tale that butterflies were fleeing the heat, adding, "In western North America, Edith's Checkerspot butterfly has shifted its range northward (by 92 km) and upward (by 124 m) during this century." Did Parmesan not tell them there was never any such migration? Or did they decide to add these fabricated distances for effect? Did Parmesan not tell them that the natural population had its most successful years during the extreme event? Did she ever mention the effects of logging? Nonetheless their paper had scientific sex appeal. This paper has now been cited in over 1315 articles, institutionalizing the illusion that rising CO_2 levels causes deadly weather extremes.

Hypothesis Obsession Syndrome

"A belief is not merely an idea the mind possesses; it is an idea that possesses the mind"

Robert Bolton

"A lie would have no sense unless the truth were felt dangerous." [880]

Alfred Adler

Although the evidence against Parmesan's extreme climate paper is damning, I want to add a few words in her defense. Some people have likened her to the Enron thieves who also kept half the information "off the books." Any clamoring for legal sanctions against bad science from either skeptics or advocates only inhibits innovative thinking. Bad hypotheses are quite common and we should always be careful about the theories we embrace; but bad hypotheses are not a crime. I do not believe she conspired to maliciously deceive her colleagues or the public. However I suspect Parmesan is a victim of what I refer to as the Hypothesis Obsession Syndrome, or HOS, which has been the downfall of many a scientist. Whenever scientists invest their time and reputation defending a hypothesis, they naturally apply it to every situation until proven wrong. They are not going to help any skeptics to prove them wrong. Letting go to examine alternative hypotheses is much easier said than done, which is why the scientific community normally encourages robust debate.

Robert Bolton wrote, "A belief is not merely an idea the mind possesses; it is an idea that possesses the mind." Once we make a choice, that choice possesses us. One of the more active areas of psychological research deals with "change blindness" and "choice blindness". An international team from Harvard, the University of Tokyo, and Lund University in Sweden cleverly demonstrated how humans are hardwired to defend their choices despite contrary evidence. Test subjects were asked to choose who was the most attractive person in a set of two pictures displayed on the other side of the table. The researchers would then retrieve the pictures and ask the subjects to explain why they made their choice. However the lighting in the room was designed to allow the researchers to switch pictures and the test subjects were handed the picture they did <u>not</u> choose. Most subjects never noticed the switch, and proceeded to explain in great detail how the picture they never chose was the most attractive.[488]

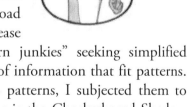

Other researchers have demonstrated how patterns can overwhelm rational thought. Our eyes and ears overload our brains with billions of bits of information. To ease the stress of information overload, we are "pattern junkies" seeking simplified scenarios. Our brains are prejudiced to embrace bits of information that fit patterns. To make my students aware of our vulnerability to patterns, I subjected them to various illusions. One of my favorite optical illusions is the Checkerboard-Shadow illusion created by Dr. Edward Adelson from MIT.

Although everyone would label square A as black (or dark) and square B as white (or light), the two squares are in reality the exact same color. As if life wasn't tough enough trying to distinguish the gray zones, our allegiance to shadows and patterns can trick us into seeing black and white when it doesn't exist. This illusion is readily available online by searching for "checkerboard shadow illusion" and I suggest you do so and then print the illusion. Carefully cut out squares A and B, so that the rest of the illusion remains intact. If you then place the cut-out squares on a blank piece of paper free of all patterns, A and B automatically reveal their true nature - identical gray. However after knowing the squares are identical, when you replace the squares back in the pattern, your mind again sees black and white. And if you switch the two squares, what you once called black is now white and vice versa.

Checkerboard-Shadow Illusion Reprinted with permission from Dr. Adelson

We are all hardwired to give extra weight to shadows and patterns. Despite our bigger brains we often respond as instinctually as an ant. Additionally our beliefs blind us, because beliefs are a form of pattern recognition. Neuroscience gives credence to the popular saying, "believe half of what you see and none of what you hear" not because other people are deviously deceptive, but because we are too easily fooled. I suspect this is why politicians typically avoid debating with facts. Faced with an overload of information, people resort to their current beliefs. Mudslinging and casting shadows on opponents more powerfully appeals to our prevailing prejudices.

As she readily expressed, Parmesan sought patterns of CO_2 climate catastrophes, therefore it was very easy for every ecological disturbance to support Hansen's doomsday predictions. In addition she believes she is saving the world. She holds a messianic vision that via assisted migration, she can lead all of the earth's creatures to an imaginary promised land with the perfect future climate. Once scientists have tied their fame and fortune to a theory, or when they believe their theory will save the world, they are much more likely to suffer from HOS. The best example of the self-deception caused by the Hypothesis Obsession Syndrome is evidenced by the scientific quest to develop nuclear fusion.

The holy grail of clean energy has been fusion energy. Fusion is the process observed in the sun when high temperature and pressure squeeze separate atoms into a single atom making a new and heavier element. In the process fusion releases light and heat. In 1958 physicists believed they had mastered fusion. Unable to account for the extra heat generated in their experimental fusion machine, the English Nobel physicist, John Cockcroft proclaimed to the world that they were "90% certain" they had harnessed fusion. This set off a worldwide celebration, and I still remember headlines proclaiming that humans would soon have limitless, clean energy. Two weeks later Japanese scientists announced they too were producing heat from fusion, and the Swedes and Russians quickly announced plans to build clones of the British fusion machine. However when one skeptical scientist tested those claims by simply reversing the electric current that drove the process, the extra heat disappeared and it became 100% certain that world's physicists had been fooled by wishful thinking.[69]

After such a public relations nightmare, fusion researched languished in obscurity until 1989 when the University of Utah announced that two highly respected chemists, Martin Fleischmann and Stanley Pons, had "successfully created a sustained nuclear fusion reaction at room temperature". Once again, the holy grail of cheap, plentiful, and clean energy was in hand and Pons and Fleischmann would save the world. However physicists, marred by decades of false alarms and wishful thinking, were doggedly skeptical. Their skepticism was confirmed when a graph that Pons and Fleischmann used in a presentation revealed that the energies levels were uncharacteristic of a fusion reaction. Pons and Fleischmann however countered they had carelessly constructed the graph for that presentation. Accordingly, when their cold fusion paper was finally published, the correct energy levels appeared in the revised graph. But a team of skeptical physicists at MIT had relentlessly perused the television footage of the laboratory during their initial press conference. They saw that the original data also had the wrong energy levels. *Pons and Fleischmann had falsified their published data.*

The past scientific achievements of Pons and Fleischmann make it difficult to dismiss them as incompetent. It was even harder to imagine that they carefully plotted to fool the scientific community, the energy industry, politicians, or the general public. Knowing that cold fusion had such global economic consequences, they most certainly understood their methods would be meticulously replicated and thoroughly tested, or else it would have no commercial value. Surely any deception would be readily exposed. Yet despite that certainty, Pons and Fleischmann were possessed by the idea that they were about to save the world. When their own data contradicted that belief, they justified changing the data "believing" they would be proven right in the future.

I have talked with a few scientists and laypeople who like Parmesan believe that rising CO_2 is condemning the world to future mass extinctions. They similarly ignore all evidence of thriving populations to focus on any negatives that support their global warming fear. Parmesan ignored the declining trends in maximum temperature and the thriving populations. She ignored all evidence that landscape change not climate change was a controlling factor. Despite the fact her extirpated population of butterflies died from cold weather, she still blamed global warming. Should laugh or should we cry at such blindness?

It is troubling enough that the focus on rising CO_2 is distracting us from the local remedies that will make a real environmental difference. More frightening is the rising demand for suppression of all debate that would expose erroneous conclusions. In March 2012 in the Huffington Post, David Suzuki published the latest in a decade of attacks on the scientific process demanding, "Deny Deniers their Right to Deny!" The threat to the scientific process by Suzuki and his ilk is no laughing matter. Asking the government to enforce just his way of thinking and "deny the deniers the right to deny," should scare us more than any fabricated extremes attributed to rising CO_2.

7

The Extreme Weather Craze and Death Valley Days

"The 5-year running mean of global temperature has been flat for the past decade." [531]

Dr. James Hansen, 2013

As the saying goes, "The coldest winter I ever spent was a summer in San Francisco." However, during the spring and autumn, the chilling fog recedes and the people of the San Francisco Bay Area are treated to some wonderfully warm days. While visiting friends on just such a day, I expressed my gratitude for the t-shirt weather. My contentment was met with cautious glances and an uneasy reply that "maybe it's too warm." These friends are good people who deeply care about our environment, and I didn't want to turn a friendly visit into a political argument, yet our contrasting emotions struck me. Instead of embracing a gift of the season, they saw an ugly omen of impending global warming doom. Knowing the local temperatures had been cooling for the past 80 years, I felt they had been victimized by the repeated attempts to advertise every heat wave as an unusual climate disruption.

Leading CO_2 advocates like Dr. Jim Hansen have repeatedly told the media that CO_2 has "*loaded the climate dice*" towards more frequent heat waves and extreme weather. Yet Hansen also admits that global warming has not increased for over a decade.[531] To explain the recent lack of warming, climate scientists now argue that natural variations have overwhelmed CO_2 warming.[938] I agree. However, to evoke a fear of climate extremes, they then make the exact opposite claim, that CO_2 has simultaneously overwhelmed those same natural variations. They can't have it both ways.

Dr. Michael Mann repeatedly argues that recent climate variability is the result of CO_2 warming that has put the "climate on steroids." Yet Mann has also written that "The Little Ice Age may have been more significant in terms of *increased variability* of the climate (emphasis added),"[404] suggesting colder conditions put the climate on steroids. Dr. Kevin Trendberth claims that every extreme weather event is connected to high levels of CO_2 and a "wetter and warmer world." Yet during the extreme cold of the last Ice Age and very low levels of CO_2, the world experienced the most rapid and extreme temperature fluctuations ever reported, the Dansgaard-Oeschger events. As illustrated in Figure 21, between 15,000 and 50,000 years ago, there were repeated episodes during which average temperatures rose and fell by 18-27°F, in just over a 10 to 50 year period.[900]

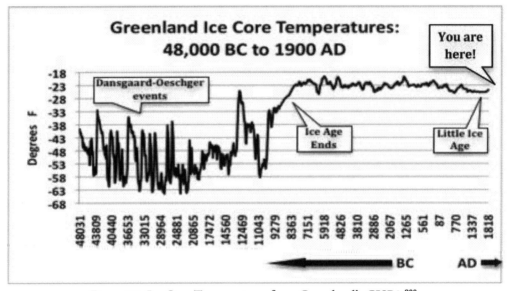

Figure 21. Ice Core Temperatures from Greenland's GISP2.[900]

The World Meteorological Organization defines a heat wave as a period when the daily maximum temperature exceeds the *average maximum* temperature by 9°F for more than five consecutive days.[92] Although Hansen, Mann, and Trenberth understand that heat waves naturally happen all the time, they argue that global warming has increased the probability that temperatures will rise above that heat wave threshold. But the global average is meaningless for local heat waves. For the United States, the maximum temperatures have never exceeded the 1930s or 1950s (see Figure 9, Chapter 3), and where my friends live, there have been decades of cooling.

If my friends had checked the nearest USHCN weather station at Santa Cruz, they would have found *a 3°F cooling trend* since the 1930s for both the adjusted and the raw maximum temperatures (see Figure 22). There was no increased probability of a local heat wave. Throughout the United States, record heat waves have similarly occurred in regions with declining maximum temperatures. Extremely high temperatures have been caused by droughts and landscape changes that dried the land and intensified surface heating. Lost heat capacity always causes temperatures to soar, regardless of the global average.

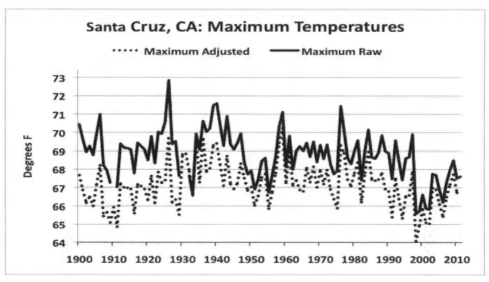

Figure 22. USHCN maximum temperatures for Santa Cruz CA

All major heat waves can be accounted for by natural weather dynamics. In the Northern Hemisphere, all heat waves are caused when the jet stream keeps cold air to the north. Although droughts are not a prerequisite, most heat waves are associated with reduced winter rains. And without exception, every heat wave is associated with a stationary High-pressure system.[34]

"Highs" always bring clear skies, drier weather, and a circulation pattern that temporarily reduces the amount of heat carried upward from the surface and back to the stratosphere. Clear skies allow greater heating by the sun. And drier weather produces drier soil. Your local weatherperson can predict possible record-breaking high temperatures in the upcoming week when he or she sees an approaching High that may get stuck in place for several days.

In most places, High- and Low-pressure systems continuously meander eastward, and a few hot days are followed by a few cool days. But sometimes weather patterns stall and High-pressure systems become stationary. When the High stalls for five days or more, it generates sweltering heat waves. Unlike Low-pressure systems, Highs resist being displaced. These "blocking Highs" cause atmospheric traffic jams that cause any trailing storms to linger longer in one location. Weather systems that normally affect a locale for just a few hours can stall and remain in place for several hours or several days. Extreme heat, rain, or snow are concentrated in one local region, causing record-setting weather. Because the exact location of these stalled weather systems changes every year, there are always record Highs and Lows somewhere on earth. As discussed later, it was also a blocking High that turned a minor hurricane into Superstorm Sandy.

Natural Drought and Natural Heat Waves

"Both natural and anthropogenic influences caused twentieth century climate change but their relative roles and regional impacts are still under debate." [554]

Dr. Judith Lean, Naval Research Laboratory

Some locations are subjected to quasi-permanent blocking-highs such as the Pacific High that generates California's sunny Mediterranean climate. Locations subject to quasi-permanent Highs also form the world's deserts, and those locations have set world records for the hottest recorded land temperatures.

On July 10, 1913, in the sparsely vegetated desert surroundings of Furnace Creek in California's Death Valley National Park, the air temperature reached 134.1°F. That temperature remains the hottest ever recorded in the western hemisphere, and the hottest July temperature ever recorded for the entire globe. Remarkably, this record high temperature occurred when the "average global temperature" was lower than today, when CO_2's contribution was trivial, and when solar activity was much lower (see Figure 23). Death Valley provides the perfect example of extreme heat caused strictly by natural dynamics.

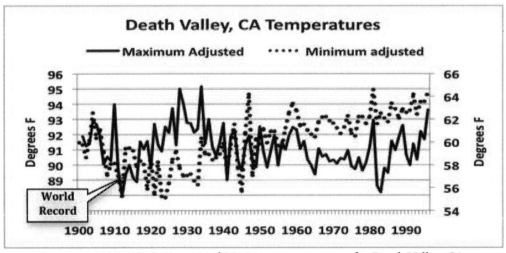

Figure 23. USHCN Maximum and Minimum temperatures for Death Valley, CA.

Death Valley's 134.1°F remained the world record high temperature until 1922 when the temperature climbed to 136°F in the desert locale of El Azizia, Libya.[†††] The record for the Asian continent was established in June 1942 in Tirat Zvi, Israel, where the temperature reached a more modest high of 129°F. The pattern of those record high temperatures on three continents is instructive. Intuitively, we would expect the hottest temperatures to be recorded near the equator. However, all three hotspots lie at latitudes between 32° and 36° N, roughly 2500 miles north of the equator, precisely where strong descending air currents produce a quasi-permanent high-pressure system. (see Figure 24).

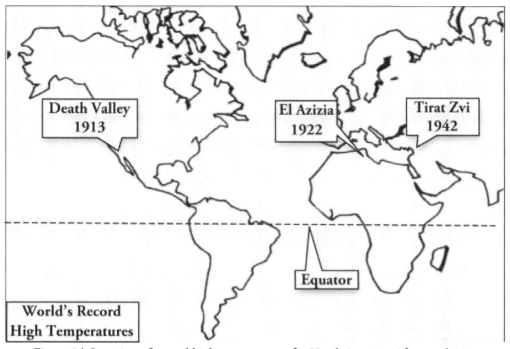

Figure 24. Location of record high temperatures for North America, Africa and Asia.

The sun's most direct, hottest rays center on the tropics, but other factors moderate the expected extreme temperature. The sun's heat creates powerful rising convection currents that carry away the tropical heat. These currents are so powerful that air in the tropics rises several miles higher than anywhere else in the world, short-circuiting the greenhouse effect and carrying heat, and sometimes water vapor, directly back to the stratosphere. Models have estimated that if daytime convection stopped redistributing surface heat, global temperatures could rise by 100°F.[91]

The rising equatorial air currents split into two circulation cells. One moves to the north and one to the south; they are referred to as "Hadley Cells" (see Figure 25). When warm air rises above the equator, it creates an area of Low pressure, and like a

---

[†††] El Azizia's record has been challenged due to landscapes changes around the weather station and possible reporting errors .

vacuum cleaner, it draws in air and moisture from the surroundings. The moisture-laden air converges near the equator and as it rises, it cools, producing rain, which further moderates temperatures.

What goes up must come down. The weight of the air carried above can only be supported by denser air near the surface. Intense currents sinking back to the earth's surface at about 2500 miles from the equator balance the intense rising convection caused by the sun's heat near the equator. The width of the Hadley cells also undergo a yet to be explained cycle of stretching towards the poles and then contracting towards the equator. The cells were widest in the 1870s, contracted to their narrowest width by the 1920s, and are now expanding again.[999] The location of the descending currents create regions of quasi-permanent High-pressure systems and any change in their location creates regional climate change. The Hadley Cells also determine the location of two of the earth's most extreme ecosystems. At the equator beneath the rising branch of the cell, rainforests form. In contrast, *beneath the descending branches, the world's largest deserts develop.*

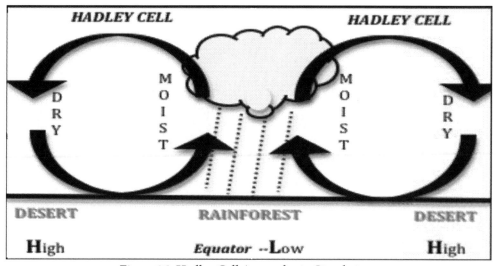

Figure 25. Hadley Cell Atmospheric Circulation

Because the equator runs through the center of the African continent, the two bands of deserts created by the descending currents of the Hadley Cells are symmetrically placed, with the Namib Desert to the south and the great Sahara Desert to the north, where El Azizia, Libya is located. Similarly, two great bands of deserts circle the globe, although less symmetrically on other continents because the shapes of the continents facilitate varying contributions of nearby ocean moisture. In southwestern North America this global pattern of descending air produces the Sonoran and Mojave Deserts and Death Valley. In South America, the pattern contributes to what is arguably the world's driest desert, the Atacama.

The extreme desert temperatures at Death Valley are not merely due to its location relative to the equator. Blocking High-pressure systems form most readily wherever cooler surfaces help the air to sink. In addition to the Hadley Cell dynamics, the relatively cold waters of the Pacific Ocean focus the descending air currents off the coast of California (see Figure 26). The blocking High prevents any moisture carried by ocean winds from reaching Death Valley and contributes to the overall dryness of the American Southwest. Mountain ranges also block moisture from reaching Death Valley, and the resulting extreme dryness permits extreme surface temperatures.

A similar High-pressure system forms in the Atlantic Ocean (called the Bermuda High or Azore High), which likewise contributes to dry conditions in the Mediterranean and northern Africa. However, because High-pressure systems in the northern hemisphere always circulate surface winds in a clockwise direction, the western side of the Bermuda High directs moisture into the eastern United States. Although Raleigh, North Carolina is about the same distance from the equator as Death Valley, it enjoys much more rain, higher humidity, lush vegetation, and more moderate temperatures.

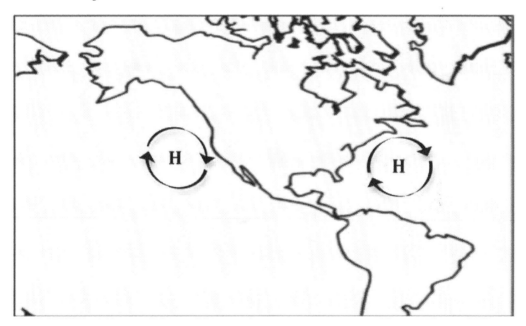

Figure 26. Position of quasi-permanent High pressure systems.

The location of the Bermuda High affects how much moisture reaches the eastern United States. Due to oscillating temperatures in the Atlantic, if the center of the Bermuda High moves westward towards the Gulf of Mexico, it drives more rains into the Great Plains and eastern United States. In contrast, when the High moves away, the eastern United States receives less rain, which promotes drought and higher temperatures in the Midwest. Similarly the western side of the Pacific High also shunts moist winds northward. A stronger High brings more rains to Oregon and contributes to the "temperate rainforests" along coastal Washington and Alaska.

The strength of the Pacific High is regulated by the temperature contrast between the land and ocean, which in turn controls the rainy and dry seasons. During the summer, the ocean is cooler than the land. This contrast strengthens the Pacific High that blocks the flow of ocean moisture and causes California's summer drought. During the winter the land surface becomes colder than the ocean, and the descending air currents are no longer focused so heavily over the ocean. This weakens the Pacific High and allows a winter rainy season. Moisture-laden winds from the Pacific can more readily sweep across California and the southwestern United States.

In addition El Niño cycles moderate the wet and dry seasons. When an El Niño warms the eastern Pacific Ocean, it weakens the High allowing more winter rains to soak California and the Southwest. In contrast, when a La Niña cools the eastern Pacific, the High strengthens. This reduces winter rains and snows and sets the stage for summer droughts and heat waves.

Trapping Heat at the Surface

"The greenhouse stays warm primarily because its glass windows prevent the wind from carrying away the heat." [992]

Dr. Michael E. Mann, Pennsylvania State University

The dry descending air currents can prevent escaping heat are far more effectively than greenhouse gases. The descending air in a High drops the "thermal ceiling" and prevent rising convection from carrying away surface heat. It that developing "dome of high pressure" that allows meteorologists to predict a heat wave. The importance of this ceiling for controlling temperatures was investigated by scientists studying greenhouse warming. Just 25 years ago physicists were mired in a huge debate. Were glass greenhouses warmer because the glass panes inhibited the escape of infrared heat waves? Or did the glass prevent warm air from rising and escaping in a normal convection current?

When I taught 8th grade science, I needed to explain the connection between CO_2, the greenhouse effect, and global warming. At the time I had adopted the trapped-infrared-heat theory. Instead of using real greenhouses to explain global warming to my inner-city students, I used a parked car as my example. I explained that the sun's visible radiation readily entered the car through the glass windows. As the rays struck the car's interior, the surface of the seats and dashboard became burning hot, and the car's heated interior increasingly emitted infrared rays. Outside the car, the sun heated the earth's surface similarly. However because the glass blocked the infrared rays from escaping, it was hotter inside the car than outside. (At the time even David Suzuki had argued that it was the carbon in the windshield that trapped the heat.)

After this real-life comparison, I would then explain that CO_2 slowed the escape of infrared rays just like the glass in their cars and in real greenhouses.

To start that lesson I first asked, "Who can tell me, when you first get into a parked car, why it is so much hotter inside the car than outside?" To my surprise the class clown shot up his hand, vigorously pleading that I call on him. I said, "OK Bobby, what's your explanation?" Bobby smirked, "It's so hot because you forgot to roll down the windows." After the rest of the class stopped giggling, I gave them the real "scientific infrared" explanation, but by then Bobby was no longer paying attention.

Life is always humbling, and I soon realized that Bobby had been far closer to the truth than I. With more sophisticated experimental techniques, physicists now agree that greenhouse walls prevent convection from carrying away the heated air. It was indeed the raised windows that caused the car's interior to be warmer.

To store heat, people alter the inner surfaces of the greenhouse. They add rocks to the floor to increase the heat capacity of the surface, much the same way as urban heat islands and deserts increase surface heat. Likewise, some add water barrels to absorb more heat and, if economically feasible, circulate water between the surface and subsurface storage tanks. This is analogous to how oceans and lakes store and redistribute heat. To minimize radiative cooling, as well as to prevent overheating during the day, shades are sometimes employed to control the heat exchange in much the same way that clouds affect temperature. And to prevent overheating, simply opening the greenhouse doors, or "rolling down the windows," allows convection to carry away the heat.

Descending air currents can act like the glass ceiling of a greenhouse. Whenever air descends it is compressed, and whenever air is compressed the temperature rises. This is called adiabatic heating (explored in a sidebar at the end of the chapter) to emphasize the fact that *no heat* is added. The important point to remember is that descending air currents always raise temperatures and this creates a layer of warmer air that may hover a few hundred meters above the earth's surface, forming a "thermal lid". Because air only rises if it is warmer than its surroundings, heated air rising from the surface stops when it reaches a layer of adiabatically heated air. Surface heat normally redistributed several miles higher is then trapped near the surface. Again, if daytime convection stopped completely, temperatures could rise by 100°F.

To be clear, I am not arguing that the global average has increased because of reduced convection. However, blocking highs and the temporary reduction in rising convection are *always* cause every "extreme" heat wave, regardless of the global average.

In fact, *cooler ocean surfaces* are linked to most extremes. Cooler ocean surfaces that develop during the cool phases of the North Atlantic Oscillation (NAO) and Pacific Decadal Oscillation (PDO) focus the descending air currents and promote more frequent blocking highs.[811,812,813,814] There is a great deal of knowledge about what causes extreme heating events, whether in 1913 in Death Valley or the 2010 Russian heatwave.[34] Simply suggesting that a recent heat wave or other extreme event has been caused by a "climate on CO_2 steroids" is not very scientific. It ignores both historical evidence and well-known weather dynamics. And it descends into fear mongering that is a gross disservice to the public.

Note: As I submit this book for publication, forecasters predict temperatures in Death Valley will approach the 1913 record high in the next few days. All the natural factors are in place as predicted. California had a dry winter, the jet stream is keeping cold air to the north and a stationary High is trapping heat. Undoubtedly many people will see this as confirmation of global warming because scientists predicted more heat waves. But these record extremes never happened during Death Valley's warmest years as global warming theory predicts. Skeptics will undoubtedly see this as a predictable natural event. Because extreme temperatures happened in 1913 when it was cooler and again in 2013 when it was warmer, suggests extreme heat waves are weather events independent of the sun and CO_2. Heat waves are weather, and not reliable indicators of climate change.

Recent Heat Waves

"It is very unlikely that warming attributable to increasing greenhouse gas concentrations contributed substantially to the magnitude of this heat wave." [94]

Dr. Randall Dole NOAA/Earth System Research Laboratory

The three major heat waves during the past decade all occurred in areas historically known to be most sensitive to blocking Highs. By 1980, climate scientists from

Harvard and Massachusetts Institute of Technology had identified the central North Pacific, the eastern North Atlantic, and the northern Soviet Union as the most likely regions to experience blocking Highs.[941] Contrary to Trenberth's "wetter and warmer" theory of CO_2 enhanced heat waves, the worst heat waves were occurring in regions dubbed "warming holes" because they had experienced a cooling trend that ran counter to modeled predictions.[93,182,487] For example, a 2004 study reported that the central United States had cooled by 0.4-1.4°F during the 20th century.[93]

A blocking High also caused extreme drought conditions throughout most of Europe in 2003. The recent shift to the negative phase of the North Atlantic Oscillation allowed colder Arctic winds to penetrate into the Atlantic, which increases the likelihood of blocking Highs that will impact Europe. Again the drought began in the cool springtime months. The resulting drier surfaces were estimated to account for about 40% of the abnormally high temperatures in Europe's summer heat wave of 2003.[717]

The Russian heat wave was also located in a "warming hole" that was susceptible to blocking Highs. Scientists reported, "The July surface temperatures for this region impacted by the 2010 Russian heat wave show no significant warming trend over the prior 130-year period from 1880 to 2009."[94] Although NASA climate scientists wrote that the 2010 summer heat wave in western Russia was extraordinary, with the warmest July since at least 1880,[94] they did not implicate CO_2 warming. Historically they reported, "The prior 10 warmest Julys are distributed across the entire [130-year] period and exhibit only modest clustering earlier in this decade, in the 1980s and in the 1930s"[94] Furthermore Moscow had just experienced a much colder than normal winter. It is unlikely that a warming blanket of CO_2 turned off in the winter and on in summer. (It is noteworthy that Death Valley's record breaking high, also followed a cold winter. The record cold temperature in Death Valley was established in January 1913.)

NASA's scientists concluded, "Our analysis points to a primarily natural cause for the Russian heat wave. This event appears to be mainly due to internal atmospheric dynamical processes that produced and maintained an intense and *long-lived blocking event* (emphasis added)." Results from prior studies suggest that it is likely that the intensity of the heat wave was further increased by *regional land surface feedbacks*. It was the drought and subsequent drying effects of the landscape that exacerbated those "land surface feedbacks."[94]

Hurricanes and Superstorm Sandy

"It is beyond me why my colleagues would utilize the media to push an unsupported agenda that recent hurricane activity has been due to global warming" [530]

Dr. Chris Landsea, Hurricane Research Division, NOAA

In 2005, Dr Chris Landsea resigned from the Intergovernmental Panel on Climate Change (IPCC) when he felt Dr. Trenberth had improperly preyed on the public's emotions by capitalizing on the misery of the victims of Hurricane Katrina. Trenberth is not a hurricane expert but Landsea is. In his resignation Landsea wrote, "It is beyond me why my colleagues would utilize the media to push an unsupported agenda that recent hurricane activity has been due to global warming. Given Dr. Trenberth's role as the IPCC's Lead Author responsible for preparing the text on hurricanes, his public statements – so far outside of current scientific understanding – led to my concern that it would be very difficult for the IPCC to proceed objectively."[530]

As scientists continued to collect data on hurricanes, it became clear Trenberth had been misled by the short-term rise in hurricane activity during the 1990s. He had assumed it must have been due to global warming and projected that trend would continue in lockstep with growing concentrations of CO_2. However the test of time supported Landsea's objections. Since satellite data became available, scientists can measure the combined number and the intensity of world's hurricanes, from which they calculate the Accumulated Cyclone Energy Index (ACE) (See Figure 27). Since the spike in hurricane activity in the Atlantic in the 1990s, the ACE has declined over the past decade. Global activity has now "decreased to the lowest levels since the late 1970s."[442]

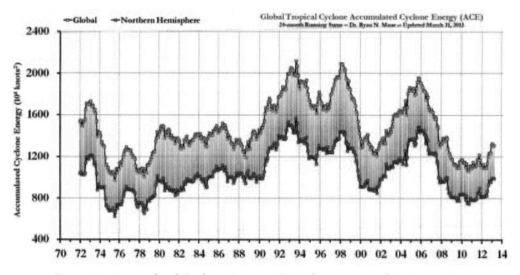

Figure 27. Accumulated Cyclone Energy ACE Index courtesy of Dr. Ryan Maue

Trenberth also published his views in the *Scientific American* article, "Warmer Oceans, Stronger Hurricanes"[550] in which he argued that warmer oceans may not increase the frequency of hurricanes, but a "warmer and wetter" world would increase the number of "extreme category 4 and 5 hurricanes." However, after Hurricane Katrina, those extreme hurricanes virtually disappeared. As the ACE index continued to fall, advocates stopped highlighting the CO_2-hurricane connection.

When Superstorm Sandy struck, however, advocates again capitalized on human misery. Just five days after Sandy had peaked, *Scientific American*'s Mark Fischetti wrote, "Did Climate Change Cause Hurricane Sandy?" and he interviewed Dr. Hansen and Dr. Trenberth. In reference to Trenberth's paper he wrote, "if you're a regular *Scientific American* reader, you might recall that another well-regarded scientist predicted behemoths such as Sandy in 2007." But Fischetti distorted the truth.[549]

Trenberth had predicted global warming would cause more Category 4 and 5 hurricanes, but Sandy was a small Category 2 storm. Trenberth had never predicted that a Category 2 storm would transform into a behemoth when it encountered cold air. Anyone can predict that there will be a heat wave or a big storm in the future and eventually be proven right. However, Trenberth's big storm occurred for all the wrong reasons. *In fact, Superstorm Sandy contradicted all the relevant global warming predictions.*

The negative phase of the North Atlantic/Arctic Oscillation allows colder air to sweep southward, cooling the north Atlantic Ocean. This induces the blocking high in the north Atlantic that forced a very minor hurricane to turn inland, which then evolved into Superstorm Sandy. The American climate models had initially predicted that this small Category 2 hurricane would pass harmlessly into the eastern Atlantic. There was no excessive warming to arouse suspicions of an extreme hurricane. However European modelers noticed a blocking High was building in the Atlantic and warned the Americans of the catastrophic consequences. As the blocking High persisted, the US modelers agreed and sounded the alarm of the approaching devastation. As Sandy approached the East Coast, it collided with cold air masses, which intensified the storm in the same way intense thunderstorms and tornadoes form when warmer air collides with colder air. Sandy did much of its damage in West Virginia and western Maryland, with heavy "thunder-snow."

Just a decade earlier, NASA scientists and scientists from Trenberth's National Center for Atmospheric Research all predicted that rising CO_2 would likely maintain the North Atlantic Oscillation (NAO) in its warm phase.[362,371] Virtually every global model had also predicted the NAO would remain in its warm phase throughout the 21st century.[886,894] A blocking High in the Atlantic was not predicted because all research had demonstrated blocking Highs occur more frequently during the NAO's negative cool phase.[845,846,885,886] *The negative NAO and the accompanying blocking high contradicted their global warming theories.*

But to keep the blame on CO_2, the advocates again flip-flopped. Fischetti's *Scientific American* article now suggested the blocking Highs formed because global warming had now caused the NAO to switch to its cool phase. As was the case for the devastating tornados that struck Oklahoma, every extreme weather event is blamed on rising CO_2 no matter how much evidence contradicts those claims. The extreme weather craze is no longer science, it is pure politics.

Superstorm Sandy's greatest damage happened when it was forced inland where a highly populated area was vulnerable to flooding during an exceptional high tide. Four hundred years ago tidal marshes and protective dunes ringed Manhattan. Over time, the marshes were filled in to create more real estate for a burgeoning population. Sand dunes that protected the coast from storm surges were lost or removed as eyesores. As Sandy veered inland, it inundated those old marshlands, but communities that had restored their protective sand dunes suffered minimal damage.

Four hundred years ago we lacked the science to inform people about the probabilities of an extreme weather event. Science will serve society best when it informs the public about the probabilities and consequences of inevitable extreme weather. *No matter how much CO_2 we sacrifice to the climate gods, we will never prevent hurricanes or superstorms.* The wisest course of action would be to stop subsidizing development on vulnerable lands and to restore the buffering dune systems. However, I have yet to talk to anyone on the West Coast who was aware of those restoration benefits. Despite contradicting all global warming predictions, we were inundated with fictitious stories about how our carbon economy wrought the misery of Superstorm Sandy.

Adiabatic Heating and Climate

The concept of adiabatic heating may sound like strange heady stuff, but it was a phenomenon well understood by more "primitive" cultures. If not for the invention of the common kitchen match, modern societies would be much more familiar with the concept. I never appreciated adiabatic heating until I met a backpacker in the Minarets just south of Yosemite. Sharing a campsite, he excitedly offered to show me his fire-stick. Understandably, I was a tad uncomfortable and worried he had been alone in the wilderness too long. So I sought quick clarification, asking if he meant a cigarette lighter. He then repeated, "fire-stick", proudly explaining he can start fires just by squeezing air in a tube. What he finally showed me is more commonly called a fire piston but nonetheless a fascinating gadget that indeed starts fires by rapidly compressing air.

You can see how a fire piston works by googling "fire piston" and watching a short video demonstration. Or you can buy one for about $15 (USD) and add it to your camping gear. In the 1800s, European explorers had observed that native people in the jungles from Borneo and Burma to the Philippines all used fire pistons to start their cooking fires.[97] By rapidly squeezing air in a small tube, temperatures rose by as much as 800°F and ignited the kindling used to start a larger fire. Because blow-darts were commonly used to hunt birds and monkeys in the jungle trees, some believe these people gained insight into the adiabatic phenomenon while boring out the bamboo tubes from which they made their dart guns.

Whether or not fire pistons were discovered independently in Europe or inspired by the stories shared by those early explorers is unclear. But Europeans who manufactured compressed air guns also noticed that air compression could emit a hot flash. Soon brass "fire pistons" and "fire syringes" were being made and patented for use in Europe's kitchens. But the invention of the handier wooden match led people to abandon the fire piston. Unfortunately, an opportunity to naturally experience adiabatic heating was also lost. Next time you use a bicycle pump to pump up a flat tire or a basketball, see if you notice the temperature difference before and after you use the pump. Although more hidden from view, adiabatic heating is a key factor governing how your refrigerator and diesel engines work.

All descending air currents are naturally compressed and cause adiabatic heating. When air currents move over mountain ranges and descend to the surface, they often cause "foehn winds", named after the Foehn winds of the European Alps. However each region gives these winds a special name like the Santa Ana's in southern California, or the Chinooks in northwestern United States. Dry foehn winds are also known as "snow eaters". During the dark winter night in Antarctica, a foehn wind can raise temperatures by as much as 90°F in only a few hours.[896] Foehn winds are responsible for the extensive ice-free regions of the McMurdo dry valleys of Antarctica. An increase in foehn storms was also responsible for the higher temperatures on the eastern side of the Antarctic Peninsula and the melt ponds that formed when the Larsen Ice Shelf collapsed.[300,321]

Descending air does not need to reach the surface to raise temperatures. If adiabatic heating creates a layer of warmer air a few hundred meters above the surface it creates a thermal lid that stops rising convection. Without rising convection to carry away the heat, surface temperatures soar. Without adding a single unit of extra heat from the sun or CO_2, natural cycles change the frequency of foehn storms and adiabatic heating. If the purpose of adjusting the raw temperature data is meant to help scientists determine how much heat CO_2 has added to the climate, then all warm temperatures caused by adiabatic heating need to be removed.

8

Beating Dead Frogs with CO$_2$

Extinct Golden Toad.
Credit: US Fish and Wildlife Service, Charles H. Smith

" one third or more of the 6,300 species are threatened with extinction." [246]

Dr. David Wake, University of California, Berkeley.

While growing up in Massachusetts, my sister and I would often take walks to a nearby pond. The chorus of chirping frogs reverberating from the pond was always a comforting symbol of struggle and endurance. No matter how daunting our problems seemed, the sound of the frogs always bred a sense of optimism. That pond would dry out each summer, then refill with the autumn rains, only to freeze completely during the winter. It seemed brutal, but every spring the frogs emerged to sing their love song.

Frogs have been incredibly resilient throughout time. Over the last few hundred million years, amphibians have survived several waves of mass extinction. The last great wave of extinction, about 60 million years ago, wiped dinosaurs from the face of the earth and 18% of all vertebrate families. Yet more amphibians endured, most likely due to the way the heat capacity of their watery habitat moderates climate change. Today, approximately one-third of the earth's amphibian species are facing extinction in what some biologists have termed the "sixth wave of extinction,"[246] and half of those extinctions have been conclusively linked to the loss of wetland habitat.

But a new wave of rapid extinctions, even where wetlands remained intact, baffled scientists for over a decade. The scientific community's efforts to solve these mysterious extinctions reveal a stark contrast between the rigors imposed on medical science versus the lax scientific standards surrounding climate change. It also reveals how global warming fervor led some scientists to *oppose* crucial conservation efforts that were our best hope of preventing imminent extinctions.

You can always recognize amphibians (i.e., frogs and salamanders) versus reptiles (i.e., lizards and snakes) by the amphibians' moist, slimy skin. To supplement their feeble lungs, amphibians absorb essential oxygen directly from the air through their skin, which must remain moist. If drinking water is unavailable, most frogs and toads have a patch on their rump that allows them to directly absorb moisture from the damp soil. Most amphibians are tied to pools of water because their jelly-coated eggs readily desiccate, and during their tadpole stage they breathe with gills. Thus, most amphibians must spend the early stages of their life cycle in a wet environment; a trait which makes them very vulnerable to the loss of global wetlands.

However, amphibians had been forced to adapt to eons of climate change cycles that had naturally dried up lakes and rivers, as well as an ever-growing population of predators hunting in their breeding ponds. A few entrepreneurial amphibians discovered that their odds of survival were better on land, and many species evolved the most amazing strategies to free themselves from their dependency on standing water. For example in Chile, Darwin's Frog lays its eggs on the moist forest floor, and the male then stands guard as they develop. As soon as the eggs show signs of emerging as wriggling tadpoles, the male swallows them; not into his stomach, but into his vocal sac. The vocal sac serves as a protected "indoor pool" in which the tadpoles grow until they metamorphose into fully developed frogs.

Throughout much of Central and South America are several species of Marsupial Frogs. Analogous to kangaroos, they grow a pouch on their backs, inside which their tadpoles develop. Most amazing of all were Australia's two species of gastric-brooding frogs. Although they spent most of their lives in water, the female protected her offspring by swallowing her eggs. Unlike Darwin's Frog, the eggs were swallowed into her stomach. Somehow, the deadly digestive enzymes and acid that normally flooded their stomach stop flowing until her tadpoles were fully developed. The adults then gave birth by regurgitation. Despite having adapted to millions of years of climate change, in the 1980s this marvel of nature became one of the first casualties of the new wave of extinction.

The male Midwife Toad guards his eggs by wrapping them around his thighs and carrying them across the landscape. When the eggs begin to dry, the male seeks water and gives the eggs a dip before venturing off again. When the tadpoles are ready to emerge, he drops them in the nearest pool to fend for themselves. In Spain, Midwife Toad populations were also mysteriously disappearing.

The Rain Frogs are petite frogs that lay their eggs beneath the leaf litter on the damp floors of tropical forests. The red-eyed Coqui, a national symbol of Puerto Rico (and a recently introduced pest in Hawaii), is a species of Rain Frog. These frogs have evolved the remarkable ability to undergo complete metamorphosis without ever leaving the confines of their eggs. However, they never evolved the waterproof eggshells of reptiles and birds, so the frogs' eggs can rapidly dry out. Some species lay their eggs in moist sand along streams. Others lay their eggs on land beneath the leaf litter. To keep their eggs moist, the thoughtful parents periodically urinate on them. Some childhoods are simply tougher than others. By avoiding ponds and streams, several species of Rain Frogs have avoided the recent wave of extinction by the water fungus, but several other species have suffered from deforestation.

Dueling Extinction Theories

"In general, however, the moderate deviations of rainfall and temperature measures from long-term averages at each site appear to be an inadequate explanation for the dramatic declines of montane frogs in Queensland. Other possible factors, especially epidemic disease, should be explored in further detail" [251].

Dr. William Laurance, CSIRO Tropical Forest Research Centre

Golden Toads (*Bufo periglenes*) had adapted to Costa Rica's dry season by spending their entire lives sequestered in moist underground burrows. The Golden Toads only emerged from their burrows in late March and April, to mate during the first few weeks of the rainy season. They laid their eggs in ponds or any temporary pool, including puddles formed by human footsteps. For the remainder of the year they retreated back to their burrows. First discovered in 1966, and inspiring the formation of Costa Rica's Monteverde Cloud Forest Reserve, this species was found nowhere else in the world. In 1987 Monteverde's biologists had counted over 1500 healthy individuals painting their breeding pools with squirming gold. Just one year later in 1988, only one Golden Toad was observed, yet not one carcass was ever found.[156]

Martha Crump and Alan Pounds had been studying Monteverde's amphibians and were understandably distraught by the rapid disappearance of the Golden Toad and several other species. Without a dead body to examine, the actual cause of death remains speculative. However, that year an El Niño had forced extremely dry conditions, and researchers were not sure if the Golden Toads had died or if they were simply waiting for wetter breeding conditions.[155] However after years of absence, it became apparent that just 25 years after their discovery, the Golden Toad had become extinct.[156,157]

Crump and Pounds had also reported that Monteverde's Harlequin Frogs had been at peak abundance in 1987 and likewise disappeared suddenly in 1988. Throughout Costa Rica in the 1970s Harlequin Frogs had been collected by the thousands and exported to Germany for the pet trade. Yet their populations were never so severely reduced as they now were inside Monteverde's newly protected boundaries. That year several other species on the preserve also suffered dramatic reductions. That such a wave of extinction could cross the borders of a preserved habitat was unnerving, and suggested a more universal killer. Climate change or disease were thought the most likely villains.

Pounds and Crump first suspected that extreme drying from a strong El Niño was the likely culprit; however, contradictory evidence evoked many doubts. Nearer to the Caribbean Sea where rain had been more abundant, frogs had been equally decimated. Furthermore, Harlequin Frogs usually lay their eggs in streams that never dried out, yet they suddenly vanished. In contrast, the number of tiny "tink" frogs increased. Tink frogs (named for their metallic call) develop inside their eggs beneath the leaf litter and were the most vulnerable to extreme drying. Golden Toads were a bigger mystery. How could an El Niño extirpate an entire species that was insulated from the weather inside their burrows?

As amphibian biologists shared their research, they realized that they were facing a global wave of extinction. Massive die-offs were not restricted to Monteverde and the effects of El Niño. Massive die-offs were observed in regions of Central and South America, Spain, North America, and Australia. In 1996, Australian researchers detected waves of die-offs that slowly spread across northern Australia. They reported that 14 species of stream-dwelling frogs, including the gastric-brooding frogs, had suddenly disappeared; in some cases in as little as three to six months.

Contradicting global warming theory, the Australian researchers reported that *the die-offs were happening at higher elevations with cooler temperatures, but not at warmer lower elevations.* Die-offs also occurred during the winter but not the summer.[248] Researchers in Central and South America also found that populations that lived at higher and cooler elevations were extirpated, while populations of the same species living at lower and warmer elevations were still thriving.[249,250] Similarly in the United States, the extirpations were happening at higher elevations in Yosemite, and during the winter in Arizona when cooler temperatures prevailed.[247]

So William Laurance from the National Institute for Research in the Amazon and his Australian colleagues hypothesized that the global population of amphibians was under attack by a rapidly spreading, exotic disease that was dependent on cool, wet conditions. They suggested that human activities such as the pet trade and invasive species had introduced and spread a deadly disease.[251]

Science should never rely on coincidences simply woven into a good story. If a scientist blames a pathogen (i.e., a bacterium, virus, or fungus) for any outbreak of death and sickness, they must satisfy a burden of proof known as Koch's postulates, first formulated over 120 years ago. First the pathogen must be found on a diseased animal and then isolated. Then scientists must culture the pathogen and inoculate a healthy animal with it. If the pathogen causes the same disease symptoms in the healthy test subjects, then it becomes a likely candidate. Finally, to prove that pathogen had caused the epidemic, researchers must then find that same pathogen on the widespread carcasses of victims of the epidemic. Environmental conditions that existed during the epidemic should also coincide with the pathogen's behavior under laboratory conditions.

In 1998, after carefully scrutinizing dead specimens from Australia and Central America, epidemiologists discovered a common killer. It was not a virus as Laurance had first suspected, but an exotic and previously unknown chytrid fungus, now named *Batrachochytrium dendrobatidis* ("Bd" for short).[504] They were then able to isolate Bd in dead frog specimens from across the globe. And when they exposed healthy laboratory frogs to the fungus, the same deadly symptoms rapidly appeared.

Having successfully isolated the Bd fungus and demonstrated its lethal effects, additional laboratory experiments soon explained why the world's frogs were killed in locations with cooler temperatures, such as higher elevations. In the laboratory, Bd was virulent between 53° and 81°F. Its optimum growth occurred between 60° to 77°F, but the fungus also survived near-freezing temperatures. In contrast, temperatures over 86°F killed the fungus,[167,168,169] which explained why populations of the same species living in warmer habitats were surviving, and why outbreaks were more common in winter than in summer. Furthermore they demonstrated that the fungus depended on a moist environment and died after drying.[167] That explained why Monteverde's stream-dwelling frogs were extirpated, but Tink frogs living in drier habitat thrived during the dry El Niño.

Once the pathogen had been identified, I expected an educational campaign to limit the chytrid's deadly spread. The pet trade and educators were often relocating amphibians, and bull frogs were being introduced throughout the tropics as a food source. Immediately after the human HIV virus was detected, public health agencies around the world embarked on a global education program to inform the public how the virus was spread. Wherever public health education was embraced, the spread of HIV was limited. That education campaign also eased the minds of a panicked public suffering from misconceptions that AIDS could be spread by mosquitos or from a cough. I didn't expect the frogs to benefit from the same extensive efforts, but an informational email to the school districts would not cost much and could enlist the support of educators.

Yet despite the biologists' lament about a sixth wave of amphibian extinction, educational efforts have been rare. In 2012 when workers from the Golden Gate National Seashore were cutting down a tree infected by a tree-rotting fungus, they stationed a biologist to hand out leaflets and answer questions to passersby to inform them why the tree was being cut. After reading the leaflet I asked why they hadn't embarked on a similar educational effort to halt the spread of the Bd fungus. The African clawed frog is a known carrier and thousands were introduced worldwide for use in labs to study embryo development, or for pregnancy testing, and for retail sale as aquarium pets. Because people are always dumping pet frogs in local ponds, educating about deadly Bd was far more critical than educating about the tree fungus. She graciously pleaded ignorance and immediately called her office. They replied there was no local Bd threat.

Hopefully recent events will open their eyes. In 2013, infected African clawed frogs were found in the ponds of San Francisco's Golden Gate Park surrounding the California Academy of Science, and every native species had been exterminated. Fifteen years after the disease was first diagnosed and likely carriers identified, there has yet to be a public education campaign.

On the other hand, Alan Pounds, the journal *Nature* and proponents of climate change actively campaigned to blame CO₂-caused warming and incite public panic. Pounds' earlier research had correctly warned that the disappearance of amphibians at Monteverde was not just a natural cycle of boom and busts.[157] However in 1999, despite the discovery of Bd and despite contradictory climate evidence, Pounds began pushing the idea that global climate change was Monteverde's great amphibian killer. Publishing in the journal Nature he argued, "The changes are all associated with *patterns of dry-season mist frequency*, which is negatively correlated with sea surface temperatures in the equatorial Pacific." He continued, "This hypothesis builds on evidence that rising sea surface temperatures have altered the climates of tropical mountains." He supported his climate argument by referring to Parmesan's Edith's checkerspot butterfly studies and argued that increased evaporation from the oceans was *"amplifying the warming in the highlands relative to the lowlands."*[154] Thus began the battle of dueling extinction theories.

The Global Warming Flip Flops

"these crashes probably belong to a constellation of demographic changes that have altered communities of birds, reptiles and amphibians in the area and are linked to recent warming. The changes are all associated with patterns of dry-season mist frequency" [154]

J. Alan Pounds 1999

"If amphibians seek warmth to combat infection, increasing cloudiness might hamper their defences. In any case, local or microscale cooling should often benefit the chytrids." [161]

J. Alan Pounds 2006

Pounds was not deterred by the fact that there was no drying trend in Monteverde's annual, seasonal, or monthly rainfall. Nor was there any trend in the variability of day-to-day rainfall. However, after dissecting Monteverde's weather data, he extracted a single statistic that correlated with increasing CO_2 levels. He calculated that during the normal dry season, from January to April, the number of "dry days" with only zero to 0.1 mm of mist had increased from about 12 to about 40 days. Pounds was splitting climate hairs. In fact, 0.1 mm is literally the width of a human hair, and a slight change in a summer breeze could easily alter any mist measurements.

Pounds' suggestion that more CO_2 caused less forest mist was immediately challenged by ecological studies. Studies from models and satellite pictures found that fewer clouds were formed due to the expanding deforested areas to the east of Monteverde.[502,503] In addition to that refutation, the mist argument was rapidly becoming irrelevant. *Evidence from around the world was mounting that Bd was the worldwide killer, and Bd preferred cooler wet habitats.* Dryness and heat protected the frogs from the deadly disease.

So Pounds then argued that that those few extra dry days had weakened the frog's immune system and set the stage for Bd infection. He argued that if his theory was correct then "widespread amphibian extinctions in seemingly undisturbed highland forests may attest to how profound and unpredictable the outcome can be when climate change alters ecological interactions."[161] Unlike the rigorous process demanded by Koch's postulates, Pounds did not need to demonstrate how a few days of subtle changes in mist had exterminated a species inside a burrow. He did not need to prove that species adapted to millennia of periodic El Niños were suddenly weakened by just 20 days without 0.1 mm of mist. Yet CO_2 advocates uncritically embraced the climate change connection, and over 900 papers cited Pounds' work, compared to the little more than 200 scientists who cited Laurance's well-tested disease hypothesis.

There was no long-term instrumental data for temperature and rainfall at Monteverde, and a few scientists questioned if those underscored dry days were perhaps just part of a longer natural cycle. Experts from Columbia University's Lamont-Doherty Earth Observatory analyzed tree cores around Monteverde and reconstructed the long-term temperature and moisture trends. They concluded, "*There was no evidence of a trend associated with global warming.*"[164]

MIT's world-renowned oceanographer Carl Wunsch has warned about attempts to circumvent the scientific process and enshrine a favored theory. "Convenient assumptions should not be turned prematurely into "facts," nor uncertainties and ambiguities suppressed…Anyone can write a model: the challenge is to demonstrate its accuracy and precision…Otherwise, the scientific debate is controlled by the most articulate, colorful, or adamant players."[486] Pounds' "CO₂-caused-warming-caused-extinction" theory exemplified what Wunsch had warned against. Without a shred of supporting evidence, Pounds' hypothesis dominated research and the media based on forceful storytelling and a powerful advocacy journal. A leading CO_2 advocate, the late Dr. Stephen Schneider, provided futuristic "evidence" to support Pounds' claim of drying mists, and *Nature* published Schneider's article in the same issue as Pounds' article. Schneider used a global climate model to create a futuristic scenario that if CO_2 doubled it "could" raise the clouds and "perhaps" cause a harmful drying effect.

Michael Mann also heralded Pounds' explanation in his book *Dire Predictions*,[992] where he highlighted both the Polar Bears and the Golden Toad as his main biological examples of global warming's catastrophic consequences. Nature and C.D. Thomas teamed up again to publish *Extinction Risk From Climate Change*[5] writing "Climate change over the past 30 years has produced numerous shifts in the distributions and abundances of species and has been implicated in one species-level extinction," referring to the Golden Toad. With nothing more than untested speculation, the Golden Toad became the poster child for extinction by CO₂–caused global warming, and Alan Pounds joined Camille Parmesan among a select group of biologists invited to serve on the Nobel-prize winning Intergovernmental Panel on Climate Change.

Around the world, rapid amphibian die-offs continued and each extirpation consistently coincided with Bd infections. As the evidence for Bd mounted, evidence for Pounds' link to global warming weakened because high temperatures and dryness killed the fungus, and protected the frogs. So CO_2 advocates simply dubbed this the *climate-chytrid paradox*. Faced with ever-mounting contradictory evidence, Pounds changed the specifics of his global warming theory. No longer was the increased "number of dry days" or "amplified warming" the killer. Pounds now reported that Monteverde's 25 year historical temperature record *revealed an approximate 2°F decline in maximum temperature* but an approximate 2°F rise in minimums. So he proposed the chytrid-thermal-optimum hypothesis, in which daytime cooling and night time warming accelerated disease development.[161]

His right hand must not have known what his left was doing. He now argued that a combination of declining maximum temperatures and an increase in cloud cover had shielded the infected frogs from the healing heat of the sun and was "fostering moist conditions."[161] He argued that sunlit mats of mosses can sometimes reach the 86°F that was known to be lethal to Bd, and those sunlit mats would have served as healing zones to naturally kill the fungus if not for CO_2.[161] However sunlit mats only matter to a very few species capable of withstanding the drying effects of direct sunlight. Besides, Pounds knew that the Golden Toads retreated to their dark burrows immediately after breeding and would never have visited those hypothetical "healing patches."

Nonetheless *Nature* readily published this newly contrived chytrid-thermal-optimum hypothesis in "Widespread amphibian extinctions from epidemic disease driven by global warming".[161] Embodying the forceful storyteller, Pounds boldly stated, "*we conclude with 'very high confidence' (99%, following the Intergovernmental Panel on Climate Change, IPCC) that large-scale warming is a key factor in the disappearances. We propose that temperatures at many highland localities are shifting towards the growth optimum of Batrachochytrium, thus encouraging outbreaks. With climate change promoting infectious disease and eroding biodiversity, the urgency of reducing greenhouse-gas concentrations is now undeniable.*"[161] To further promote this "new" climate optimum hypothesis, *Nature* added a companion opinion piece singing the praises of Pounds' "elegant idea".

Ironically the declining maximum temperature refuted his previous theory that "amplified temperatures" had stressed the frogs and made them more vulnerable to disease. Clearly, Pounds was manufacturing any possible link to rising CO_2 levels. Earlier research had documented that the Golden Toads had always emerged from their burrows when their breeding pool temperatures were in Bd's optimal range.[155,165] If an optimal temperature triggered the deadly disease, the frogs should have died decades earlier. The slight change in temperature was irrelevant. It was the introduction of the disease from other locales that caused widespread extinctions.

Some scientists suspected Pounds' correlations with climate change were simply due to a lack of statistical rigor. In a 2008 paper, "Evaluating the links between climate, disease spread, and amphibian declines"[173] the researchers demonstrated just how easy it is to generate meaningless statistical correlations. In response to Pounds' link to global warming they wrote, "*Numerous other variables, including regional banana and beer production, were better predictors of these extinctions.* Almost all of our findings were opposite to the predictions of the chytrid-thermal-optimum hypothesis."[173]

Changing our carbon footprint will never ever remove Bd's preferred range of temperatures from the world. Some locations may be more optimal than others, but wherever and whenever that 53° to 81°F range occurs, the fungus will grow and spread. Whether man-made or natural, the most climate change could ever do is shift the location or the season when Bd does its killing. It was the ease of modern day transportation, and uneducated people who assisted the spread of disease carriers that allowed Bd to rapidly find new locations with acceptable climates. The best solution for conservationists was to slow the spread of the disease and to use captive breeding wherever extinction was imminent. But Pounds unconscionably attacked this solution.

Denigrating Conservationists

"There is something fascinating about science. One gets such wholesale returns of conjecture out of such a trifling investment of fact."

Mark Twain Life on the Mississippi

"To suggest that this alone can halt the extinctions undermines scientific credibility and engenders false hope and complacency among voters and consumers. Biodiversity loss warns that humanity's life-support system is crumbling." [158]

J. Alan Pounds

Fortunately, biologists trying to save the frogs understood the real danger and published elsewhere in journals not dominated by climate change advocacy. Seventy-six amphibian experts eventually agreed on an amphibian recovery plan, and set out to rescue species most likely to be endangered by the spreading wave of Bd fungus. They targeted regions where the climate suited Bd's growth, and sought out regions nearest the latest wave of the disease's advance. Their efforts have been overlooked by the media and advocacy journals, but their success is a tribute to the power of good science.

Reminiscent of the wave of introduced diseases brought by Conquistadors that extirpated millions of native Incas and Aztecs, Central and South American amphibians were under the attack of a rapidly spreading fungus. Karen Lips had been surveying amphibians in Central and South America and had tirelessly warned of the impending dangers of spreading Bd. In 2008 she reported, "Available data support the hypothesis of multiple introductions of this invasive pathogen into South America and subsequent spread along the primary Andean cordilleras. *Additional analyses found no evidence to support the hypothesis that climate change has been driving outbreaks of amphibian chytridiomycosis*".[171] Martha Crump, who had originally worked with Pounds analyzing the demise of the Golden Toad, now fully grasped the disease's devastating potential.[159] After the sudden appearance of Bd in Panama and the onset of mass die-offs, these biologists estimated the rate and direction in which the disease would spread. Lips predicted that the next wave of extinctions would soon strike El Valle, Panama and assembled a team of volunteers from Zoo Atlanta. They flew to Panama and airlifted 600 live frogs of potentially threatened species to safety just before Bd's predicted arrival ravaged amphibian populations months later.

The hope now is that captive breeding will provide those species with the opportunity to evolve natural immunity, so eventually they can be released back into the wild. Fortunately, natural selection typically causes new virulent diseases to evolve into less deadly forms. If a strain of the chytrid fungus kills its hosts too quickly before the fungus can reproduce, it eliminates its most deadly genomes. On the other hand, because the disease kills the frogs that are the most vulnerable, any surviving frogs with more resistant genetics slowly repopulate their old habitat. Eventually, a balance evolves where more resistant amphibians and a less virulent disease coexist. Before the age of modern transportation, this evolutionary process happened within a limited area. However if a disease is spread around the world before a balance evolves, the most virulent forms spread a trail of tragic consequences. Species with small populations in a restricted habitat, like the Golden Toad and relatives of the Harlequin Frog, are most vulnerable. A single introduction of the disease can rapidly wipe out the entire species.

Yet somehow Lips' valiant actions threatened Pounds and he published articles attacking those conservation efforts. In the journal *Science*, Pounds denigrated the airlift efforts, "To suggest that this alone can halt the extinctions undermines scientific credibility and engenders false hope and complacency among voters and consumers. Biodiversity loss warns that humanity's life-support system is crumbling. Those who realize this may become responsible global citizens, demanding sound governance and accountability."[158] Pounds and his fellow advocates appeared less worried about saving frogs and more concerned about maintaining a climate of fear and its political leverage.

The rapid spread of the chytrid disease still continues worldwide. Although powerful journals like *Nature* and *Science* advocated Pounds' climate hypothesis, and funds were continuously diverted to test Pounds' ever-changing hypotheses, only Laurance's 1996 hypothesis of a rapidly spreading novel disease has stood the test of time. In 2012 researchers in the Sierra Nevada documented the fungus' spread through three lake basins around Sequoia National Park. Only after the fungus suddenly appeared did the local frogs go extinct. These experts again found no support for the Pounds' global warming hypothesis.[174] So much for Pounds' forceful storytelling and his "very high confidence" (99%, following the Intergovernmental Panel on Climate Change) that global warming was the driver of amphibian extinctions.

For those interested in the scientific detective work that unraveled the Bd epidemic, I highly recommend the 2009 book *Extinction in Our Times: Global Amphibian Decline*,[159] coauthored by Pounds' old colleague from Monteverde, Martha Crump. While Crump sings the praises of the researchers whose tireless efforts identified the disease, the journal *Nature* and Pounds again teamed up to discredit the book and the well-established disease hypothesis.

Pounds wrote, "James Collins and Martha Crump try to reassure us that these vanishing creatures are not warning of large-scale environmental deterioration like canaries in a coal mine, but are simply telling us that they themselves are in trouble. A book blaming a fungus for the disappearance of amphibians from wild places wrongly downplays the role of environmental change."[160] But Collins and Crump had most definitely stated that in addition to the fungus-caused deaths, scientists must counteract the other factors threatening the environment. They wrote, "*We now recognize commercial exploitation, introduction of exotic species, and land use as ongoing causes of amphibian declines*". But that was not the "environmental change" that Pounds and *Nature* were trying to exploit. They want us to believe "humanity's life-support system is crumbling" solely due to rising levels of CO$_2$.

In 2011, *Nature* published another article by Camille Parmesan who suggested we end the climate debate, "By over-emphasizing the need for rigorous assessment of the specific role of greenhouse-gas forcing in driving observed biological changes, the IPCC effectively yields to the contrarians' inexhaustible demands for more 'proof', rather than advancing the most pressing and practical scientific questions."[534] Then, as if science had proven that CO$_2$ had killed the Golden Toad she wrote, "*Species' extinctions have already been linked to recent climate change; the golden toad is iconic*."[534]

Indeed, the Golden Toad is iconic of the recent attempts to link rising CO$_2$ to extinctions based on weak and non-existent evidence. It is iconic of repeated attempts to force a global CO$_2$ perspective and evoke a climate of fear at the grave expense of sincere conservation efforts. Understanding how to limit the transmission the deadly fungus is "the most pressing and practical scientific question," and blaming CO_2 warming is the biggest distraction. The illusory politics of the Golden Toad demonstrate why public debate about climate change and "demands for more proof" are more important now than ever.

9

The Great Drought Debates and the Power of El Niño

"The model seems to miss some of the dynamics that drive large droughts." [939]
Dr Jason Smerdon, 2013, Columbia University's Lamont-Doherty Earth Observatory

Dr. Jim Hansen is another forceful storyteller who captured headlines by prophesying devastating droughts of biblical proportions and promising that your salvation will come only by reducing CO_2 emissions. In a 2012 *N.Y. Times* op-ed piece titled "Game Over for the Climate," Dr. Hansen restated that CO_2 could kill off half of all species, and our civilization was at dire risk. Then capitalizing on the recent droughts in the United States, he painted a landscape devastated by record-breaking droughts that will wither crops as if devoured by locusts. He divined that semi-permanent droughts will smite us from Texas to North Dakota with an ever-widening Dust Bowl. And so spoketh his models. Hansen wrote, *"If this sounds apocalyptic, it is. This is why we need to reduce emissions dramatically."* [183]

However Hansen's dramatics are not supported by a great many of his colleagues. Dr. Martin Hoerling is a research meteorologist specializing in climate dynamics at NOAA's Earth System Research Laboratory. He publicly countered Hansen: "The claim in the Hansen NYT piece that the Midwest would be a dustbowl in coming decades thus runs contrary to peer reviewed literature and recent assessments by the U.S. Global Research Program that emerged from the synthesis of current understanding by an expert team of scientists." He continued, *"Facts should, and do, matter to some. The vision of a Midwest Dustbowl is a scary one, and the author [Hansen] appears intent to instill fear rather than reason."* [212]

Hansen's ominous vision is inspired by the overly simplistic notion that CO_2-caused global warming will increase summer evaporation and dry our soils, resulting in widespread drought. For starters, his model has the tail wagging the dog. It was the lack of winter rains that initiated the drought by early spring, long before summer evaporation came into play. Droughts are exacerbated by, but rarely *caused* by, warmer temperatures. Due to a loss in the landscape's heat capacity, warmer temperatures are "a response to drought, rather than a factor in forcing drought."[492,490] In his rebuttal, Hoerling also reminded Hansen that the recent Midwest drought occurred in a "warming hole" where temperatures had been decreasing over the past century.[93]

> ### Hansen's Model Simplified:
> more CO2 = more heat = more evaporation = apocalyptic drought

It is the transport and distribution of moisture, controlled by ocean cycles such as El Niño and La Niña that cause most droughts and floods. Floods in Asia typically occur simultaneously with droughts in the American southwest, and vice versa. While the media focuses on one swing of the see-saw, globally there has been no increase in droughts for the past 60 years.[490] In addition to ocean cycles, lost wetlands and dried landscapes remove vital sources of moisture required for convective summer rains. Contradicting Hansen's notion of increased evaporation, climate scientists suggest, "It is more plausible that evaporation actually decreases during a drought because of less precipitation."[490,491,492] Dryness always causes higher temperatures (see Chapters 5).

Although it is well accepted that El Niño cycles cause a see-saw pattern of droughts and floods, Hansen's global climate models still fail to accurately simulate those cycles. Despite the over emphasis on CO_2, as of 2012 our state-of-the-art models could link no more than 4% to 6% of recent droughts to rising CO_2 levels. *Natural climate variations accounted for the other 94%.*[496] Furthermore the same models that projected drought by evaporation failed to accurately simulate the past 50 years of drought. The models simulated a rapidly drying United States between 1950 and 2000, but in reality it was wetter due to more frequent El Niños. Likewise, all the models from the Intergovernmental Panel on Climate Change had predicted a wetter African Sahel. Instead the Sahel suffered extreme droughts and famine.[243] Still the advocates claim the greenhouse effect will be more visible over the next two decades and want us to keep the faith.

Short-range weather models have made the greatest strides in climate prediction because they incorporate the most recent climate conditions and scale their predictions to local conditions. Yet even these more focused models struggle to predict droughts from one year to the next. For example, in the spring of 2000, based on their best statistical predictors, the National Weather Service issued a drought alert for the Midwest, then cancelled the alert by midsummer as the Midwest experienced wetter than normal conditions.[34]

Hansen's doomsday preaching also aroused fears that CO_2-driven droughts were already driving parched wildlife into extinction. In reality, we should be celebrating the successful joint efforts by conservationists and hunting groups who have worked hard to improve wetland habitat. Despite reduced wetlands during the most recent La Niña-caused droughts, the US Fish and Wildlife Service reported that in 2011 the wetland dependent ducks of North America filled the skies with record abundance. *The overall population was 43% higher than the 1955-2010 long-term average.* Similarly the bog-loving Moose is also expanding throughout North America. Until 1980, Moose in New England were restricted to the most northern parts of New England and absent from Massachusetts. As marginal farmland was abandoned and forests returned, over a thousand Moose now live in the western part of Massachusetts.

Historic Droughts

"[L]and degradation factors are consistent with the anomalous nature of the Dust Bowl drought!" [95]

Dr. Benjamin Cook, Lamont-Doherty Earth Observatory

Warmer temperatures do not cause droughts. The hot tropical rainforests are among the wettest places in the world. In contrast, the driest region in the world is the McMurdo Dry Valleys of Antarctica, where temperatures remain far below freezing throughout most of the year. And despite Hansen's suggestion that we are living in climate hell, compared to the last thousand years we are living in a golden age of less drought.[190,193,194,206] Tree stumps submerged beneath Lake Tahoe speak of unimaginable drought during colder times in an era when the atmosphere held 30% less CO_2.[225,127] Tree-ring studies reveal that droughts equal to the 1930s Dust Bowl and 1950s have occurred once or twice every century during the past 300–400 years, and a sustained mega-drought (a period of more frequent droughts lasting several decades) happens once every 500 years.[220]

Central Africa suffered extreme droughts during the Little Ice Age.[241] The effects of Little Ice Age mega-droughts also caused the collapse of the city of Angkor in Cambodia, and the Khmer empire, and coincided with the disintegration of nearly all of the major regional kingdoms of southeast Asia.[189,193] The Great Victorian Drought during the cool 1870s resulted in horrendous famine in southeast Asia and caused the death of tens of millions of people, prompting widespread rebellions against the colonial French and British.

In North America, severe droughts lasting decades were centered around 1000 AD, 1500 AD, and 1800 AD.[494] Reconstructions using lake and stream deposits as well as tree rings revealed a series of mega-droughts each lasting 20–40 years over a 400-year period.[195] Reconstructions of California's Sacramento River during the past 1000 years show the period beginning around 1350 AD was the driest 50-year period and the period beginning around 1140 AD was the driest 20-year period. The greatest frequency of extreme low river flow for the Colorado River occurred in the 19th century with "extreme event years in the 1840s and 1850s."[499]

More recently, studies around Glacier National Park (GNP) indicate the late 1800s suffered a series of droughts lasting more than 10 years, with the single most severe dry period occurring from 1917–41.[495] That drought caused GNP's immense Sperry Glacier to lose 60% of its mass between 1900 and 1950.[47] All those severe droughts have nothing to do with rising CO_2 or increased evaporation. They are better accounted for by changes in the El Niño cycles and the position of the Hadley Cell (see Chapter 7).[231]

Droughts occur irrespective of atmospheric CO_2 levels. Their inevitability demands that we become a more resilient society, and that we act to insure the resilience of our wetlands and water supplies. We cannot control the El Niño cycles but we can learn from past land-use mistakes. Healthy watersheds and wetlands more readily absorb heavy rains and minimize floods. Healthy watersheds also store more water underground and augment our reservoirs. The slow release of subsurface water during drier periods sustains fisheries and nourishes the vegetation that sustains wildlife.

To date, two of our Sierra Nevada meadows have had their watersheds restored. Although 2012 was an extremely dry year, both meadows stayed wetter longer than I have ever observed during the 20 years prior to the restoration. The billions of dollars spent to demonize CO_2 could more realistically improve the planet's health if it went to restoring streams and wetlands.

Human history has littered the landscape with collapsed civilizations that were either unable to adapt to droughts and floods or who exacerbated those cycles by landscape abuse. It was not an unusually severe reduction in the rains that precipitated the Dust Bowl. It was the destruction of the natural landscape by unsuspecting wheat farmers that elevated the Dust Bowl era to one of the greatest ecological disasters of the century. Nineteenth century surveys of the southern Great Plains had called the area "No Man's Land" or the "Great American Desert". That region was naturally prone to periodic droughts, and considered inappropriate for agriculture. Unaware that recent rains were a product of a natural ocean cycle, prospective settlers were seduced by a 20-year wet phase.

The government enticed farmers with land ownership under the Homestead Act. To further encourage the settlement of the "Great American Desert," government and university scientists speculated that a permanent trend to a wetter climate had now begun. To explain the increased rainfall, several scientists surrendered to the prevailing bias and theorized that the "rains follow the plow;" this idea was readily promoted by greedy land speculators and government officials.

Within two decades, wheat farmers had removed drought-tolerant, moisture-holding buffalo grass from 41,000 square miles, an area greater than the state of Ohio. When La Niña conditions brought a drought, neither the remaining buffalo grass nor wheat could retain enough moisture or hold the soil in place, and the dust storms began. Like a rolling mountain range, clouds of dust 7000 feet high and 200 miles wide buried the land. One 24-hour storm moved more soil than was excavated from the entire Panama Canal.[497] Better agricultural practices and the government's purchase of withering farmlands to create National Grassland preserves were instrumental in stopping the cycle of destruction.

A thousand years ago, the Mayan civilization sustained 10 times more people than inhabit the Yucatan Peninsula today. Introduced disease and severe droughts were their undoing. As La Niña conditions reduced rainfall by 40%, the Mayans could no longer adapt and the end of their world came earlier than their calendar predicted.[209] Evidence from Tikal, Guatemala reveals that the Mayans had battled water scarcity long before the rains failed. They employed sophisticated technology including dams, reservoirs, and sand filtration systems. However their technological resilience was not enough and they may have unwittingly exacerbated the drought's effects. As the Mayan metropolises grew, they paved over ever-widening areas. Rainwater that had normally penetrated the surface and recharged the springs that fed their reservoirs was now shunted away by those covered surfaces.[209] (Likewise, modern-day urbanization quickly shunts rainfall into sewers to dry the local landscape.)

Similarly it was the combination of drought and land abuse that forced the Anasazi in the American Southwest to abandon their homes, leaving the empty cliff dwellings of Mesa Verde and Chaco Canyon as ghostly reminders of a once-vibrant society. The growing Anasazi civilization had increasingly deforested their surroundings, which would exacerbate the looming drought's local effects.[498] The rooted tree stumps in the middle of Mono Lake to the east of Yosemite National Park are evidence that region-wide mega-droughts were the final tipping point for the Anasazi.

Civilizations located in great river valleys survived those droughts; Cahokia became the thriving center of the Mississippian civilization. The remnants of this culture can be seen at Illinois' Cahokia Mounds State Historic Site near St. Louis. The Cahokians heavily deforested their surroundings to build stockades and temples dubbed "Woodhenge," as well as to stoke the fires that supported a copper industry, and to keep warm during the growing cold. In 1250 AD, Cahokia's population equaled that of London or Paris. However when the rains returned, deforestation promoted heavy flooding that led to the city's rapid demise. Archaeologist Charles Mann wrote in his book *1491*, "the kings who gained their legitimacy from claims to control the weather, would face angry questions from their subjects" when the catastrophic floods arrived.

Causes of Drought

"[T]he North American medieval megadroughts are part of a global hydroclimatic regime linked to persistent La Niña–like conditions in the tropical Pacific." [195]

Dr. Celine Herweijer, Columbia University

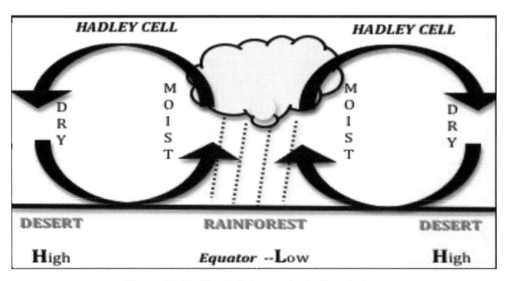

Figure 28. Hadley Cell Atmospheric Circulation

In the simplest terms, droughts and floods are caused by variations in the global pattern of rising and descending air currents. Rising air currents bring rains and descending air currents bring droughts. Annually, tropical rain forests experience wet and dry seasons due to shifting Hadley Cells (see Figure 28). As the sun's position migrates north and south relative to the equator, so does the position of the Hadley Cell's rising and sinking currents. Wherever the moist rising air is centered, there is a rainy season; wherever the descending air strikes there is a dry season.

The Pacific Ocean undergoes short-term cycles every two to seven years that also shift the position of rising and sinking air currents. El Niño shifts the location of floods one year and drought the next. El Niño cycles also drive the Pacific Decadal Oscillation (see Figure 31) which promotes approximately 20-year cycles of more frequent El Niños and approximately 20-year cycles of more frequent La Niñas. More frequent La Niñas caused mega-droughts in the American Southwest. The droughts that devastated the Great Plains, as well as the Mayans and Anasazi over a thousand years ago, were all associated with the relatively cold waters that formed in the eastern Pacific Ocean when La Niña conditions strengthened the blocking High-pressure system.[186,191,198,409]

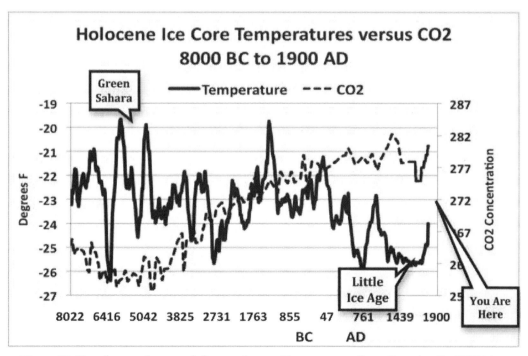

Figure 29. Ten thousand years of climate change. Temperatures from Greenland's GISP2 ice core. CO2 concentrations from EPICA ice core.

There are also drought-causing cycles that happen over periods of thousands of years. The positions of the sun and the Hadley Cells shift due to the wobble of the earth's axis. As seen in Figure 29, despite rising CO_2 levels there has been a 6000-year cooling trend punctuated with dramatic warm spikes. Six thousand years ago, northern Africa was a bountiful grassland dubbed the Green Sahara. As the earth's wobble shifted the focus of the sun, the Hadley Cells shifted south and descending air currents increasingly hammered northern Africa. Rich savannahs withered into the greatest expanse of desert on earth. The creation of the Sahara Desert can be considered the mother of all droughts, and it had nothing to do with global warming.

The El Niño-La Niña oscillation

"Of central importance to drought formation is the development of cool "La Niña-like" sea surface temperatures in the eastern tropical Pacific region" [206]

Dr. Edward Cook, Lamont-Doherty Earth Observatory

"The IPCC has not paid enough attention to natural variability, on several time scales, especially El Niños and La Niñas, the Pacific Ocean phenomena that are not yet captured by climate models, and the longer term Pacific Decadal Oscillation (PDO) and Atlantic Multidecadal Oscillation (AMO) which have cycle lengths of about 60 years." [938]

Dr. Kevin Trenberth, National Center for Atmospheric Research

I visualize the El Niño-La Niña cycle as an oceanic version of the Rock of Sisyphus. The Greek gods condemned King Sisyphus to push a rock up a hill for eternity. Each time Sisyphus approached the summit, the weight of the rock overwhelmed him and the rock rolled uncontrollably back to the bottom. Sisyphus was then forced to start over and over again. Similarly during a La Niña phase, the Pacific trade winds steadily push ocean waters uphill, concentrating the heated tropical waters into world's greatest reservoir of warmth, the Indo-Pacific Warm Pool (see Figure 30). This causes the sea level to rise on the Pacific's western side and drop on its eastern side.

Winds maintain that mountain of water, but when those winds weaken or reverse, the warm pool waters roll "downhill" towards the Americas. This eastward flow of warm water is called the El Niño phase, and causes the eastern Pacific to rapidly warm every two to seven years. The resulting change in ocean temperatures then causes the global zones of High and Low pressure to oscillate. The alternation between an El Niño and La Niña has been termed the "El Niño Southern Oscillation", or ENSO. Just 50 years ago an El Niño was considered a curious abnormality. Now climate scientists recognize its enormous control of global climate.

Warm pools typically hover at approximately 83° to 89°F, which is a critical threshold for ocean evaporation and deep atmospheric convection.[285] At that temperature, any additional energy from the sun readily promotes more evaporation rather than raising the ocean's temperature. The convection currents rising from the warm pools transfer moisture and heat from the ocean to the air. While much of that evaporated moisture falls back as rain in the vicinity of the warm pool, *the warm pools serve as the headwaters of earth's "atmospheric rivers" that flow out from the tropics.*

Streaming through the sky, atmospheric rivers carry water and heat poleward to drier and cooler lands. At any given time three to five gushing streams, each carrying as much water as 10 Mississippi Rivers, rise from tropical warm pools and meander towards the poles. As the Pacific's warm pool waters slosh back and forth across the ocean, it alters the path of the atmospheric rivers. And it is the path of these rivers that determines where floods will most likely occur. Nearly every extreme rainfall event is located where either hurricanes or atmospheric rivers make landfall. [178,179,180]

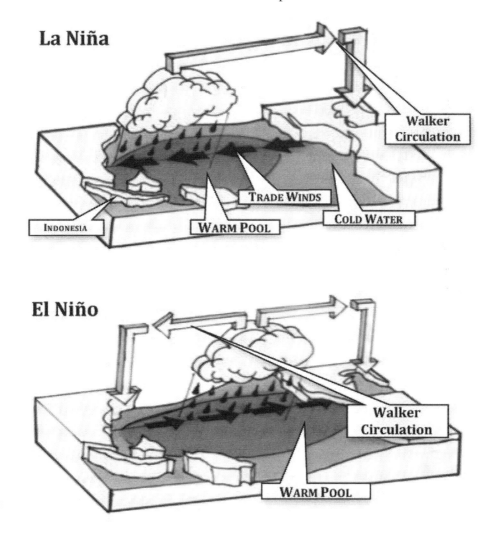

Figure 30. El Niño Cycles and the relocation of Warm Pool, Rains and Descending Dry Air

As illustrated in Figure 30 (upper panel), during a La Niña phase stronger trade winds sweep heated surface waters from the eastern Pacific causing cold waters from below to rise to the surface. This makes the surface in the eastern Pacific Ocean *7 to 18°F colder* than the warm pool in the west. Because colder surfaces cause the air to sink, this region encourages dry, descending air currents and strengthens the Pacific high pressure off the coast of California (see Chapter 7).

The temperature and pressure contrast creates an east-west circulation pattern called the Walker Circulation, with rising air and low pressure over the warm pool and sinking dry air over cooler surfaces. During a La Niña, the Walker Circulation strengthens the surface trade winds that blow from the colder east towards the warmer west. The stronger winds concentrate the warm pool in the far western Pacific, and Southeast Asia is inundated with rains. Simultaneously, the descending branch of the Walker Circulation delivers drought-like conditions to extensive regions of the Americas.

In contrast, during the El Niño phase (see Figure 30, lower panel) the trade winds weaken and can temporarily reverse direction, unleashing the warm pool. As warmer waters flood the eastern Pacific, it brings rains to the coast of North and South America. Peruvian fishermen were first to notice that a warm current travelled down the coast from Ecuador around Christmas. They called this warm current El Niño ("the boy") in honor of Jesus' birth. Although researchers have used different definitions, in general any extreme warming of the eastern equatorial Pacific is called an El Niño. The earliest documented extreme El Niño occurred in the 1890s when the flood of warm ocean water carried crocodiles from Ecuador down the coast to Peru, and heavy rains transformed the Peruvian deserts back to grasslands.[410]

As seen in Figure 30, when the warm pool shifts eastward during an El Niño, dry sinking winds will dominate over Southeast Asia bringing widespread drought. During the 1998 El Niño, the World Food Program had to assist Indonesians as their rice crops failed countrywide, and Indonesia was overwhelmed with rampant forest fire. In contrast, heavy rains fell across the west coast of the United States, and floods occurred in California wherever the atmospheric rivers made landfall.[176,179] For eons, as the warm pool sloshed back and forth across the Pacific, and the rising and descending air currents in the Walker Circulation relocated, alternating droughts and floods have sorely tested wildlife and humanity. You can readily recognize any ill-informed hype whenever the media portrays droughts in the southwest United States and heavy rains and floods in Southeast Asia as a climate gone crazy. That see-saw pattern of drought and floods has happened for millennia and is absolutely what climate scientists expect.

Monsoons

"A significant link between the Indian monsoon and wide range of large scale features of the global climate, such as El Niño and Southern Oscillation (ENSO), has been recognized in numerous previous studies."

Dr. Vishwas Kale, University of Pune

Monsoons are likewise driven by rising and descending air currents. However, the pattern is controlled by seasonal changes that unequally affect land and ocean surface temperatures. As the sun "moves" northward during the summer, the continents heat up faster than the oceans. Relative to the ocean, a warmer land surface increases rising convection and lowers the pressure over the continent. As at the equator, that lower pressure acts like a vacuum cleaner that draws in moist air from surrounding regions. Unlike Southeast Asia, which is synonymous with heavy monsoon rains, the blocking High pressure system in the eastern Pacific prevents California from experiencing summer monsoons (see Chapter 7). However, further east, summer monsoons will penetrate much of the United States.

The atmosphere does a very poor job of storing heat. So the pattern of rising and sinking air quickly reverses during the winter. Due to the higher heat capacity of the ocean, as soon as the summer sun retreats, the land cools faster than the oceans. The colder land surface now causes the air to sink over the continent, and this creates a higher pressure that spreads drier, colder winds across the continent. This wintertime reversal of winds is linked to the wintertime occurrence of an El Niño.

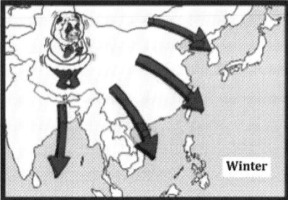

Periods of low solar activity heat the land less, and lower sunspot activity has been correlated with weaker summer monsoons.[232] The weakest monsoons correlated with the sunspot minimums that punctuated the Little Ice Age[233] while the strongest monsoons of the 20th century correlated with the peak sunspot activity between 1930 and 1950. Accordingly, researchers speculate that global warming may actually increase the summer monsoon rains[222,551] and that could offset any predicted CO_2-caused evaporation.

The water evaporated from the oceans and transported by the summer monsoon winds is the lifeblood for Asia's ecosystems and agriculture. However just a mere 10% change in moisture is the difference between droughts and floods.[193] While the summer sun affects the strength of the monsoon winds, El Niño cycles determine how much moisture the monsoons will carry. An El Niño shifts the atmospheric rivers westward, depriving the monsoons of much-needed moisture. It was not just the cold of the Little Ice Age that caused the famines that hastened the end of China's Ming Dynasty,[234] and the collapse of most southeast Asian kingdoms. It was persistent El Niño-like conditions.

Mega-droughts and the Pacific Decadal Oscillation

"The East India drought of 1790 to 1796 occurred during the great El Niño of the late 18th century, which was felt worldwide and resulted in widespread civil unrest and socioeconomic turmoil around the globe." [231]

Dr. Edward Cook, Lamont-Doherty Earth Observatory of Columbia University

"Consistent with previous studies, I found that precipitation over Southwest North America is highly correlated with Sea Surface Temperatures in the tropical Pacific Ocean on ENSO [El Niño] and longer time scales." [993]

Dr. Aiguo Dai, National Center for Atmospheric Research

Although the droughts and heavy rains caused by an extreme El Niño event typically last for only one year, El Niño or La Niña-like conditions can occur more frequently, sometimes persisting for several years in a row. The persistence of any one phase induces mega-droughts. Greater solar activity during the Medieval Warm Period increased the strength of the trade winds and tipped the balance to more frequent La Niña-like conditions, inducing mega-droughts in the American Southwest.[186,409] Conversely, low solar activity during the Little Ice Age reduced the trade winds. A more evenly heated ocean surface created more El Niño-like conditions, and the mega-droughts cycled to Asia.[198]

The longer term pattern of alternating ocean temperatures is dubbed the Pacific Decadal Oscillation or PDO.[126,151] During the negative or cool phase of the PDO, the heated waters pile up in the western Pacific warm pool and the eastern Pacific cools. The relatively cooler eastern Pacific and relatively warmer western Pacific increases the east-west temperature contrast and strengthens the trade winds encouraging more persistent La Niña-like conditions.

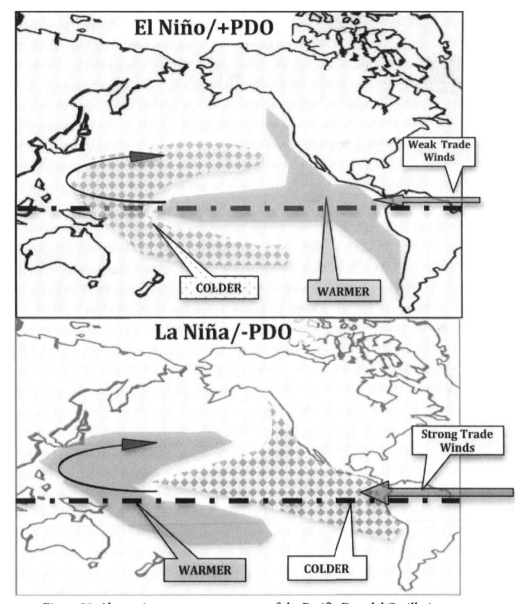

Figure 31. Alternating ocean temperatures of the Pacific Decadal Oscillation

In the simplest terms, the PDO cycle begins to shift as each El Niño delivers more warm water to the eastern Pacific. After each El Niño event, some warmer and saltier water remains below the surface (see egg experiment, Chapter 5). Each winter when the surface cools, those warmer waters can float to the surface,[920] re-emerging to reproduce a pattern of ocean temperatures similar to the recent El Niño (see Figure 31, upper panel).

The warmer surface temperature in the eastern Pacific reduces the east-west temperature differences and weakens the Walker circulation and the trade winds, promoting more frequent El Niños, and the ocean's surface temperatures switch to the warm positive PDO phase. (see Figure 31, upper panel)

As the intruding subsurface heat is ventilated, the cycle begins to reverse back to the negative cool PDO. As the eastern Pacific cools, the temperature contrast increases and strengthens the trade winds. Stronger winds push more heated water into the western Pacific reinforcing more frequent La Niña-like conditions and the ocean's surface temperatures switch back to the cool negative PDO phase (see Figure 31, lower panel).

Each phase of the PDO may last 20 years or more depending on the strength of the sun. Although technically the PDO Index is a measure of the difference in temperature between the eastern and western regions of the Pacific Ocean, it is useful to view the PDO as a measure of the frequency of El Niño events. In the 1940s the PDO abruptly switched to the cool La Niña phase. Between 1950 and 1976, there were nine consensus La Niña's but only three El Niño's. Consequently the Great Plains of the United States endured severe droughts in the 1950s, while southeast Asia was wetter.[186] In the 1970s, the PDO switched to the El Niño phase and from 1977 to 1998, there were seven consensus El Niño events but only one La Niña. Global temperatures rose and the western USA became wetter.[408,496]

As seen in Figure 32, the average precipitation at three weather stations in central New Mexico undulates to the beat of the Pacific Decadal Oscillation. Superimposed on the PDO pattern are annual variations in rainy and dry years determined by short term El Nino cycles. Nevertheless on average, a negative PDO causes more La Niñas and delivers less rainfall while a warm positive PDO delivers more rains. There is no increasing drying trend associated with rising CO_2. Because the pattern of ocean surface temperatures determines the general location of droughts and floods, when climate models specify the ocean surface temperatures for a given year, they are usually able to replicate the rising and falling air currents and the general location of most droughts.

A recent NOAA report found the severe drought of 2012 in the United States was caused by natural weather variations when a High-pressure system blocked the summer monsoons from transporting moisture into the Great Plains.[904] Kevin Trenberth, who blames all extreme weather on a "wetter and warmer world" driven by rising CO_2, oddly attacked the NOAA report and defended the global warming perspective by suggesting the lack of snowfall in the Rocky Mountains had contributed to drier air.[905] But the lack of snowfall and dry Rocky Mountains is precisely what is predicted by the cool phase of the PDO, supporting the report's conclusions that the drought was caused by natural weather variations.

Most extreme climate events occur when a La Niña and a cold PDO phase coincide, or when an EL Niño and a warm PDO phase coincide.[131,245,436,437,438] When a La Niña and a cold PDO coincide, the southwestern United States experiences the most severe droughts and increased fire danger. For example, each phase of the PDO persists for about 20 years, but cycles of El Niño and La Niña alternate every two to seven years. Thus the coincidence of both a La Niña and the cool phase of the PDO has only occurred about 29% of the time. However since the 1700s that 29% coincided with 70% of all major fires in Rocky Mountain National Park. Colorado's 2012 wildfire season was no exception.[130]

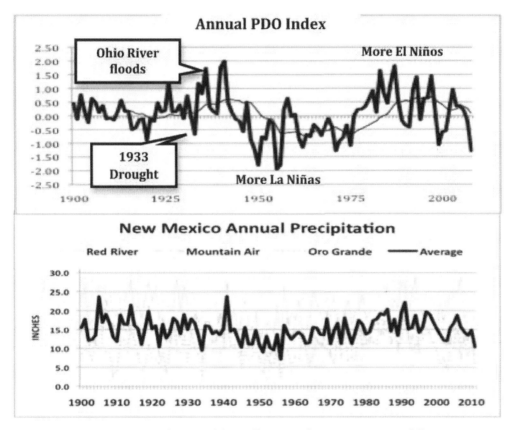

Figure 32. Pacific Decadal Oscillation and New Mexico Rainfall

Scientists advise that there is a "need to better understand the physical processes" behind the Pacific Ocean's temperature oscillations, so that climate models can better simulate rainfall processes.[500] In 2012 researchers wrote, "If nature exhibits such strong natural variability of tropical Pacific sea surface temperatures on centennial time scales, then assumptions that the observed trend over the past century is a response to radiative forcing [CO_2] are tenuous. *It could in fact be that the observed trend over the past century and a half is merely reflective of internal variability. If so, it could strengthen or weaken in the future as the natural variability evolves.*"[226]

This growing understanding of the El Niño/PDO cycles has similarly led other scientists to conclude, "Regardless of whether or not the rapid recent oceanic warming has occurred largely from anthropogenic or natural influences, our study highlights its importance in accounting for the recent observed continental warming. *Perhaps the most important conclusion to be drawn from our analysis is that the recent acceleration of global warming may not be occurring in quite the manner one might have imagined.*"[216]

The next twenty years will reveal the relative power of CO_2 versus these El Niño/PDO cycles. As the solar activity is dropping and the PDO is entering its cool phase, natural cycles predict a halt to the warming, despite rising CO_2. So far that is exactly what we are observing, but the time period is still too short to provide definitive answers.

10

Is "Obama the Denier" Killing the Pika?

Pika, courtesy of Connie Millar

"Another species on the brink — thanks to human-caused global warming — is abandoned"

Joe Romm

"The belief that one's own view of reality is the only reality is the most dangerous of all delusions."

Paul Watzlawick

Pikas are not found in the eastern United States, where I grew up, so I never saw my first Pika until the 1970s while backpacking in the Uinta Mountains of northeastern Utah. We had camped on the edge of a lush meadow in a broad canyon. Under a waning gibbous moon, we sat around a small fire, eating our freshly caught trout and rice pilaf. As we squabbled about how to divvy up the last ration of Hershey chocolate bars, from just the other side of a row of pines, the bellow of an Elk pierced the growing darkness, making my chest quake.

The empty silence that alternated between each Elk bugle somehow accentuated the faint squeaks coming from the talus slope behind us. It was a new sound to my ears and the rhythm and shifting locations of those peeps evoked images of elfin creatures playing a land version of Marco-Polo as they popped out of various crevices. As I strained to listen, I was shook again from another burst of bugling. After the Elk finally ambled on, I tried to put a face on those peeps, but it was too dark. The next morning I scoured the rocks and discovered a hamster-like animal carrying leaves and flowers in its teeth to make hay piles for the winter. It was my first encounter with the pika, a cousin of the rabbits nicknamed the "whistling hare" or "boulder bunny".

In 2010 Joe Romm of Climate Progress blogged, "So long Pika, we hardly knew ya. Another species on the brink — thanks to human-caused global warming — is abandoned". Romm was mad that Federal and State scientific agencies had found no scientific proof to support lawsuits to list the pika as a species endangered by rising CO_2 levels. Romm is another advocate who believes CO_2 causes all things evil, and that everyone who disagrees is a denier. The scientists working for the U.S. Fish and Wildlife Service, California Fish and Game, and the International Union for the Conservation of Nature (IUCN) will likely be added to his list of climate deniers. But Romm was right on one point: he hardly knew the pika, or the wealth of scientific studies indicating pikas are thriving. Instead Romm and CO_2 advocates uncritically embraced a few papers by Dr. Erik Beever who had argued global warming was driving the pika up to the mountain tops and over the climate cliff to extinction.

The Advocates' Case for Death by CO_2

"It is misleading of the CBD to claim to be scientifically astute yet perpetrate in press releases the untruthful image that pikas perish when ambient temperatures reach 78°F. They do not die at these temperatures; they retreat to the cool interstices of the talus."

Dr. Andrew Smith, Arizona State University

The Center for Biological Diversity (CBD) is a group of environmental lawyers who specialize in lawsuits claiming various groups of animals are dying from rising CO_2 levels. In October 2007, the CBD submitted a petition to the U.S. Fish and Wildlife Service seeking endangered species status for the pika. The CBD's press release alleged, "Climate change is spreading its heat death zone higher into the mountains, jeopardizing the species' survival. In the Great Basin mountains, researchers have found that the range of the pika is retreating upslope at an accelerating pace. More than a third of documented populations in the Great Basin have gone extinct in the past century, and climate experts predict temperatures in the western United States in this century will increase twice as much as they did in the past century, perhaps more. This will prove devastating for pikas living at lower elevations and lower latitudes of the West.....Our oil addiction is driving the American pika and many other species to extinction," "The pika's survival hinges on achieving immediate reductions in greenhouse gas emissions, but we're running out of time." [103]

Despite their dramatic appeal, the federal courts rejected the CBD's petitions because they lacked scientific evidence, so the CBD stepped up their attack by also calling President Obama a denier in a February 2010 press release titled "Obama Administration Denies American Pika Endangered Species Act Protection: Small Alpine Mammal Declining Due to Global Warming."[903] Accusing Obama of "ignoring science and the law," they complained that "[t]he Obama administration has blocked Endangered Species Act protection for other climate change-imperiled species and has made little progress on overall listings." "During its first year, the Obama administration listed only two species under the Endangered Species Act, compared to an average of eight species per year under George W. Bush, and 65 species per year under Bill Clinton."

But why would a beleaguered Obama administration "ignore science" and risk alienating his environmental allies? Was Obama "fooled" by experts like Dr Andrew Smith and Connie Millar who had presented a plethora of evidence that the pika is flourishing? Was it possible that Obama's decreased number of endangered species listings was the result of years of hard work by earlier conservationists who had accurately listed most of the species that were truly in need? The CBD's meaningless comparison of administrations was simply an attempt to embarrass and bully Obama, a treatment afforded to all "deniers" who dare to disagree.

To make their case, the CBD cited the research of pika expert Dr Andrew Smith and warned "brief exposure to temperatures of 78°F or warmer can cause death." In stark contrast Dr. Smith argued the pikas were thriving and that the CBD had twisted his research responding, "It is misleading of the CBD to claim to be scientifically astute yet perpetrate in press releases the untruthful image that pikas perish when ambient temperatures reach 78°F. They do not die at these temperatures; they retreat to the cool interstices of the talus."[111]

As was the common practice in the 1970s, Smith had performed a "lethality experiment" to measure the limits of the pikas' heat tolerance. On three different nights, a pika was trapped and subsequently "confined at dawn in a large wire mesh cage." Each animal died around noon when the temperatures reached 78°F. However it was direct exposure to the sun that killed Smith's pika, not the surrounding air temperature.[109] It is the same reason the Occupational Safety & Health Administration advises workers to seek the shade to prevent heat illness and death; the lack of shade killed those pikas.

When running free, pikas retreat to the shade of the talus slopes (rock piles) they call home. Hidden away beneath the boulders, the sun's rays can only heat the surface of the rocks, not the pikas. Air warmed by the rocks rises and carries most of that heat upward and away. Underneath the rocks, denser colder air from the previous night has either settled into the various nooks and crannies, or slowly flowed to the low end of the talus, creating a natural air conditioned area. If grazing has not removed the vegetation, pikas will bathe in the cool draught draining from the bottom of the talus.[110] On especially hot days, pikas simply take a siesta. They will readily switch their activities from daytime to evening.

In the winter, cold air can settle into the talus and threaten the pikas with cold stress. However, each summer pikas make several hay piles, and researchers speculate that hay piles are not only a supply of winter food, but also a supply of warmth. As many unsuspecting farmers have learned, the decay process in wet hay can generate enough heat to burn down a silo. Furthermore where there is adequate snow, the snow creates an insulating blanket. Heat generated from decaying vegetation warms the air and slowly wafts upward. At higher levels in the talus, heat chimneys develop wherever this rising warmth concentrates and melts a hole in the overlying snow. In the winter, pikas can move higher to take advantage of that rising warmth. Our family behaved much like the pikas. During hot New England summers before the days of air conditioning, we migrated down to the basement family room, which was always several degrees cooler than the upstairs. During the winters, we migrated back upstairs, where it was always warmer and less expensive to heat.

Nonetheless the CBD insists global warming and 78°F temperatures were killing pikas and their "proof" was Dr. Erik Beever's study "Patterns of apparent extinction among isolated populations of pikas (Ochotona princeps) in the Great Basin"[100]. Beever had imitated Parmesan's butterfly study and revisited 25 isolated areas where pikas had been documented to exist earlier in the 20th century. He found that 28% of those previously documented colonies were vacant, which he claimed represented "apparent extinctions" due to climate change. However he had no way of knowing when the pikas had last occupied those sites or why they were absent. Without decades of annual visits, there was no way of knowing if this 28% vacancy rate was just average, improving, or worsening. He also had no way of knowing how often a site was abandoned and then recolonized.

Like Parmesan's Edith checkerspots, pikas also live in meta-populations. The total population consists of several scattered satellite populations. At any given time a small population will suffer extirpation (a local extinction). Extirpations can happen due to a lack of food, too much snow, an efficient predator like a weasel or rattlesnake, disease, or old age. In captivity, pikas only live six to seven years, so each territory has a high turnover rate. Once vacated, the habitat of an extirpated population lies in wait for dispersing young to recolonize it. The young are driven away each year by their territorial parents. Dispersing in random directions, they require a bit of luck to find a vacant territory.

As Beever's title indicated, he was studying small, isolated populations that were the least likely to be recolonized.[100] In his first study, the best predictor for the presence or absence of pika was not temperature, but the size of the talus patches. As would be expected, smaller rock patches had fewer neighbors to supply replacement young and thus there was a higher vacancy rate. In contrast, the large talus slopes typical of the Sierra Nevada hold several adjoining territories, so the supply of dispersing young is much greater and vacant territories are more easily found. In the Sierra Nevada there is a very low vacancy rate of just 2%.[99] However to minimize recolonization, Beever purposefully avoided locations that were too near the Sierra Nevada.

Beever's paper soon garnered tremendous fanfare from global warming advocates. It was just the type of study that Parmesan and the journal *Nature* had encouraged. In a 2006, Parmesan cited Beever's study to support her contention that climate change was driving animals upward and northward. She wrote "In the Great Basin of the western United States, 7 out of 25 re-censused populations of the pika (Ochotona princeps, Lagomorpha) went extinct since being recorded in the 1930s (Beever et al. 2003). Human disturbance is minimal because pika habitat is high-elevation talus (scree) slopes, which are not suitable for ranching or recreational activities. Extinct populations were at significantly lower elevations than those still present."[114] However, as had become commonplace, Parmesan was again blind to any land use changes and only embraced interpretations that spoke of climate catastrophe.

In stark contrast to Parmesan's retelling that "human disturbance is minimal," Beever had actually reported that every one of his extirpated sites had been subjected to grazing. Grazing of vegetation at the base of talus slopes has been known to force pikas to move higher up the slope in search of food.[101] It was true that grazing is not an issue in more forested habitat of the high Sierra Nevada where pikas are thriving. But grazing was most definitely a problem in the Great Basin where Beever and Parmesan blamed global warming.

Beever had also written that humans directly impacted three of the seven "extinct" populations. At one site, half the talus had been excavated and used for road maintenance. At another site, the talus area was used extensively as a dumpsite. Carvings in aspen tree trunks at the third site suggested extensive human use since at least the 1930s, and Beever "found numerous gun shells on taluses there." Those three sites accounted for almost half of the "apparent extinctions". Furthermore one of his seven "extinct" populations had been recolonized when he surveyed it a second time.

Like Parmesan, Beever did not use local temperatures. However five of the seven "extinct" populations were located in the northwestern extreme of the Great Basin, not in the southern extreme as predicted by global warming theory. Furthermore, the maximum temperatures at the nearby Cedarville USHCN weather station revealed that maximum temperatures had been decreasing since the 1930s (see Figure 33). If heat truly were the killer, then those populations more likely died around 1940. If not, the pikas had already survived temperatures much hotter than those today. However to make his global warming case in a later paper, Beever presented a "cut-off" graph with a trend starting in 1945 which created an out-of-context warming trend. And instead of local temperatures, he used the Great Basin average.

Beever also separated thriving neighbors from those supposedly "killed by CO_2." In another paper, Beever wrote about additional populations at Lava Beds National monument that were just 93 miles away from five of his extinct sites. Beever reported, "given the recent extirpation of pikas from low-elevation sites,…. current persistence of pikas in Craters and Lava Beds National Monuments is noteworthy."[105] At Lava Beds the average elevation of existing pika was about 900 feet lower than the average elevation of three nearby extinct sites. And although he had blamed high temperatures for the Great Basin vacancies, *at Lava Beds the pika were surviving where temperatures averaged an additional 3.6°F higher*, and precipitation was 24% less.[105]

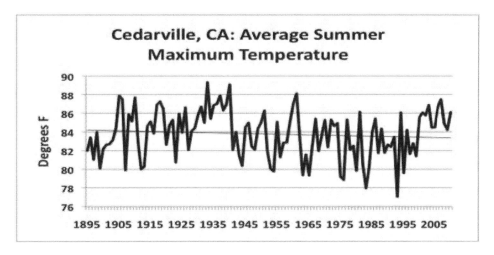

Figure 33. USHCN Cedarville CA maximum temperatures 1895-2011.

More curious, in a subsequent paper Beever wrote, "*Climate change metrics were by far the poorest predictor* of pika extirpation (emphasis added)." Nor did he find a correlation with the stress of maximum temperatures, writing, "Although pikas have been shown to perish quickly when experimentally subjected to high temperatures, our metric of *acute heat stress was the poorest predictor of pika extirpations* (emphasis added)."[112] Because maximum temperatures had revealed no acute heat stress, Beever adopted the term "chronic heat stress" which was just a more alarming way to say the average temperature. By including a rising trend in minimum temperatures and limiting the start data of is temperature trend to 1945, he finally got a correlation with rising CO_2 levels.

Although Beever's earliest studies had admirably examined a host of confounding factors, he soon focused only on global warming. In a 2011 paper, he reported "a nearly five-fold increase in the rate of local extinction and an 11-fold increase in the rate of upslope range retraction during the last ten years, compared with the 20th Century."[113] Although this report literally left some students tearfully concerned, the most horrifying aspect of his report was how the peer-review process accepted his abuse of statistics. Pikas were being massacred only in a virtual reality created by bad statistics.

Although the purpose of his later study was to evaluate how pikas had changed elevation during a century of climate change, he eliminated from his calculations all new observations of pika found at lower elevations. In the 1990s he found six sites where pika were observed at lower elevations than ever reported. In his follow up studies in the 2000s, he found another four sites at lower elevations. Without ever knowing if those new findings represented pikas recolonizing an abandoned territory or if they were migrating lower, he arbitrarily argued that those pika were just missed during previous surveys. Therefore he assumed that pikas had always lived there.

However, that assumption violated all the rules of statistical analysis. Statistics evaluate how often your results could happen by pure random luck. Instead, his statistical machinations guaranteed that the pikas would always move upward, never downward. The peer review process should have rejected this study, not celebrated it as proof of global warming.

Like many global warming studies, Beever's was guided by Hansen's 1988 predictions that animals will be forced northward "by 50 to 75 km per decade". When applied to elevation, the predictions indicate that animals will move upslope 30 meters per decade. But pikas easily move 100 meters in their daily adventures. Any small change in the elevation from where they first had been observed says very little about their response to climate. Yet "If you torture the data long enough, it will confess."[994]

Of the 16 locations where Beever had found existing pikas, he used just 10 to generate his 11-fold increase in the rate of upslope flight from warming. *Sites where pikas were found at lower elevations or where the elevation had not changed were not used*, and he unapologetically presented this biased data.[113] Beever compared historic elevations at which pikas had first been observed versus the elevations where he observed pikas in two new surveys. All sites were surveyed in the late 1990s and again in the early 2000s. I could not replicate his published calculations based on the results in his paper, so I emailed him, requesting the exact numbers which he provided immediately. Below are four of the more egregious examples of how the selective use of data created the illusion of pika fleeing upslope when in fact they were found at lower elevations.

Mustang Mountain Survey		
Historic 1933 Elevation	**1990s Elevation**	**2000s Elevation**
3048 meters	2865 and 2743 m	2773 m

Elevation change from historic documents: lower by 275 meters

Beever's calculated change: Zero change. Mustang Mountain was not used to create the 11-fold rise in average elevation

Long Creek Survey

Historic 1928 Elevation:	1990s Elevation	2000s Elevation
2387 meters	2188 m	2234 m* (2776)

Elevation change from historic documents: <u>lower</u> by 154 meters or more

Beever's calculated change: <u>higher</u> by 542 meters

*Because he observed just one individual at the 2234 m elevation, he considered this individual "anomalously disjunct from the species' typical distribution within the site." So Beever pretended that pika weren't there and used the 2776 m elevation to calculate the large upward movement.

Cougar Peak Survey

Historic 1925 Elevation:	*1990s Elevation*	*2000s Elevation*
2416 meters	2073 m	2222 m

Elevation change from historic documents: <u>lower</u> by 343 meters (in 1990) or lower by 194 meters (in 2000)

Beever's calculated change: <u>higher</u> by 149 meters.

Although the two recent surveys observed pika at elevations lower than historic elevations, Beever subtracted the 1990s from the 2000s to report an upward retreat of 149 meters. (This site was originally one of the seven sites considered to have gone extinct, but pikas were either missed or had recolonized. The site now hosts a robust pika population.)

Thomas Creek Survey		
Historic 1956 Elevation:	**_1990s Elevation_**	**_2000s Elevation_**
2377 meters	2743 m	2686 m

Elevation change from historic documents: _higher_ by 309

Beever's calculated change: _higher_ by 309 meters, but note how the treatment differs from Cougar Peak.

If Beever had similarly subtracted the 1990s from the 2000s the elevation was lower by 57 meters. He was apparently choosing whatever elevation created the biggest rise.

Beever never tried to hide his statistical choices. To his credit, he was always very upfront about them in all our conversations and in his publications. And from our phone conversations and email exchanges, my impression remains that Erik Beever is a sincere and honest person. However I can only conclude he was HOS-ed; the Hypothesis Obsession Syndrome had claimed another victim. Such statistical chicanery could only be accepted so readily because it supported the prevailing bias that animals must be fleeing upslope to escape CO_2 warming.

The Case for Thriving Pika

I've come loaded with statistics, for I've noticed that a man can't prove anything without statistics. No man can.

Mark Twain

"The truth that is suppressed by friends is the readiest weapon of the enemy."

Robert Louis Stevenson

During a trip to the desert ghost town of Bodie, California, I was surprised to find pikas lived there as well. The discovery of gold in the 1800s had brought a flood of human immigrants who had hastily constructed a community in the Great Basin desert just to the east of Lake Tahoe. Miners had industriously hollowed out the surrounding hills searching for gold, but when the mines failed to produce more gold, the human population at Bodie slowly went "extinct". However in the eyes of the pikas, the remaining piles of rocky debris were just as inviting as natural talus and the pikas quickly colonized them.

My previous Uinta experience with pikas had been in a more verdant montane habitat with lush vegetation, far removed from human disturbance. Near the Sierra Nevada Field Campus, pikas also inhabit moist talus slopes surrounded by luxurious summer growth. To see pikas in such a stark high desert setting, occupying piles of human generated debris, challenged all preconceptions.

Pikas are busy all summer, gathering plants and making hay piles for the winter. Although elsewhere pikas are fond of tender herbaceous plants, at Bodie they make piles of sagebrush and bitter brush that are considered inedible and toxic to most other mammals. However as their hay pile "cures," the toxins apparently help preserve the plants' nutrients, and eventually the toxins breakdown into harmless chemicals. To maximize the nutrition from plant food, pikas are the ultimate recyclers. They excrete caecal pellets, which they eat later. The caecum is a pouch between the large and small intestines that houses bacteria which help digest difficult plant material. During the caecal pellet's second run through the digestive tract, pikas can more efficiently extract the plant's nutrients. (The human appendix is believed by some to be a remnant of a caecum that was more useful in our ancient past).

Curious about the rates of extirpation and recolonization for pikas living in Bodie's scattered ore dumps, pika expert Dr. Andrew Smith conducted the only available study that can evaluate trends in pika vacancy rates. Although pikas had abandoned a set of ore piles on Bodie's south side, on the northern edge of town, Smith tracked the vacancy rates of 76 ore piles from 1972 to 2009. As expected for a meta-population, during those 37 years Smith observed 107 local extinctions, balanced by

106 re-colonizations.[98] Like pika habitat elsewhere in the Great Basin, on average 30% of the ore piles were unoccupied at any given time, but that vacancy rate was highly variable. Some years the vacancy rate was as high as 52%, and other years as low as 11%. In his first survey in 1972, Smith found that 82.3% of the ore piles were occupied by pika. In 2009, pika again occupied 82.8% of their possible sites.

Dr. Andrew Smith is not only one of the world's leading authorities on pikas, he is currently the Chair of the International Union for Conservation of Nature's (IUCN) Species Survival Commission for the Lagomorph[‡‡‡] Specialist Group. As IUCN's chair, he is responsible for compiling the Red List[§§§] status of the world's endangered lagomorphs. From our conversations, it was clear Dr. Smith is an ardent believer in climate change, but he was extremely disturbed with the way the CBD had misrepresented the truth.

In his letter to the California Department of Fish and Game testifying *against* the CBD's petition to list the pika as endangered,[111] Smith warned that such an unsupported petition "comes at a time when the public is becoming increasingly skeptical of endangered species legislation, and when Congress is contemplating serious negative changes to the Endangered Species Act. The ESA is a landmark piece of legislation and one of the most substantial country-level acts to preserve biodiversity in the world. California legislation to protect endangered species is similarly important. Thus, it is incumbent upon us to ensure that endangered species determinations be made based on solid scientific evidence, so that those who may seek to undermine these legislative attempts are not given ammunition to complete their vendettas."

Smith's letter then proceeded to refute every argument by the Center for Biological Diversity asserting that pikas were endangered. He concluded his rebuttal letter with, "I grimace at the hyperbole of the current PR campaign to make the pika an endangered species, as I similarly decry the loss of scientific objectivity and/or the failure of those embarking on this campaign to recognize that the USFWS, State of California and IUCN have all objectively not listed the pika as endangered. *I teach the next generation of conservation biologists, and it is an affront that I have to instruct them to worry not only about the flank of those who are climate change and endangered species deniers, but now also those who purport to support these issues.*"

Dr Smith was not the only pika researcher with evidence to refute the CBD's hype of a CO_2 "death zone" pushing the pika higher up the mountains. The CBD's contention that CO_2 warming "will prove devastating for pikas living at lower elevations and lower latitudes of the West" was being refuted from all corners of the

---

[‡‡‡] Lagomorpha is a scientific category - an order - that groups all the closely related families of rabbits, hares and pikas. It is similar to the category of carnivores, which includes all the families of dogs, cats, bears, etc
[§§§] The IUCN Red List evaluates the status of the world species from "Least Concern" to "Critically Endangered

American west. Due to climate change concerns, the US Forest Service's Connie Millar extensively surveyed pika habitat throughout the Sierra Nevada and the Great Basin. In contrast to Beever's 27 sites, she examined 420 sites of which 67% were definitely occupied, and 27% that showed activity but occupancy was not verified by a visual observation during their rapid assessments. Only 6% were classified as "old", or vacated, sites. She also reported, "The relative number of old sites, the vacancy rate, increased from the Sierra Nevada eastward into the Great Basin ranges. In the Sierra Nevada the vacancy rate was just 2%, in the southwestern Great Basin ranges it increased to 17%, and was highest, 50%, in the central Great Basin ranges."[99] Pikas were thriving in the Sierra Nevada and southern Great Basin, and she suggested that the larger percentage of unoccupied sites in Beever's central Great Basin was most likely due to the greater difficulty recolonizing isolated sites with small amounts of suitable habitat.[102]

In the southern Rocky Mountain region just east of Beever's study area, another independent study reported, "Results from a survey of 69 sites historically occupied by pikas indicate that only four populations have been extirpated within this region over the past few decades"[104] That is a vacancy rate of less than 6%.

In contrast to the CBD's claims that pika were dying at low elevations and fleeing to higher elevations, Millar found new pika colonies at elevations much lower than ever previously documented. The benchmark for wildlife abundance and distribution in California had been Joseph Grinnell's surveys from the early 1900s. But Millar recently found active pika colonies several hundred meters lower than Grinnell had documented. In total, 19% of the currently known populations are at lower elevations than ever documented by any study during the early 1900s.[110] Her surveys also increased the number of documented locations for living pikas, and revealed that pikas had adapted to a much wider array of climates and weather patterns than previous studies had portrayed.[102] Further north in the Columbia River Gorge, another independent researcher also found pikas at much lower elevations and surviving at temperatures much higher than the models had predicted.[106,107]

When the CBD lawsuit claimed, "More than a third of documented populations in the Great Basin have gone extinct in the past century," they ignored abundant undocumented pikas living at higher elevations, and the overwhelming evidence from hundreds of other sites arguing that pikas are thriving at lower elevations. Yet Greg Loarie, an attorney with Earthjustice representing the CBD transformed Beever's small sample of vacant sites into continental wide death and destruction, *"We've already lost almost half of the pikas that once inhabited the Great Basin,* and scientists tell us that pikas will be gone from 80 percent of their entire range in the United States by the end of century (emphasis added)."[903] I am very curious from what anatomical region Loarie pulled those statistics.

Dr. Smith countered, "Millar and Westfall (2010) documents 420 sites of pika occupancy, largely in the western edge of the Great Basin. These sites extend over 2,060 m of elevation; include 11 mountain ranges, and 10 geomorphic habitat categories. Many sites extend the distribution of pikas in the region to lower elevations than previously known. I have discovered additional low-altitude sites with Millar, and her database on pika distributions in the region has now been expanded to over 600 sites." Smith continued, "Remarkably, and inexplicable to me, rather than to embrace this finding, the CBD (Shaye Wolf) wrote a critical rebuttal to the journal AAAR contesting these data."

But the CBD's response should be no surprise to Smith. The CBD was not defending the pika, they were defending their lawsuit and global warming theory. The CBD claim that we "already lost *almost half of the pikas* (emphasis added)." only sheds light on their integrity and says nothing about the abundance of pikas.

Such distortions are why Dr. Smith rightfully fears the CBD's tactics will only jeopardize the Endangered Species Act, and I agree wholeheartedly. Such distortions are why I too fear our environmental concerns have been hijacked. Instead of spending money dealing with frivolous law suits that only line the pockets of lawyers, our tax money would be better spent constructing fences around talus slopes where overgrazing threatened Beever's pika. Such abuse of the Endangered Species Act to promote CO_2 advocacy will surely polarize the electorate further and serve to weaken the ESA.

Yet despite the ever-mounting evidence of thriving pikas at lower elevations, people hear only what they want to hear. And if you repeat something often enough, people will believe. In 2012, *Science News* published the article "Animals on the Move" and highlighted the American pika with an inset reading, "*The American Pika is second to only the polar bear as a symbol of a warming climate's effects on animals. As their habitats have changed, pikas have hightailed it upslope* (emphasis added)."

Indeed the plight of the pika and polar bear are very similar. Both are examples of the incessant repetition of bad science and bad statistics.

11

Gray Whales, Cycles of "Doom" and Alfred Hitchcock's Inspiration

Gray Whales as Climate Indicators

"a <u>late retreat</u> of seasonal ice may impact access to prey for pregnant females and reduce the probability that existing pregnancies will be carried to term."

2011 Report of the Sub-committee on Bowhead, Right and Gray Whales

I often hike the coastal bluffs south of San Francisco. The spouts of migrating Gray whales are always a source of optimism that humans are becoming better environmental stewards. Gray whales are another conservation success story. In 1845, Captain Charles Scammon had been hunting Elephant Seals when he discovered the first known Gray whale breeding lagoon in Baja, Mexico. Gray whales provided more oil than seals, and when confined to their breeding lagoons, hunting was as easy as shooting fish in a barrel. By 1875, the estimated global population of 20,000 Gray whales had been decimated.

Although a growing petroleum industry had reduced the demand for whale oil and relaxed the hunting pressures, a few relentless whalers still pursued the approximately remaining 1,000 whales. Unable to fully recover, the International Convention for the Regulation of Whaling legislated protection in 1946 and the US Endangered Species Act added protection in 1973. Remarkably, by 1994 Gray whale numbers had rebounded to equal historical estimates, and the IUCN currently lists them as a species of "least concern".

Over the past 30 years I have seen two dead whales washed up on local beaches. From 1995 to 1998, the natural mortality rate based on the number of beached Gray whales from Alaska to Mexico averaged 41 per year, but that number suddenly leapt to 283 in 1999 and then 368 in 2000. A 700% jump in dead whales was clearly a cause for concern, but no one was sure what had caused this episodic die-off that stranded so many half-starved whales from Mexico to the Bering Sea.[520]

As many are prone to do, the California Gray Whale Coalition immediately blamed global warming for the sudden strandings: "Gray whales are entirely dependent on climatic factors. Their prey, (amphipod macrocephela) needs very cold water to grow and survive. In 1999/2000, almost half the Gray whale population died and starvation appeared to be the major cause." To encourage you to press the "donate now" button, they then wrote, "2007 is the sixth consecutive year of melting sea ice in the Arctic with scientists predicting a new and steeper rate of decline." They concluded that the whales' "future survival is grim. One of the first casualties of climate change in the Arctic is likely to be the Gray whale."

Of course all organisms are "dependent on climatic factors." However the coalition assumed only CO_2-induced global warming causes abrupt climate change. The link between global warming and abrupt climate change is still theoretical speculation favored by media sensationalism. However, there is an overwhelming abundance of scientific evidence that abrupt climate change is regularly caused by a natural cycles such as the Pacific Decadal Oscillation (PDO). Because the winds, ocean currents, and marine life all reorganize when the PDO changes phase, marine biologists refer to such changes as a "regime shift". So what killed the whales?

The first clue that CO_2 paranoia had trumped objective science was the absurd claim that "half" the whale population had died. Half calculates to about 10,000 whales versus the actual 2-year count of 651 dead whales. Second, they narrowly focused on an episodic tragedy but ignored a bigger and brighter picture. Despite the fact that observers were now on high alert, in 2001 and 2002 the number of stranded whales dropped to just half of the yearly average, with only 21 and 26 stranded whales, respectively. The population has now recovered fully and most appear well-fed.[523] Did climate change cause those two years of higher mortality, or did climate change aid their recovery?

Although the coalition linked the population decline to the loss of summer sea ice in the Arctic Ocean, that statistic means precious little to the Gray whales. Unlike the filter feeding baleen whale, Gray whales primarily suction amphipods[****] and other bottom dwellers from the shallow sea floor of the Bering Sea and neighboring Chukchi Sea. The converging currents over the shallow Bering Sea ensure a constant supply of upwelled nutrients that supports copious supplies of phytoplankton,[††††] which in turn supply a robust food web not found elsewhere. So each year Gray whales make a 10,000-14,000 mile round trip from their breeding lagoons in Baja Mexico to the Bering and Chukchi Seas to feed. It is believed the whales fast after they leave Arctic waters.

Scientists have documented that "summer arctic ice extent is a poor indicator of Bering Sea ice extent."[527] This has been confirmed, as Bering Sea ice has expanded for the past decade, reaching record extents in 2012, and winter sea ice remains above average. Furthermore, reduced ice does not cause starving whales; just the opposite. Research indicates that too much sea ice is deadly because it denies the whales and their calves access to their requisite shallow feeding grounds.[516] Less ice also means more plankton. In 2007, plankton production was 23% greater than the 1998-2002 average. The most recent studies show that during periods of less ice, phytoplankton productivity increased by 30% in the whales primary feeding grounds.[519] More plankton usually produces more food for bottom-dwelling clams and shrimp-like amphipods and thus more food for Gray whales and walruses.

Researchers had already warned that because the whales had rapidly recovered to historic highs, they had pushed their favored food supplies to the limits of sustainability.[431,522] Most believe that the whales are now at the ocean's absolute carrying capacity, with the population fluctuating between 20,000 and 22,000. When the number of whales increase beyond that carrying capacity, they over eat and reduce their amphipod supply. Less food reduces the whale population and brings the whales and amphipods back into equilibrium.

Subsequent studies have found the overall abundance of amphipods is still high enough to sustain the current whale populations, so climate change did not cause a widespread deterioration of the whales' food.[552] However events such as the 1999 La Niña can trigger episodic events that rapidly eliminate a local food supply. Researchers have reported that phytoplankton blooms in the whales' feeding grounds in the Bering Sea can be so great that the rain of dead bodies and subsequent decay depletes the oxygen and suffocates the bottom dwellers.[518] Additionally, La Niñas cause episodes of upwelling that brings nutrients to the surface but also draws

---

[****] Amphipods are shrimp-like creatures. Gray Whales prefer the bottom dwelling ampeliscid amphipods.

[††††] Phytoplankton are floating, photosynthesizing algae-like organisms. Zooplankton are small floating animals.

suffocating, oxygen-deprived waters onto the shallow ocean shelves.

Ocean Regime Shifts or Omens of Doom?

"Accept the regime concept for marine ecosystems - a wealth of historical evidence suggests regime shifts are a natural and recurring part of marine ecosystems" [514]

2005 advisory report - North Pacific Marine Science Organization

The Pacific Decadal Oscillation reorganizes marine ecosystems approximately every 20 years, and is known to cause ocean food chains to temporarily boom and bust. These cycles have often been misinterpreted as omens of doom but they readily explain the sudden incidences of whale strandings followed by their rapid recovery. Phytoplankton are the foundation of the ocean's food web. Like land plants, phytoplankton need water, nutrients, and sunlight to photosynthesize. Living in the ocean, water is obviously not a problem. Seasonal sunlight is usually guaranteed when not blocked by sea ice. The one critical factor that is never guaranteed is the nutrient supply. The oceans' natural fertilizers are continuously sinking into the darkness of the ocean's depths.

When, where, and how those nutrients are brought back to the sunlit surface determines the state of the ocean's ecosystems. The immense expanse of open ocean lies over great depths where access to nutrients is always limited, and ocean productivity is usually low. Smaller species of phytoplankton inhabit open oceans and support a relatively sparse but stable and complex web of marine life that is highly adept at filtering food and recycling limited nutrients.[410]

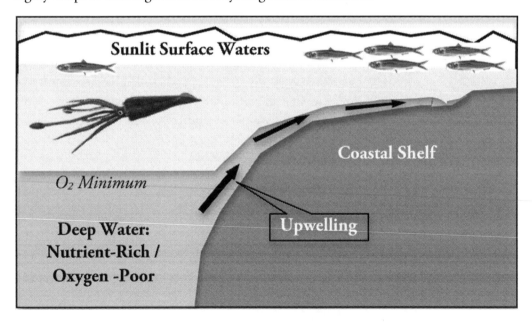

In contrast, whenever the winds and currents remove the ocean's upper surface layer, it allows cooler, nutrient-rich waters from below to upwell as a replacement and fertilize the sunlit layers. Upwelling is particularly strong along the coasts, where replacement water can only come from below. Shallow coastal shelves also prevent nutrients from sinking to inaccessible depths. Over shallow shelves like the Bering Sea, winds can more easily mix the surface and bottom waters. Unlike the open ocean, the coastal waters support huge blooms of bigger phytoplankton like diatoms, greater swarms of zooplankton, and more abundant fish. Cycles of El Niño and the PDO dramatically alter the degree of nutrient upwelling causing periodic booms for some species and busts for others.

Sardines and anchovies are small, short-lived fish that rapidly respond to changing ocean conditions. They are a critical link in the food web between plankton and larger fish and birds. Anchovies are "biters," feeding on the larger and more concentrated plankton that occur in regions of vigorous upwelling. In contrast, sardines are mostly "filter feeders" that are more adept at feeding on the smaller, more sparse plankton commonly found in more open waters. During periods of low upwelling, anchovy numbers decline and, partly due to reduced competition, the sardine populations expand towards the coast. When upwelling is renewed during the next cycle, anchovies flourish and sardine populations decline.[553]

Dr. Francisco Chavez is the senior scientist at the Monterey Bay Aquarium Research Institute. He honed his scientific skills studying the effects of El Niño on the fisheries of his native Peru. Because of the similarities in ocean temperatures between a one-year El Niño event and the approximately 20-year warm phase of the PDO, he likes to call the warm PDO phase El Viejo (the old man). Similarly, because of its effect on the fisheries throughout the Pacific, he also calls it the sardine regime. Conversely, he calls the cold PDO phase that resembles a La Niña, La Vieja (old woman), or the anchovy regime.

He reports, "In the Pacific Ocean, air and ocean temperatures, atmospheric carbon dioxide, landings of anchovies and sardines, and the productivity of coastal and open-ocean ecosystems have varied over periods of about 50 years. In the mid-1970s, the Pacific changed from a cool 'anchovy regime' to a warm 'sardine regime.' A shift back to an anchovy regime occurred in the middle to late 1990s. *These large-scale, naturally occurring variations must be taken into account when considering human-induced climate change and the management of ocean living resources* (emphasis added)."[37]

The Peruvian fishermen are acutely aware how each El Niño cycle alters upwelling and the abundance of fish. The Peruvian anchovy fishery was considered one of the richest in the world. During the more common La Niña-like conditions, stronger westward-blowing winds sweep away the upper layers of warm waters inducing high rates of upwelling and rich plankton blooms. Despite intensive harvests, throughout the mid 1900s the Peruvian fisheries were hailed as a model of successful management, by both biological and economic standards.[413]

But that success was deceptive. The cool La Niña phase of the PDO had induced vigorous upwelling. Still an extreme El Niño can abruptly shut down upwelling every three to seven years. El Niño's flood of warm water acts as a thermal lid, preventing cooler, nutrient-rich waters from reaching the sunlit surface. Upwelling doesn't stop completely but is confined to more local and coastal hotspots where winds and currents can maintain a supply of nutrients.[553] During periodic El Niño episodes, the fishermen sought out the local refuges. The life altering power of an El Niño was evident in 1965. The food chain suffered a temporary bust, which not only depleted anchovies but also caused seabird abundance to decline by 75%. When upwelling resumed, the fish stock rapidly rebounded, and the bountiful Peruvian anchovy fishery remained the envy of the world until 1971.

The 1972 El Niño caused another crash in the Peruvian anchovy fishery, but this time there was no rapid rebound. Unbeknownst at the time, the ocean currents were transitioning into the warm, El Niño phase of the PDO. Peru's coastal Humboldt Current slowed, El Niños became more frequent, and upwelling was widely reduced. Peru's celebrated anchovy fishery collapsed and remained depressed for several decades. Unaware of the 20-year PDO cycle, fishermen continued to deplete the anchovies in the remaining refuges of local upwelling only to deplete the fishery further. The admirable management practices that had been hailed for maintaining high abundance just a few years earlier now metamorphosed into an example of human ignorance and greed.

Indeed, they were unaware of the PDO and its effect on climate and fisheries. The PDO was a natural phenomenon that would not be named for another two decades. Although the government imposed restrictions that protected the refuge populations from further exploitation, the regulations did not promote a recovery. However, as the PDO transitioned back to its cool phase, the anchovy populations have now returned and are approaching their previous levels of abundance.

The abundance of Peru's anchovies and sardines abruptly alternated during the mid 1970's and again in the late 1990's. When fishery biologist noticed a similar seesaw in salmon abundance and other fish species between Alaska and Oregon/Washington, they finally recognized the cyclical behavior of the PDO.

In 1915 Alaskan salmon fisherman had suffered their worst harvest, but further south the Columbia River fisheries had experienced unprecedented abundance. (The Columbia River forms the border between the state of Washington and Oregon.) In 1939 there was a sudden reversal of fortune. Bristol Bay Alaska reported the greatest salmon run in history while the Columbia River fisheries had their worst. The fickle finger of fate reversed the situation again in the 1970s. Bristol Bay reported a salmon disaster, and Columbia River harvested the greatest run of Chinook salmon since counting began. By 1995 Alaska was again boasting record breaking salmon harvests, while off the coast of Oregon the spring Chinook fishery shut down and west coast Coho salmon fishing was banned.[414] Since 1999, the salmon fisheries are reversing once again and salmon are now increasing in their southern ranges.

The reason for the seesaw in salmon abundance becomes clearer when we see how differently the main currents deliver nutrients to the two regions. As seen in Figure 34, the major currents diverge in this region. During a La Niña phase of the PDO, the eastern Pacific cools, causing the trade winds and High Pressure system to strengthen which in turn speeds up the California Current. More cold water enters the California Current and cold-water species are pushed further south. Due to the Coriolis effect (explained at the end of the chapter), a faster equator-bound California Current pumps water to the west and away from the coast, which increases coastal upwelling. Although not shown in Figure 34, the exact same dynamics occur with the equator-bound Humboldt Current off the coast of Peru. A stronger Humboldt Current also increases upwelling, which causes Peru's anchovies to boom.

The PDO similarly disrupts life on land. As discussed in Chapter 9, the megadroughts of the American southwest are associated with the cool La Nina PDO,[927] and those megadroughts contributed to the crash of the pueblo cultures. Archaeologists have suggested that as the cold PDO dried up rivers, native people migrated towards the coast where the faster California Current was enhancing upwelling and marine life. Archaeologists studying the coastal Chumash people of southern California uncovered an increase of violent deaths as migrating tribes fleeing the drought were drawn to increasing abundance of marine resources for which they violently competed.[928] Since the year 2000, there has been a similar increase in inland droughts accompanied by increased marine abundance.

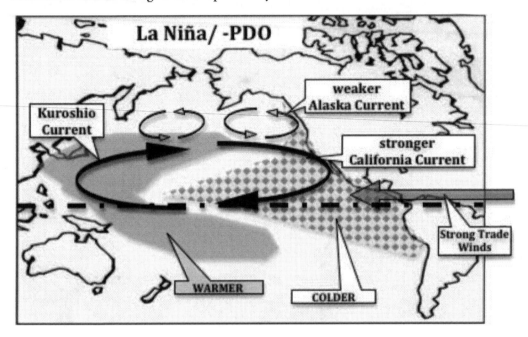

Figure 34. The cool or negative PDO phase and northern Pacific Ocean currents

Regime Shifts and Popular Culture

"The realization that jellyfish populations have been pulsing globally at decadal scales should lead to a broadening of the search for the drivers of change." [507]

Dr. Robert H. Condon, Marine Environmental Sciences Consortium

During the recent PDO warm phase between 1976 and 2000, numbers of "warm-water" sardines increased along the coast of Peru and California. As the California Current slowed down, sardines and other warm water species expanded northward. It was a phenomenon not seen since the previous warm phase from 1925-1946[417] when California's sardine fishery boomed, creating a heyday for Monterrey, California. However the sardine fishery suddenly collapsed when the PDO switched to the cold La Niña phase around 1946. The PDO's abrupt impact on Monterrey, California's sardine fishery was the basis of John Steinbeck's classic book *Cannery Row*.

The PDO's switch in 1946 also set the stage for another cultural classic. Sooty Shearwaters are sea birds that mostly breed in New Zealand and then migrate to the northern Pacific to feed in the upwelling zones. When the PDO is in its warm El

Nino phase, the shearwaters concentrate nearer Japan and the Bering Sea. When the PDO switches to the cool La Nina phase, they concentrate more along the California coast.[426,428] In 1961, the renewal of intense upwelling along the coast of Monterrey produced increasingly robust plankton blooms that attracted hundreds of thousands of shearwaters. However, plankton blooms also produce natural toxins, like the notorious "red tide." A peculiar toxin, domoic acid (produced in diatoms), accumulates in the zooplankton and small fish that the shearwaters eat. Domoic acid causes "shellfish amnesia," making the birds disoriented and head for land. Hundreds of shearwaters crashed into buildings, pavement, and innocent bystanders. These squadrons of kamikaze shearwaters alarmed the citizens of Monterrey, and newspaper reports of this bizarre event inspired Alfred Hitchcock's iconic film "The Birds."[432]

Most newspaper journalists who write "scientific columns" lack a science background. Like Hitchcock, they are inclined to tantalize their audiences by transforming unusual natural calamities into captivating tales of wildlife gone crazy. For example, increasing numbers of jellyfish recently evoked fearful media stories of abrupt climate change with stories like "Global warming, pollution and human activity in marine habitats are not generally regarded as good things — unless you're a jellyfish."[506] Although some portray booms in jellyfish as an omen of developing ecological chaos,[515] the most recent research shows that jellyfish around the world also undergo approximate 20-year cycles of boom and bust[507] There was a similar rise in jellyfish that clogged both fishermen's nets and the intake pipes that cooled power plants during the PDO's last cool phase. These blooms raised such concerns that the government passed the Jellyfish Control Act of 1966 to "control or eliminate" troublesome jellyfish. Ocean researchers now write, "The realization that jellyfish populations have been pulsing globally at decadal scales should lead to a broadening of the search for the drivers of change."[507]

Despite their bad reputation for stinging, jellyfish are vital links in the food chain. Their blooms are great news for endangered leatherback sea turtles that have struggled to recover in the Pacific. The leatherback's biggest threat has been human raids that at times plundered nearly 90% of the eggs laid on known nesting beaches.[517] Not only are jellyfish good for the turtles breeding in Costa Rica and Mexico, leatherbacks that nest in Indonesia will swim across the Pacific to feed on the jellyfish blooms along California's coastal upwelling.

Dead Zones and the Red Devil

"The expansion of Dosidicus' range does not appear to be directly linked to a regional increase in sea-surface temperatures." [447]

Dr. Louis D. Zeidberg Monterey Bay Aquarium Research Institute

Upwelling has another misunderstood downside. The boom in coastal marine life produces a rain of dead bodies that sink below the sunlit surfaces. The bacterial decay of those corpses consumes whatever scant oxygen is available, causing a zone of minimal oxygen 300-900 meters below the surface. When waters from those "oxygen minimum zones" are upwelled onto shallow coastal shelves, they can suffocate the bottom dwellers.[420,422] Paradoxically, a cornucopia of life near the surface can suffocate crabs, shrimp, and other sea-floor dwellers.

Dr. Chavez and others report that oxygen minimum zones have been increasing for over the past hundred and fifty years, largely due to increased upwelling cycles. The warming of the oceans began in the 1850s as solar activity increased, and the improved ocean productivity was accompanied by an expansion of oxygen minimum zones. Increased solar heating favors stronger trade winds that produce La Niña-like conditions and more upwelling.[143,144,409,419] In contrast, during the colder Little Ice Age, low solar activity correlated with lower ocean productivity and reduced oxygen minimum zones.[410,419]

In 2002, fisheries managers observed that the ocean floor off Oregon's coast was littered with dead fish. When fishermen in the area hauled their crab pots to the surface, they were stunned to find more than 70% of their crabs were dead. A region that once teemed with bottom dwelling fish and invertebrates suddenly went lifeless. However the crabs had to be alive when they crawled into the traps, so they must have been killed by a sudden episodic event and upwelling most likely caused a sudden intrusion of oxygen deficient water. Some dead zones such as one at the mouth of the Mississippi River have been generated when humans flushed unusual amounts of nutrients into the rivers. However the oxygen minimum zones off the coast of Oregon, as well as one extending from Peru to the equator, are far more extensive and these zones have been created by natural cycles of upwelled nutrients.

CO_2 advocates capitalized on these natural dead zone events, pointing to models that had predicted rising CO_2 levels will cause warmer waters that will hold less oxygen.[515] They argued that a warmer ocean surface will sit on top of the cooler nutrient-rich waters and inhibit any mixing of surface oxygen into deeper waters. Those generalized dynamics of a theoretically warmer ocean are true. However, the sea floor suffocation was not caused by warmer, oxygen-deprived surface waters near the surface, but from more ancient oxygen-depleted waters rising from the depths.[421,423] The hypothetical CO_2 connection fails because the surface waters over Oregon's "death zones" have been cooling for the past decade. *The paradox of cooling surface waters and larger oxygen-deprived zones cannot be explained by global warming, but the PDO and increased upwelling can readily explain it.*

Most global climate models have not yet incorporated the PDO's effects. Global models still fail to reproduce the observed east-west pattern of alternating warmer and cooler ocean surfaces. Instead most global climate models simulate a uniform east-west surface temperature, as did Hansen's earlier models that launched heightened CO_2 concerns.[2] Such failures have prompted scientists to now warn, "There appears to be a disconnect in this aspect of the models that needs to be addressed" [372]

Nonetheless the Los Angeles Times wrote, "Oxygen-starved waters are expanding in the Pacific and Atlantic as ocean temperatures increase with global warming, threatening fisheries and other marine life."[424] To support their misguided interpretation the journalist referred to the growing presence of the "Red Devil", aka the giant Humboldt squid *(Dosidicus gigas), which tolerates low oxygen.* However it is the renewed cycle of vigorous upwelling and abundant marine life during the PDO's boom cycles that attracts the squid.

The reddish squid giant earned its diabolic nickname for its voracious appetite, occasional attacks on scuba divers, and unrepentant cannibalism. The Red Devil's primary residence is in the Humboldt Current near Peru due to more reliable upwelling. However it travels daily between deep colder waters with minimum oxygen and warmer waters on the coastal shelves, so most scientists doubt they migrate in response to temperature change.[411,448] The squid's main constraint is food. In less than one year the giant squid hatchling grows 5 or 6 feet and gains 100 pounds. In order to achieve such rapid growth, it must hunt in the richest upwelling zones.

Because they live for just one year, giant squids must seek robust food supplies in order to rapidly reach sexual maturity and lay the eggs for the next generation. If food is abundant, they grow bigger and mature a little later. If food is more limited, they are smaller and mature a couple of months earlier. Due to the year-to-year uncertainty of ocean upwelling, each female will float 1 to 13 million eggs and will shed them anywhere and anytime.[425] Whenever food becomes abundant, the squid population rapidly multiplies. Consequently, with the recent shift to more upwelling associated with the cool phase of the PDO, giant squids have proliferated from Chile to Oregon, promoting more popular horror stories.

The boom in squid benefits the squid specialists, like the Pacific sperm whale. Moby Dick was a sperm whale, and hunters nearly drove that species to extinction with the tenaciousness of Captain Ahab. Although whale hunting has been prohibited, the population has yet to recover to historic levels. But there is encouraging news. Despite the uncertainties from our best surveys, there have been recent indications that sperm whale numbers have begun to increase.[523] Likewise, the squid-eating Bryde's whale which is also associated with vigorous upwelling has coincidentally increased on the west coast of North America.[524] Although this is all evidence of a richer food web, one local TV station portrayed recent sightings of the giant Humboldt squid as one more tale of dread where "global warming is already wreaking havoc with nature."[430]

Predicting Natural Regime Shifts

"Lower productivity of the coastal marine ecosystem, associated with a climate regime shift in 1976-1977, likely caused large, but unforeseen, impacts on population abundances and trophic structure in near shore benthic communities." [132]

Dr. Sally Holbrook, University of California, Santa Barbara

"These large-scale, naturally occurring variations must be taken into account when considering human-induced climate change and the management of ocean living resources." [37]

Dr. Francisco Chavez

These "unusual" responses by marine life are providing scientists with confirmation that regime shifts happen every 20 to 40 years, as had been predicted thirty years ago. For example, the Southern California Bight extends from Santa Barbara down to San Diego, and on a map it looks as if a "bite" had been taken from the coastline. The Bight is very sensitive to changes in the California Current and has attracted several marine studies. A team of researchers led by Dr. Sally Holbrook had reported, "In the Southern California Bight, a large temperature increase occurred during 1976-1977 when annual surface temperature rose by an average of nearly 1°C [1.8°F] above the average for the previous 1.5 decades." Pop culture blamed human-caused climate change[416] and interpreted the increase in warm-water species expanding northward as confirmation of Hansen's global warming predictions. In Parmesan's 2003 IPCC paper, "A Globally Coherent Fingerprint of Climate Change Impacts Across Natural Systems,"[133] she cited Holbrook's work to imply confirmation of global warming theory.

Holbrook however had been more skeptical. The temperature change was not gradual as one would expect from rising CO_2 levels. Instead it was a "jump shift" that is expected from a "regime shift." Before 1976, there was no warming trend, and ocean temperatures fluctuated around a lower average. Then after 1976, temperatures jumped higher and then fluctuated around a new higher average, but with no further warming trend. Holbrook cautioned, "The steep abundance declines on all levels were events that are not obvious predictions from present models of climate change." In contrast to Parmesan's interpretation, Holbrook predicted that the California Current would regain its intensity and revert to cooler temperatures. She concluded the following decades "would provide a natural 'test' of our hypotheses".[415]

Around 1999, the PDO again entered its La Niña phase, the California Current strengthened, and temperatures along the Southern California Bight reversed. Since 2000, temperatures have declined, and several species of fish that had once moved northward are now retreating southward. Above all other environmental factors, the changes in fish abundance has correlated best with the PDO regime shifts.[134] Between 1998 and 2003, other researchers reported that phytoplankton and zooplankton biomass doubled off central California and "zooplankton biomass off southern California has increased to values not seen regularly since the 1970s."[417]

Those scientists also reported "*the transition between the strong El Niño event in 1997–1998 and the 1998–1999 La Niña was possibly the most dramatic and rapid episode of climate change in modern times.*" [417] Mean summer ocean temperatures off the coast of Oregon decreased by 2°F beginning in 1999. Temperatures at some locations off the California coast fell by nearly 18°F between 1998 and 1999, and coastal sea levels were the lowest in at least 65 years. Warm-water fish like sardines declined and the more cold-loving anchovies and smelts increased by an order of magnitude. Indeed Holbrook's natural regime shift hypothesis was confirmed. Most likely it was this dramatic reorganization of the oceans in 1999 that caused the stranding of so many Gray whales.

Ocean Regime Shifts Cause Abrupt Climate Shifts

"Observations from the Bering Sea are good indicators of decadal shifts in climate, as the Bering is a transition region between the cold, dry Arctic air mass to the north, and the moist, relatively warm maritime air mass to the south" [985]

Dr. James Overland, NOAA/Pacific Marine Environmental Laboratory

"when the PDO value changed from dominantly negative to dominantly positive values, a sudden temperature increase across Alaska was observed." [508]

Dr. Gerd Wendler, Alaska Climate Research Center, University of Alaska, Fairbanks

Abrupt ocean regime shifts cause abrupt climate shifts. The ocean surface temperatures determine the strength and location of rising and sinking air currents (see Chapters 7 and 9). So shifting ocean temperatures rapidly alter high and low pressure systems that distribute the earth's heat and moisture. Global warming models have failed to predict those shifts. For example, climate scientists with the IPCC had identified northwestern North America and Siberia as the world's two most rapidly warming regions.[297] From 1950 to 1999 the average winter temperatures increased by 5°F nearly tripling the global average and advocates embraced that warming as evidence of CO_2-amplified climate change. However that warming also coincided with the PDO's shift to its warm phase.[121] Now that the PDO has shifted back to its cool phase, Alaska and the Bering Sea have become the earth's most rapidly cooling regions.[508]

The PDO alters Arctic climate by modulating the strength and location of the Low-pressure system that slides across the Aleutian Islands from the Bering Sea to the Gulf of Alaska. It is appropriately called the Aleutian Low. "Lows" circulate the winds counterclockwise as illustrated (see Figure 35). Climate studies conclude that the strengthening of the Aleutian Low is almost invariably associated with a warm phase of the PDO.[445]

In 1976 when the PDO shifted to its warm El Niño phase, the Aleutian Low strengthened and more frequently occupied the location illustrated in the upper panel of the Figure 35. The Low pumped more warm water through the Bering Strait and more warm air into Alaska. As a result, the annual temperatures increased by 5°F compared to the PDO's cool La Niña phase.[434] More specifically, this particular location of the Aleutian Low accounted for 50% of all "warm" months, and never allowed a colder than average month. On average, it raised regional winter temperatures 4-7°F above normal.[445]

The location of the low during PDO's warm phase also opposes the cold north winds that typically blow ice southward from the Arctic Ocean, so Bering Sea ice extent was also reduced. Without the insulating cover of sea ice, the oceans ventilated more heat. Winter temperatures in Nome, Alaska hover at -10°F, and winds blowing across exposed +28°F ocean waters can deliver an Arctic "heat wave.

Arctic amplification refers to period when the Arctic warms at a rate two to three times faster than the global average. Such rapid warming cannot be explained by rising concentrations CO_2, so advocates ironically emphasize the local climate perspective while still blaming rising CO_2. Arctic amplification is nearly a universal phenomenon of all global climate models. The models suggest warmth caused by rising CO_2 reduces snow cover, which allows the land surface to heat more rapidly. The models also suggest CO_2 warming melts more sea ice, allowing more heat to ventilate to the surface. However rapid warming in the Arctic has not followed the steady rise in CO_2, but has occurred only during the PDO's warm cycles. Several climate scientists now believe that "*the sudden changes in the Arctic temperature trends around 1940 and 1970 suggest that other factors besides slowly varying concentrations of greenhouse gases and aerosols, or solar changes, could have played a significant role*". In addition they report, "Arctic warming from 1910–1940 proceeded at a significantly *faster rate* than the current 1970–2008 warming."[657]

When the PDO shifted to its cool phase, "arctic amplification" suddenly disappeared from the Bering Sea and Alaska. When the PDO enters its cool phase, the Aleutian Low weakens and often "splits" as illustrated in the lower panel of Figure 35. An intervening High-pressure system forms, which circulates the winds in a clockwise manner and enhances the southward flow of cold air and ice. This atmospheric circulation pattern accounted for 38% of all colder-than-average months and caused temperatures in the eastern Bering Sea to drop 4-7°F below normal.[445] In 2013 with the PDO in its cold phase, Siberia's temperatures plummeted so low that it "left thousands without heat when natural gas liquefied in its pipes and water mains burst."[528]

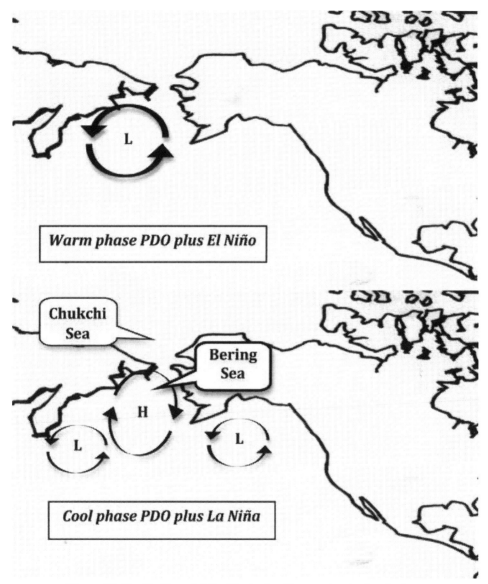

Figure 35. Pacific Decadal Oscillation's affect on Arctic circulation.

Since the PDO reversal, the average Alaskan temperatures have cooled by 2.3°F over the past 10 years. In keeping with the advocates' love for extrapolating meaningless trends far into the future, this means that by the year 2100, Alaska will be 23°F colder. However climate scientists admit, "it cannot be decided whether this is a climatic shift during the first decade of the 21st century or if it represents decadal-interdecadal variability."[508] Whatever proves to be the case, clearly whenever the PDO shifts, it overwhelms any theoretical CO_2-warming.

Climate models had predicted that the Bering Sea ice extent would be about 25 percent less than the 1979–1988 average by mid-century.[555] In contrast, after a lag of a few years since the PDO shifted, Bering Sea ice has been rapidly expanding each winter.[527] By 2012 Alaskan headlines bemoaned the extreme cold and record Bering Sea ice: "Sea ice cover in the Bering Sea was well above normal for much of the season, and reached a record high extent in March 2012. In addition, ice surrounded the Pribilof Islands, tiny volcanic islands in the middle of the Bering Sea, for a record number of days this winter."

The Aleutian Low links the Pacific Decadal Oscillation with the Arctic Oscillation (henceforth AO) and together these cycles alter how the winds distribute heat in the Arctic. The shifting AO affected Arctic sea ice in three ways. First the winds increased the amount of warmer water flowing through the Bering Strait melting ice in the Chukchi Sea, as seen in Figure 36. Second, the shift in the AO increased the below-freezing winds blowing from Siberia. These cold winds expanded the open waters of coastal polynya along the Siberian coast.[535,536] Unprotected by insulating ice, the winds stirred the waters and raised warmer waters from below (see Chapter 5). Scientists have demonstrated that even after the intrusion of warmer waters had stopped, the winds still bring warmer waters to the surface, reducing sea ice and raising surface temperatures.[484] Lastly, the shifting winds pushed thick, multiyear ice trapped in the central Arctic out into the Atlantic.[535,536] Scientists have determined the ice export from the Arctic was low in the 60's, the late 80's and 90's, and particularly high during 2005–2008.[925]

Where thicker ice remained and ventilation was inhibited, there was no warming trend. Until the AO shifted, Arctic air temperatures were cooling. Researchers measuring air temperatures over the Arctic Ocean in the 1980's and 90's reported, "we do not observe the large surface warming trends predicted by models; indeed, *we detect significant surface cooling trends over the western Arctic Ocean during winter and autumn.* This discrepancy suggests that present climate models do not adequately incorporate the physical processes that affect the polar regions (emphasis added)."[538]

After the winds removed the thicker ice, new replacement ice was thinner and more easily melted each summer, and heat readily ventilated from the ocean depths. *Arctic sea ice is currently behaving more like Antarctic sea ice (see Chapter 12).* Antarctic oceans never contained much thick multiyear sea ice, so each summer Antarctic sea ice melts much faster than Arctic sea ice. Yet each winter the Antarctic sea ice has steadily expanded.

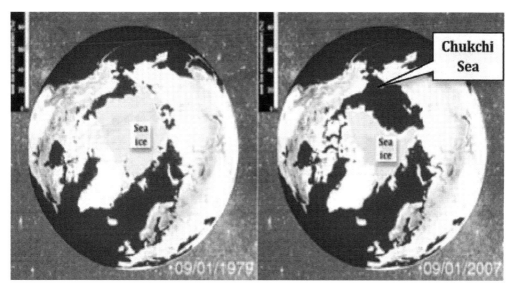

Figure 36. Satellite Comparison of Arctic Sea Ice: September 1979 (left), September 2007 (right)

As the evidence continues to unfold, the real control knob of climate change appears to be El Niño and ocean regime sifts like the Pacific Decadal Oscillation. Not only is sea ice affected by the PDO, but similarly the duration of ice cover on freshwater lakes and streams has been increasingly correlated with the phases of the PDO [435,441] If the growing Antarctic sea ice and Bering Sea ice are an indication of things to come, ice cover in the Chukchi Sea will be next to recover, followed by the rest of the Arctic seas. The AO has now switched to its cool phase and after a lag of a few years the winds should begin to trap and build thicker multiyear ice that resists summer melting. Several studies show that changes in the Aleutian Low are transmitted to the North Atlantic with an approximate five-year delay,[556] and the cool phase of the AO also explains the recent cold and snowy European winters.

In contrast to predictions of a natural recovery, CO_2 advocates predict an arctic sea ice "death spiral." On December 14, 2010, Dr. Michael Mann and seven other scientists wrote a letter to Secretary of the Interior Ken Salazar, arguing that global warming was a threat to polar bears (see Chapters 14 and 15). They wrote, "Under current greenhouse gas emissions trends, Arctic summer sea ice has been projected to disappear in the 2030s or before, as reported by several recent studies." So the next 15 years will provide another natural experiment to test the power of the PDO hypothesis versus CO_2. Will Arctic sea ice begin to increase or disappear by 2030?

The Coriolis Effect and Upwelling

The general rule is any wind or ocean current moving from the equator towards the poles will curl to the east. Conversely, any current travelling from the poles toward the equator will curl to the west (see Figure 37).

The Coriolis effect is caused by changes in the speed of the earth's surface. If your car is travelling at 60 miles per hour, so are you. When you jam on the brakes, the brakes stop your car, but you continue to travel at 60 mph until something stops you. It is safer to have your seat belt stop your motion instead of the steering wheel, the windshield, or a tree.

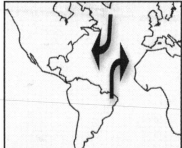

Figure 37. Coriolis effect on the direction of winds and currents.

Likewise, air and water at the equator are traveling about 1000 miles per hour from the west to the east, which is the speed and direction of the equator's rotation. However, if you straddled the North Pole, your feet would travel just 10 feet in 24 hours. Essentially, as you travel from the equator to either the North or South Poles the speed of earth's surface is slowing from 1000 mph to almost zero. Any wind or ocean current that has acquired a faster eastward speed of the earth's surface, and is not wearing a seat belt, will continue towards the east as the surface below slows down. Thus all poleward currents curl to the east relative to the earth's slower surface.

Conversely, any current that has acquired the slower speed of the earth's surface nearer the poles will curl towards the west, because the speed of earth's surface accelerates as we approach the equator. It is similar to being thrown backwards when the car accelerates. As the rising air of the Hadley Cells draws surface winds towards the equator, those winds curl to the west, generating the east–to–west Trade Winds. Similarly as the equator-ward waters of the California Current or Peru's Humboldt Current speed up, more water is also pumped westward away from the coast due to the Coriolis effect. As the surface waters are pumped away from the coast, subsurface water upwells as a replacement.

Winds descending from the Hadley cell and travelling towards the poles will curl from west to east. So the prevailing wind affecting Europe, northern Asia, and most of the United States are westerlies, and most storms in those regions travel from west to east. It is the Coriolis effect that similarly causes High and Low pressure systems to rotate.

12

Top Ten Reasons Rising CO_2 Has Not Harmed Adelie Penguins

"The location of research stations near colonies has led to reductions in suitable ground for breeding, excessive visits to colonies and disturbance caused by aircraft movements although the impact of disturbance in relation to environmental conditions appears to vary with location."

The IUCN Red List of Threatened Species

There have been several attempts to suggest Adelie penguins are suffering from global warming. In February 2012 "The fate of the Adelie Penguins, A message from Al Gore" was posted to his website, "The Climate Reality Project." Al Gore reported, "As temperatures rise along the West Antarctic Peninsula and the winter sea ice blankets the ocean three months fewer per year than 30 years ago, the local ecosystem is in danger. Everything from the base of the food chain – the phytoplankton (microscopic plants and bacteria) and krill (shrimp like creatures), to one of the continent's most iconic inhabitants, the Adelie penguins, are under threat…There is an important lesson for us in the story of the Adelie penguins. In Antarctica, as elsewhere, subtle changes in the local environment can have devastating impacts on all the living beings that depend on it. As the global climate continues to change, we can expect to hear different versions of these kinds of impacts many times over."

Regretfully, similar catastrophic tales are indeed being told many times over. The World Wildlife Fund's website says, "sea ice has been disappearing, and penguin populations along with it". NOAA has a series of "educational videos" called *Ocean Today*. Apparently designed to create dread, it focused on one small area where 80% of the penguins have been lost, yet they failed to mention that

everywhere else, Adelies are thriving. There are 10 very good reasons that demonstrate their horror stories have strayed far from reality. And there is indeed "an important lesson for us in the story of the Adelie penguins, " but it's a story only penguin lovers and climate skeptics will enjoy. The Adelies only struggle with local climate change, not global warming.

#10. Adelies Are More Abundant Than Ever

Across 95% of Antarctica's coastline, the number of Adelie penguins has mulitplied.[266,347] At DuDu, populations of Adelies increased "between 1984 and 2003 at a rate of 1.77% per year."[307] In the Ross Sea, home to 30% of the world's Adelie penguins, populations tripled between the 1960s and the mid-1980s. Although populations dipped in the late 1980s, the increasing trend resumed in the 1990s.[308]

From a global perspective, global warming has benefitted the Adelie penguins, and the International Union for the Conservation of Nature (IUCN) lists their population as increasing. Only on the western side of the Antarctic peninsula, a mere 5% of the Antarctica coastline, have the Adelies declined; that is the one place advocates focus our attention. The decline is strictly a local issue. The peninsula is the one sector that is most sensitive to El Niño cycles and the Pacific Decadal Oscillation. During the PDO's last cool phase, the peninsula's breeding populations of both Adelie and Chinstrap Penguins quintupled.[317] However, paralleling the 1976 switch to a positive PDO and more frequent El Niños, the penguin populations around the peninsula abruptly declined.

#9. Adelies Abandon Breeding Colonies With Too Much Ice

"If the Adélie Penguin is faced with a walk of more than a couple of kilometers on a regular basis, its colonies will disappear" [253]

Dr. David Ainley

Emperor and Adelie penguins are both considered "ice-dependent". However the Adelies use sea ice in a much different manner. Adelies never breed on ice as the Emperors do. Instead, as the returning springtime sun begins to thaw the coastline, they swim ashore and clamber up gentle, rocky slopes to breed. Although Adelies are remarkably more agile, they lack the tenaciousness of the dawdling Emperor marathoners. If Adelies are forced to walk more than three to five km over fast-ice, they will abandon their breeding site.[266] Furthermore, most studies report that years with heavy sea ice lowers the Adelies' population size and breeding success.[278,266,307,315,316] Because Adelies abhor long walks over coastal ice, breeding colonies typically border reliable polynya (see Chapter 4) with quick access to open water. Open waters also promote greater plankton blooms, and polynya are centers of robust food chains.[390,360]

#8. Adelies Depend On Winter Sea Ice Which Is Increasing

"Antarctic sea ice area exhibits significant decreasing annual trends in all six [model] ensemble members from 1950 to 2005, in apparent contrast to observations that suggest a modest ice area increase since 1979."[543]

Dr. Laura Landrum, National Center for Atmospheric Research

Each year the Adelies in the Ross Sea complete a 7800 mile round trip from their breeding grounds to the edge of the winter ice pack and back to their breeding grounds.[359] The winter is the only time Adelie penguins are dependent on sea ice. Adelies need light to hunt and therefore depend on winter sea ice located north of the Antarctic Circle. Although CO_2 affects Arctic and Antarctic sea ice equally, Antarctic sea ice has been expanding (see Figures 38 and 39), and Adelies spend the winter on increasingly abundant ice floes in the dim light north of the Antarctic Circle.

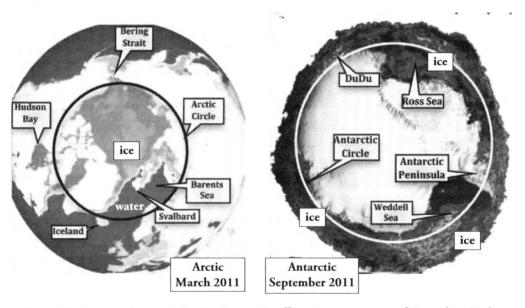

Figure 38. Arctic vs. Antarctic Sea Ice Extent. Satellite pictures courtesy of Cryosphere Today, University of Illinois.

The extent of Antarctic sea ice is controlled by two factors. Cold winds originating from the cold interior of the continent blow ice away from the coast and drive it equator-ward. Sea ice continues to expand until it reaches the warmer waters at the edge of the encircling Antarctic Circumpolar Current (ACC, see Figure 40).

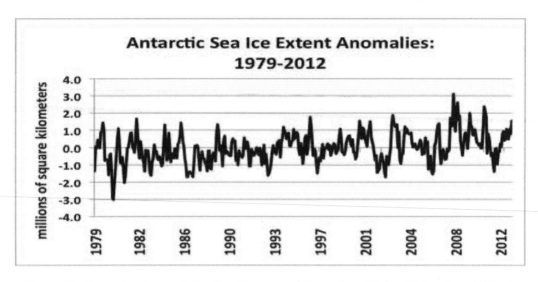

Figure 39. Increasing Antarctic Sea Ice. Courtesy of Cryosphere Today, University of Illinois

The ACC marks the contested boundary where warm waters driven southward by subtropical winds collide with cold coastal waters pushed equator-ward by Antarctica's continental winds. The exact position of the ACC varies slightly as the current meanders in response to the push-of-war between opposing winds. *Unrestricted by continents, the ACC is the world's greatest and most powerful current, moving a hundred times more water than the all the earth's rivers combined.*

Due to the earth's rotation and Coriolis effect (see Chapter 11), the subtropical winds curl towards the east, powering the west-to-east flow of the ACC. The strength of the ACC insulates Antarctic waters from any intrusions from warm tropical waters, such as those that have been melting sea ice inside the Arctic Circle (see Figure 38). Due to the insulating barrier of the ACC, the Antarctic pack ice symmetrically extends far beyond the Antarctic Circle and Antarctic sea ice continues to increase. The ACC's oceanic barrier was first established when continental drift separated Antarctica from the other continents millions of years ago. This allowed unimpeded flow and as the ACC strengthened, Antarctic waters cooled dramatically.

Species requiring warmer water soon became extinct. Today, the encircling ACC still maintains this formidable thermal barrier that has thwarted invasions by cold-blooded marine species. Since the establishment of the ACC, true sharks, true crabs, and some families of barnacles are uniquely absent inside the ACC,[288] and many of Antarctica's remaining cold-blooded species are found nowhere else. In contrast, the Arctic Ocean has been invaded by many North Atlantic and Pacific species that can persist at lower depths in warmer subsurface waters.

Each winter, Antarctic winds push the sea ice equator-ward and by September, 16 to 17 million square kilometers of sea ice cover the Antarctic Ocean, nearly 40% of the southern hemisphere's ocean surface. In contrast, because continents surround the

Arctic Ocean and constrain the winter's ice expansion, the maximum extent of Arctic sea ice in 1979 covered only about 15 million square kilometers.[††††]

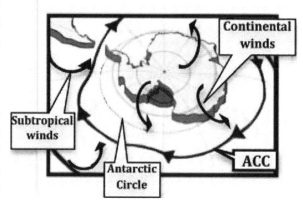

Figure 40. The ACC - Antarctic Circumpolar Current

Counterintuitively, despite more extensive winter ice, Antarctica's sea ice retreats much more rapidly each summer. Because Antarctic sea ice consists mostly of thinner first-year ice, it quickly shrinks to a mere one or two million square kilometers. Even during the Arctic's "historic" summer lows of 2007 and 2012, *the Arctic still retained two to three million square kilometers of sea ice, nearly twice as much as the Antarctic's seasonal low.* Despite this rapid summer melting, each winter Antarctica's sea ice faithfully returns each winter and sea ice extent continues to increase (Figure 39).

#7. The Food Web Is Improving

"natural environmental variability associated with inter-annual and decadal-scale changes in ENSO [El Niño] forcing must be considered when assessing impacts of climate warming in the Antarctic Peninsula–Weddell Sea region "[351]

Dr. Valerie Loeb 2009, Moss Landing Marine Laboratories

Early researchers feared that rising CO_2 levels would cause less sea ice and reduce the supply of krill, shrimp-like animals that are the cornerstone of the entire Antarctic food web. Initial research found that less sea ice correlated with less krill and logically assumed rising CO_2 would destroy the food chain. However there was another paradox. On a local level, researchers observed that less ice allows more sunlight to penetrate the water, which always promotes more photosynthesis and boosts productivity, and thus less ice also increased krill numbers and the stability of the entire food chain.[335,390] Globally, ocean productivity has increased by 4.1%.[333,334] The cause of the confusion was El Niño.

It is now known that cycles of El Niño and the PDO also create cycles of upwelling

---

[††††] Measurements of sea ice extent differ depending on what concentration of ice cover is used as the threshold between ice and "no ice". For example, by using a lower concentration, some authors report that Antarctica's maximum coverage reaches 20 million km². Here we use statistics supplied by the University of Illinois' website *The Cryosphere Today* to allow an accessible comparison of the Arctic and Antarctic

(see Chapter 11) along the Antarctic Peninsula. Those upwelling cycles cause krill populations to boom and bust. Upwelling decreased and krill populations plummeted during the positive Pacific Decadal Oscillation (PDO) with more frequent El Niño's. In contrast during the cool phase of the PDO, more La Niñas induced more upwelling of nutrients onto the shallow shelves of the western peninsula. The same researchers who had once reported that krill had plummeted due to less sea ice now believe that the decline was largely driven by more frequent El Niños.[351] Due to the current trend towards more La Niñas and more upwelling of nutrients, researchers are now reporting richer plankton blooms and more krill.[349,351, 356,357,358]

Furthermore, due to enlightened conservation and the reduced demand for blubber, we can celebrate the widespread recovery of Antarctic's krill-eating wildlife. There has been a slow but steady rebound in Blue whales, and a booming recovery of Humpback whales that are increasing by 5% a year along the peninsula.[353] The islands just north of the peninsula are home to over 95% of the krill-eating Antarctic fur seals. Previously driven to the edge of extinction by commercial sealing, these populations have recovered rapidly. Since 1990 the fur seal populations have grown by 6 to 14% per year and are now so numerous, the IUCN lists them as a species of "Least Concern".[354] During the last negative PDO, the number of the krill-eating Adelie penguins quintupled, so there is good reason to believe the Adelies along the peninsula will soon increase like elsewhere in Antarctica.

#6. Winds Control the Adelies' Peninsula Habitat

"While snow accumulation patterns are a primary driver of variation in population trends among colonies, the effect of snow accumulation is outweighed by proximity to human activities near Casey."

Dr. P.K. Bricher, University of Tasmania

Winds from the cold Anatarcic interior have blown so persistently and so reliably for millions of years that Emperor and Adelie penguins evolved breeding strategies that depend on access to the open water polynyas maintained by those continental winds (see Chapter 4). In contrast, the southward winds that drive the ACC periodically speed up and slow down, a phenomenon dubbed the Antarctic Oscillation (or Southern Annular Mode). Due to its close proximity to the ACC, the Antarctic Peninsula is uniquely impacted by the winds blowing from the north, which can compress ice against the shore and block the Adelies access to open water.

For example, in 2002 when strong winds from the north compressed sea ice against the peninsula's shore, the local population of Adelie penguins "experienced the largest recorded between-season breeding population decrease and lowest reproductive success since they were first observed 30 years ago." Most birds were forced to either defer breeding or suffered higher chick mortality.[300]

Similar wind events explain the paradox of why less ice has only been detrimental for Adelie penguins along the peninsula. Elsewhere when the winds blow ice away from the coast, less ice is beneficial. Typically less ice means more open leads and bigger polynya, and easier access to open water for feeding. Although the north winds statistically created three months of less sea ice on the peninsula's west side, a detailed examination revealed that "less ice" was a misleading average statistic. The coastal regions actually experienced much longer sea-ice seasons (lasting about seven to eight months) because the winds had compacted offshore ice onto the coastline.[302] Offshore, these windswept waters experienced the much shorter sea-ice season to which Mr. Gore referred. However, the collapse of Adelies had been caused by the longer ice season along the coast that denied the penguins easy access to the water.

Shifting winds further disrupted the Adelies' breeding season by affecting snowfall. Because Adelies are so adverse to heavy ice during their breeding season, we would expect them to breed much later in order to avoid the dangers of persistent coastal ice and late snowfalls. However, an early breeding season synchronizes their feeding with spawning krill that migrate offshore each summer to drop their eggs in the warmer waters. Instead Adelies adapted to the dangers of heavy snowfall and the resulting melt waters that can drown their chicks by building "comfy" nests from piles of glacial pebbles that drain quickly and elevate their chicks above deadly melt waters.

Adelies also choose their nest locations carefully. Populations are absent from the sides of islands that are regularly clogged with circulating sea ice even if food is more abundant on that side. Instead, they always nest on the sides of an island where currents keep the coastal waters open. They also choose microclimates where the swirling winds sweep snow from the surface and prefer sites on slightly higher grounds and less likely to flood.

Their sensitivity to snow accumulation was demonstrated by an unintentional experiment. On Cape Hallet, on the western side of the Ross Sea, buildings were erected in 1959 as part of a joint research effort between the United States and New Zealand. Unwittingly, those buildings altered the wind patterns and caused an increase in snow accumulation downwind where Adelie penguins had established a breeding colony. The Adelies quickly abandoned those sites. When scientists later abandoned the research station, the buildings were removed, which reestablished the previous wind patterns. The snow accumulation dwindled, and the Adelies quickly recolonized.[312]

Unlike the rest of the continent where there has been no change in snow accumulation trends, ice core data revealed that since 1850 snowfall over the peninsula has steadily increased, doubling over the past 150 years.[381] Despite increasing snowfall, the number of the peninsula's Adelies quintupled from 1930 to 1970. Adelies adapted to rising snowfall by choosing breeding sites with microclimates that minimized snow accumulation. When the Pacific Decadal Oscillation and the Antarctic Oscillation swung to positive phases during the 1970s, the winds became stronger and the primary wind direction shifted from the north to the northeast. This caused snow to accumulate more heavily on the southwest side of any significant landscape features.

A study of abandoned colonies around the Palmer Research Station located on the western side of the peninsula discovered that 86%, or 18 of 21, of the recent "extinct" colonies had been located on the southwest side of large rock mounds and cliffs. In contrast, 55 of the 66 remaining colonies (83%) occupied sites in areas other than the southwest side, where snow never accumulated as heavily. Researchers concluded the Adelies' "decline has been related to the effects of local topography and wind direction on changes in the patterns of snow accumulation in the vicinity."[313] Although CO2-driven models erroneously predicted that both the Arctic and Antarctic Oscillation would remain in their positive phases, the Arctic Oscillation has cycled back to its negative phase, and the Antarctic Oscillation is also trending back to its negative phase. When the winds shift again on the peninsula we should expect the Adelies to adapt accordingly.

#5. Adelies Thrived During Warmer Times

"Two subsequent periods of abandonment at 5000-4000 years Before Present correlate with cooling episodes that caused unfavorable marine conditions for breeding penguins. Most modern colonies were established only within the past 2000 years."[267]

Dr. Steven Emslie, North Carolina University

Adelie penguins thrived in warmer temperatures. Because Adelies breed on land, they produce rich layers of freeze-dried carcasses, addled eggs, fecal material, and regurgitation that can be identified and dated by indentured graduate students. The Ross Sea is home to 38% of the world's Adelie penguins. During a much warmer period about 4000 years ago (see Figure 41) Adelie penguins enjoyed a heyday that researchers dubbed the "Penguin Optimum."[396]

In addition to a warmer Penguin Optimum, recent climate change on the peninsula is not unprecedented. On Anvers Island on the peninsula's west coast, several Adelie colonies had been recently abandoned. Examining long-term climate change, researchers determined the island is covered by more ice now than 700 to 1000 years ago. They found that extensive loss of ice is not unprecedented and has occurred at least three times in the past 5000 years.[378]

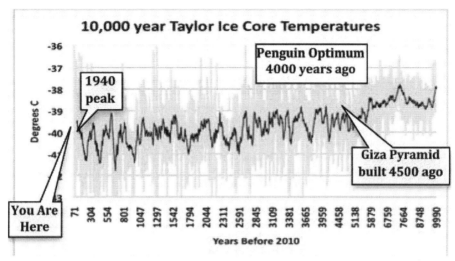

Figure 41. Antarctic Ice Core Temperatures. Raw data from Steig 1998.[361] Black Line 20 year running average.

Ice cores also indicate that the decade from 1930 to 1940 was the warmest of the 20th century for western Antarctica, and that the current warming trend began about 200 years ago.[323,325] During the 20th century, Antarctic temperatures rose just 0.36°F despite the rapid warming of the peninsula.[323] The 0.36°F increase is the within the bounds of the sun's contribution, and isotopes found in the cores reveal that observed changes in Antarctica's climate correlate closely with solar activity.[401] As solar activity declines and CO_2 increases, the next two decades will again provide greater insight to the relative impact of those two factors. However, a weakening sun adequately explains the growing sea ice and cooler Antarctic temperatures elsewhere.

#4. Rapid Warming on the West Side of Peninsula is Due to Winds and Ice.

"We can show that atmospheric warming and reduction in sea-ice duration coincide in a small area on the west of the Antarctic Peninsula, but here we cannot yet distinguish cause and effect."[297]

Dr. David Vaughan, British Antarctic Survey

The rapid warming on the western side of the peninsula startled several climate researchers, and advocates warned that it was an omen of things to come. Paradoxically, most of the continent has cooled since the 1980s[326,380]. The warming on the peninsula is another example of how local conditions amplify natural climate change. The peninsula, located in the southeastern Pacific, catches the full force of every warm El Niño event.[299] Ice core data revealed that average temperatures for the western Antarctic and peninsula reached their greatest peak during the El Niño events from 1939-42.[323] Temperatures then plummeted in the 1950s as the PDO coincidentally shifted to the cool phase. Temperatures peaked again around 1999 but failed to surpass the ones recorded in the 1940s. They have been slightly cooling since the PDO shifted to its cool phase as seen at the Faraday weather station (see Figure 42).

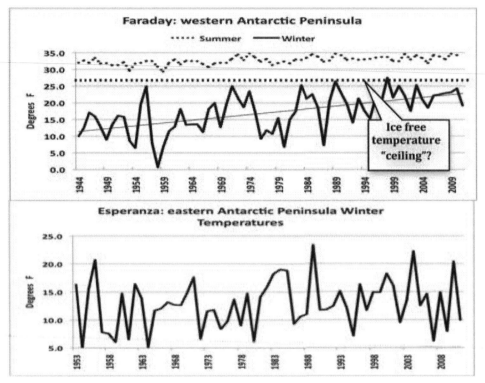

Figure 42. Comparison of western peninsula (Faraday, upper panel) to eastern peninsula (Esperanza, lower panel). Courtesy of British Antarctic Survey.

The Esperanza weather station is located on the tip of the eastern side of the peninsula and 120 miles closer to the equator. Here, winter temperatures average 10°F colder compared to the Faraday station on the western side (see Figure 42). The unexpected difference is due to ice cover. The Coriolis effect causes winds blowing from the continent's interior to curl from east to west, making the coastal ice circulate counterclockwise around the continent. The peninsula blocks this flow of ice. As seen in a satellite picture taken in March 2012 (see Figure 43), the circulating sea ice converges on the eastern side of the peninsula in the Weddell Sea. Like trapped ice in the Arctic, these thicker layers resist summer melting. The greater ice cover blocks ventilating heat, making the eastern peninsula much colder.

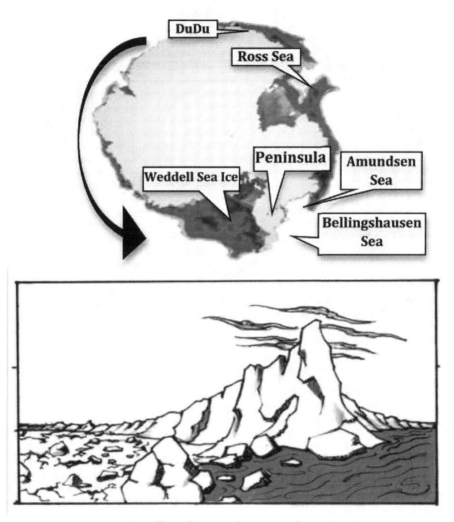

Figure 43. Effect of Peninsula on Circulating Sea Ice

Heat-releasing polynyas typically form on the west side of an island or peninsula because circulating ice cannot replace ice removed by the wind. The peninsula similarly promotes more open waters in the Bellingshausen and Amundsen Seas,[299] and because open waters ventilate over 100 times more heat than ice-covered waters[289], the western side of peninsula averages 9° to 18°F warmer than the eastern side just 100 kilometers away.[375]

Advocates often focus on the rapid 10° to 12°F rise of the Antarctic Peninsula's temperatures at Faraday station. However Faraday's rapid warming is restricted to the winter. During the winter there are wild 15° to 25°F swings from year to year, determined by how much ice is swept from the surface. In summer when there is no ice cover to control heat ventilation, those wild temperature swings are absent (see

Figure 42, upper panel). Faraday's warmest winter temperatures occur during the most ice-free years, and temperatures consistently reach a "ceiling" that plateaus around 25°F. Warmer temperatures are mostly a function of the winds that compress the ice and create more open waters that ventilate heat. On the eastern side of the peninsula at Esperanza station, warm winds from an El Niño still create warm spikes, but due to more persistent sea ice there is no winter warming trend. *Rapid climate change is strictly a local and seasonal phenomenon.*

Adelies avoid the heavy ice and cold temperatures on the eastern side of the peninsula; breeding colonies are rare on all but the northernmost tip. Adelies are still quite common on ice-free islands further to the north of the Weddell Sea and on the western side of the peninsula.

#3. Warming Events without Added Heat

"At any time of the year, instances of strong, gusty southwesterly winds can occur on time-scales of a few hours to a week. The strong wind events are characterized by warming (especially during winter, when valley cold pools are disrupted and temperatures can rise by up to 50°C [90°F])"[896]

Dr. Daniel Steinhoff, Byrd Polar Research Center

The peninsula generates another paradox. The eastern tip of the peninsula experiences abrupt warming events during the summer not observed on the western side. The Antarctic Peninsula is an extension of the soaring South American Andes, separated only by Drake's Passage. So the towering peninsula blocks eastward-flowing winds that drive the ACC. Normally, winds blowing from the west to the east hit the peninsula and are diverted northward around it. However, during the positive phase of the Antarctic Oscillation, winds strengthened and began flowing up and over the peninsula. When winds are forced over this towering mountainous barrier, foehn storms erupt on the lee side causing rapid warming with 15° to 40°F spikes in a matter of hours[374] (Foehn storms raise temperatures without adding heat. See Adiabatic Heating on page 108). This causes a slight warming trend in the summer at Esperanza station as well as rapid melting of a nearby glacier.

The same winds that compressed ice against the coast and caused the Adelie penguins to abandon colonies on the west side of the peninsula caused a foehn storm over the Larsen Ice Shelf. The sudden appearance of melt ponds just before the shelf collapsed testified to rapid adiabatic heating.[300,321] These winds also halted the circulation in the Weddell Sea and likely lowered the sea level temporarily, adding further stress to the floating ice shelf.

Foehn storms also explain one of Antarctica's greatest mysteries. In the McMurdo Dry Valley temperatures rarely rise above freezing. Furthermore the meager snow fall quickly sublimates[§§§§] without producing melt water. *Yet there is enough melt water produced each summer to maintain liquid lakes below the ice.* Researchers have determined that short-lived summer foehn storms can temporarily raise temperatures above the freezing point to produce enough melt water to supply those lakes. Some studies have shown that even during the dark winter, adiabatic heating from a foehn storm can raise temperatures by 90°F. Even more intriguing, during the coldest years of the last Glacier Maximum, those lakes reached their highest levels. Adiabatic heating is the most likely explanation for abundant meltwater.[923,926] The frequency of foehn storms has also been connected to ocean oscillations. It has been calculated that a 1% increase in foehn storm frequency raises the average temperature by 1°F.[373] Similar warming from foehn winds is observed around the world, such as in the Alps and Carpathian Mountains of Europe.[377]

#2. A Natural Experiment Reveals CO_2's Effect is Trivial

The Antarctic Peninsula's extreme temperature shifts caused by wind and ice make it impossible to tease apart any contribution from rising CO_2 levels. However the South Pole during the winter is one of the rare places on earth where climate change is relatively free of the multitude of confounding factors that cause warming elsewhere. It is the only place where CO_2 unarguably controls the temperature.

Skeptics and advocates battle over contributions from the primary greenhouse gas - water vapor. However Antarctica's extreme cold squeezes all moisture from the air, so we can eliminate any significant effects of water vapor on the South Pole's climate. CO_2 is the only remaining greenhouse gas. Similarly, land surface changes and urbanization have affected weather stations around the world, but we can eliminate any land surface change at the South Pole.

Skeptics also argue that changes in ocean oscillations like the PDO have caused higher temperatures by redistributing heat. But the South Pole is far from the coast, so the ocean's contributions are statistically insignificant. Furthermore the flatter terrain of the high plateau does not induce adiabatic heating by foehn winds, and the slower speeds of the nascent continental winds have a minimal effect on the cold surface layer.

Some scientists argue ozone depletion has caused a cooling effect, but the ozone hole is not a factor in the winter and does not form until sunlight returns in the spring. The winter darkness also eliminates any effects of a variable sunlight or reflection. *Thus virtually every significant confounding climate factor is eliminated at the South Pole*

[§§§§] Sublimation is the process during which ice changes to water vapor without entering a liquid water phase.

during the winter.

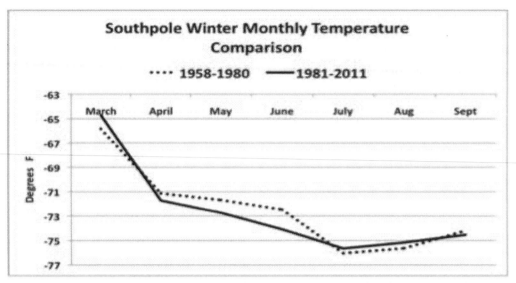

Figure 44. Winter temperatures at Amundsen-Scott station, South Pole. Courtesy British Antarctic Survey http://www.antarctica.ac.uk/met/gjma/

As the sun disappears after the autumn equinox in March, South Pole temperatures plummet to below -70°F. Between the equinoxes, any further drop in winter temperatures is slowed by CO₂'s greenhouse effect. The South Pole's winter temperature depends almost exclusively on the balance between incoming and outgoing long-wave radiation, and incoming radiation is supplied by CO₂ in the warmer air layers that hover above the cold surface.

By comparing temperatures averaged for the periods before and after the 1976 PDO regime shift (see Figure 44), we see absolutely no winter warming and perhaps an insignificant cooling at the South Pole. There is not a trace of "polar amplification," nor a trace of global warming.

#1 Only Models Are Killing Penguins

"During recent decades, surface temperatures decreased significantly over most of Antarctica." [380]

Dr. Drew Shindell and Dr. Gavin Schmidt, NASA 2004

"The important thing is to make sure they're losing the PR battle. That's what the site [Real Climate] is about." [806]

Dr. Michael Mann, Pennsylvania State University

The Adelie penguins join a growing list of species listed as threatened or endangered despite abundant and increasing populations. In 2012, the IUCN up-listed the penguins from a species of least concern to "Near Threatened," writing, "it is thought to be threatened by the effects of projected climate change, *primarily through future decreases in sea ice concentration* (emphasis added)." However Antarctica's sea ice concentration has defied the models and has steadily increased (see Figure 39). The IUCN's new designation is clearly not based on evidence, but based on faith in model projections. This faith is surprising in light of the fact that Antarctica represents the models' greatest failures. For example, as of 2012 climate scientists using an ensemble of IPCC models reported, "Antarctic sea ice area exhibits significant decreasing annual trends in all six ensemble members from 1950 to 2005, *in apparent contrast to observations that suggest a modest ice area increase* since 1979."[543]

In 2002, scientists wrote that the Antarctic Peninsula had warmed by several degrees over the past several decades, "while the interior of the Antarctic continent has exhibited weak cooling."[548] In 2004, NASA scientists attempted to adjust their models to account for surface temperatures that had *"decreased significantly over most of Antarctica* (emphasis added)."[380] They suggested changes in ozone had created the paradox. Because models driven by CO_2 tend to warm everything evenly, most models fail to accurately simulate opposing local trends for the same reason they fail to capture the alternating temperature cycles in the Pacific Ocean. When the models added enough heat from CO_2 to make the peninsula warm, the models also make East Antarctica warm, contradicting observations.[326]

Some advocates solved the Antarctica cooling paradox by using a starting date with the coldest temperatures. In a 2006 study, climate scientists reported, "Starting dates of 1966-82 have negative trends" but, "the choice of 1958 as a starting year produces the near-maximum possible positive trends over the Antarctic continent."[326] By starting the trend in the 1950s they created a warming trend for the whole continent.

In 2009 RealClimate's Dr. Eric Steig coauthored "Warming of the Antarctic ice-sheet surface since the 1957 International Geophysical Year", and the journal *Nature* adorned its front cover with a bright red map of Antarctica to promote this warm trend. Not only did Steig's methods choose the dates for *the near-maximum possible positive trend,* they used an averaging method that homogenized the extreme warming from the peninsula across the entire continent. That made it appear as if the whole continent had warmed more uniformly. By such averaging techniques, the cooling paradox of the last two decades and the effects of local topography were eliminated, creating the appearance of a uniform warming trend consistent with predictions based on rising CO_2.

It became quite apparent that this "new and improved" view of Antarctica's climate was driven by politics. Just a year before, Steig had coauthored a paper in which ice core data had shown the warmest decade on the peninsula occurred 1936-45 and was associated with strong El Niños.[323] After the PDO shifted to a cool phase, temperatures plummeted to the extreme lows of the 1950s. If the starting point began in 1940, even the Antarctica peninsula would show no warming.

The paper's statistical techniques were soon challenged,[327] and further analyses reaffirmed past research that warming was concentrated over the peninsula. They argued that Steig's coauthor Michael Mann had used statistical techniques inappropriate for Antarctica's diverse climate, and sparse data sets. Anything touched by Dr. Michael Mann draws the quick ire of the skeptical community and Steig's paper became a flash point for more conspiracy theories. Michael Mann is also the cofounder of the website RealClimate which I regularly visited to get their version of climate change.

Coincidentally I had happened to visit the website just as Dr. Gavin Schmidt posted "Warm reception to Antarctic warming story," in which he naturally praised Steig and Mann's new paper. I was one of the first three people to post a comment; I suggested that it would be more informative to discuss the start dates of these oscillating trends and that the past two decades of cooling still needed to be addressed. My post was quickly stricken from their website. It was clear these scientists were more interested in the PR battle than in honest scientific discussion.

Gavin Schmidt's opening paragraphs revealed the political nature of the website. After he praised the media for their widespread coverage of their paper, he made it appear that only uninformed skeptics believed Antarctic was cooling. He wrote, "The most prevalent peg was the fact that the study appeared to reverse *the 'Antarctic cooling' meme that has been a staple of disinformation efforts* for a while now (emphasis added)." That was a very weird thing to say if you consider that just five years earlier Schmidt had coauthored a paper trying to model the observed cooling trend that previous models had failed to simulate. Was it also "disinformation" when Schmidt wrote in 2004, "*during recent decades, surface temperatures decreased significantly over most of Antarctica*"?[380] Everyone, including Schmidt, knew Antarctica had been cooling – a fact the CO$_2$ theory had failed to predict. Unable to adequately explain the cooling, they got rid of the cooling trend by clever averaging and disavowing their previous admissions of cooling.

Recent attempts to explain Antarctica's expanding sea ice further illustrates the absurd lengths that advocates have gone to in order to deny contradictory evidence. My favorite is a 2007 paper, "Increasing Antarctic sea ice under warming atmospheric and oceanic conditions."[541] They argued that *warming causes more ice*. They reasoned that global warming causes more freshwater, which can freeze more readily, and that the layer of freshwater insulates the surface from ventilating heat.

Freshwater *does* freeze more readily, but if more melting causes more freezing, then why hasn't the melting Arctic sea ice caused the Arctic ice to also expand. Such speculative papers flood the peer-reviewed literature and erroneously get cited as scientific evidence. As Mr Gore warned, "we can expect to hear different versions of these kinds of impacts many times over."

13

Walruses, Whales and Arctic Wisdom

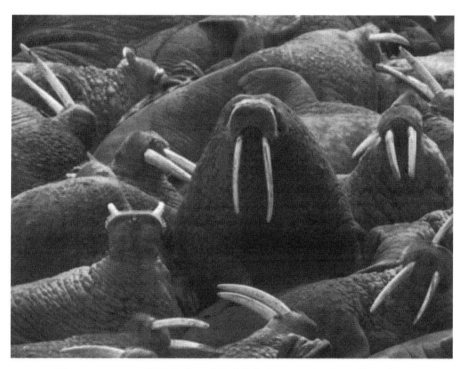

Photo courtesy of US Fish and Wildlife Service. Credit Bill Hickey.

Successful Walrus Conservation

The walrus is another example of improving environmental stewardship. Valued for its oil and ivory tusks, the Pacific walrus was subjected to intense commercial slaughter in the mid 1800s, and by the early 1900s, many worried they would soon go the way of the dinosaurs. Although population estimates have always been highly uncertain, as hunting was progressively limited, Pacific Walrus populations "increased from 50,000 to 100,000 animals in the late 1950s to more than 250,000 animals by 1985," and they are believed to have now reached their maximum carrying capacity.[557] As walrus numbers rebounded, they have crowded together at historic coastal haul-outs (Haul-outs are land locations where walruses congregate when not swimming). However some advocates are using the walrus' recovery as evidence of ecological disruption caused by global warming and the loss of sea ice. But their fears would vanish if they had a more historical perspective.

In 1923 Captain Joseph Bernard published an account in the *Journal of Mammalogy* about the inspiring conservation efforts he had observed in the village of Ingshong on the Siberian coast.[558] There the wisdom of walrus conservation, dressed in the trappings of shamanic beliefs, had fostered a dramatic comeback in local walrus abundance.

When Capt. Bernard had first visited the village of Ingshong, he met an ordinary hunter named Tenastze. Eighteen years later, Tenastze had become Chief. His rise to the top began when he gathered together the men of Ingshong and neighboring villages to discuss a decade of failed walrus hunts and disappearing herds. Walruses had once come to rest on their beaches in countless numbers, but the beaches were now empty. Tenastze believed that there was no one in the village looking after the spirit of the walrus and summoned a small group of shamans to peer more deeply into the problem.

After days of extended drumming and an induced trance, the shamans reported that indeed someone had offended the spirit of the walrus and poisoned the land. To break the spell of evil, the people had to choose a strong chief who promised to guard the walrus' spirit.

Their first step was to sacrifice the first walrus that presented itself to the village's hunters. After ritualistic preparation, its skull was placed on a long stick. Holding the other end of that stick, the strongest man in the village would attempt to lift the skull in response to each question. Like a shaman's version of the Ouija board, questions were directed to the walrus spirit. If the strongman was unable to lift the skull, it was a negative answer. If the spirits wanted to respond positively, the spirits imbued the man with enough strength to lift the skull. One by one, the names of all the men vying to be the new chief were offered to the walrus spirit. Only when the name Tenastze was spoken could the strongman lift the skull. (Although I love the story's ending, the skeptic in me can't help but wonder if Tenastze paid off the strongman.)

Now in charge, Tenastze quickly designated a round-the-clock guard to insure that the walruses were not disturbed. When the walruses first appeared in the coastal waters, fires were not allowed and alcoholic drink was forbidden. Shortly thereafter, a lone venturous walrus finally settled on their beach, and spent the night undisturbed. After each feeding foray, that walrus returned again and again and each time brought more and more walruses. By the time the autumn sun was retreating south, and the winter freeze beginning, several hundred walruses had come ashore. Only then were the people allowed to take their allotted kill; most walrus were permitted to go away unharmed. The walruses seemed unaffected by this limited hunt, and the next year many more came ashore. As the years passed, the herd grew to such proportions that villagers told Bernard, "last year the beach was so crowded when the walruses hauled there, many walruses were crushed to death just from overcrowding."[558]

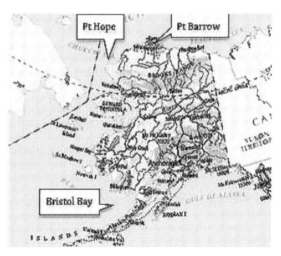

In 1925 Bernard again wrote in the *Journal of Mammalogy*, advocating for walrus sanctuaries in Alaska to the south of Barrow.[559] He contrasted the more conservation-minded village of Ingshong to the settlement of Point Hope on the Alaskan Coast. Thirty years before, the walruses had hauled out by the thousands and some would even wander into town. However the traders, whalers, and Inuit of the settlement were all too quick to shoot any weary walrus coming ashore. Subsequently, for the last twenty years live walruses had become a rare sight on that beach.

The European settlers of that time had embarked on a withering onslaught, motivated by a lucrative ivory market. In just a few decades the only surviving walruses were the ones that had learned to avoid coastal haul-outs, finding greater safety on the ice floes or more remote islands. Nomadic Inuit hunters showed no greater restraint than the Europeans. They followed the wary walrus herds out onto the ice floes. Although walrus meat was highly valued, ivory tusks brought much greater returns. Along the 200 miles of shoreline near Pt Barrow, Alaska, Bernard counted 1000 walrus corpses washed ashore. One third of the corpses still retained their tusks; although shot, they had managed to slip into the waters before the hunters could cleave their tusks. The nightmare was likely far greater than evidenced by mere shoreline counts. If Bernard counted 1000 rotting carcasses washed ashore by the westerly winds, how many more were carried by the currents out to the Arctic Ocean, or to other distant beaches?

From 1900-1930, the annual harvest of Pacific walrus averaged 5000 per year. Despite growing concerns voiced by Bernard and others, that figured doubled to 10,000 per year between 1930 and 1950. The Pacific walrus was seemingly headed for extinction. Fearing this may be the last chance to observe living walruses, Francis Fay began compiling one of the most complete accounts of the ecology and biology of the Pacific Walrus for the US Fish and Wildlife Service. After more than two decades of research, "The Ecology and Biology of the Pacific Walrus" was published in 1982.[560]

The 1950s were the 20th century's nadir of walrus abundance. Over-hunting of whales and walruses had been so severe, the native Yupik of the St Lawrence Island found themselves on the verge of starvation. The Yupik had dodged an earlier threat of extirpation in 1879 when disease was introduced by visiting whalers. When John Muir and a Smithsonian naturalist visited the island they were horrified to find huts strewn with hundreds of dead bodies. There were few survivors. Although the Yupik population had only rebounded to just one-third of their pre-epidemic population, the slaughter of whales and walruses now denied the surviving Yupik adequate sustenance. According to Fay, "If remedial food supplies had not been provided by Federal and State governments, the islanders probably would have been afflicted again by starvation and death in 1954-55."

When the walrus were plentiful in the 1800s, they had hauled out in great numbers on beaches. Fay reported that of "numerous coastal hauling grounds that were used on the Siberian coast in the early part of the century, only three remained in use by the mid-1950's." There were just too few Tenastze to guard the walruses. Thanks to hunting restrictions, the walrus rebounded. As populations returned to historical peak abundance, they began returning to former coastal haul-outs. Most recently walruses returned to an Alaskan beach about 140 miles southwest of Barrow. It was the general location that Captain Bernard wanted protected as a walrus preserve, and news of the walruses' return would have certainly caused the good captain to celebrate. But not the global warming advocates. A stampede, most likely provoked by a hunting polar bear, left several trampled walruses. *Although historically tramplings had been associated with great abundance, advocates spun it as proof of deadly CO_2.*

The Huffington Post published the following: "ANCHORAGE, Alaska — Trampling likely killed 131 mostly young walruses forced onto the northwest coast of Alaska by a loss of sea ice, according to a preliminary report released Thursday." "Obviously it's a real tragedy, and it's one we're going to see repeated more and more as the climate warms and the sea ice melts," said Rebecca Noblin, staff attorney at the Center for Biological Diversity (CBD). The CBD had petitioned to list walrus as threatened or endangered because of increased CO_2 levels. The article makes the bold claim, "Were it not for the dramatic decline in the sea ice, the young walruses at Icy Cape most likely would be alive on the ice and not dead on a beach," said WWF

[World Wildlife Fund] biologist Geoff York."

However, by all historical accounts, land haul-outs were very common in a time of abundant sea ice. The lawyers and advocates were ignoring (or ignorant of) Bernard's 1925 lament that *"Thirty or forty years ago in various places along the Alaskan coast walruses were known to haul-out in countless numbers* (emphasis added)."[559] It's also doubtful they had ever read Fay's mid-century accounts in which death by trampling was listed as one of the *"top 3 natural causes of death to walrus calves exceeded only by deaths caused by killer whales and polar bears* (emphasis added)."[560]

Fay's research had compiled numerous reports depicting far greater mortality from trampling. Those deadly events happened when animals either hauled out in panic when pursued by killer whales, or when stampeded by attacking polar bears or humans. For example, in 1975, researchers reported a large number of dead animals during a stampede from a traditional hauling ground at Cape Blossom on Wrangell Island. *The low-flying aircraft of the researchers had caused that stampede.*[560]

In the heavy ice year of 1979, Fay examined the remnants of the greatest trampling tragedy yet recorded. On Punuk and St Lawrence Island, "At least 537 animals died at one haul-out area," and approximately 400 other carcasses washed ashore from other locations. Nearly all of the dead were extremely lean, having less than half as much subcutaneous fat as healthy animals examined in previous years." St Lawrence Island and the Punuk islands lie directly in the migratory path of the walrus' southward journey from their summer feeding grounds in the Chukchi Sea to their wintering areas in the Bering Sea. The tramplings were spread out over both traditional haul-out locations on the Punuk Islands and in "four other locations on St. Lawrence Island where locals claimed they had not been seen in recent memory." A more thorough investigation unearthed abundant old carcasses and bones and laboratory dating techniques revealed those "new" haul-outs had been very active in the early 1900's before hunting pressures decimated their populations.

The Demise of the Atlantic Walrus

All evidence indicates that walruses have always hauled onto land even during the severe ice conditions of the Little Ice Age. It was overhunting that drove walruses from the beaches, and this is clear from historical accounts of the first encounters between walrus and European hunters on the pristine Svalbard archipelago. In archaeologist Robert McGhee's superb book on the Arctic, *The Last Imaginary Place*[631], he devotes an entire chapter to the "rape of Spitsbergen" (Svalbard's largest island) and vividly documents the excesses of European harvests and glimpses of previously untouched Arctic wildlife.

Photo courtesy of US Fish and Wildlife Service. Credit John Sarvis

Svalbard is located about 180 kilometers to the east of Greenland across the Fram Strait. Each year the Arctic winds remove much of the Arctic's sea ice through the Fram Strait, sending ice southward to melt in the northern Atlantic. The Arctic ice piles up on the frigid northern half of Svalbard, in contrast to its ice-free southern half. In March, sea ice has reached its maximum extent and thickness, but the warm nutrient-rich waters can keep Svalbard's south side ice-free. Those nutrient-rich waters once sustained an awe-inspiring profusion of life that has yet to fully recover from overhunting.

Although ancient hunters had reached the Arctic 5000 years ago, they never reached the islands of the Svalbard archipelago. It remained pristine until the Europeans first discovered the islands in the 1500s. In 1596, the Dutch explorer Willem Barents is believed to be the first person to ever set eyes on Svalbard and the Barents Sea now bears his name. Barents wrote about feasting on the eggs laid by the Barnacle goose, which was the biggest scientific news of the times. Until Barents' discovery, the Barnacle goose was the poster child for the theory of spontaneous generation. No European had ever seen a Barnacle goose egg. Yet every winter the Barnacle goose returned from its arctic breeding grounds to become one of the most abundant birds in Europe. It was a devious twist to the old question, "Which came first, the chicken or the egg?" There was no egg. So their knowledge gap was filled with the prevailing bias of the time: the Barnacle goose appeared by spontaneous generation.[631]

Despite Barents' important contribution to scientific thinking, the Arctic showed him no mercy. Sharing the fate of many early explorers, he was trapped by unpredictable winter ice and died while overwintering on an Arctic island. But the news of a stupendous Arctic bounty spread. Eight years after Barents' discovery, the English Muscovy Company set sail to harvest Svalbard's abundant meat and furs. Their ships' logs provide vivid accounts of massive herds of "sea horses" resting on the beaches. From company records, biologists estimate that the Svalbard Archipelago alone supported close to 25,000 walruses before European hunting began. That's thousands more than currently populates the entire Atlantic sector today. By trapping the walrus on the beaches, within just six hours they butchered six to seven hundred walruses, and filled their boat with tusks and hides. But even more

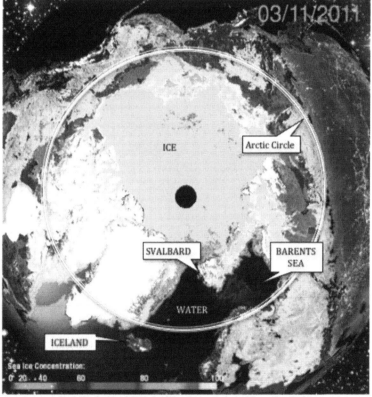

Arctic Sea Ice March 2011. Satellite picture courtesy of Cryosphere Today

valuable were the 11 tons of oil for cosmetics and oil lamps that were highly prized by Europeans battling the frequent bouts of extreme cold that punctuated the ongoing Little Ice Age. Walruses and even polar bear were boiled to render their oil.[631]

The walrus survived the first wave of hunters because Europeans quickly turned their harpoons on a far greater source of oil, Svalbard's whales. The logs from those early walrus hunts spoke of an "endless pool of whales," as did Henry Hudson's during his ill-fated search for the Northwest Passage. After the whales were virtually eliminated by the 1800s, hunters again focused on the walrus; the most vivid description of their hunting techniques were preserved in Sir James Lamont's 1852 *Seasons with the Sea Horses*: "On one venture, after discovering a herd of several thousand walrus reposing on the land, four boats carried 16 men armed with lances. They stalked the shoreline in order to place themselves between the walrus herd and the ocean. As the first wave of stampeding walrus tried to enter the water, they were

Photo courtesy of Dr. James Kelley

killed or injured creating a row of dead bodies inhibiting the escape of the others. With lance or axe in hand, the crews marched forward and descended on the trapped herd, killing the rest. A total of 900 walrus were killed that day."[631]

The hunters also mastered the technique of luring in any walruses that had successfully fled to open waters. Manipulating the walrus' family devotion, hunters captured and tortured a calf. The calf's barking and agonizing grunts pulled on the heartstrings of the fleeing herd. As the entire herd returned to rescue the calf, they entered into harpoon range. Lamont described one harpooned mother that continued to tow their hunting boat while she valiantly carried her calf under her flipper and tusks, desperately trying to shuttle it to safety. Such gallantry prompted Lamont to praise "the wonderful maternal affection displayed by this poor walrus."

Several northern European nations rushed to avail themselves of Spitsbergen's cornucopia of marine life, sending warships to protect the hunters. The frenzied competition led to the destruction of Svalbard's wildlife. Although most wildlife had already been eliminated, the 1920 treaty of Spitsbergen finally ended the tragedy of the commons and the "rape of Spitsbergen". In 1986 when McGhee went to Svalbard to search for any evidence that early Inuit or more ancient Tuniit may have reached the island, he only found evidence of the European overkill. Massive whalebones abounded, and beaches were littered with tusk-less walrus skulls. The birds had returned to the ponds and cliffs, while the reindeer and fox were now more common. But the beaches that once sheltered thousands of walrus were still empty and silent.

Walrus Summer Migration

The notion that walruses only haul-out on land when deprived of ice is a story that would have been laughed at just 30 years ago. Previously it was thought that ice denied walruses access to their hunting grounds. Walrus require shallow seas where they suction the seafloor for shellfish. As late as 1982 scientists stated, *"the maximum absence of ice in the Chukchi Sea beneficially influences the population of the Pacific walrus permitting the animals to use vast feeding grounds in the summer and autumn seasons* (emphasis added)." [561] Walruses do not require sea ice to hunt. Like Gray whales, they are associated with Arctic sea ice because it covers their food supply, and the current patterns of walrus migration support that view.

Unlike most females, thousands of male walruses never follow the receding ice pack but instead migrate southward to ice-free waters of the southern Bering Sea. Around Bristol Bay, Alaska, walruses readily forage up to 130 kilometers from their nearest haul-out site. The walrus' main constraint is the water's depth; they avoid regions where depths exceed 60 meters. Throughout the summer, adult males rest at their land haul-out sites for several days at a time between their offshore foraging trips which last four to ten days."[562] Swimming at normal swim speeds of 10 km/hour, walrus can cover the entire span of most shallow sea shelves in a few days, so there is little need for ice floe transportation. The males that do migrate north generally abandon the sea ice in spring and congregate on land haul-outs along the coasts of Russia and Alaska.[562,563]

Alarmists suggest the increasing use of land haul-outs is a sign of disaster, caused by the loss of sea ice. However all the evidence argues that as walrus populations increase, so does the use of land haul-outs. It is a sign of the walrus' successful recovery. When the Pacific walrus was teetering on the edge of extinction, "no walruses were observed along the Alaska Peninsula", and only about a thousand animals were recorded at Walrus Island in Bristol Bay Alaska.[562] By 1960 both Russia and Alaska had instituted protective measures and within 20 years, walrus populations rebounded to pre-exploitation levels. As the numbers grew, they began to reoccupy traditional land haul-outs. *By 1980, the numbers of walrus hauling out on Walrus Island in the Pribilofs had grown from 3,000 to 12,000.*[562]

The use of land haul-outs still varies annually and (although poorly studied) is likely due to fluctuations in food supply. Massive herds suctioning the sea floor will eventually deplete a local food supply. Furthermore, regime shifts such as the Pacific Decadal Oscillation alter the winds and currents that deliver nutrients. Most likely the productivity of ocean floors also oscillate in approximate 20 year cycles. For example, at Cape Pierce in southern Bristol Bay, more than 12,000 walruses were hauling out on the beaches each summer in the 1980s. Then suddenly most walruses disappeared for over two decades. Recently they have been returning to Cape Pierce and as of 2008, their numbers increased to over 5000.[563]

More curious is the fact that these walruses are not content to just clamber out onto the nearest vacant piece of solid real estate and hunker down in an exhausted heap. The walruses of Cape Pierce appear to enjoy jaunty bouts of adventurous hiking.[564] They also developed a fondness for climbing to the top of grassy plateaus. Unfortunately when they decide to reenter the water and feed, they sometimes charge off on an ill-advised shortcut. Some biologists have suggested that because they are limited by poor eyesight, they are just following their sense of smell and a direct line back to the ocean. Others suggest they are easily spooked by human disturbance or aircraft and stampede in a blind panic. Whatever the reason, between 1994 and 1996 over 150 bulls launched themselves into an undulating swan-dive. Lacking Greg Louganis' grace, they plunged from the cliffs to their deaths 150 feet below. Only a few lucky ones were cushioned by their late brethren's blubber, got a favorable bounce, and continued to the sea. Biologists have now erected a fence, hoping to deter other neer-do-well thrill seekers from taking the same fateful path to the top of the plateau.

The Pacific Walrus is now believed to have recovered fully to its historic population of about 200,000, but surveys have been limited and therefore carry great statistical uncertainty. However in the Atlantic there is no question this subspecies has never recovered from the human quest for blubber and ivory. Large herds had once hauled out on islands and the mainland beaches as far south as Sable Island off the coast of Nova Scotia, Canada. All those southern populations were completely exterminated. The early walrus population along the St. Lawrence River alone has been estimated at over 100,000. In contrast, today the entire Atlantic subspecies is confined to waters further north. No longer migratory, they typically reside in polynya, and their total population is a mere 20,000.[565] With such low numbers, stories of trampling are rare from the Atlantic sector. A beach packed with walruses is evidence of better conservation, not global warming doom.

Successful Bowhead Whale Conservation

The recent loss of ice has improved Arctic productivity by allowing greater blooms of phytoplankton.[519] This bloom has also sustained the recovery of the endangered Bowhead whales. Like the walrus, Bowhead whales are always associated with ice, but are not dependent upon it. The greatest plankton blooms happen as soon as the ice melts, which opens the waters to sunlight. Nutrients are in relatively short supply and quickly consumed by plankton. When plankton die, they quickly sink to darker depths.

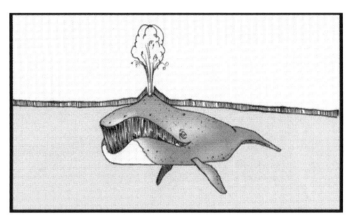

So Bowheads engage in risky beneath-the-ice maneuvers in order to reach those open waters at the "crack of the Arctic dawn". This gives them access to the initial spring flush of concentrated plankton that fills the Arctic polynya. To reach those polynya, Bowheads successfully navigate unreliable ice-choked waters. If an open-water lead freezes over, they can crack open a breathing hole in the new ice. If the winds close the lead with thicker ice, they can press against the fractures with their blowholes and continue to breathe as they migrate. However such derring-do also exposes them to sudden ice entrapment. Recent studies have found that Bowhead whales in the Beaufort Sea may provide 3 to 50% of an individual polar bears' total caloric intake.[566]

Despite their adaptations for navigating ice-clogged waters, the Bowhead have been divided into eastern and western populations by the congested ice within the Canadian Archipelago. Every year both populations follow the retreating ice from the Pacific and the Atlantic into the Arctic Ocean, but neither navigates through the Canadian Archipelago to intermingle or cavort with the other population. The migration barrier is partly caused by the Canadian Archipelago's thick multi-year ice that clogs passageways between the maze of islands. That thick ice also prevents the high plankton productivity***** found elsewhere and thus reduces any incentive for the whales to traverse the Northwest Passage, even though ships have done so for over 60 years. But the Bowheads had done so in the recent past.

Archaeologists have found several fossil whalebones scattered among the islands. This has led to a consensus that there was much less Arctic ice 3,000 to 10,000 years ago. Using carbon dating techniques, they determined that the Bowhead ranged into the Canadian Archipelago between 10,000 and 8,000 years ago. Then after retreating during a cold spell, they once again entered between 5,000 and 3,000 years ago. The most recent excursions into ice-free waters were dated around 1,500 years ago around the Medieval Warm Period.[581,696]

***** Productivity refers to the concentrations of phytoplankton that serve as the foundation of the food chain. Satellites measure productivity by estimating the amount of green chlorophyll

The Bowhead's under-the-ice tactics were well understood by Inuit hunters but not by credentialed scientists, and that lack of knowledge resulted in severe miscalculations of abundance, and management disagreements. However those shortcomings were rectified by community-based management. Community-based management has been evolving as the Inuit have successfully fought for more control of their own resources. In 1999, Canada established the territory of Nunavut, which translates as "our land" in the Inuit language. Nunavut stretches along the Arctic Ocean from the western Ellesmere Island and the western Hudson Bay westward to the eastern edge of the Beaufort Sea. The government policy of Nunavut emphasizes the use of Inuit knowledge—Inuit Qaujimajatuqangit [I can't pronounce that so I just say "IQ"]—for all decisions affecting Nunavut. The Inuit's superior knowledge of the Bowheads highlights why Inuit knowledge must be incorporated into all wildlife management decisions.

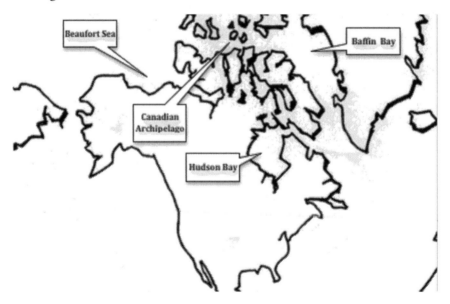

Due to overharvesting through the early 20th century, Bowhead whales were truly on the brink of extinction. In response, the commercial hunting of Bowhead whales along the Canadian Arctic was banned in 1951. Subsistence hunting continued until 1979, but it was restricted under the Cetacean Protection Regulations of the Fisheries Act. After extensive debate improved our understanding of the science, a limited licensed subsistence hunt was eventually renewed in Nunavut in 1996.[906]

Whaling was restricted due to a genuine concern by credentialed scientists whose models had led them to believe that there were far too few Pacific Bowhead. When the Inuit first petitioned to hunt the Bowhead in the 1980s, they argued that the Bowhead population had recovered to sustainable numbers, safely permitting limited subsistence hunting. They insisted the scientists had grossly underrepresented the whale's abundance by the faulty design of their "systematic" surveys. It is not exactly clear how the Inuit counted, but by coalescing the observations of their entire community, they insisted there were three times as many Bowhead as the scientific models had suggested. Unlike the current debate over polar bear management, the future of Bowheads was not clouded by the politics of global warming, mostly because more open water benefits plankton and whales. However, increased subsistence hunting was still not readily accepted.

Many non-Inuit were suspicious that Inuit whalers had simply manufactured a higher population estimate, insinuating the Inuit's estimates were a self-serving calculation driven by their desire to hunt more whales. Off hand comments often portrayed Inuit estimates as mere hunches that lacked written documentation and verifiable dates of their observations. IQ was not considered on par with the calculations of more "objective" credentialed scientists and there were murmurings by some who mocked the idea that "primitive" estimates could ever compete with sophisticated statistics and scientific models.

But scientific surveys frequently suffer from a wide range of biases. Models are often just the best guesses of a small group of scientists that are then translated into numbers and equations. The data that feeds those models are often limited and highly uncertain. In order to achieve statistical significance, surveys must be repeated at the same place during the same time of season. Although this allows a statistical comparison from one year to the next, a small sample from a strictly defined area fails to capture the reality of highly migratory populations. Movements of arctic populations vary with the winds and currents, and animals will relocate as needed. In a world of virtual statistics, the movement in and out of any given study area can be easily misinterpreted as a population decrease or increase. For example, in 2009 scientists could not locate a herd of 270,000 caribou. It was hard to imagine how so many animals could just disappear, and scientists suggested they had been killed by global warming. Two years later the herd was rediscovered in an unexpected location.[932]

In the 1970s, during the Bowhead's spring migration, scientists had perched on hilltops, or pressure ridges in the ice, and counted whales as they migrated north through the open leads along the north coast of Alaska. They erroneously assumed that when the winds changed and ice temporarily closed those leads, the whales stopped migrating. When the winds shifted and the leads reopened, the count continued. Based on that assumption, the scientists modeled that only 2000-3000 Bowhead whales existed and thus were still endangered.

The Inuit whalers had always ventured much further out on the ice. Their IQ developed from a much greater array of observations and opinions from a widespread community whose very survival depended on their collective knowledge. IQ argued that when open leads closed, the whale migration still continued. The swirling pack ice always generates chaotic but sufficient springtime cracks and leads, which provide whales enough opportunities to breathe. The whales were not restricted to the large open leads along the coast that credentialed scientists had been monitoring. The Inuit whalers argued that despite their systematic scientific approach, researchers were blind to more than half of the migrating whales.

After several friendly discussions between "credentialed scientists" and the Inuit "citizen scientists", scientists from Cornell's Macaulay Library of Natural Sounds employed undersea acoustics to estimate populations, while aerial surveys were extended further offshore. Lo and behold, these new survey methods detected many more "hidden" whales. The new estimates suggested there were as many as three times more Pacific Bowhead whales than had been previously calculated, and that the population ranged between 6000 and 8000. After subsistence whaling was allowed, the Bowhead population has continued to increase. As of 2001 the International Whaling Commission estimated a population of 10,500 whales, growing at a net rate of about 3.2% per year.

Such collaboration between "credentialed scientists" and whaling "citizen scientists" not only improved our scientific knowledge of Bowheads, it clearly illustrated that by bringing all the stakeholders together, a more complete knowledge unfolds. New models emerged based on all observations, which were then scientifically tested by further observation. The whalers brought more eyes, increased observing time, and a hunter's wisdom to the discussion. Their observations corrected the false presumptions built into the early computer models. As all computer modelers recognize, limited knowledge is the most deadly bug: GIGO – garbage in, garbage out.

The new scientific understanding of Bowhead whale migration was only possible because all sides sat down in civil debate. The Inuit call this "kappiananngittuq" or "a safe (or non-scary) place" where all matters can be discussed. (I can't pronounce that word either.) Unfortunately, it is a lesson not eagerly embraced when science becomes politicized. Power struggles and adversarial lawsuits supersede the quest for more complete knowledge. Although most Inuit also claim it is "the time of the most polar bears", the Inuit's' voices go unheeded (see Chapter 14). Likewise in the more "civilized" lands south of the Arctic, most advocate scientists refuse to sit down with any skeptics in public debate.

Reminiscent of cold war politics, advocate climate scientists have erected a "CO_2 Curtain" to insulate their views, and refuse to debate with the broader population. One of the most recent examples occurred on a 2013 John Stossel show. Stossel sought a scientific debate between CO_2 advocates and skeptical scientists. Dr. Roy Spencer, the U.S. Science Team leader for the Advanced Microwave Scanning Radiometer on NASA's Aqua satellite, was the skeptical scientist. However, advocate scientists "circled the wagons" and refused to debate Spencer face to face. Advocates like Kevin Trenberth have consistently advised against debating skeptics so that no credence is given to alternative viewpoints.[478]

In contrast to demeaning comments against Dr. Spencer in the media wars, behind closed doors climate scientists had expressed tremendous respect for Spencer's integrity. When advocates criticized an earlier paper by Spencer and pointed out possible flaws in his interpretation of the satellite data, in the spirit of "kappiananngittuq" Spencer listened and subsequently corrected those errors. In a Climategate email, Dr. Thomas Peterson from the National Climatic Data Center observed the process and wrote to climatologist Dr. Phil Jones at the University of East Anglia, "I must say that the way they [skeptical scientists Dr. Roy Spencer and Dr. John Christy] reacted to this news and the plans they drew up to address it reflects very well on their character and scientific integrity."

Despite Spencer's acknowledged integrity, climate modeler Gavin Schmidt was the only advocate who agreed to appear on the Stossel show, but only if there was no face-to-face debate with Spencer. Perhaps that was because Schmidt had also published failed predictions that the Arctic Oscillation would likely remain positive due to rising CO_2 levels,[362] or because Schmidt expressed views that the Inuit are in denial.[933] Whatever the reason, Spencer had to leave the room so Schmidt could present his views without being challenged. Schmidt then departed before Spencer could return. Such sophomoric antics only belittle the scientific process.

By refusing to enter a "climate kappiananngittuq", self-serving advocate scientists avoid addressing contradictory observations and alternative interpretations that might expose the many uncertainties and move climate science forward. They also alienate half of the earth's stakeholders and politicize the debate. Abraham Lincoln wisely assembled a "team of rivals" with widely contrasting views to guide our country through its most divided and hostile times. Similarly our government would be wise to create a climate kappiananngittuq where all rival stakeholders can respectfully debate face to face. The debates can be posted to the internet to increase accessibility, and a global community of truth checkers can expose any falsehoods. Public debates in the spirit of a climate kappiananngittuq would promote confidence in the real science and expose any deceptions by either side. As the Inuit have demonstrated, credentials and peer-reviewed publications never guarantee the accuracy of a scientific interpretation. It takes a whole village.

14

Inuit and Illusions in the Time of the Most Polar Bear

"No known environmental or other factors are currently posing a significant or immediate threat to polar bears overall." [647]

Daniel Shewchuk, Nunavut's Minister of Environment, 2010

There is a polar bear paradox. Most Inuit argue, "it is the time of the most polar bear."[619] CO_2 advocates argue that polar bears are endangered.[584] In 2010 Nunavut's Minister of Environment Daniel Shewchuk wrote, "Inuit hunters have a close relationship with the land and wildlife. They have observed that the overall population of polar bears in Nunavut is not declining as some suggest, but rather is thriving. No known environmental or other factors are currently posing a significant or immediate threat to polar bears overall. Furthermore, Inuit knowledge and science corroborate that the species can and will adapt to changing and severe climatic conditions, as it has done for centuries."[647]

Image Courtesy www.naturespicsonline.com

In contrast, Kassie Siegel, staff attorney for the Center for Biological Diversity (CBD) who sued the United States to list the polar bear as endangered wrote, "The Arctic sea ice melt is a disaster for the polar bears…They are dependent on the Arctic sea ice for all of their essential behaviors, and as the ice melts and global warming transforms the Arctic, polar bears are starving, drowning, even resorting to cannibalism because they don't have access to their usual food sources." In 2008, Lawrence McGinty of Independent Television News interviewed polar bear expert Andrew Derocher. Derocher is the chairman of the IUCN's Polar Bear Specialist Group (PBSG) and he warned the PBS audience that global warming was leading polar bears to extinction. He predicted, "It's clear from the research that's been done by myself and colleagues around the world that we're projecting that, by the middle of this century, two-thirds of the polar bears will be gone from their current populations".

However, the claims of the CBD and Derocher, whose fame and fortune have been intimately tied to climate alarm, are built on several illusions. The Inuit maintain that the bears are not starving, they are not drowning, and any cannibalism is just a family tradition. They perceive the hyped anecdotes of cannibalism and the "myth of the drowning bears" as one more attempt to mislead international power brokers and usurp the Inuit's local control. After reading the evidence in the next two chapters, I believe you will agree with the Inuit.

Declining Population Illusions

"Models that predict rapid increases or decreases in population size would not mirror reality" [593]

PBSG expert Steve Amstrup

When polar bear expert Mitch Taylor and the Canadian Wildlife Service surveyed populations in the Baffin Bay region (west of Greenland) from 1983-1989, they estimated there were only 300 to 600 bears. The Inuit hunters protested that his estimate was much too low, and that the resulting quota was unfair. So Taylor and Inuit hunters sat together in "kappiananngittuq" (see Chapter 13) to discuss the problem. The Inuit pointed out that his studies had been performed during a time and in a place that overlooked a large proportion of the population. Thus Taylor's model had incorrectly extrapolated a smaller population.

To Taylor's credit, he redesigned his survey based on the hunters' recommendations. After further observation and analyses, he raised the population estimate to 2074 bears. Although Taylor and the Inuit had increased the estimate of the Baffin Bay population to over 2000, Taylor wrote that the increased abundance did not reflect a jump in the population, but was simply a better estimate based on a better study design. He believed "the population was stable or slightly increasing."[618]

It is worth noting that while Taylor gives the Inuit hunters the credit for redesigning the study, Derocher's PBSG website doesn't. The website simply suggests the erroneous estimate was realized when "work in the early 1990s showed that an unknown proportion of the subpopulation is typically offshore during the spring." Later, PBSG scientists suspected there was excessive hunting by neighboring Greenlanders. So after incorporating the higher rates of suspected human harvest into the model, the current population estimate was lowered to about 1600 bears. Although the drop in numbers was also due to a more inclusive model, the PBSG website tags the Baffin Bay population with a big red "Declining" designation, and warming advocates erroneously point to "declining" Baffin Bay bears as another casualty of CO_2.

Polar bear estimates are often more political than scientific. Overall Taylor agrees with the Inuit, writing, "Generally, polar bears currently appear to be abundant as, or more abundant, as they have ever been in modern times."[818] Such beliefs drew the ire of the advocates, so Derocher barred Taylor from recent PBSG meetings because, as he reportedly said, "it was the position you've taken on global warming that brought opposition."[620]

NASA climate modeler Gavin Schmidt, a moderator for Michael Mann's RealClimate website, had been invited along with Martha Stewart to promote Derocher's view that global warming is killing polar bears. After returning Schmidt gave a lunchtime seminar in his NASA office, which he posted to YouTube.[933] But it was clear Schmidt was more interested in promoting global warming theory than protecting polar bears. He began by comparing a picture of a bark beetle and then a polar bear asking his audience, "Which would make a better icon for global warming?" When asked about the perceptions of the native peoples, he dismissed the Inuit's assertion of thriving bears by suggesting they were in "heavy denial."

When the United States listed polar bears as a "threatened" species, many people were suspicious because by all accounts the bear populations had been growing wherever prudent hunting quotas were installed. Anyone familiar with the scientific literature would agree that polar bears are as abundant as they have ever been and that conclusion is documented below.

-The *Committee on the Status of Endangered Wildlife in Canada* listed Canada's polar bears only as a species of "special concern". In making that designation they reported that population models had projected that only 4 of 13 subpopulations (approximately 28% of 15,500 polar bears in Canada) have a high risk of declining in the next 36 years. Although some declines in Western Hudson Bay and Southern Beaufort Sea were attributed to climate change, *most declines were attributed to unsustainable harvest* in Kane Basin and Baffin Bay. In contrast, seven subpopulations *(43% of the total population) are projected to be stable or increasing*. Trends could not be projected for two subpopulations (29% of the total population).[609]

- Derocher's PBSG website designates the Davis Strait population as "declining". However based on 1980 estimates of 900 bears, the population has more than doubled. By 1993 that estimate rose to 1400 and by 2007 the estimate stands at about 2150 bears.[612] If you click on the comments to find the rationale for listing them as "declining" you would find only empty speculation: "New estimates of natural survival and current harvest suggest the population *may begin to decline*. Scientific and local knowledge suggest the population has significantly *increased* in the past."

- PBSG expert Oystein Wiig studied bears of Svalbard, and in 1998 published: "The population was totally protected in 1973 and probably *doubled in size* from 1970 to 1980"[611]

- The Fox Basin encompasses the northern end of the Hudson Bay. In 1996 studies estimated the bear population to be 2119 and then raised to 2300 bears in 2004.[614] The results from a recent aerial survey published in 2012 now estimate that the Fox Basin embraces about 2580 bears.[613] Instead of listing this population as increasing, or at least stable, Derocher's PBSG "hid" their thriving population with an odd "data deficient" designation.

- Only 333 bears were believed to inhabit the Gulf of Boothia in 1984 but the numbers quadrupled by 2000. Estimates of 900 were established in the 1990s and "following the completion of a mark-recapture inventory in spring 2000, the subpopulation was raised to 1523 ± 285 bears"[615]. Although those studies would support the Inuit claims of increasing bears, the PBSG designated this population as "Stable."

- The Lancaster Sound subpopulation was estimated at 2541 ± 391 based on an analysis of both historical and current mark-recapture data in 1997. The PBSG writes that population is considerably larger than the previous estimate of 1675.[616] However they oddly listed this population as declining.

- The Western Hudson Bay population is one of only two populations that the *Committee on the Status of Endangered Wildlife in Canada* referenced as declining possibly due to climate change. PBSG expert Ian Stirling had published a paper in 1999 calculating that the population had grown from about 500 bears in 1981 to about 1100 bears in 1997.[590] Although the western Hudson Bay is the best-studied population in the world, changing survey methodologies made those statistical estimates highly uncertain, prompting Derocher to warn "models may not prove applicable to other polar bear populations unless large and unbiased samples are obtained." Still, Derocher also estimated this region held about 1000 bears in 1995 and believed "the population had been lower during the 1960s".[575] The Canadian Wildlife Service's model later suggested that the number of bears had dropped from about 1100 in 1994 to about 950 in 2004. They predicted the number of bears would continue to drop to as low as 600 in the next 15 years due to global warming. However the latest aerial survey by the Nunavut government, "Western Hudson Bay Bear Aerial Surveys, 2011" *estimated that the population now stands at over 1000 bears.*[572] Instead of celebrating the good news, Derocher's PBSG website still lists these bears as declining.

- The only other population that is believed to be declining with a possible connection to climate change is the South Beaufort Sea polar bears. However, in 2001 PBSG expert Steven Amstrup had published that the Southern Beaufort Sea population had increased from approximately 500 females in 1967 to over 1000 in 1998. Assuming females represented half the total, Amstrup believed the total population likely exceeded 2000 bears. However for the purpose of setting safe hunting quotas he decided to be conservative and officially designated the population at 1800 bears.[593]

Derocher, Ian Stirling, and Steven Amstrup are the three leading advocates that argue polar bears are suffering from global warming. In a very strange turn of events, Amstrup suddenly ignored his South Beaufort Sea research where the bear population had doubled. In order to counter the perception of a growing polar bear population, he wrote, "it is important to emphasize here that despite an absence of scientific information regarding worldwide population trends over the past several decades, many in the general press have claimed that polar bear populations worldwide have grown. *Dykstra (2008) thoroughly examined these media accounts, and verified that they have no scientifically established basis* (emphasis added)." [591]

Amstrup's own published science stood in stark contrast to his claim that Dykstra had '*verified that there was no scientific basis*' for a growing population. Curiouser and curiouser, Dykstra was just a journalist carrying out a modern version of the ol'shillin-the-audience trick. "Dykstra's proof" was based on interviews with none other than Amstrup and Derocher. Amstrup *verified* his claim of *no scientific basis* based on Dykstra's interview with Amstrup. This is not the way to build trust in the experts.

From 2006-10 Amstrup co-authored several papers from a single study of South Beaufort Sea bears suggesting that the population had suddenly declined and was in danger of extinction. The highly questionable results again contradicted Amstrup's earlier conclusions.[593] Due to several troubling inconsistencies, the South Beaufort Sea bear population is examined in more detail in later sections of this chapter.

The City Dump Illusion

"In the year of 2005 the dumped closed. This resulted in a significant reduction in the number of polar bears handled each season." [621]

Daryll Hedman, Manitoba Conservation

In 2005, the Inuit raised their hunting quotas for bears around the western Hudson Bay because their community had observed more bears in more places than ever before. So PBSG's Ian Stirling from the Canadian Wildlife Service and NASA climate scientist Claire Parkinson teamed up to rebut the Inuit interpretation in a 2006 paper. Unfortunately their opening tactic was to marginalize Inuit IQ (also known as TEK, Traditional Ecological Knowledge) as unscientific, writing, "For the majority of populations in which the quotas were increased, the estimates of population size, and the sustainable quotas from them, were determined on the basis of *scientific studies* (mark-recapture, survival rates, and reproductive rates). *However, in four populations—Western Hudson Bay, Foxe Basin, Baffin Bay, and Davis Strait — Inuit traditional knowledge was the primary information source that influenced the quota increase* (emphasis added)." [586]

Their paper then continued to emphasize supposed "shortcomings" in the Inuit's method for estimating wildlife and implied that because the Inuit didn't publish or write down their results, it invalidated their observations. "Unfortunately, few hunters or other residents in Nunavut have documented the actual numbers of bears they have seen over time, the dates or locations of their sightings, or the approximate age and sex composition of bears perceived as problems. Nor do we have other information that could be evaluated independently, such as the physical condition or fatness of problem bears killed or the number of trips to the same areas during which no or few bears were seen."[586] Then after briefly giving lip service to Inuit IQ and acknowledging it had been generally proven accurate, they argued that Inuit had been fooled by an illusion. Stirling and Parkinson argued, "the earlier loss of sea ice was forcing more bears from the ice and into villages." Bear populations hadn't really increased, the Inuit were just encountering more bears because global warming had deprived the bears of critical sea ice habitat.

Stirling and Parkinson then presented data showing that an increase in problem bears in Churchill correlated with a trend in less summer sea ice. They predicted, "If the open water period becomes progressively longer due to earlier sea ice break-up and later ice formation, we anticipate further changes in distribution, behaviour, and condition of the bears, leading to an increase in human-bear conflicts."[586] But their prediction failed after 2004.

In contrast, the Inuit argued that increase in problem bears in Churchill had been caused by a growing tourist industry and Churchill's growing city dump. Close the dump and the human-bear conflicts would decrease even if there was less sea ice. Near our research station in Sierra City, California, we experienced a similar problem with black bears that was caused by the unrestricted access to our local dump. When dump access was eventually closed, the bear problem virtually disappeared. Likewise as the dump theory had predicted, when the Churchill dump closed in 2005, the number of troublesome bears plummeted.

Daryll Hedman who heads the Polar Bear Alert Program in Churchill reported that before the town dump was closed in 2005, the average number of problem bears handled was 80 a year. The highest number of problem bears in one season was 176 in 2003. After the dumped closed, the number of problem bears that needed handling plummeted. By 2011, the average number of problem bears was just 50 per season despite less summer sea ice and a growing bear population.[621] However advocates have repeated their scenario that shrinking ice is causing increased human-bear conflicts,[569,584] but all their graphs stop in 2004 without ever incorporating the new data. Nearly a decade later to support his catastrophic views, in 2013 Derocher again used only pre-2005 zombie data to maintain the illusion that global warming had been driving bears into town, not the dump.[583.]

The Cannibalism Illusion

"Generally, polar bears currently appear to be abundant as, or more abundant, as they have ever been in modern times."[818]

Dr. Mitchell Taylor, Department of the Environment, Government of Nunavut

Although PBSG advocates repeatedly denigrate Inuit knowledge as anecdotal evidence,[622] to counter the growing evidence of more abundant bears, Derocher and his ilk have retreated to relying on nothing but anecdotal evidence, like cannibalism.[584] Previously most PBSG experts thought cannibalism increased when the density of bears increased. In 1995, PBSG expert Steve Amstrup wrote, "We have also observed that larger bears often chase smaller bears away from kills, and sometimes even kill them" and then suggested that male polar bears may regulate the population by eating younger bears. This was supported by numerous anecdotal reports by Inuit who regularly observed large males eating smaller bears, and numerous other reports.[592] Likewise in 1999, Derocher reported 2 observations of cannibalism on Svalbard: "In the first, an adult male killed three young cubs at a den site and consumed one of them. In the second, an adult male actively pursued, killed, and consumed a dependent yearling" He too suggested that when the population reached its carrying capacity after recovery from overhunting, cannibalism in Svalbard became more common.[603]

Nansen had published observations of cannibalism in 1904, long before global warming filtered our perceptions. In 1985 Mitch Taylor published a compilation of over 20 scientific reports of cannibalism between 1970 and 1982.[617] Near the western edge of the Beaufort Sea, Taylor reported a cub decapitated by a large male, and another male killing an unprotected yearling after his mother had been drugged and immobilized by researchers. In 1984, a 23-year old male was observed eating a 17-year old female. Tracks in the snow revealed the male stalked and killed the female. In 1973, the two ungrateful 2-year-old cubs of a drug-immobilized mother took advantage of her temporary state of unconsciousness and ate her! There were two other reports of bears eating their drug-immobilized brethren.

Scientists had also suggested that cannibalism was the best explanation for the high levels of the trichinosis parasite in polar bears. Usually the parasite spreads when a predator eats infected meat, but the bears' main prey, the ringed seals, have extremely low levels of the trichinosis parasite. So the high rate of trichinosis in polar bears was attributed to polar bear cannibalism. Furthermore the scientific consensus has always suggested that females with cubs and smaller sub-adults avoid areas inhabited by large males in order to minimize cannibalism.

Inuit have always insisted that the bear's cannibalistic behavior hasn't changed for millennia. Whether or not the bears are overcrowded, or if they experience years of heavy ice or years of open water, big bears simply eat smaller bears. Sara Nelson interviewed Nunavut leaders in Rankin Inlet to the north of Churchill and they lamented, "it is wrong to connect the bears' behavior with starvation". Inuit Association president Jose Kusugak didn't mince his words, "It makes the south – southern people – look so ignorant. A male polar bear eating a cub becomes a big story and they try to marry it with climate change and so on, it becomes absurd when it's a normal, normal occurrence."[633]

The sudden cannibalism hype has raised questions regarding the effects of global warming politics on the PBSG's integrity. For example, in addition to reporting that he had observed large male bears chasing and sometime eating smaller bears, Amstrup also reported finding a female who had been killed and eaten by a large male and another death caused by two fighting males.[592] But those published observations were suspiciously "forgotten" as Amstrup later hyped "*unprecedented*" cannibalism caused by global warming. He now wrote, "During 24 years of research on polar bears in the southern Beaufort Sea region of northern Alaska and 34 years in northwestern Canada, we have *not seen other incidents* of polar bears stalking, killing, and eating other polar bears. We hypothesize that nutritional stresses related to the longer ice-free seasons that have occurred in the Beaufort Sea in recent years may have led to the cannibalism incidents we observed in 2004."[607]

Later Amstrup also contradicted his nutritional-stress-from-less-sea-ice story. He co-authored another paper that had measured the body condition of bears along the South Beaufort Sea where the hyped *unprecedented* cannibalistic remains were observed. There was no nutritional stress. There was no trend in the body condition of adult males and despite the added strain of motherhood, the females' body condition had improved.[573]

Nonetheless, cannibalism headlines suddenly appeared everywhere like CNN's "*Polar bears resort to cannibalism as Arctic ice shrinks*." Amstrup's cannibalism anecdote was repeated again and again in the PBSG's 2009 proceedings and they warned of increasing cannibalism in the future. In the CBD's law suit and congressional testimony, they too argued, "bears are starving, drowning, even resorting to cannibalism". But neither our carbon footprint nor shrinking sea ice will ever control cannibalism. As the Inuit understand, cannibalism is simply a way of life for all bears.

For example in a 2007 study, researchers had reported several cases of cannibalism writing, "Infanticide cases that resulted in a complete litter loss occurred in or near dens, and in 2 of 3 instances the mother was also killed and thus was not available for mating. One of the sites showed evidence of fighting and the female likely was killed while defending the cub." "Although there likely are multiple factors contributing to infanticide, it seems reasonable to assume that an increased density of bears increased encounters."[623]

Despite the fact that this observed uptick in cannibalism had occurred simultaneously with the recent loss of Arctic sea ice, this was a study of black bears in Ocala, Florida. As in the Arctic, hunting restrictions had led to an increased bear density, which increased the chance of bears encountering one another. The greatest cause of cub mortality was infanticide. The Florida cubs had a 46% chance of surviving their first nine months of life and adult bears caused nearly one-third of those deaths. Likewise another black bear study in Arizona found that 50% of the deaths were due to cannibalism.[628] Indeed there are numerous cannibalism accounts for all three species of North American bears.

If cub survival is dependent on the degree of cannibalism, then cannibalism in the Arctic may actually be less common than elsewhere. According to data from the *Committee on the Status of Endangered Wildlife in Canada*, cub survival for Canada's populations averaged 60%,[609] compared to 46% for Florida's black bears. Likewise in the same paper, which PBSG expert Stirling had theorized that the earlier breakup of Hudson Bay's sea ice was causing a population decline, Stirling also reported that cub survival had increased from ~45% in 1990 to over 70% in 1997. Polar bear cub survival in western Hudson Bay averages 71%[609] which is comparable to black bear cub survival of 73% in Shenandoah National Park[626] and 62% in Great Smoky Mountains National Park,[625] where bears are fully protected.

Any reports of increased polar bear cannibalism is likely due to better conservation. Before stricter hunting regulations were imposed, trophy hunters had sought the biggest, baddest bears that a bush pilot could find. As a result, the biggest males rapidly disappeared from the population. Just after the period of heavy trophy hunting ended between 1970 and 1973 the oldest harvested bear "was only 11 years old, and the next oldest bears were both 8 years old."[624] By the late 1970s, the proportion of harvested bears 10 years of age or older had increased to 20-30% for males. This increase in older male bears alone, no matter what the environmental conditions, would increase the probability of cannibalism.

The Declining Body Condition Illusion

"Weight gains experienced by pregnant bears during spring hyperphagia can be large. Solitary, and presumed pregnant, females in summer were often obese to the point of inhibiting locomotion." [627]

Dr. M. A. Ramsay, University of Alberta

Virtually every claim that less summer ice has been detrimental to the polar bears' body condition, hinges on a 1999 study by PBSG's Ian Stirling in the western Hudson Bay. He reported that the Body Condition Index (henceforth BCI) for adult males and females had been steadily declining (Figure 45).[590] However that decline stopped after 1997. As would be expected from a population affected by cycles in prey abundance, the polar bears' condition undulates. Since 1997 the BCI improved but Stirling and other PBSG experts have kept this contrary data "off the books." I accidentally discovered the unpublished data presented in Figure 45 when viewing a presentation given to the Inuit.[820].

Any correlation between Hudson Bay sea ice and polar bears' condition has been fleeting. Sea ice was increasing from 1980 to 1990, yet those years correlated with the largest drop in their BCI.[590,634] Furthermore data before 1987 are problematic so researchers have ignored Hudson Bay population estimates before 1987, stating estimates were biased by incomplete sampling. (If pre-1987 data is used, then the population had clearly doubled since 1981.[590]) So assuming that incomplete sampling had also biased the BCI estimates prior to 1987, I have shaded the those years in Figure 45. Since 1985 there is no declining trend for body condition. However no matter what starting data is chosen, since 1997 BCI has improved. It is disingenuous for Stirling and Parkinson to discredit Inuit IQ for the lack of published data, and then refuse to publish their own contradictory evidence. This disconcerting tactic of not publishing all available evidence was used for Parmesan's butterflies (see Chapters 2 and 6) and Beever's pika (see Chapter 10).

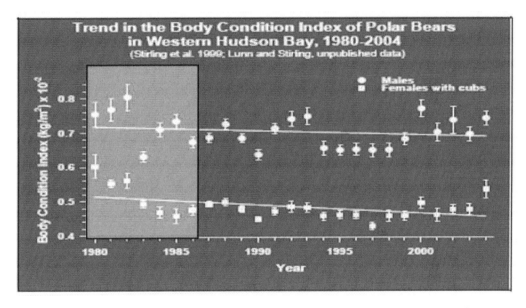

Figure 45. *From "Management consultations for the Western Hudson Bay (WH) polar bear population,"[582] Masking of first 7 years added for this book.*

Determining the condition of a polar bear population is complex. Individual weights depend on the bear's age and the time of year when measurements are taken. One adaptation to a temporary or unreliable food supply is the ability to rapidly store fat during times of plenty. Unconstrained by social etiquette, polar bears indulge in binge eating, or hyperphagia. During a period of just two months from late March through May, most polar bears can triple their weight by feasting on baby Ringed seals (see Chapter 15). Weight gains experienced by pregnant bears during spring hyperphagia can be so large, females in summer are often obese to the point of inhibiting locomotion. Researchers reported that one 17-year-old female with three cubs-of-the-year was handled in November 1983 when she weighed just 218 lbs. The following July, she was without cubs, probably pregnant, and weighed 903 lbs, a four-fold weight change in just eight months.[627] However her gain may have been even greater. All bears lose weight during the winter season of heavy ice; she likely continued to lose weight from November until March or April when the first seal pups appeared.

Estimating body condition is biased by many factors. Primarily, unequal proportions of pregnant females skew the data. Furthermore as bears get older they get bigger and heavier. Averaging weights is meaningless unless the size of the bear is also considered. So to offset the effects of size on weight, polar bears researchers normally use a Body Condition Index. The BCI divides the weight by a measurement derived from the bear's length. Inappropriately, in their rebuttal of the Inuit, instead of reporting the improved body condition of all bears,[586] Stirling and Parkinson abandoned body condition altogether to cherry-pick a more agreeable but less reliable statistic. They used only the chimeric weights of lone females.

Elsewhere, advocates also buried improving body conditions to emphasize declines. The United States Geological Survey's (USGS) study of bears in the Beaufort Sea population warned of impending polar bear extinction by the end of the century. From 2001 to 2003, bears had enjoyed a very high year-to-year survival rate ranging from 92% to 99%, which researchers admitted would increase the population.[601] However for just the years 2004 and 2005, they estimated the survival rates had suddenly dropped as low as 77%, and if that 77% rate persisted, they argued the bears would perish. Typically, such a rapid drop in the survival rate "does not mirror reality."[593] It meant that over 400 bears along the South Beaufort Sea had died each year from starvation. However there was no such evidence of a mass die-off or any starvation.

To push the idea that recent ice loss had caused nutritional stress, Amstrup and his co-authors highlighted cherry-picked statistics to suggest bears were starving. In the abstract they wrote, "Declines in mass and BCI of sub-adult males, declines in growth of males and females, and declines in cub recruitment suggest that polar bears of the Southern Beaufort Sea have experienced a declining trend in nutritional status."[602]

However sub-adult males comprised a mere 5% of all measured bears. The abstract failed to mention that the body condition for 95% of all the other bears, both adult males and females, sub-adult females as well as all cubs, showed no signs of nutritional stress. *In contrast, adult females represented about 34% of all captures, and despite being under the most stress due to an eight-month fast while giving birth and nursing their cubs, their body condition had improved.* To read this good news you had to search the results section: "There was no trend in mass of adult females during the study, but the mean BCI of females increased over time". They also wrote there was "no trend in mass or BCI of adult males over time." Likewise, "There was no trend in mean BCI of sub-adult females over time," and "there was no trend in the mass of the cubs."[602] So why did these experts focus on just 5% of the population?

Their abstract also implied "a decline in cub recruitment" to support their model's uncharacteristic dive in survival rates. But that too was an illusion. Recruitment compares the number of cubs in the spring with the number of cubs in the fall. Their observed results found that the number of cubs per female had increased between 1982 and 2006 during the spring. This would be expected. When the female BCI increases, they usually produce more cubs.[638,639] However Amstrup and his coauthors argued there was a decline in cubs during the fall, and thus a decline in recruitment. *However they had not surveyed in the fall since 2001.*[602] They were again using zombie data.

They also introduced a new measure of the bears' "condition". Averaging the length of all adults, they had detected males were 3.4 millimeters shorter each year, and argued the bears were suffering "declines in growth." This is literally splitting hairs. The thickness of the fur or variations in the length of the tail cause far bigger differences in length. In fact the length of the tail was not an actual measurement but had to be modeled due to inconsistent measurements techniques. Furthermore, there was a high level of transiency, and bears in different regions have significantly different measurements.[596] Despite tremendous ambiguities, those few millimeters became their "proof" that polar bears had suffered from rising CO_2 levels.

The Illusion of Drowning Bears

"bears that were sick sought a firm substrate on which to rest and ultimately die." [592]

PBSG expert Steve Amstrup

In his 2008 paper, "Polar Bear Conservation in Canada: Defining the Policy Problems," Douglas Clark discusses how the *"myth of the drowning polar bears"* has been used to disenfranchise the Inuit. Polar bears are "not only indicators of climate change impacts, but also powerful symbols for mobilizing public interest and pressuring governments to act on climate change".[635] The myth fortuitously appeared in 2006, as anecdotal evidence to support the USGS model that Beaufort Sea polar bears had suffered unprecedented mortality.

A researcher flying over the South Beaufort Sea surveying Bowhead whales reported seeing four (maybe three) *floating* bears. With the help of Andrew Derocher they crafted the floating bears into a fanciful tale that helped support his catastrophic theories,[598] and published, "Observations of Mortality associated with Extended Open Water Swimming by Polar Bears in the Alaskan Beaufort Sea." Before the days of advocacy science when more rigorous examination was demanded, the editors of peer-reviewed journals would never have allowed such an assumptive title. The cause of death was unknown and the bear carcasses were never collected or examined.

Stating that the bears had been swimming was pure speculation as was any assumed direction. The only reliable fact we can possibly deduce from their report was that the floating bears were too fat to sink. Yet these unexamined floating bears have been championed ad nauseum as martyrs of global warming. Amstrup, Derocher and Stirling coauthored papers that not only repeat the myth of the drowning bears, but later encouraged a more untestable hypotheses arguing that when researchers cannot find a radio collar it likely means the bears drowned due to global warming.[584,668] Untestable hypotheses are simply not science.

Why were four floating bears so readily raised to the level of scientific evidence? The advocates' model suggested survival dropped to 77% in the year 2004, and that required 400 yet-to-be-found, starved-to-death bears. In contrast, the body condition of most Southern Beaufort bears had been stable or improving. So to convince the public and the courts that bears were endangered, the USGS scientists wrote "several recently observed mortalities were directly related to sea ice retreat, or appeared related to changes in food availability that *may be* associated with sea ice retreat. In autumn of 2004, four polar bears were observed to have drowned while attempting to swim between shore and the distant pack ice."[573] This isn't merely misleading; it is outright fabrication. No one observed those bears swimming anywhere or knows whether they drowned. In contrast, the only confirmed observations of a bear actually drowning are from 2007, when two bears fell into water and drowned after being drugged by researchers.[630] And suggesting starving bears were swimming out to sea contradicts well known behavior. At that time of year most bears are typically swimming towards the coast.

In 1995, Amstrup tracked all his radio-collared bears to determine why they had died. Although bears are exceptionally strong swimmers, they are known not to swim out to sea when weak with hunger. Amstrup reported that *"bears that were sick sought a firm substrate on which to rest and ultimately die* (emphasis added)."[592] Furthermore as summer sea-ice declines, an increasing proportion of the Southern Beaufort Sea bears come on land during the autumn open-water period. Their return to the coast parallels the migration of the ringed seal. The seals return to the coast after spending the summer offshore in the open ocean. As the sun disappears following the September equinox, coastal ice will form rapidly, so the seals must create their winter breathing holes before the ice thickens.

There is a more likely scenario for the floating bears. September is the height of the whaling season, and whalers are often forced to shoot a few bears in defense of life and property when bears overrun their whale flensing station. Those bears often fall into the water and are carried out to sea. Although the advocates had speculated the bears had drowned "while attempting to swim between shore and the distant pack ice," just the opposite was likely occurring. Other bears in that region were all swimming towards the whale carcasses. Over 80% of all bears surveyed in September in the Beaufort Sea were within nine miles of a whale carcass. Accordingly in the mythical drowning paper, live swimming bears as well as two dead floating bears were found very close to Barter Island.[598] The town of Kaktovik on Barter Island is the traditional whaling center of that region. The carcasses on Barter Island draw swarms of polar bears. Over "68 % of all polar bears observed on the Beaufort Sea coast occurred at Barter Island alone."[637] This was confirmed by another study reporting that the "majority (73%) of polar bears observed in 2000-04 were located within 12 km of Barter Island."[636]

There have been previous reports that whalers had been forced to kill multiple bears competing for their whale. Since 1995, any bear killed in self-defense would count against a village's quota, and thus there may be an incentive not to report such a kill. With abundant whale meat, there is no need to take a polar bear for subsistence. The Inuit prefer to use their allotted bear quota to bring outsiders into their village for a guided hunt which is far more valuable and often provides the only source of money that allows trade with the rest of the world.

The incessantly repeated anecdote of the drowning bear exposes the hypocrisy of a few PBSG experts. Martyn Obbard wrote "that one of the difficulties of integrating TK [Traditional Knowledge or IQ] with scientific knowledge is the uncertainty of anecdotal observations and how much they can be extrapolated to broader trends". Yet while expressing disdain for Inuit anecdotes, PBSG experts repeated the "drowning" tale in seven papers, including their 2009 "Proceedings of the 15th Working Meeting of the IUCN/SSC Polar Bear Specialist Group," edited by Martyn Obbard.

PBSG experts demonstrated the "proper way to extrapolate anecdotes to broader trends." They extended the isolated observations of four floating bears and extrapolated it into a major die-off. First they calculated the proportion of the Beaufort Sea that was not surveyed. Because only 1/7th of the area had been surveyed and because they speculated that global warming was forcing all bears to swim, they multiplied by about 7 to conclude "as many as 27 bears died."[598] This conclusion was totally unverifiable but was repeated several times. Obbard was correct. The Inuit would never "extrapolate to broader trends" in that same excessive manner.

Finally, although the greatest extent of Arctic open water in modern history unarguably occurred in 2007 and again in 2012, there have been no more floating bears peppering the seascape. In contrast, Russian PBSG experts studying the bears on Wrangel Island in the Chukchi Sea provided more contrary evidence. Wrangel Island is home to one of the largest known denning areas in the Arctic. Several traditional walrus haul-outs are also found on Wrangel. In 2007, the greatest decrease in sea ice cover was observed in the waters surrounding the island and just west of the Beaufort Sea's floating bears. Due to the lack of ice, researchers observed the greatest number of "stranded" polar bears on the island. However contrary to the starving-bear theory, there were no signs of nutritional stress. Anticipating the seasonal haul-out of walruses, the bears concentrated on land where they were easily observed. The researchers determined that less than 5% of the Wrangel Island bears were designated skinny or very skinny. That compared very favorably to the 7 to 15% of skinny bears observed in previous years with heavier ice. Furthermore they determined that not only did 29% of all bears look "normal", the remaining 66% were fat or very fat. No bears were observed desperately swimming out to sea. In contrast, when disturbed by researchers they often fled into the sea, and then quickly returned.

The Illusion of Objective Science

"[R]adiotelemetry data show that individual bears may not be uniformly available for capture." [593]

PBSG expert Steve Amstrup

Unlike the Inuit, who spend all year hunting throughout polar bear country and then process their observations from discussions within a widespread community, the dire forecast of impending extinction relies on a "mark and recapture" method by:

- a small group of scientists

- in limited study areas

- during a very short period of time.

Despite the denigrating remarks by credentialed PBSG scientists, the Inuit methods are no more subjective than a scientific mark and recapture study. The subjective bias involved in interpreting data the USGS' South Beaufort Sea scientific study was most glaring.

Mark and recapture studies calculate population abundance based on estimations of how many marked animals survive between years. For a population to grow, the number of surviving cubs must outpace the number of dying older bears. If survival rates go down so does the population. For example, realizing the great uncertainty in calculations of survival, PBSG expert Steven Amstrup reported three different population estimates for bears along the South Beaufort Sea. If he assumed the adult bears had an 82% chance of surviving into the next year, the models calculated the population was 1301 bears. If survivorship was 88%, the abundance climbed to 1776 bears. If he estimated survivorship at a more robust 94%, then polar bear abundance climbed to 2490. [608] Thus depending on apparent survival rates, a mark-and-recapture study may conclude that the population has doubled, or that it has suddenly crashed.

Here are the basics of any mark and recapture study. Assume the fenced-off area is your study area. For statistical reasons you ignore observations outside that designated area. During the first year, you reach into your study area and capture four bears, which you then mark by painting a big white cross on their chests. (Researchers first painted big numbers on polar bears for easy identification from a helicopter, but the tourism industry complained that it ruined photographs. They now use discreet ear tags and a tattoo under their upper lip in case the tag falls off.)

The next year you return to your study area and randomly capture four more bears. However only two of them are marked with a white cross. Now the researcher must decide what happened to the two missing bears that were marked last year. Did they die or did they avoid detection? Assuming they avoided detection, then survival is estimated to be 100%. Since the two recaptured bears represent *half of last year's marked bears,* the models assume the four bears captured during the study's second year similarly represent about *half of the total* population. So the models estimate that there were at least eight bears within the study area.

However the calculations change if the researcher assumes the missing marked bears died. In this case, it means that in the second year you captured *every possible marked bear.* So your model assumes that you also captured every possible bear in the study area. Now the model estimates that there were only about four bears living in your study area. Because the survival rates are greatly affected by this guesswork, these estimates are called "apparent survival rates."

To appreciate the magnitude of the problem in estimating apparent survival rates, imagine a human mark-and-recapture study in which the local supermarket is your study area. For statistical reasons, you can only use observations inside your defined study area to determine whether or not your neighbors are alive or dead. (Because you recognize your neighbors' faces, there is no need to add ear tags.) How often do you see your neighbors in that store? Although my neighbors and I shop at the same supermarket 2 or 3 times each week, 52 weeks a year, I don't see 90% of them at the supermarket more than once every 5 to 10 years. If I was doing a human mark and recapture study, and did not see my neighbors after 5 years, my model would assume most of my neighbors had died! Fortunately for Inuit hunters, they are not bound by such scientific limitations.

Apparent survival rates are heavily biased by any migration in and out of the study area. The earliest mark and recapture models were tested on rodent populations, and the statisticians warned that barriers should be erected to prevent the rodents from moving. Otherwise all statistical calculations were totally unreliable. In keeping with the human analogy, if I prevented migration and trapped all my neighbors in the supermarket, it would be more obvious when they died. But that tactic is impossible for people, and likewise for highly migratory polar bears.

Unlike other bears that defend a territory with reliable resources, polar bears *never defend territories*. They walk and swim across great distances and will congregate wherever the Arctic's ever-shifting food supply becomes most abundant. Polar bears are globetrotters with variable ranges within extensive regions.[605] A study of radio-collared female bears denning on Wrangel Island determined that after the bears left the island they travelled an average distance of about 3700 miles.[606] A similar study with bears from western Alaska reported annual movement of about 3400 miles.[604] To put those distances into perspective, in one year a polar bear could leave the polar bear watching capital of the world in Churchill Manitoba and travel to Dallas Texas, do an about face and return to Churchill before the year was complete. Although much of their travel is confined within a less extensive region, one radio-collared female was observed in Alaska in late May and tracked to Greenland by early October.[641] Such wide-ranging movements allow rapid adjustments to the Arctic's annually varying food supplies. However it presents great difficulties for any mark and recapture study. Deciding if a bear was travelling or died thus becomes guesswork, and the amount of guesswork increases with shorter studies.

Instead of erecting barriers, a small percentage of female bears are equipped with radio collars. (Males have such big necks the collars will slide off. Young bears outgrow their collars too quickly and could choke themselves to death. So typically only adult females are collared.) Because collared bears can be tracked, there is no guesswork unless the batteries die. If a radio-collar remains in one spot for a long time, researchers locate the collar and determine if the bear died or just lost the collar. The vastly more accurate survival-rate data produced by collared bears is called "biological survival". Researchers use biological survival to evaluate the accuracy of "apparent survival". For example, if a large percentage of collared bears survived but moved out of the study area, then researchers assume a similar percentage of marked bears had also moved away. In that case, a low apparent survival rate was an illusion most likely due to temporary migration, not death.

Amstrup diligently followed up his earlier study on the apparent survival of South Beaufort Bears using radio-collared bears over a 12-year period. It turned out that his high-end apparent survival estimate of 94% was still too low. If only natural deaths were used, polar bears had a 99.6 % biological survival rate.[592] Most bears died at the hands of hunters. If death at the hands of hunters was also considered, then biological survival was still higher than apparent survival, but fell to 96.9%. In 2001 Amstrup concluded that the South Beaufort Sea population was increasing and the current hunting quotas insured a growing population.

Perhaps it was the growing pressure from adversarial lawsuits, and speculation that the polar bears were endangered from CO_2 warming, but in the series of USGS publications coauthored by Eric Regehr, Stirling, and Amstrup, they suddenly emphasized the illusion of apparent survival and downplayed biological survival to suggest the polar bears were facing extinction by the end of the century.[573,547,599,600,601] Their study was far too short, covering just six years, and only the last two years resulted in low apparent survival. Low apparent survival in the final years can be caused by yet another illusion. Bears marked in the earlier years have more time to return to the study area and thus have a higher and more realistic apparent survival.

During the first three years of this "extinction" study, the researchers reported apparent survival ranging from 92-99%[574]. The higher estimate was the same as the biological survival rates of Amstrup's radio-collared bears. However apparent survival dropped dramatically for the last two years of the study. Most disturbing, researchers kept the biological survival rates off the books writing, "radiotelemetry captures present methodological difficulties." So they excluded that data from critical statistical tests![573] Despite knowing that biological survival rates had never rapidly changed before,[593] and despite knowing more bears were outside their study area in 2004 and 2005, the USGS report argued polar bear survival dropped from 96-99% in 2003, down to 77% in 2004,[574] and the 2004 estimate was a sign of impending extinction.

In their first report, Regehr, Stirling, and Amstrup demonstrated high integrity in their analyses and were upfront about the problems of their models, writing, "the declines we observed in model-averaged survival rates may reflect an increase in the number of "emigrants" toward the end of the study, and not an actual decrease in biological survival, and they noted male bears had exhibited unusually high transiency.[573] In subsequent reports it became clear that when apparent survival rates were high, only 24% of the collared females had wandered outside the study area. In contrast during last two years of the study when apparent survival plummeted, the number of collared bears wandering outside the study area had nearly doubled to 47% in 2005 and 36% in 2006.

For their subsequent reports, the USGS brought in Dr. Hal Caswell who would also model the Emperor penguins into extinction (see Chapter 4). Using the very same data they argued that high transiency had no effect and simply wrote, "High proportions of radio-collared bears in the sampling area, 53% in 2005 and 64% in 2006, suggest that the low survival estimates in 2004 and 2005 did not reflect increased movement out of the study area."[600] But clearly collared bears had demonstrated increased movement out of their study area. Although radio-collared bears comprised 10% of all captures, they never published their biological survival rates. Perhaps that was because rumor had it biological survival exceeded 97% and that would contradict the extinction story!

As their re-analyses of the same data evolved, it became clear advocates were maneuvering to create a statistical link between sea ice and bear survival. Not only did survival magically drop to 77% with the "new and improved" models, the link to sea ice also suddenly improved. The first paper reported, "In our analysis of the 2001–06 data, "we did not find clear evidence for a relationship between sea ice coverage in the SBS [Beaufort Sea] region and survival."[573] After tweaking the models, 4 years later they wrote, "In the most supported models, polar bear survival declined with an increasing number of days per year that waters over the continental shelf were ice free." Even their choice of the term "ice free" was questionable. What they had really measured was regions where there was less than 50% sea ice, which is normal in many sections during the summer. So why label "49% ice cover" ice-free?

Their new model required about 400 bears to die each year, which is more than ten times the deaths of previous years, Yet there was no evidence of mass die-offs. Female body condition was improving and the percentage of cubs had increased. So hyped anecdotes of "unusual" cannibalism and four floating bears suddenly appeared.

Maternity dens were another example of the hype. In past decades maternity dens on the pack ice were so rare, researchers discounted all such reports. Everywhere else bears den on land. A den on the shifting pack ice may move over 500 miles during the winter and take the mother and her cubs far from good seal habitat. When it was finally proven that some bears were indeed denning on the pack ice in the Beaufort Sea, the consensus was that heavy human hunting had driven them away from the coast. Cubs had been sought as food for sled dogs. With hunting restrictions in place, bears began to return and in 1994 Amstrup wrote "the increase we observed in land denning may have resulted from a decline in hunting of denning areas that began decades ago."[632] But Amstrup flip-flopped one more time. He recently coauthored a paper arguing bears were now *forced* ashore "in response to reductions in stable old ice, increases in unconsolidated ice, and lengthening of the melt season."[629] To repeat the words of Kivalliq Inuit Association president Jose Kusugak, "they try to marry it with climate change and so on, it becomes absurd" …"It makes the south – southern people – look so ignorant."[633]

International Politics versus the Inuit

The International Union for Conservation of Nature (IUCN) wisely states, "Protected areas and threatened species could most effectively be safeguarded if local people considered it in their own interest to do so. Working with rather than against local people is a major working principle for IUCN." But in total contradiction of their professed goals, the anecdotal claims of problem bears, cannibalism, and drowning bears have been used to discredit and dismiss the Inuit's contention that it is the time of the most bears. Many Inuit are deeply angered and feel the polar bear myths have been used to undermine their observations and usurp their local control. Although there has been an increasing effort to incorporate Inuit knowledge, most Inuit believe their knowledge of polar bears and arctic wildlife continues to be ignored and discounted.

In 2009, the Inuit presented two resolutions to the IUCN's Polar Bear Specialist Group: 1) Population Estimates to Include Local Knowledge and Inuit Qaujimajatuqangit [IQ] and 2) Basic Requirements for Sound Conservation Management which recommended the systematic cooperation and inclusion of Inuit, Inuvialuit, and Inupiat in all aspects of polar bear management and research. PBSG scientists rejected both of those proposals, arguing that the Nunavut government already required them to honor IQ even though it was clear these Nunavut requirements were given lip service and then ignored. The rejection smacked of elitism and racism. Passing those resolutions would have shown well-deserved respect for Inuit expertise. On the other hand, dismissing the proposed resolutions insured that Derocher and his like-minded PBSG experts could control the flow of information being disseminated worldwide.

The Inuit have long been victimized by "southern people's" politics. Initially Inuit people had suffered from bouts of kidnapping during the whaling period. Later the "legal" relocation of indigenous families became a tactic employed by all the "polar bear countries" in an international chess match to stake claims on Arctic resources. In 1925, Denmark relocated families in Greenland to counter any Norwegian claims to the island. The following year the Soviet government moved a small Eskimo community to Wrangel Island in order to replace an occupation of Alaskan Eskimos that had been established there by American interests. The relocation of families was also a crucial cold-war tactic by Canada to insure their claims on the Arctic, but not just against any Russian threats, but more so from perceived encroachments by the United States.[631]

In 1944, Henry Larsen, a staff sergeant in the Royal Canadian Mounted Police, became the first to navigate the Northwest Passage from the west to east and back again. This celebrated feat greatly strengthened Canada's claims to Arctic lands, and offset any potential Scandinavian claims based on Norway's Roald Amundsen's successful crossing of Canada's Northwest Passage in 1903-06. However the US military bases built during World War II were now perceived as a threatening foothold. So in the 1950s Larsen was put in charge of relocating several Inuit families to Grise Fiord and Resolute Bay in the far northern reaches of the Canadian Arctic. Grise Fiord is known by its Inuit name that means "the place that never thaws." Although these were strategic places in ongoing international maneuverings, it was a region long abandoned by the Inuit's ancestors. Government stories of an unspoiled land where hunting was more bountiful enticed Inuit families to leave the milder climates of their villages along the central Hudson Bay. Government officials sealed the deal by suggesting there was absolutely no risk and promised a swift return passage if the families found their new settlement unsatisfactory.[631]

But it was a promise that Canadian officials never intended to keep. Ironically, the woman who played Nanook's wife in the popular 1930s documentary "Nanook of the North" and her son (who was fathered by the documentary's producer) were among the families relocated to Grise Ford. Although "Nanook of the North" had enthralled Americans and Europeans with a glamorized depiction of Inuit resilience and adaptability, their new settlements doled out such incredible hardships their resilience was severely tested. The struggles of those families have now been well documented in the book, *The Long Exile: A Tale of Inuit Betrayal and Survival.* It was the film producer's granddaughter, daughter of his half-Inuit, half-Caucasian son, who finally forced the Canadian government to own up to their betrayal. The Canadian government finally made a public apology in 2008 and paid reparations to the offended families.[631]

Although the relocation of Inuit families was purely tactical and politically self-serving, Canadian scientists supported the move based on archaeological remains of settlements that had been abandoned centuries ago when the climate was much warmer and the whales had yet to be decimated. The Canadian media portrayed the relocation as a humanitarian effort dedicated to protecting the "unspoiled Inuit society" from the evils of a modern world. While the relocated Inuit suffered tremendously, Canadian newspapers glamorized the move. Canadian Broadcast Company filmed the drop-off and the *Toronto Sun*, the *Montreal Gazette* and the Hudson Bay Company's paper, *The Beaver,* "all published glowing accounts of the new, improved lives the Inuit were living". Even *National Geographic* journalist Andrew Brown was sent to interview Canadian officials about this wonderful humanitarian effort.[631]

While the media interviewed government officials, who dutifully waxed profusely about the relocation's success, no one ever interviewed the Inuit. As McGhee wrote, "Had they been asked, the Inuit might well have told the reporters and Departmental officials that while the hunters were away, the women and children were often forced to survive on bannock and thin broth made from seal heads, and that everyone regularly went hungry and thirsty. The group on the Lindstrom Peninsula might have pointed out that the women of the camp were having to walk miles out on the floating pack to chip freshwater ice from bergs mired in the floe and at the Resolute Bay camp, they might have mentioned that no large game ever came on to the island and that they had been reduced to sneaking up to the air-base rubbish dumps under cover of darkness and stealing the remains of the pilots' packed lunches in order to stave off starvation".[631]

Now in the 21st century the Inuit feel once again they are victimized by the international politics of climate change and the CBD's lawsuits. If anyone asks, most Inuit would tell you "it is the time of the most polar bears!"

15

Resilient Bears and 10,000 years of Rapid Climate Change

Photo courtesy of US Fish and Wildlife Service. Credit Susanne Miller

"The extra energy elevated early Holocene summer temperatures throughout the Arctic 1.3°C above 20th century averages, enough to completely melt many small glaciers throughout the Arctic, although the Greenland Ice Sheet was only slightly smaller than at present."

Dr. G. H. Miller, Institute of Arctic and Alpine Research

Polar bear researchers Derocher and Stirling have repeatedly warned that widespread polar bear extinctions are likely by mid century because models predict temperatures may rise by 2° to 4°F. However, all ecological evidence supports the Inuit's counterclaim that polar bears "can and will adapt to changing and severe climatic conditions, as [they have] done for centuries."[647] And all paleoclimate evidence indicates the Arctic was much warmer in the recent past.

The climate variability throughout the Arctic is extraordinary, hosting the world's most extreme change of seasons. When the sun reappears for a few summer months, daylight can linger for 24 hours. A frozen world thaws, and the open waters invite throngs of whales, walruses, seals, and birds. However the sun soon retreats and shrouds the Arctic in months of darkness. The advancing sea ice chases the summer visitors southward to more open waters and envelops those that dare to linger too long in an icy tomb. Second only to dramatic seasonal extremes are the extremes wrought by El Niño cycles, building unusually heavy ice in one region and raising temperatures in others.[661] Because the polar regions always lose more heat than the summer sun can provide, the Arctic would be a much colder and more forbidding place if not for heat imported from the tropics. *Every change in the delivery of that heat due to ocean oscillations magnifies Arctic climate change more than anywhere else on the planet.*

To survive these extremes, polar bears have evolved several adaptations. 1) Because ocean cycles alter their prey's abundance, polar bears never defend territories like other species. Instead they remain mobile, and can cross the Arctic in a single season. 2) Polar bears indulge in extreme hyperphagia when food is abundant. Two months of binge eating can sustain them for the remainder of the year. 3) Polar bears have no set period of hibernation. Only pregnant females predictably enter maternity dens for the winter. All others remain active. They briefly seek shelter dens when needed and enter "walking hibernation" when food is scarce. 4) Polar bears are highly individualistic. They adapt to whatever food supply is present. Although the ringed seal is the most reliably encountered prey, diets vary between regions and populations, as well as amongst individuals within a region.

Genetic evidence tells us that the polar bear is an ancient species that has *experienced multiple glacial cycles.*[646] The resilient polar bear has survived 100,000-year ice-age cycles, when Arctic temperatures plummeted to 36°F colder than today.[645] The intervening warm periods, known as interglacials, were warmer and produced less summer ice. Summers averaged 9°F warmer than today yet polar bears survived.[645]

Extreme rapid warming events punctuated the most recent ice age between 48,000 BC and 11,000 BC. Greenland ice core temperatures fluctuated by 18 to 27°F in a 10 to 50 year period during what scientists call Dansgaard-Oeschger events.(see Figure 46) After the Arctic ice sheet melted and the Bering Sea reconnected with the Arctic Ocean, more muted temperature swings, known as Bond Events, persisted during the most recent 10,000 years.[706] In some regions, *the Arctic has cycled between 7°F cooler and 9°F warmer than today over periods of just a few hundred years.*[682] Most recently, Alaska and the Bering Sea have swung from the world's most rapidly warming region during the 1980s and 90s to the most rapidly cooling region of the last decade (see Chapter 11). Equally intriguing, while temperatures along the western Hudson Bay recently warmed by 1.4°F per decade, along the adjacent eastern Hudson Bay and the Baffin Bay temperatures cooled by 1.4°F.[804]

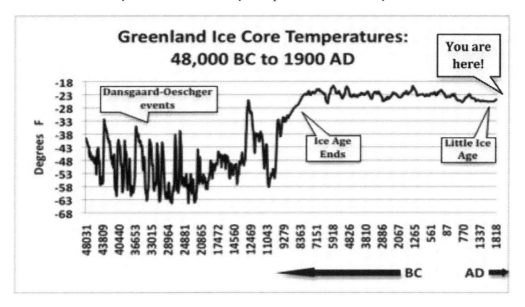

Figure 46. Rapid Climate Change during last Ice Age

The effects of such great variability have been harsher on climate modelers than it has been on the bears. The recent retreat of Arctic ice has been far greater than predicted by CO_2 warming. After observing rapid ice retreat, NASA climate scientist Jay Zwally predicted accelerated melting and an ice-free Arctic by the summer of 2012. However, the Arctic Ocean still retains more sea ice each summer than Antarctica's oceans, and there sea ice is increasing.

In 2010 an international collaboration of climate scientists led by Dr. Vladamir Kattsov published "Arctic sea ice change: a grand challenge of climate science." They wrote, "Until concentrations of Green House Gases reach higher values, climate signals from natural variability may be comparable in magnitude to those from external forcing [i.e. CO_2]."[643] Other researchers observed that recent warming in the western Hudson Bay was induced by stronger winds from the south and conceded,

"It remains to be seen whether these changes in atmospheric circulation might be ascribed to human actions or simply to natural climate variability."[805] Scientists taking measurements from Russian drifting ice stations and by dropsondes from US Ptarmigan weather reconnaissance aircraft in the 1990s concluded "In particular, we do not observe the large surface warming trends predicted by models; indeed, we detect significant surface cooling trends over the western Arctic Ocean during winter and autumn. This discrepancy suggests that present climate models do not adequately incorporate the physical processes that affect the polar regions."[538] (Dropsondes are weather balloons that fall from a plane to the ground.)

Furthermore heavy ice has been shown to be more detrimental to bears, and to the entire Arctic food chain. If recent research implicating natural ocean cycles and sunspot cycles are correct, the bears may soon suffer from more ice. *With less solar heating and ocean cycles reverting to cool phases, Arctic sea ice may return to the thickness of the 1970s within the next 2 decades.* Scientists at the Harvard-Smithsonian Center for Astrophysics and elsewhere are demonstrating that small changes in solar heating alter the temperature contrast between the equator and the poles and thus the patterns of ocean circulation. That altered circulation rapidly adds or subtracts the amount of heat transported into the Arctic.[485,656,706,785,790,793,794,798]

Cycles of Intruding Warm Water Improve the Arctic Food Chain

"Annual primary production in the Arctic has increased yearly ... Should these trends continue, additional loss of ice during Arctic spring could boost productivity >3-fold above 1998–2002 levels" [579]

Dr. Kevin Arrigo, Stanford University

Advocates have implied that the loss of thick, multiyear ice in September is denying the polar bears the icy platform from which they hunt seals. However in reality, less summer ice has a negligible effect on hunting but a decisively positive effect on the bears' main prey. The bears' most important feeding period extends from March to June when bears binge on breeding ringed seals. This is the time when sea ice is most important, but unlike the highly publicized reductions in September ice, the reduction in springtime ice has been quite minor. *On the other hand, those summer periods of more open water have undeniably benefitted the whole food chain.*

The Arctic Ocean is relatively poor in nutrients, and relies on ocean cycles that import nutrients from the Bering Sea and the Atlantic. The intruding warm and nutrient-rich currents also cause less ice, which promotes more photosynthesis. Between 2003 and 2007, productivity in the Arctic Ocean increased by 23% relative to the 1998-2002 average. In the Siberian sector where the greatest loss of summer ice occurred in 2007, there was a 3-fold increase in ocean productivity.[676] When phytoplankton increase, zooplankton flourish,[678] treating whales, sea birds and young Arctic cod to a bountiful feast.[678,680] In addition to more food, the warmer surface temperatures stimulate the "cold-blooded" Arctic cod to grow faster and bigger, and bigger fish are better able to survive the winter. Fishery scientists have concluded, "*at least in the short term, the lengthening of the ice-free season presently observed in Arctic seas could result in improved recruitment and larger populations of Arctic cod.*"[677] The intruding warm Atlantic waters also provide a winter refuge for the Arctic cod that gather in huge numbers at the warmest depths.[679]

More Arctic cod means more food for ringed seal, harp seals, harbor seals, beluga whales and several species of seabirds. Ringed seals must feed intensively in the open waters of summer to store the fat needed to survive the winter and they suffer when sea ice is slow to break up. *In 1992 when breakup of sea ice was delayed by 25 days, the body condition of all ringed seals declined.*[673] In contrast during the most recent decade with more open water, the number of ringed seal pups in the western Hudson Bay tripled relative to the 1990s.[673] With more seal pups the polar bears' body condition also improved. Stirling and his PBSG colleagues observed that recent improvement but never published it.[582] (see Chapter 14, Figure 45.)

Thicker Ice Causes Fewer Ringed Seals

"Heavy ice conditions in the mid-1970s and mid-1980s caused significant declines in productivity of ringed seals, each of which lasted about 3 years and caused similar declines in the natality of polar bears and survival of subadults, after which reproductive success and survival of both species increased again." [624]

Ian Stirling, PBSG expert, Canadian Wildlife Service

Because a larger body size conserves heat more efficiently, animals living in polar regions are typically the largest among related species. (i.e., polar bears and Emperor penguins) Paradoxically, the ringed seal is the smallest yet most abundant of all Arctic seals, and they remain in the Arctic all winter. Both males and females are featherweights (weighing in at about 110-150 pounds) compared to the male Pacific walrus (weighing in at approximately 3500 pounds). The secret to this tiny seal's success is the relative warmth of the ocean's water (+28°F or higher). Seals avoid deadly -20°F air temperatures by staying in the water. *In fact, for most of the year, ringed seals spend more than 90% of their time swimming, inaccessible to polar bears.*[675] Even during the winter when seals are tethered to their breathing holes, they never spend more than 20% of the time out of the water. Although most polar bears remain active all winter when ice is most abundant, the bears continue to lose weight because the odds are slim that they will stumble upon a seal resting on the ice.

However, the bear's odds improve during seals' breeding season. For about 6-8 weeks from late March through May, ringed seals spend about 50% of their time hauled out on the fast-ice, giving birth and nursing their pups in lairs just beneath a layer of snow.[675] During their extensive nursing period, adults and pups are most vulnerable to bears and foxes. Consequently female polar bears emerge from their maternity dens at just the right time to dine on fat, helpless ringed seal pups. *Scientists have estimated that about 80% of the ringed seals consumed by polar bears are pups.* And during those few months of binge eating, bears gain 80% or more of their annual weight, by plundering every ringed seal nursery they can sniff out.[624]

After the surviving pups are weaned, adult ringed seals seek out ice edges and floes where they can lay in the sun and molt their skin during two weeks of peak sunlight in June. Although not as vulnerable as baby seals, molting seals spend 60% of their time on the ice. However once their molt is complete, *ringed seals are swimming in distant open waters from July through October, far from the jaws of hungry bears.* But with the passing of September's equinox, the sun begins to fade and adult seals return to the coast to stake out their winter territories. And savvy polar bears line the coast in anticipation.

The seals must arrive before the new ice thickens in order to develop a series of breathing holes. Younger seals that cannot claim a territory either migrate to more open waters to the south or seek the open waters of Arctic polynya. (see Chapter 4 for polynya and fast-ice details). While waiting for the ice to form, seals feed on the abundant cod that aggregate in huge numbers in warm shallow bays. When the fast-ice first forms, the seals use their heads to punch open holes in the thin ice. Then as the fast-ice thickens, they must constantly chew and claw at the ice to maintain their breathing holes throughout the winter.

Because seals require thinner ice to create their breathing holes,[674] *areas dominated by thick multiyear ice always sustain far fewer seals and far fewer bears.*[590,595,685] In regions like the northern Canadian Archipelago, winds pile ice against the shoreline. The winds crumple the ice and heave layers of thin ice into piles of thick rubble. The ice rubble resists melting and sets the stage for thicker multiyear ice to increase in the following years. Climate scientists have detected various cycles that alternately drive thick ice out of the Arctic or confine and compress the ice.[821,536] These cycles range from 6 to 20 years and are associated with the North Atlantic Oscillation/Arctic Oscillation. So bears and seals must remain mobile in order to adjust to these multiyear cycles of ice formation.

Since the mid 1990's, Arctic sea ice has been behaving more like Antarctic sea ice (see Chapter 12) and that has been good news for plankton, cod, seals, and bears. When the Arctic Oscillation swung to a positive phase, thicker multiyear ice was blown out from the Arctic into the north Atlantic.[535,536] As a result the thinner replacement ice now melts more rapidly each summer. Some have suggested this is cause for alarm, but biologically it is highly beneficial. In the Antarctic, where ice is not constrained by continents, thick multiyear ice is always scarce yet Antarctic sea ice has expanded to its greatest limits during the most recent decades. At places like Barrow Alaska, between December and March, winter air temperatures range from -15°F and -52°F.

Similar temperatures around the Arctic guarantee that ample fast ice will always form and ringed seals will always have breeding habitat. *However the loss of thicker Arctic ice, and the concomitant increase in thinner summer ice benefits feeding ringed seals, which in turn increases the polar bears' all-you-can-eat dining habitat.*

In 2012, PBSG experts Stirling and Derocher published "Effects of climate warming on polar bears: a review of the evidence." To illustrate the importance of ringed seal pups they wrote, "In the mid-1970s and again in the mid-1980s, ringed seal pup productivity plummeted by 80%

Photo courtesy of NOAA, credit Shawn Dahle

or more for 2–3 years…. A comparison of the age-specific weights of both male and female polar bears from 1971 to 1973 (productive seal years), to those from 1974 to 1975 (years of seal reproductive failure), demonstrated a significant decline in the latter period."[584] Without argument, bears always benefit from more seal pups, but Derocher's retelling of the seals' decline in a section titled, "Why progressively earlier breakup of the sea ice negatively affects persistence of polar bear subpopulations" was highly deceptive! *The seals' productivity had plummeted because the Arctic had cycled to a year of heavy ice,* not due to "a progressively earlier breakup."

Instead of directly mentioning the heavy ice connection, Stirling and Derocher simply referenced Stirling's 2002 paper. In that paper he wrote, "*Heavy ice conditions* in the mid-1970s and mid-1980s caused significant declines in productivity of ringed seals, each of which lasted about 3 years and caused similar declines in the natality of polar bears and survival of subadults, after which reproductive success and survival of both species increased again."[624] In 2012, Stirling coauthored another paper with a seal researcher. They discussed the cycles of decline in the 1970s and 1980s and again in the 1990s. *All declines were caused by heavy ice years.* Their paper then proposed that "the decline of ringed seal reproductive parameters and pup survival in the 1990s could have been triggered by unusually cold winters and heavy ice conditions that prevailed in Hudson Bay in the early 1990s, through nutritional stress".[673] Yet in their 2012 "review of the evidence", Stirling and Derocher implied that the declines were caused by "*a progressively earlier breakup* (emphasis added)." How do such blatant false fabrications pass peer-review?

Stirling also reported a coincidental 10-year cycle of freshwater input from the Mackenzie River. Excess fresh water directly affects the Arctic cod and thus the seals. The specific density of the cod's eggs allows the eggs to float in the warmer surface layer where oxygen and plankton are most abundant. However when thicker layers of fresh water cover the surface, the eggs sink deeper below the surface where development is inhibited. (See "floating eggs" in Chapter 5). This is why Stirling also hypothesized the decline in bears' body condition (BCI) in the 1990s may have resulted from recently completed hydroelectric projects that had flooded the bay with an excessive amount of fresh water.[590] Although the disruption to the region's fisheries has been a common complaint of the native peoples, global warming theories garnered all the attention. But global warming does not explain the 10-year cycles that cause seal abundance to fluctuate, which in turn causes polar bear abundance to oscillate.[673,784,788]

Reproductive Cycles for Seals and Polar Bears

"the exceptional significance of Wrangel Island as a survival refuge for polar bears during ice free seasons confirmed the hypothesis that an ice-free ocean provides alternative food resources for polar bears by transferring large quantities of marine food material into coastal ecosystems."

N.G Ovsyanikov, PBSG expert, Wrangel Island State Nature Reserve

Stirling and Derocher's review linked declining polar bear cub survival to progressively earlier breakup of the sea ice, but their arguments again relied on zombie data. They accurately reported cub survival had plummeted from over 70% in 1980 to 48% in 1992. *However they failed to mention 1992 was a heavy ice year.* They also failed to mention that *cub survival quickly rebounded.*[590] Survival increased to over 70% from 1993 to 1998 and the 2008 *Committee on the Status of Endangered Wildlife* in Canada reported that cub survival averages a healthy 66%.[609]

Their "review of the evidence" also suggested declining birth rates in the Hudson Bay were evidence of impending doom but those rates were also out of context. All researchers for seals and bears, including Stirling and Derocher, have long reported that birth rates change depending the population's carrying capacity.[792] When populations are reduced below the region's carrying capacity, both bears and seals respond by reproducing at an earlier age and reproducing more often. Conversely, as populations increase, the birthrates decline. A similar response has been observed in humans. Human birth rates have fallen precipitously over the past 100 years, yet no one will argue the human population is now threatened because fewer babies per female are born.

Any cycle that weakens the food chain will reduce the region's carrying capacity and bears and seals will respond with lower birth rates. This natural mechanism keeps the population in harmony with the food supply. During years when seals are abundant or during years when overhunting had reduced the bear population, the bears have responded with elevated birth rates. The bears' birthrates then declined whenever their population ballooned or when seal populations withered.

Although Derocher and Stirling now paint that decline as the effects of deadly global warming, they (again) failed to publish all the details. Stirling had written earlier, "To date, this declining trend does not constitute a threat to the population: even in the late 1980s, when natality was at its lowest, the rates *were still higher than the upper range of values* reported for bears elsewhere in the Arctic (emphasis added)." [590] In other words, despite a complete loss of ice every summer, the Hudson Bay has been more productive than areas with thick summer ice.

The ice-free season in the Hudson Bay and Foxe Basin provides two benefits: it insures ample thin autumn ice required by breeding ringed seals, and it permits the summer immigration of Beluga whales, harp seals, and harbor seals into the bay. Any bear that failed to get its fill of ringed seal pups in the spring, can supplement its diet with these open-water immigrants.

Scientists can now determine a bear's diet by taking samples of fat from the rump of a (heavily sedated) polar bear. Each prey species has a highly specific combination of essential fats. By analyzing those unique fats, they can tell what the bears have eaten. Using this method scientists have determined that ringed seals provide about 70% of the bear's diet in the Hudson Bay. The remainder of the diet consists of resident Bearded seals, Harbor seals that typically avoid ice, and Harp seals and Beluga whales that immigrate into the bay during the open-water season. Elsewhere the Lancaster Sound population dines on Beluga whales nearly as much as they eat ringed seals. Belugas are frequently trapped by rapidly advancing winter ice. In the summer Belugas also herd cod into shallow embayments but get helplessly stranded when the tide goes out. In the South Beaufort Sea, ringed seals account for 15% to 70% of the bears' diet, while Bowhead Whales contribute from 2% to 52%, and Beluga Whales from 1% to 33%, with percentages varying widely amongst individuals.[688,689,690,691,692]

In the Davis Strait off the coast of Labrador, polar bears will binge on baby Harp seals that breed on the pack-ice. Harp seals are another conservation success story. Since sustainable hunting regulations were imposed, they increased from less than 2 million in the 1970s to over 5.5 million in the 1990s and the bear population grew accordingly.[792] Contrary to popular global warming theory, Harp Seals are now spreading south. In the 1980s only 5 seals were reported on Sable Island off the coast of Nova Scotia. By 1994 the Harp Seal population had ballooned to over 1100.[791]

In Foxe Basin just north of the Hudson Bay, ringed seals make up about 50% of the diet. In addition to harbor seals, harp seals and bearded seals, walruses contribute 7% of the bears' diet.[688] Wherever walruses are abundant, they are preyed upon by bears. Along the Laptev Sea polar bears have been observed making pits behind piles of driftwood, in which they hide and wait for walruses to come ashore.[560] On Wrangle Island the bears wait on ice-free shores, anticipating the traditional haul-outs to feast on any exhausted walrus that lumbers ashore. *Researchers have remarked that such varied hunting behavior explains how polar bears have thrived during the past 10,000 years when summer sea ice was much less prevalent than today.*[694]

Polar Bears Survived the Warm Climatic Optimum

Stirling and Derocher's 2012 "review" warned that unless rising temperatures are limited to ~2.2°F, "polar bears will likely disappear from the southern portions of their range within 30–40 years."[584] Yet climate history reveals polar bears have survived longer and warmer periods throughout the last 10,000 years. Evidence from Greenland ice cores (see Figure 47) clearly show that the Arctic climate was much warmer than today.[772,773] The past 10,000 years are called the Holocene. *Because early researchers believed that warmer temperatures were beneficial,* Scandinavian scientists named an exceptionally warm period from about 7000 to 3000 BC the Holocene Climatic Optimum.

In the tropics, studies of the Great Barrier Reef found that the coral growth was also optimal and water temperatures were over 1.5°F warmer about 6000 years ago.[760,762] At the same time, pollen and vegetation studies from Siberia and China[761,799] all indicate that summer and winter temperatures were magnified in the Arctic, as temperatures were as much as 15°F warmer. Nearly all accounts estimate that during the Optimum, summer temperatures in the Arctic ranged 8°F to 18°F higher than today.

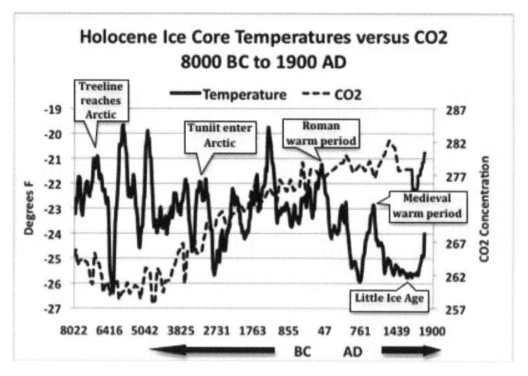

Figure 47. Greenland's GISP2 Holocene ice core temperatures

For the most recent millennia, temperatures from Pacific Warm Pool suggest tropical temperatures today and during the Medieval warm period were about the same.[200] A 2011 ice core study concluded, "warmer temperatures were the norm in the earlier part of the past 4000 years." With century-long intervals of temperatures that were 1.8°F warmer than the 2001-10 decade, they concluded, "the current decadal mean temperature in Greenland has not exceeded the envelope of natural variability over the past 4000 years."[809]

Although Greenland's GISP2 ice core data does not capture changes in sea ice, there are 3 notable points that stand out:

1) Arctic temperatures have declined since the Optimum with more prolonged cold periods that culminated in the most recent Little Ice Age.

2) About every 1000 years, there are significant warm spikes.

3) *The cooling trend was undeterred by the slight rise of CO_2 and the warmest temperature spikes occurred during the lowest levels of CO_2.*

Several studies correlate the alternating warm spikes and cold periods with changes in solar activity, prompting climate scientists to suggest "significantly more research into the potential role of solar variability is warranted."[743] However, whether or not the warm spike of the Medieval Warm Period was greater than the most recent warm spike has spawned a ferocious debate. Advocates argue that the 20th century warm spike is unprecedented and thus "proof" of CO_2 warming. They point to Dr. Michael Mann's "hockey stick" reconstruction as evidence (see Figure 49). Despite a plethora of contradictory evidence, Dr. James Hansen's more apocalyptic scenarios argue that the "global temperature in year 2000 has reached at least the Holocene maximum."[744] Who to believe?

Tree-line evidence

"Over most of Russia, forest advanced to or near the current arctic coastline between 9000 and 7000 yr B.P. and retreated to its present position by between 4000 and 3000 yr B.P.[Before Present]" [697]

Dr. Glen MacDonald, University of California, Los Angeles

Ancient tree-lines provide the best evidence of a much warmer Holocene Optimum. Freeze-dried stumps scattered across the Arctic tundra stand like tombstones honoring a much warmer past. Analyses of the stumps' ages reveal that tree-line reached the shores of the Arctic Ocean about 9000 years ago.[697] Then as Holocene cooling progressed, the tree-line retreated to its current position around 3000 years ago, over a hundred miles south of the Arctic coast. Based on the temperatures that now limit the current tree-lines, *researchers estimate the Arctic coast was 4° to 12°F warmer between 9000 and 4000 years ago.*[697]

The Tuniit (also called the pre-Dorset or paleo-eskimos and unrelated to the Inuit) entered the Arctic's ancient forests about 5000 years ago hunting caribou and muskoxen with bows and arrows. Archeological evidence reveals that a warmer climate permitted the Tuniit to occupy the now frigid coasts of northern Ellesmere Island just west of Greenland. They lived in tents, which they heated with firewood that was then more abundant.[631] By comparing the fossil evidence of temperature-sensitive phytoplankton that layer the sea floor sediments, researchers determined that the Tuniit alternately abandoned and colonized the Arctic coast many times in synchrony with 100-year climate cycles.

From about 6500 to 2600 years ago, temperatures cycled from lows 3.5°–7.5°F cooler than present, then suddenly jumping to highs that averaged 9°F warmer than today. Similarly sea ice concentrations ranged from two months more sea ice, to four months more open water than presently observed. The warming events took about 50–100 years and often lasted about 300 years before colder intervals intervened for as much as 500 years.[682] During the colder intervals, the Tuniit abandoned the coast and followed herds of muskoxen and caribou southward. About 1,000 years ago, the Inuit entered the Arctic and drove Tuniit from most of their former lands. In 1902, the last of the Tuniit were living on South Hampton Island just north of the Hudson Bay. But with the same frightful speed that exterminated other native Americans and modern frogs (see Chapter 8), disease introduced by sick European whalers exterminated the Tuniit in a matter of weeks.

The Little Ice Age (LIA) was the Holocene's most recent and coldest interval. Global cooling stretched from the poles to the equator and temperatures in the Pacific warm pool dropped by as much as 1.8°F,[200] and fish abundance off the coast of Peru reached its lowest levels in 1000 years.[419] Tree-lines were driven lower and new growth was inhibited. If you backpack in the high country of the Sierra Nevada, you will occasionally see fossil stumps dotting a barren hillside above the current tree-line. A 1997 study in Sequoia National Park found that "Tree-line elevation was higher than at present throughout most of the last 3500 years."[698] In the Ural Mountains (which divides Asia from Europe), researchers found thousands of more than 500-year-old dead trees that grew before the LIA struck. In contrast, remnants of any new trees that could have sprouted during the LIA were almost entirely absent.[699]

Although the Holocene cooling trend caused the above-ground tree-line to retreat, viable rootstocks of many species remained underground. Trees that advance into a new territory require ideal conditions for seedlings to get established. However, ancient rootstocks allow trees to suddenly emerge whenever local conditions are mild enough to promote growth. For example the world's oldest-known living tree, a Norway Spruce, was recently discovered in Sweden. Although the living 13-foot high trunk emerged relatively recently, it had sprouted from the same rootstock that has persisted for nearly 10,000 years. Scientists found four different "generations" of above-ground remains with ages that dated 375, 5660, 9000 and 9550 years old.[700]

Other fossilized trunks at currently treeless elevations in Sweden indicate that Scandinavian temperatures during the Holocene Optimum were 6°F warmer than now. More recently, temperatures derived from Scandinavian tree-rings indicate that the warmest 30-year period over the past 2000 years was the "Roman Era" over nineteen hundred years ago. Temperatures of the Roman Era averaged about 1.8°F warmer than the 1950-80 average (see Figure 48). Two thousand years of tree-ring temperatures have steadily declined as predicted by changes in the sun's orbit. Most interesting is that the most recent Scandinavian warm peak was not during the 1990s. Similar to trends in the maximum temperatures in California's Sierra Nevada, peak warming also occurred from 1918-47.[705]

Sea Ice Evidence

By studying the processes of beach formation, scientists observed that coastal sea ice shelters beaches from eroding waves. In contrast, when ice was absent, beach erosion was significant. Combining geological evidence from beach formation and patterns of driftwood delivery, they concluded the Arctic (and thus the bears), must have experienced more open water throughout the Holocene Optimum. *They reported,* *"Multiyear sea ice reached a minimum between ~8500 and 6000 years ago, when the* *limit of year-round sea ice at the coast of Greenland was located ~1000 kilometers to the* *north of its present position."*[684] Fossil whalebones and driftwood relay very similar stories, suggesting the Canadian Archipelago was ice-free during 3 extended periods: between 10,000 and 8,000 years ago, between 5,000 and 3,000 years ago and most recently around Medieval Warm Period 1,500 years ago.[581,696] The deposition of driftwood and whalebones on the islands of Svalbard told a similar story for the entire Arctic Ocean.[695]

The Betrayal of the Wooden Thermometers

"No current tree ring based reconstruction of extratropical Northern Hemisphere temperatures that extends *into the 1990s captures the full range of late 20th century warming observed in the instrumental record."*

Dr. R.R. Wilson, University of Edinburgh

"It is important to remember that locally few regions exhibit statistically significant warming. Highly *significant at the hemispheric level, but not great at the local level."*[806]

Dr. Phil Jones, University of East Anglia

Because modern thermometers are typically placed near human disturbances, it is difficult to determine how much current land use changes have affected current instrumental temperature measurements (see Chapter 3). Even in the small village of Barrow Alaska, researchers have reported that "urban" heating had raised winter temperatures by 4° to 9°F higher than the uninhabited tundra.[000] Furthermore, reliable instrumental data does not extend much earlier than the 20th century, so scientists rely on tree-rings from both living and fossilized trees to reconstruct temperatures dating back a thousand years. Because researchers sample locations at the uninhabited tree-line, tree-ring temperature measurements are relatively unaffected by human disturbance. Because properly calibrated tree-rings allow scientists to reconstruct past temperatures, climate scientists travelled worldwide collecting tree-ring data in order to put the current climate change in a historical framework *and the results have contradicted CO$_2$ theory.*

Most tree ring studies suggest that temperatures have declined since the 1950s. In addition to the 2012 study of Scandinavian trees (see Figure 48),[705] tree rings from around the world presented similar patterns of declining summer temperatures in Siberia,[702] Carpathian Mountains in Poland and Slovakia,[723] Nepal and Katmandu,[729] Tien Shan in China[711], British Columbia,[730] Northern Quebec,[732] the Yukon, and South Island of New Zealand,[731,721] In fact a 2007 paper by 10 leading tree-ring scientists reported that every tree-ring study has yielded temperatures that are lower than what the current instrumental data suggests. They wrote, *"No current tree ring based reconstruction of extratropical Northern Hemisphere temperatures that extends into the 1990s captures the full range of late 20th century warming observed in the instrumental record."*[714]

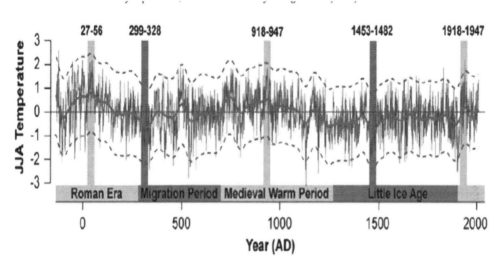

Figure 48. 2000 year summer temperature reconstruction of northern Scandinavia. Warmest 30-year periods are highlighted in by light gray bars (i.e. 27-56, or 1918-1947) and coldest 30-year periods are highlighted by dark gray bars (i.e. 1453-1482) Reprinted from Global and Planetary Change, vol. 88-89, Esper, J. et al, Variability and extremes of northern Scandinavian summer temperatures over the past two millennia, 2012, with permission from Elsevier.[705]

Dr. Keith Briffa had collected data "from trees sampled at more than 300 locations spread across the Northern Hemisphere."[708,735] He was among the first to report that tree ring temperatures disagreed with instrumental temperatures since the 1950s and published *"Trees tell of past climates: but are they speaking less clearly today?"* He chose to interpret this recent decline of tree ring temperatures as "a dramatic change in the sensitivity of hemispheric tree-growth to temperature forcing."

Who to believe? If the tree ring data is reliable, then past temperatures were indeed much warmer than today, and our urbanized instrumental measurements have exaggerated climate warming. Alternatively, if the trees had suddenly "lost sensitivity" and the instrumental data accurately reflects natural temperatures, then the trees are acting like wooden-headed deniers. Tree ring data would then over estimate past temperatures. That would mean the recent global warming is worse than we thought. However suggesting insensitivity casts significant doubts on the whole science of tree-rings. Climate scientists have called this enigma the "divergence problem."[707] Many CO_2 advocates argue that trees suddenly became less responsive to their environment around 1950, while *other scientists have questioned the calibration techniques and biases in the instrumental data.*

A sudden onset of "temperature insensitivity" seems highly unlikely from a biological, chemical and evolutionary perspective. Many of the sampled trees had either lived through warmer times or were genetic clones from rootstocks that survived the Holocene Optimum. Furthermore the Arctic had undergone a similar warming period in the 1930's when Arctic temperatures exceeded the temperatures of the 1980's and 90's when the most recent tree-ring samples had been collected.[412] In 2004 climate scientists wrote, "*The huge warming of the Arctic that started in the early 1920s and lasted for almost two decades is one of the most spectacular climate events of the twentieth century*" and because "*the ongoing present warming has just reached the peak value of the 1940s, this has underpinned some views that even the present Arctic warming is dominated by factors other than increasing greenhouse gases.*"[412]

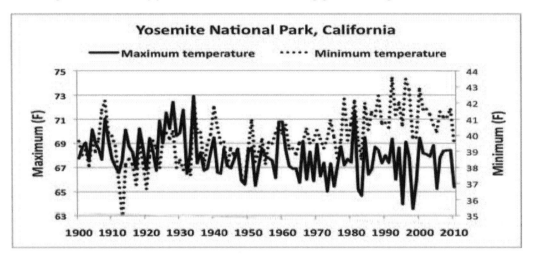

There was no divergence between tree rings and instrumental data during peak temperatures in the 1930s and 1940s, so there is no reason to believe less extreme temperatures had suddenly induced "temperature insensitivity." It may be possible that pollution had affected the trees, but the lichens that grow on trees are far more sensitive to pollution. From my observations, pollution at the tree line is insignificant and by most accounts, since the passage of the Clean Air Act in 1970, air quality has been improving. Furthermore in several places both instrumental maximum temperatures and tree rings all peaked in the 1930s and 1940s. [702,705,734]

What had changed since 1950 was the disproportional influence of the minimum temperature associated with creeping urbanization and increased data homogenization. Trees do not photosynthesize during the darkness of pre-dawn when the minimum temperatures are recorded. Physiologically, it is the summer maximum temperatures that should correlate best with tree ring growth. As seen throughout most of California and much of the USA, instrumental temperatures based on just maximum temperatures have not surpassed the 1940s as did temperatures from ice core data on the Antarctic peninsula.[323] Therefore several scientists suspected that the "divergence problem" arose from using an average temperature that had been skewed by the minimum. New studies found when the maximum temperatures were used, the trees and instrumental data agreed.[720,721,707]

Another possible contribution to the divergence problem is that "an adjustment process on steroids" had tainted the instrumental data by creating artificially steep temperature trends (see Chapter 3). A 2012 study criticizing the adjustment process reported, "results cast some doubts in the use of homogenization procedures and tend to indicate that the global temperature increase during the last century is between" *0.7°F for raw data and 1.3°F for adjusted.*[727] *Adjustments boosted temperatures 160%!*

Adjustments are also very subjective and vary between agencies. For example, a prominent researcher was reconstructing temperatures from tree rings near the village of Dawson in the Yukon Territory but found a significant divergence between instrumental and tree ring temperatures. There were two official temperature records to choose from and both had been homogenized. The divergence was reduced when she used data from the Historical Canadian Climate Network (HCCN). *The HCCN data suggested a rising average trend of 2.5°F /century. In contrast, the Global Historical Climate Network amped up the trend to about 8°F/century.* Although the smaller trend reduced the divergence problem, based on the advice from NOAA's David Easterling (who coauthored the extreme climate paper with Parmesan; see Chapter 6), the trend of about 8°F/century was used "*because he believed it better reflected the warming trend* of the 20th century observed at other stations in this general region (emphasis added)."[79] To explain the resulting divergence while still embracing their homogenization procedures, researchers are forced to declare the trees insensitive to climate change. Because tree ring reconstruction models could not verify the adjusted temperatures it "compelled a number of researchers to eliminate recent decades from their calibration modeling, effectively shortening the available periods for direct calibration and verification-testing between tree rings and climate"[79]

Michael Mann is most noted for his reconstruction of past temperatures known as the "hockey stick" as illustrated in Figure 49.[†††††] The "hockey stick" representation was highlighted by Al Gore in "An Inconvenient Truth" and was an icon featured by the Intergovernmental Panel on Climate Change (IPCC). It was the hockey stick's rapidly rising 20th century temperatures that has evoked widespread fears of a climate out of control. For that reason it has also been a lightning rod for skeptics and the subject of many books and blogs. The pros and cons of the hockey stick have been deeply delved into in a skeptical book by Montford[801] and a book in his own defense

---

[†††††] Data downloaded from KNMI Explorer, NH [K] NH temperature reconstruction, Mann et al, Science 2009 (326) 1256-1260 doi:10.1126/science.1177303, 1850-2006 PC-filtered instrumental observation

by Mann[802].

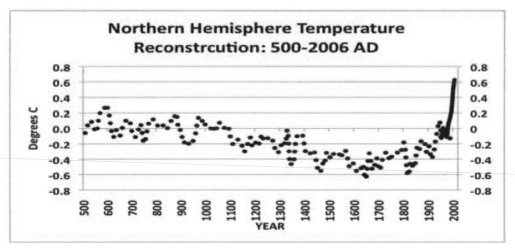

Figure 49. Michael Mann's reconstruction of Northern Hemisphere temperatures.

My concern is that to make this iconic "hockey stick," Mann simply eliminated the divergence problem. He only included tree ring evidence (the dotted line) up to the 1950s. He then overlaid the global average of the adjusted instrumental data (the solid line) to make a chimeric representation of climate change. In the Climategate emails this was known as "Mike's *Nature* trick" (because it was published in *Nature*) to "hide the decline." Many skeptics mistakenly thought he was hiding the decline in the instrumental temperatures, but they were mistaken. However, Mann's methods did obscure the major disagreement between trees, human instruments and data adjustments.

The power of one graphic's virtual reality is startling. Mann's chimeric hockey stick representation of a global average suggests the polar bears are suffering from rapid warming. To publicize his interpretation, Mann ventured to the Hudson Bay. Reporting that he had witnessed undernourished bears he commented, "For the first time in my life, I actually saw climate change unfolding before my eyes. It was a sobering moment, and one I'll never forget."[895] In contrast, research at the time of Mann's visit, indicated the condition of the polar bears of the Hudson Bay had been improving and the population was increasing[572] (see Chapter 14). Who to believe?

Nonetheless it is always local temperatures, never some chimeric average, which affects all organisms. When Dr. Jeff Severinghaus emailed IPCC scientists about the divergence problem, he asked why the tree rings had not revealed any warming. CO_2 advocate Phil Jones replied, "It is important to remember that *locally few regions exhibit statistically significant warming.* Highly significant at the hemispheric level, but not great at the local level." The Scandinavian instrumental and tree-ring temperatures from the Arctic tree-line are a better reflection of what Arctic wildlife has actually experienced in the Atlantic sector of the Arctic. Again at the local level there is no worrisome warming, and this is also seen in tree ring studies around the world.

A recent 2012 paper, "The extra-tropical Northern Hemisphere temperature in the last two millennia: reconstructions of low-frequency variability"[822] published the graphs of over 91 paleoclimate studies using tree-rings and other temperature proxies from 1500 to 2000 AD. With the author's permission I am presenting the first 64 graphs from his Figure 2. The temperatures on the right hand side vary because some axes represent actual temperatures while others represent temperature anomalies. Nonetheless if the graph curves upward then so did the temperatures. The far right hand side of each graph always represents the most recent temperatures from 1900 to 2000 AD. Many studies show temperatures rising from the 1800s to 1950, but very few show a rise after that period. I ask you to count how many tree ring studies reveal a jump in temperature from 1950 to 2000 like Mann's hockey stick.

I suspect that most people would agree that only a small minority of studies approximate anything close to looking like a hockey stick, reinforcing Dr. Jones' admission "It is important to remember that *locally few regions exhibit statistically significant warming.*" Global warming is not global.

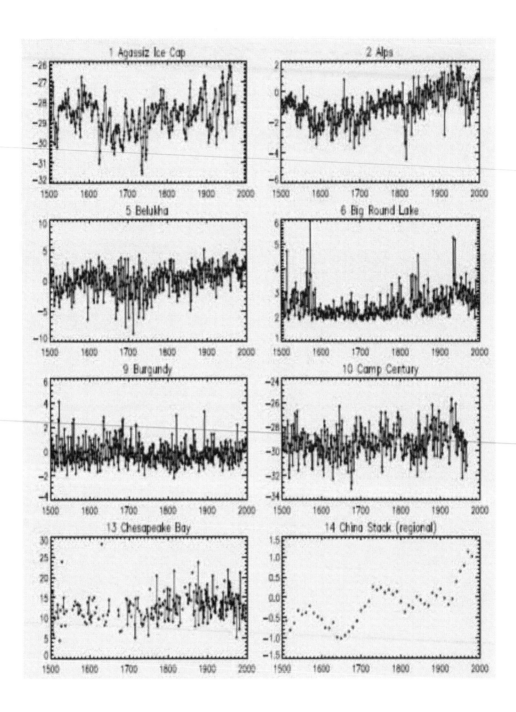

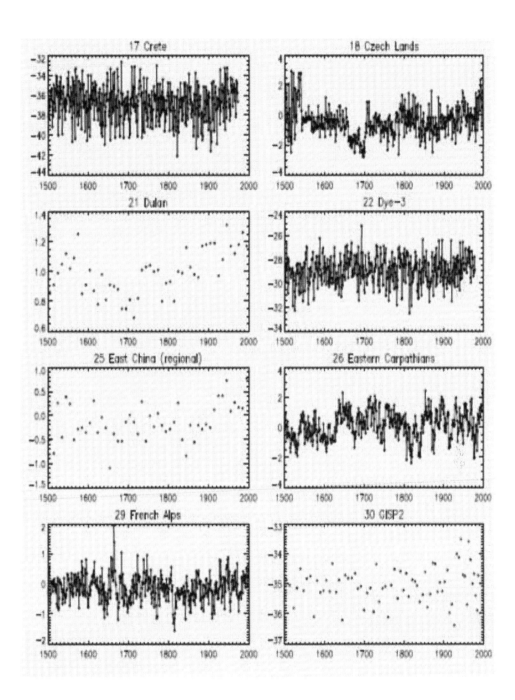

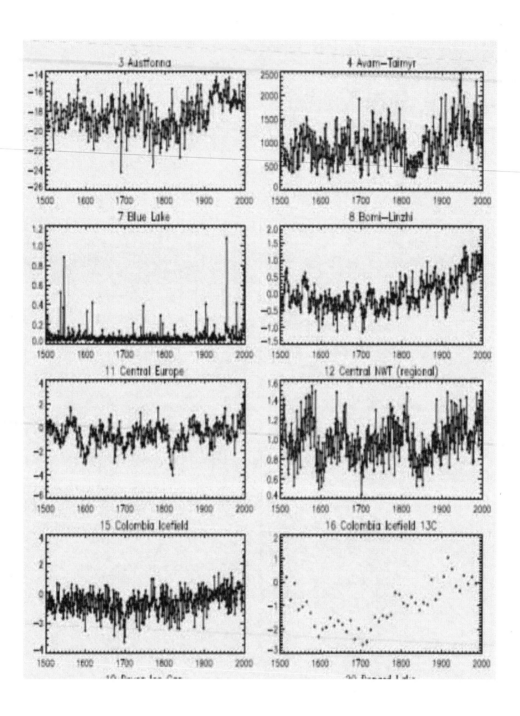

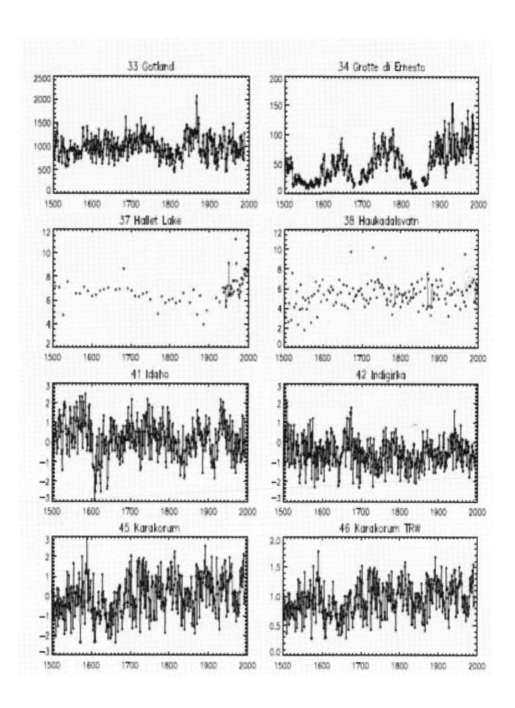

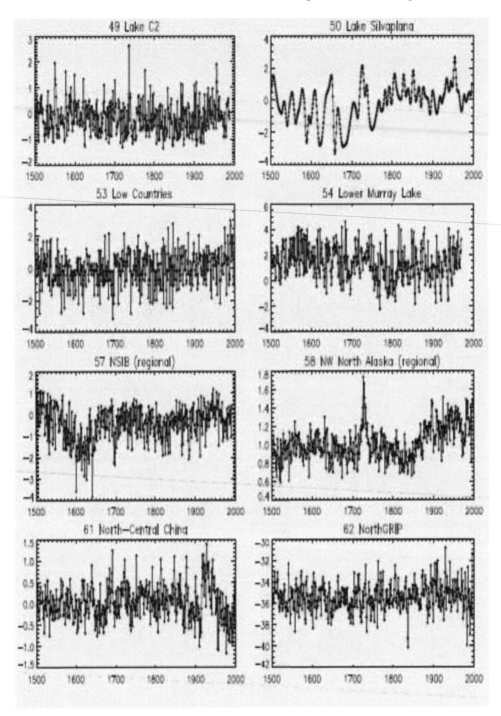

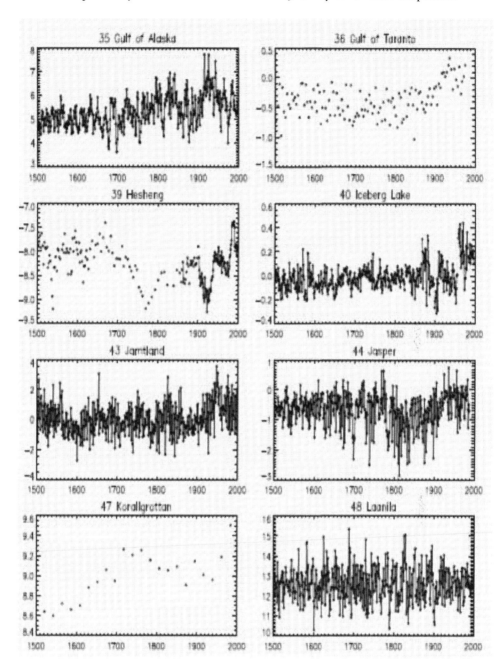

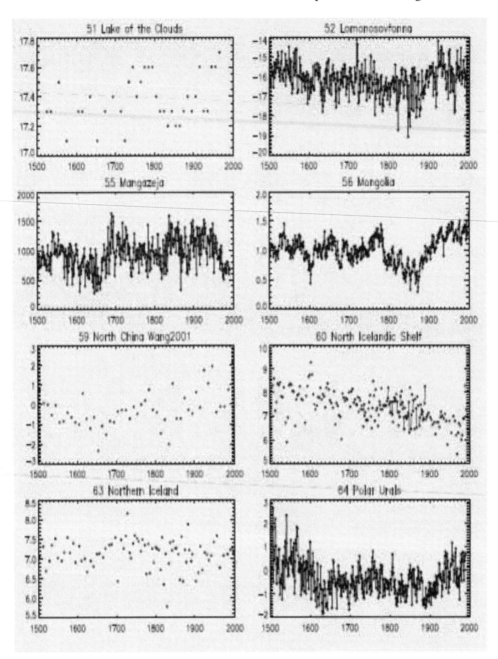

16

Many Ways to Shrink a Glacier

Kilimanjaro: Freeze Dried

"The near extinction of the plateau ice in modern times is controlled by the absence of sustained regional wet periods rather than changes in local air temperature on the peak of Kilimanjaro." [532]

Dr. Georg Kaser, Tropical Glaciology Group, University of Innsbruck

"Melt dominates where precipitation is high and sublimation dominates where precipitation is low." [853]

Dr. Summer Rupper, Brigham Young University

Kilimanjaro's shrinking glaciers illustrate another conflicting diagnoses arising from a local versus a global perspective. In 2004, Dr. Geoff Jenkins, Head of the Climate Prediction Programme at England's Hadley Centre sent an email to his colleague and CO_2 advocate, Dr. Phil Jones. Jenkins was worried about the credibility of the advocates' arguments that Kilimanjaro was a victim of global warming. He wrote,

"…we have been concerned that people often use the melting glacier on Kilimanjaro as an example of impacts of man-made warming. you may have seen some stories countering this on the sceptics websites. I got philip brohan to look at temps there (see attached) and there isnt any convincing consistent recent warming in the station data. but your gridded CRUtem2V does show a recent warming. presumably that is because (as philip suggests) the gridded stuff has influences from quite a large radius, and hence may reflect warming at stations a long way from kilimanjaro? would you agree that there is no convincing evidence for kilimanjaro glacier melt being due to recent warming (let alone man-made warming)? be grateful for your help, cheers"

Advocates had been misled by Jones' averaging techniques that had obscured the more critical local temperature. Advocates were further led by assertions by Dr. Lonnie Thompson who published that the glaciers on Kilimanjaro had begun growing over 11,000 years ago and had survived both the Holocene Optimum and periods of drought lasting 300 years. Blaming global warming Thompson warned, "The disappearance of Kilimanjaro's ice fields, expected between 2015 and 2020, will be unprecedented for the Holocene."[850] Al Gore's *Inconvenient Truth* soon elevated the shrinking glaciers of Kilimanjaro to icon status of CO_2-caused warming.

However Thompson's interpretation was soon contradicted. Other researchers found vegetation debris at the base of new ice cores that indicated that the glaciers had disappeared several times during the past 10,000 years. *Furthermore the glaciers were rapidly retreating, even though automatic weather stations at the foot of the glacier reported that air temperatures never rose above the freezing point.* (That was the reason for Jenkins' email about *the lack of any warming*.) The latest research suggests that due to the lack of moisture, the glaciers disappear every 160 years despite below-freezing air temperatures. Kilimanjaro's recent retreat was not at all unprecedented, and not due to global warming.[532]

In 2006, I attended the AAAS meeting (American Association for the Advancement of Science) in San Francisco. Lonnie Thompson was scheduled to speak, and I was eager to hear his explanation why Kilimanjaro was shrinking while glaciers from southwestern Norway, parts of coastal Alaska, Patagonia, Karakoram, and Fjordland of the South Island of New Zealand were expanding. Because there was no longer a consensus, I expected a lively debate. Instead either the AAAS president, or the editor of their journal Science introduced the session confidently proclaiming, "there is no more debate" to the roaring approval of the crowd. Later Lonnie Thompson presented a pictorial tour of the dramatic retreats of the world's glaciers. During the follow-up question period, Thompson was asked if he could link rising CO_2 to shrinking glaciers. Thompson paused as he carefully chose his words. "*We know that rising concentrations of CO_2 correlate with retreating glaciers.*" Next question. That was the extent of the discussion about the causes of shrinking glaciers.

In contrast, several experts have documented how other factors correlate with Kilimanjaro's shrinking glaciers. One expert wrote, "climatological processes other than air temperature, control the ice recession in a direct manner. *A drastic drop in atmospheric moisture at the end of the 19th century* and the ensuing drier climatic conditions are likely forcing glacier retreat on Kilimanjaro."[827] Another paper concluded that their research "provides a clear indication that solar radiation is the main climatic parameter governing and maintaining ice retreat since ca. 1880."[828]And yet another paper concluded, "it is likely that ice has come and gone repeatedly on Kibo's summit plateau [a peak on Kilimanjaro], throughout the Holocene. Such cyclic behavior is supported by evidence that demonstrated changes in precipitation simultaneously drove shrinking glaciers at high elevations and declining lake levels at lower elevations.[532] Another researcher emphasized that logging had disrupted the forest's transpiration rates that normally wick ground water to the surface, further drying the region. They argued, "long-term ice retreat at the summit of Kilimanjaro therefore is most likely to be influenced by changes in local land-use."[829]

How can glaciers shrink when temperatures are below freezing? The answer is sublimation. When the air is dry, there is a one-way flow of water molecules from the ice to the air. Even in the darkness of an Antarctic winter with -60°F temperatures, snow and ice disappear due to sublimation. The sun's high-energy short-wave radiation will speed that process – even though air temperatures are far below freezing. We can visibly distinguish ice loss caused by prolonged sublimation versus melting caused by higher air temperatures. In the cartoon, the snowman in the middle represents the original condition. On the left, only the side of snowman directly struck by the sun has been sublimated away by shortwave radiation. Analogous to a sunburn line that develops between the sun and shade, sunlight chisels a sharp angle in the ice. In contrast, when air temperatures rise above freezing, the entire surface melts, leaving rounded, oozing shapes as depicted by the snowman on the right.

The melting from just a week of warm air temperatures can erase any sharp features generated by decades of sublimation, so the presence of sharp angled ridges and chiseled features are the telltale signs of extended periods of below freezing air temperatures.

Because rates of sublimation vary between sunlit surfaces and shaded surfaces, angles align with the sun. Kilimanjaro's vertical walls are so sensitive to solar radiation that east-facing sides erode more quickly than west-facing sides. This is due to the afternoon clouds that develop and lessen the afternoon sun's intensity. Once a cavity is formed in the ice, it traps and reflects light, which accentuates sublimation. Sharp structures known as *penitentes* are one telltale sign of subfreezing sublimation (see Figure 50). Similarly so are the sharp ridges and deeply lined vertical cliffs of Kilimanjaro (see Figure 51).

Figure 50. Penitentes. Photograph made freely available by the European Southern Observatory. Penitentes ice formations at the southern end of the Chajnantor plain in Chile. August 25, 2009.

Elsewhere, glaciers resting on steep slopes consist of two general zones with different local climates. The upper "accumulation zone" experiences colder temperatures and heavier snowfall. The weight of the accumulated snow and ice drives the glacier down to a lower elevation "ablation zone" where temperatures are higher and melting exceeds accumulation. The size of these glaciers is determined by the balance between growth in the accumulation zone, primarily driven by snowfall and sublimation, versus decay in the ablation zone which is primarily driven by warmer air temperatures.

In contrast, Kilimanjaro's plateau glaciers rest completely in the accumulation zone and the plateau prevents any redistribution of ice. Drier air increases sublimation and also allows more solar radiation to reach the surface, further increasing the glacier's decay. Without a deep snowpack, unprotected vertical walls relentlessly sublimate away. And whenever landscape features fragment the glacier and expose more vertical surfaces, the glacier decays more rapidly.

For Dr. Georg Kaser (a glacier expert from the University of Innsbruck, Austria), Kilimanjaro provided a superb natural laboratory in which to observe the glacier's "decay rate" independent of warm air temperatures. Without heavy wet years and a deep snowpack, he calculates that Kilimanjaro's plateau glacier can shrivel from its maximum size and disappear in just 160 years, solely due to below freezing sublimation. That averages to a loss of 30,000 square meters per year, without any "warm air melting."[532]

Figure 51. Kilimanjaro's northern glacier from NASA photo #8103310189

Not being glacier experts, Kevin Trenberth and Phil Jones relied on experts like Kaser to compile the IPCC report. Kaser's emails[806] clearly explained to them why global warming was not driving the retreat of Kilimanjaro's glaciers.

> "The plateau glaciers retreat from their vertical walls where no accumulation is possible and since they do so, there is no way to find an equilibrium besides disappearance. The vertical walls are a result of cold temperatures, high sublimation, and strong solar radiance. There is no way to replace the retreat by ice dynamics on the flat summit plateau." Kaser concluded, "*All studies which investigate tropical glacier retreat and climate show the dominance of changes in energy and mass balance terms are related to the atmospheric moisture content rather than locally measured air temperatures(emphasis added).*"

It was also well known that many small glaciers from the Little Ice Age, had disappeared between 1850 and the 1940s, such as the glaciers on Europe's Iberian peninsula.[908] Kaser noted many small glaciers will continue to disappear (likely before Kilimanjaro's) adding, "well known and studied glaciers in the Andes like Chacaltaya, Charquini and Pastoruri will also disappear soon. *This is not because of a particular regional climate feature but just because they were already small when retreats started* (emphasis added)." [806] Elsewhere glacier experts note that wherever precipitation is low, sublimation drives the retreating glaciers.[853]

Even hardcore CO_2 advocates like Michael Mann have admitted warming temperatures did not cause Kilimanjaro's retreating glaciers. In his book *Dire Predictions* there is a chapter titled "The Vanishing Snows of Kilimanjaro, An Icon of Climate Change?" In the face of overwhelming scientific evidence, Mann wisely acknowledged that retreating glaciers were not caused by global warming but instead had been impacted by changes in precipitation patterns. However, Mann still managed to implicate CO_2 stating that melting glaciers "...are tied to larger-scale climate change. In this sense human influence on climate is probably responsible for the imminent demise of Kilimanjaro's snows, even if warmer regional temperatures alone are not."

But Mann's *"probably responsible"* argument falls far outside the scientific process and into the realm of opportunistic story telling. To suggest Africa's 5000-year drying trend or dry cycles caused by ocean oscillations are driven by CO_2 is ludicrous, and unsupported by the scientific community. The rapid rate of decay of Kilimanjaro's vertical walls abides by simple natural physical processes independent of CO_2. Biochemist Isaac Asimov wrote, "The only constant is change," and science education is best served by empowering the public with the knowledge about what causes that change. Instead, Mann and other advocates tirelessly try to convince the public that all climate change is due to human influence and rising CO_2. Such overzealous advocacy is a public disservice.

Solar Cycles

"The timing of the onset of glacier retreat (mid-nineteenth century) conflicts with mean annual temperatures based on instrumental data [Jones et al., 2001] and with paleo-temperature reconstructions [Mann et al., 1999] that show no clear warming until the beginning of the twentieth century" [867]

Dr. Christian Vincent, Laboratoire de Glaciologie et de Geophysique de l'Environnement

"comparison between the Great Aletsch glacier and the residual 14C records supports the hypothesis that variations in solar activity were a major forcing factor of climatic oscillations in west-central Europe during the late Holocene." [998]

Dr. Hanspeter Holzhauser, University of Zurich

Counterintuitively, the earth is closest to the sun in January during the northern hemisphere's winter. We experience cold winters despite being more than 3 million miles closer to the sun because the tilt of the earth's axis points the northern hemisphere away from the sun. In 50,000 years the earth will again be closest to the sun in July. The earth's axis also wobbles, which determines which hemisphere receives the most heat. These orbital changes are collectively called Milankovitch cycles and most scientists believe they drove the 100,000-year ice age cycles.

The intensity of sun's output (solar flux) also varies in 11-year sunspot cycles. The intensity of the 11-year cycles also varies in 88- and 120-year cycles. The 20th century experienced a sunspot maximum that arguably produced the highest level of solar flux in a thousand years. In contrast, the Little Ice Age was dominated by sunspot minimums. Sunspot cycles are associated with cycles of advancing and retreating glaciers and have also been shown to affect ocean circulation that redistributes tropical heat.[138,843]

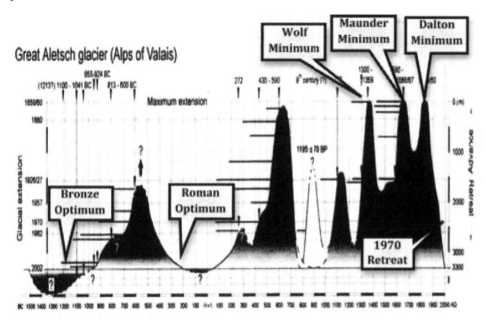

Figure 52. Three thousand year record of the Great Aletsch glacier. Reprinted from The Holocene, vol. 15/6, Holzhauser, H. et al, Glacier and lake-level variations in west-central Europe over the past 3500 years.[998] 2012 with permission from Sage publications. (Call-out boxes added)

Scientists calculate that the world's glaciers were smaller for more than 60% of the last 11,000 years, primarily due to warming effects of the Milankovitch cycles.[848] The lowest point in glacier extent appeared during the Holocene Optimum. During that time all of Norway's glaciers disappeared at least once,[833] and Greenland's glaciers retreated past the positions they occupy today.[862] After the optimum ended about 5000 years ago, glaciers began to grow in dramatic spurts. The long-term cooling trend dubbed the "neo-glaciation" is driven by Milankovitch cycles. Superimposed on this cooling trend are dramatic spikes in glacier advances associated with sunspot minimums and retreats associated with sunspot maximums. (see Figure 52.)

As illustrated by the rhythm of Europe's largest glacier, the Great Aletsch glacier, the last 3500 years were punctuated by progressively stronger glacier advances, followed by rapid retreats. The dark peaks of Figure 52 represent the length of the Aletsch glacier. The baseline represents the past 3500 years and the current position of the glacier.

The Great Aletsch glacier is fairly representative of all large glaciers in the European Alps. During the Bronze Age Optimum around 1400 BC, the Aletsch glacier was about one mile shorter than today. The glacier expanded slightly but during the Roman Optimum between 200 BC and circa 50 AD, it rapidly retreated to a position slightly less than today's position. The most recent retreat of Alpine glaciers has exposed Roman coins and other artifacts where Roman outposts once guarded ice-free passes. Expanding glaciers rapidly covered those outposts during the Migration Period around 450 AD, but abruptly retreated again during Medieval Warm Period beginning circa 700 to 800 AD. The most extensive period of glacier growth occurred during the Little Ice Age beginning circa 1300 and ending circa 1850 AD.

The Little Ice Age (LIA) marked the coldest period in the last 10,000 years, and provided the most extensive glacier advances. Each advance coincided with a sunspot minimum. Yet even during the LIA, glaciers rapidly retreated at rates similar to today when solar activity increased. In the 1800s glaciers began to rapidly retreat as we approached a new sunspot maximum, causing most small glaciers to disappear by 1950. The rate of the Great Aletsch's recent 200-year retreat appears very similar to earlier LIA retreats when CO_2 had little impact, suggesting a similar cause. With the sun suddenly approaching a new minimum, if sunspot cycles did drive past advances and retreats, we would predict glaciers will begin to advance in the next decade. How the glaciers respond to this new minimum will help scientists separate the effects of sunspot cycles from CO_2.

In addition to orbital cycles and sunspot cycles, water vapor and aerosols control how much sunlight actually reaches the surface. The amount of water vapor in the atmosphere is driven globally by El Niño cycles[899] and regionally by other ocean oscillations. Despite two decades of declining solar flux, a University of Girona study reported, "Solar radiation in Spain has increased by 2.3% every decade since the 1980s. This increase is linked to the decreased presence of clouds."[996] The solar radiation record for the Alps shows that in the 1940s global shortwave radiation over the summer months was 8% above the long-term average and significantly higher than today, favoring rapid glacier mass loss. Experts reported, "Snow and ice melt was stronger in the 1940s than in recent years, in spite of significantly higher air temperatures in the present decade. Dimming of solar radiation from the 1950s until the 1980s is in line with reduced melt rates and advancing glaciers"[85]

Advocates argue that the recent retreat of the world's glaciers is evidence of rising air temperatures due to increasing CO_2. Although rising air temperatures definitely increased melting in the ablation zone, the rhythm of advancing and retreating glaciers has been independent of CO_2 concentrations and global temperatures. If Mann's hockeystick reconstruction of the Little Ice Age temperatures is correct, the small drop in global temperature during the LIA was not enough to cause the glaciers to advance. Furthermore the rapid retreat of glaciers in the European Alps began in the 1800's before global temperatures had sufficiently risen. Several researchers call this the *Little Ice Age paradox*.[867] It appears more likely that rapidly retreating LIA glaciers were driven more by sunspot cycles, changes in moisture and the resulting increase in sublimation.

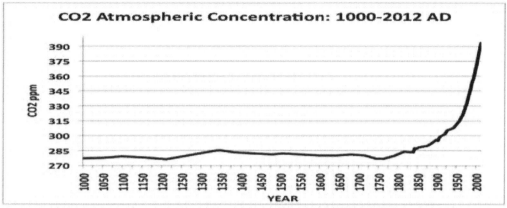

Figure 53. Carbon Dioxide Concentration Since the Medieval Warm Period

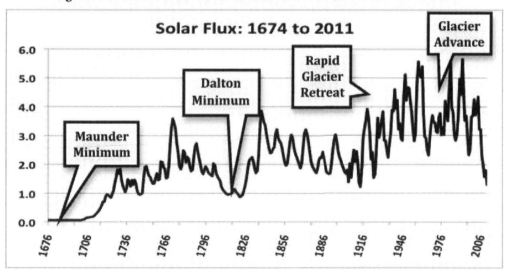

Figure 54. Three hundred year record of Solar Flux

Because the varying strength of the sun's magnetism alters the proportion of carbon14 (^{14}C) and beryllium (^{10}Be) (cosmogenic isotopes[‡‡‡‡‡]) scientists can track

---

[‡‡‡‡‡] Cosmic rays striking the earth's atmosphere create several common isotopes. A highly active sun creates a magnetic shield that blocks cosmic rays. Geologic layers with lower proportions of cosmogenic isotopes indicates a very active sun.

changes in the strength of the solar flux far beyond written records of sunspot observations. The pattern of solar flux correlates well with major advances and retreats.[787]

Observations by the Swiss Glacier Monitoring Network lend additional support to the sunspot theory. When solar flux dipped between 1960s and 1980s, most glaciers around the world stopped retreating, and many glaciers started advancing. In 1980 sixty-three glaciers in the European Alps advanced, twelve remained stationary and just twenty-six continued to retreat. It is not clear why some glaciers behaved differently, however many glaciers often respond to a climatic change only after a 10 to 20 year lag period. Or perhaps some were located in a dry "rain shadow" where sublimation continued to dominate. Nonetheless the pattern of retreating and advancing Alpine glaciers does not follow the steady rise in CO_2, but undulates with cycles of the sun and ocean oscillations (see Figure 55).

Figure 55. Proportion Retreating Glaciers from the Swiss Glacier Monitoring Network

Ocean Oscillations and Snowfall

"The claim that Himalayan glaciers may disappear by 2035 requires a 25-fold greater loss rate from 1999 to 2035 than that estimated for 1960 to 1999. It conflicts with knowledge of glacier climate relationships, and is wrong."[808]

Dr. J. Graham Cogley, Trent University

The supply of moisture unarguably contributes to the patterns of glacier advance and retreat. Researchers observed that Europe's Little Ice Age glaciers did not advance synchronously with global temperatures because the North Atlantic Oscillation (NAO) alternately delivered moisture between northern and southern Europe.[833] Similarly during the 1980s and 1990s when the North Atlantic Oscillation was positive, it pushed winter storms northward, and the glaciers in Scandinavia advanced while glaciers in the Alps retreated. *Due to this see-saw effect, a 2005 study calculated no overall change in the mass of European glaciers*[855] as the loss of mass by glaciers in the Alps had been offset by an increase of mass in Scandinavia. Researchers also reported, "Snow and ice melt was stronger in the 1940s than in recent years, in spite of significantly higher average air temperatures in the present decade. This paradox was explained by the Atlantic Multidecadal Oscillation and its effect on water vapor and precipitation.[85,86] Several researchers have correlated the advancing Little Ice Age glaciers with a 25% increase in precipitation.[823,824,852,867]

Ignoring ocean cycles and their effect on precipitation, the Intergovernmental Panel on Climate Change (IPCC) assumed retreating glaciers were simply driven by rising levels of CO_2. They announced with high confidence that the Himalayan glaciers would disappear by the year 2035 and perhaps sooner if the Earth keeps warming at the current rate. Those alarming IPCC claims rightfully stirred a disbelieving crowd of skeptics across the blogosphere and within the scientific community as well.

In contrast, a 2012 study has now confirmed that the Karakoram glaciers of the western Himalaya have been growing over the past decade.[807] Curiouser and curiouser, several authors had published that Karakoram glaciers had been increasing years before the IPCC predicted their imminent disappearance.[839] Karakoram covers about 45% of the Himalayas and is home to the second tallest peak in the world, K2. The Karakoram is also home of the Kutiah Glacier, which holds the Guinness world record for the fastest surging glacier. *In 1953, the Kutiah Glacier advanced 7.4 miles in just 3 months.*

The growing glaciers of the Karakoram suggest the IPCC was too narrowly focused. They had misinterpreted regional climate change as an example of global climate change. The Pacific Decadal Oscillation affects the Asian monsoons and how much moisture reaches the eastern Himalayan glaciers and those glaciers had indeed been shrinking. However they were not shrinking at a rate that would even approach disappearing in our children's children's lifetimes. Experts investigating the IPCC's alarming prediction reported, "The claim that Himalayan glaciers may disappear by 2035 requires a 25-fold greater loss rate from 1999 to 2035 than that estimated for 1960 to 1999. *It conflicts with knowledge of glacier climate relationships, and is wrong.*"[808]

The paradox of growing glaciers in Karakoram and shrinking glaciers in the eastern Himalaya is difficult to explain by a uniform blanket of CO_2 or a global temperature increase. However the path by which moisture is delivered to each region readily explains the difference. The Karakoram receives most of its moisture from westerly winds, while the eastern Himalaya accumulates snow during the summer monsoons. Most climate scientists agree that any future changes in monsoon intensity will have an important effect on Himalayan glaciers,[712,851,852,853,854] and the strength of the  monsoons correlates with the Pacific Decadal Oscillation (PDO). Asian droughts were more frequent during the warm phase of the PDO that persisted from 1976 to the early 2000s (see Chapter 9).

A 2012 study also determined that temperatures in the Karakoram Range have been cooling,[712] especially during the summer.[839] However the lack of widespread instrumental data makes any estimate of temperature trends unreliable and tree-ring studies have suggested there is cooling in some places and warming in others.[868,869] A 2003 study found no warming in the 20th century in either the tree rings of Nepal or the instrumental temperatures at Katmandu.[711]

The Pacific Decadal Oscillation similarly controls the general pattern of rains and snowfall in the mountains of western North America. While glaciers in the southern Sierra Nevada shrunk, the glaciers on Mt Shasta nearer the Oregon border continued to grow.[835] A 2006 study reported a general retreat of the glaciers on Oregon's tallest peak, Mt Hood, since the end of the Little Ice Age, but those glaciers ebb and flow according to the PDO. "Mount Hood's glaciers experienced two periods each of retreat and advance. Glaciers retreated between 1901 and 1946 in response to rising temperatures and declining precipitation. A mid-century cool, wet period led to glacier advances. Glaciers retreated from the late 1970s to the mid-1990s as a result of rising temperatures and generally declining precipitation. *High precipitation in the late 1990s caused slight advances in 2000 and 2001* (emphasis added)."[836] Washington's Mt Rainer recorded a similar cycle of heavy snow accumulation and glacier advance between 1945 and 1976, with a subsequent melt back after the PDO entered its warm phase.[870]

While most photographs of shrinking glaciers compare the years circa 1900 with the present, those pictures can be misleading. The audience does not see how the glaciers ebbed and flowed during the intervening years. For many glaciers the greatest rate of retreat occurred during the first half of the 20th century when the effects from CO_2 were trivial. The greatest retreat of Montana's Sperry Glacier in the Glacier National Park happened by the 1940s after a prolonged drought. Between 1850 and 2005, the Sperry Glacier lost 77% of its total area, about 2.9 square kilometers. However 81% of that loss happened before 1945.[495] Likewise the greatest retreat of the Darwin Glacier in California's Kings Canyon National Park happened before 1950.[834]

In New Zealand advancing and retreating glaciers also correlate with El Niño cycles. Scientists reported that the two large glaciers, the Franz-Josef and the Fox glaciers have been growing. These glaciers are located on New Zealand's western divide and get more moisture during El Niño events. In contrast, on the east side, El Niño brings drought and there the glaciers are shrinking.[871] The IPCC was well aware that glaciers were growing in several regions including the Himalaya. Kaser advised the IPCC,

> "In some regions moderately increased accumulation observed in recent decades is consistent with changes in atmospheric circulation and associated increases in winter precipitation (e.g., southwestern Norway, parts of coastal Alaska, Patagonia, Karakoram, and Fjordland of the South Island of New Zealand".

Nonetheless the IPCC preferred to spread an alarming story of glaciers disappearing by 2035 or sooner.

Ocean Regime Shifts and Warm Currents

"we find no direct evidence to support the claims that the Greenland ice sheet is melting due to increased temperature caused by increased atmospheric concentration of carbon dioxide. The rate of warming from 1995 to 2005 was in fact lower than the warming that occurred from 1920 to 1930." [657]

Dr. Petr Chylek, Los Alamos National Laboratory

"The warming in the 1920s and 1930s is considered to constitute the most significant regime shift experienced in the North Atlantic in the 20th century." [803]

Dr. Kenneth Drinkwater, Bjerknes Center for Climate Research

Shifting ocean oscillations have increased the flow of warm Gulf Stream waters that eventually bathe the coast of Greenland and islands in the Arctic Ocean. These warm currents melt the bottoms of any glaciers that terminate in the ocean. Greenland's largest outlet glacier, Jakobshavn Isbrae, drains about 7% of the Greenland ice sheet and generates 10% of the Atlantic's icebergs. Most believe that it was an iceberg from Jakobshavn that sunk the Titanic. During the Holocene Optimum, Jakobshavn had retreated further than its present day terminus and remained that way for almost 7000 years. During the Little Ice Age, Jakobshavn rapidly advanced several kilometers beyond today's terminus.[862]

The glaciers' most rapid 20th century retreat occurred between 1920 and 1950, followed by an advance in the 1970s and then a renewed retreat in 1998. Again the NAO and Atlantic Multidecadal Oscillation's influence on warm ocean currents explains this cyclical behavior better than a rising global air temperature. Air temperatures along western Greenland have not exceeded the peaks of the 1940s.[657]

The rapid retreat of Jakobshavn between 1920 and 1940, as well as in the 1990s, corresponds to North Atlantic regime shifts during which warm waters from the Atlantic were pushed into the Arctic. Marine biologists wrote, *"The warming in the 1920s and 1930s is considered to constitute the most significant regime shift experienced in the North Atlantic in the 20th century."*[803] Fishery biologists observed that "species of fish such as cod, haddock and herring expanded farther north while colder-water species such as capelin and polar cod retreated northward. The maximum-recorded movement involved cod, which spread approximately 1200 km northward along West Greenland." The warm water and associated species lingered for 2 more decades before retreating in the 1960s.

There has been a new cycle of warm waters entering the Arctic and many advocates claim it is caused rising CO_2 but researchers have cautioned, "To fully prove the effects of global warming, future changes in the marine biota must exceed those recorded in the 1950s and 1960s."[740] And so far they have not.

Several studies suggest current Arctic temperatures are very similar to the last cycle. A 2006 study of Greenland's land surface temperatures noted, "We find that the current Greenland warming is not unprecedented in recent Greenland history. Temperature increases in the two warming periods are of a similar magnitude, however, *the rate of warming in 1920–1930 was about 50% higher than that in 1995 – 2005.*" They concluded, "we find no direct evidence to support the claims that the Greenland ice sheet is melting due to increased temperature caused by increased atmospheric concentration of carbon dioxide." [657,733] Finally, a 2003 paper from researchers at the International Arctic Research Center in Alaska and the Arctic and Antarctic Research Institute in Russia noted that low-frequency cycles make it very difficult to determine the contributions of CO_2 to Arctic warming. Their study determined that Arctic temperatures in the 1930s and 1940s were exceptionally high, approximately 0.3°F higher than the maximum in 2000.[655]

The greatest loss of Arctic Sea ice in the past 30 years occurred in the Barents Sea near the Russia island of Novaya Zemlya. Glaciers on the island also retreated during the 1920-1930 regime shift, accounting for most of the lost ice mass. Experts reported, "the glaciers completed 75 to 100% of the net twentieth-century retreat by 1952."[796]

The changes in glaciers, fish, sea ice and the tree ring temperatures captured by the Scandinavian studies all agree that the period from about 1920 to 1950 was most likely the warmest the Arctic has experienced. It is not clear what other temperatures advocates have averaged in order to create the dramatic hockeystick interpretation of unprecedented climate change, but it seems quite certain that unprecedented global warming is not global and natural cycles offer a better explanation for regional climate change.

17

Communicating Science

I haven't failed. I've identified 10,000 ways this doesn't work.

Thomas Edison

"That is the way of the scientist. He will spend thirty years in building up a mountain range of facts with the intent to prove a certain theory; then he is so happy with his achievement that as a rule he overlooks the main chief fact of all—that all his accumulation proves an entirely different thing."

Mark Twain

Science is more than a collection of facts or viewpoints that need to be memorized. Science is a process of questioning and testing. Schools that simply force students to remember a list of vocabulary words, facts and theories are not promoting the scientific process; they are simply indoctrinating students with the current dogma. The most vital aspect of scientific education is teaching students how to think creatively and critically. We need to teach students how to design a study that separates confounding factors and how to make predictions that will test the validity of their thinking. We must also teach students how to embrace the lessons of inevitable failures. We often learn more by being wrong. Our understanding becomes muddled when a prediction is "right" for all the wrong reasons.

Communicating science requires demonstrating the skills needed to engage in fruitful discussions with a diverse group of thinkers. It is from those discussions we gain a broader perspective and a more well-rounded understanding. Better communication fosters better science. The greater the diversity of minds that can focus on a problem, the more likely the best solution will emerge.

A growing global community of interconnected minds has sped the development of science in all arenas. Back in my youth when televisions used vacuum tubes and computers were just being transistorized, the advent of giant mainframe computers raised fears that only governments and the rich would have access to that computing power. Yet within thirty years human creativity and the entrepreneurial spirit placed far more computing power in the hands of the great majority of the global citizenry. A global community of entrepreneurial thinkers will likewise solve our energy problems in an environmentally friendly way.

Dr. Temple Grandin understands the power of a diversity of mindsets. She overcame the hardships of autism to become an innovative leader in the animal husbandry industry. She has been actively campaigning to "encourage diversity in modes of thinking so that we aren't losing the special talents of people who might contribute greatly to research and development by offering unique perspectives."

The First Lady Michelle Obama offers similar sage advice. In a 2013 commencement address, she urged graduates to reach out to people with different political beliefs, saying "the country would benefit from the conversations…If you're a Democrat, spend some time talking to a Republican, and if you're a Republican, have a chat with a Democrat. Maybe you'll find some common ground, maybe you won't." However she predicted they would learn something if they reached out "with an open mind and an open heart…And goodness knows, we need more of that, because we know what happens when we only talk to people who think like we do. We just get stuck in our ways."

However in the arena of climate change, we are definitely stuck in our ways. In a world where every one understands the benefits of diversity, a group of entrenched climate scientists have actively sought to prevent all face to face debates and label all skeptics who challenge their dogma as deniers. Why is suppressing skeptical thinking ever considered an acceptable tactic that could ever benefit the scientific process? Sound science is never so fragile that it needs to be protected. Respectful debate encourages us to synthesize a multitude of perspectives that can then provide more satisfactory solutions. Suppressing that debate only communicates the methods of tyranny, not the methods of science.

Cycles of Scientific Stagnation

All schools, all colleges have two great functions: to confer, and to conceal valuable knowledge.

Mark Twain

"The strongest oak of the forest is not the one that is protected from the storm and hidden from the sun. It's the one that stands in the open where it is compelled to struggle for its existence against the winds and rains and the scorching sun".

Napoleon Hill

Scientific disciplines often travel through cycles of discovery and growth where new ideas are sought and embraced and thoroughly discussed. Eventually a new scientific perspective evolves with improved explanatory powers for whatever perplexing phenomenon was in question. The proponents of those improved views are soon elevated to positions of authority. However once entrenched, there is a tendency to protect that authority. Instead of Feynman's ideal scientists trying to prove themselves wrong as quickly as possible, they now try to prove themselves right by any means necessary. Research supporting and protecting their viewpoints are promoted while little tolerance is afforded competing ideas.

John Muir suffered from such a cycle in the field of geology. His humble observations were attacked by the head of the US Geological Survey and Harvard professor Josiah Whitney. Whitney was an excellent geologist for whom Mount Whitney was named. Muir was a naturalist with a simple but deep desire to understand how the world worked. Based on careful observations, Muir wrote popular articles suggesting glaciers had formed Yosemite Valley. This contradicted Whitney who had wedded his lofty reputation to a more catastrophic theory. Instead of trying to prove himself wrong and test Muir's hypotheses, Whitney chose to protect his status by denigrating Muir. Muir was attacked as an amateur who lacked the authority of a credentialed geologist. As evidence mounted, Whitney's attacks intensified, and he dismissed Muir's ideas as flights of fancy from an "ignorant shepherd". But Muir continued to write for popular magazines and newspapers and eventually attracted the attention of other geologists. It has been Muir's ideas that have withstood scientific process of rigorous cross-examination and the test of time. And no one has done more to protect the environment than Muir.

The highly respected Linus Pauling learned little from Whitney's ugly hubris. Pauling had won the 1963 Nobel Peace Prize. He was unquestionably a genius who had won a second Nobel Prize in chemistry for his theories on electro-negativity that explained how atoms bonded to form molecules. If not for a careless error later noticed by Watson and Crick, he would have earned a third Nobel Prize, and the honor of discovering the structure of DNA. A colleague told me that the joke circulating around the Linus Pauling Institute was if he had read his own text book, he would have earned his third Nobel.

Despite his peace prize, Pauling went to war against a fellow scientist who had simply reported observing a crystal with a shape that Pauling's models deemed impossible. In the 1980s Dan Shechtman humbly claimed that he had observed "quasi-crystals."

Quasi-crystals have unusual symmetries that were not predicted by Pauling's models. Instead of embracing a new observation, Pauling tried to suppress it. Pauling repeatedly commandeered the stage at scientific conferences and shouted to the crowd, "Danny Shechtman is talking nonsense. There is no such thing as quasi-crystals, only quasi-scientists."

The head of Shechtman's research group and a so-called "friend," handed him a textbook suggesting that by reading it he would recognize his errors. Shechtman replied that he taught classes with that book, but it didn't change what he saw. However Pauling's belittling of Shechtman was a powerful tool of suppression. Shechtman recalled. "I was thrown out of my research group. They said I brought shame on them with what I was saying."

Likewise journals rejected his initial attempts to publish his findings on the grounds that such a heretical paper was of no interest to the scientific community. A few years later, with the help of a few supporters, he finally published his observations along with a theory describing why it was possible. The result was the scientific equivalent of a religious miracle that healed the blind. By publishing an alternative view, he removed the blinders of the prevailing bias and suddenly everyone started seeing quasi-crystals. Quasi-crystals are now an important component of surgical instruments and in 2011 Dan Shechtman won the Nobel Prize in chemistry for his discovery. The deferential Shechtman suggests, "A good scientist is a humble and listening scientist and not one that is sure 100 percent in what he reads in the textbooks."

Shechtman's story illustrates two powerful points. People see only what they think they should see. Shechtman's publication simply gave them permission to see things that were always there. Conversely those who want to maintain their authority, will work hard to prevent others from thinking outside their box. Dr. Trenberth's speech paradoxically titled "Communicating Climate Science" exemplified such a tactic. He advocated against debating "deniers" to ensure alternative views do not gain any credibility. He understands alternative views, right or wrong, give others permission to think differently.

The second lesson is the power of character assassination. "Quasi-scientists" are less apt to get funding, as would be the case for anyone associating with such a person. After Pauling labeled Shechtman, his friends tossed him from his research group simply to protect themselves. Shechtman's only sin was not recanting an observation. Scientists can be a jealous and vengeful lot. Words like ignorant shepherd, quasi-scientist and deniers have been wielded like a club by those in authority for the same reason entrenched powers have branded their opposition as heretics, infidels, or traitors.

To protect their authority against alternative views, the entrenched German scientists pieced together a consensus to publish "One Hundred against Einstein". Today's entrenched climate scientists now use the term "denier" to warn other scientists that they jeopardize their careers if they dare speak skeptical thoughts that challenge their authority. When Dr Eduardo Zorita spoke out against some manipulative practices by entrenched climate scientists he acknowledged, "By writing these lines I will just probably achieve that a few of my future studies will, again, not see the light of publication."[988]

Denying Uncertainty and Denigrating Skeptics

"So far, no one has been able to provide a compelling answer to why climate change seems to be taking a break. We're facing a puzzle."[997]

Dr. Hans von Storch, University of Hamburg, 2013

"One of the biggest uncertainties in the projection of future climate is our understanding of climate sensitivity."[968]

Dr. James Pope, Royal Meteorological Society

"they [skeptics] want to continue a 20-year assault on climate research, questioning basic science and promoting doubt where there is none."[982]

Dr. Michael Mann, Pennsylvania State University

A growing number of scientists acknowledge that our climate models have failed to simulate the past 10 years of climate change. Most climate scientists admit, "We're facing a puzzle".[997] In contrast a few advocates like Michael Mann accuse skeptics of "promoting doubt where there is none."[982] I hoped the growing uncertainty would prompt prominent climate scientists to engage in a more open scientific process. For fleeting moment, I thought more open debate was emerging when I heard that skeptic Marc Morano and advocate Michael Mann had debated on the BBC's World Service News Hour. But after reading the transcripts, it became clear the purpose of the show was not to foster debate, but to portray Michael Mann as a victim of skeptic attacks. When Morano alluded to contradictory research the commentator shut him off. After Morano spoke, it was not the science that Mann attacked. Mann indulged in exactly what he claimed was being done to him. Mann said "literally everything Morano said was untrue...he spreads malicious lies...[he] uses language that makes it sound like we should be subject to death threats, that we should be literally harmed or killed...he's a hired assassin". When Morano got to speak again, he too turned to personal attacks.

Instead of debates that promote science education, we are bombarded with dialogues that we would be best confined to a Jerry Springer show. Mann's statements reflect a pervasive tactic to profile all skeptics as bad people, and some now suggest skeptics deserved to be exterminated. Professor Richard Parncutt drew the wrath of skeptics when he wrote "In this article I am going to suggest that the death penalty is an appropriate punishment for influential Global Warming deniers." On Joe Romm's Climate Progress someone posted "an entire generation will soon be ready to strangle you and your kind while you sleep in your beds." Dr. James Hansen called for the chief executives of large fossil fuel companies to be put on trial for high crimes against humanity and nature.

Not to be outdone England's skeptic James Delingpole drew the wrath of CO_2 advocates when he suggested, "The climate alarmist industry has some very tough questions to answer: preferably in the defendant's dock in a court of law, before a judge wearing a black cap." In England black caps were only worn by judges when handing out death sentences.

Naomi Klein frames the scientific debate as a battle between good and evil people, "If you have an egalitarian and communitarian worldview, and you tend toward a belief system of pooling resources and helping the less advantaged, then you believe in climate change." In contrast she categorizes skeptics as selfish "deniers" suggesting, "The stronger your belief system tends toward a hierarchical or individual worldview, the greater the chances are that you deny climate change and the stronger your denial will be."[456]

Such is the sad state of public "scientific" discussions. We are not using the media to educate the public about science. We are using a pretense of "science" to denigrate political and personal opponents while a cycle of suppression by a few entrenched scientists has hijacked the scientific process.

Let me review a 30 minute snapshot that illustrates problem. A few decades ago I watched broadcasts of Newton's Apple to glean ideas for classroom science demonstrations, but it now appears that the show's host Ira Flatlow has been enlisted to politicize science. On Science Friday in March 2012, Flatlow interviewed Dr. Michael Mann. To begin the show Flatlow said, "Just last month, leaked memos, allegedly from the Libertarian think-tank The Heartland Institute, surfaced on the Internet. The memos revealed a plan to reshape the discussion about climate change as taught in classrooms. This is the latest battle in the war over climate change, a war that my next guest, climatologist Michael Mann, knows all too well." The first red flag was the implication that anyone teaching alternative viewpoints was part of some evil plot to reshape education.

Michael Mann then spoke,

> "Well, you know, for really more than two decades now, there has been an effort by vested interests and some of the groups that advocate for them to try

to discredit the science underlying human-caused climate change. And in many cases, that effort has taken the form of character attacks against scientists themselves. And I have found myself at the center of those attacks.....I realized was that many of those who were seeking to disagree or discredit that research were not engaging in sort of the good-faith rules that scientists engage in when we challenge each other, when we try to disprove each other, when we try to move the science forward."

To accuse others of not playing by "good-faith" rules was both amusing and unsettling. The revelations from the climategate emails had clearly shown that instead of engaging in debate to move the science forward, Mann had fervently worked behind the scenes to discredit two skeptical Harvard astrophysicists, Dr. Willie Soon and Dr. Sallie Baliunas, who challenged Mann's conclusions by simply compiling over nearly 100 studies that suggested the Medieval Warm Period was warmer than today.

Because Dr. Soon and Dr. Baliunas's 2003 paper received widespread attention, Mann and his fellow colleagues embarked on a campaign to discredit them. He pressured the journal that published their study, suggesting the editor was too easy on skeptics and had not engaged in proper peer review even though the paper had been reviewed by 4 other experts. He pressured like-minded editors of the journal to resign in support of his "unprecedented global warming" interpretation and hinted that he and his colleagues would boycott the journal for allowing skeptical views to be published. He then sought out politically allied Harvard administrators to disavow the two scientists. A few years later when the BBC ran an article in which scientists described how the Pacific Decadal Oscillation could slow down global warming, Mann discussed ways to constrain any similar articles. It was these behind the scenes activities that made Mann a primary target of the skeptics. When Mann portrays himself as a victim of class warfare and he has just decided now to "fight back", those comments only raise a red flag of insincerity and deceptive propaganda.

To offset the damage done by the climategate emails, Mann now portrays all challenges to his personal interpretations of climate change as if they were seditious attacks against the real "truth" and all of "science". However it was not just skeptics who complain about Mann's tactics. Other climate scientists have expressed similar disapproval of Mann's attempts to suppress alternative viewpoints.

In 2009 climatologist Dr. Eduardo Zorita blogged that Michael Mann, Phil Jones and Stefan Rahmstorf should be barred from the IPCC process reporting, "research in *some areas of climate science has been and is full of machination, conspiracies, and collusion*, as any reader can interpret from the CRU-files. ... *The scientific debate has been in many instances hijacked to advance other agendas* (emphasis added)."[988]

Dr. Edward Cook's research detected evidence of the Medieval Warm Period in New Zealand, but because that research was similar to what Soon and Baliunas had reported, Mann raged against those findings. Dr. Cook wrote in an email, "In all candor now, I think that Mike is becoming a serious enemy in the way that he bends the ears of people like Tom with words like "flawed" when describing my work and probably your and Keith's as well. This is in part a vindictive response to the Esper et al. paper. He also went crazy over my recent NZ paper describing evidence for a MWP [Medieval Warm Period] there because he sees it as another attack on him. Maybe I am over-reacting to this, but I don't think so."

Ironically just one week after appearing on Science Friday it became clear who was not playing by good-faith rules. The memos that Flatlow and Mann had highlighted to incriminate the Heartland Institute as well funded provocateurs and agents of climate misinformation were actually forged by fellow CO_2 advocate Dr. Peter Gleick. The hypocrisy was heightened further by the fact that Dr. Gleick had just been appointed Chair of the prestigious American Geophysical Union's Task Force on Scientific Ethics.

Dr. Gleick defended his forgery saying, "My judgment was blinded by my frustration with the ongoing efforts — often anonymous, well-funded, and coordinated — to attack climate science and scientists and prevent this debate, and by the lack of transparency of the organizations involved. Nevertheless I deeply regret my own actions in this case. I offer my personal apologies to all those affected." Is that the way our top climate scientists should fight back?

How could Gleick possibly blame skeptics for preventing "this debate"? Indeed all this backstabbing and subterfuge could be easily eliminated by making climate science more transparent. Yet several climate scientists have only released their data after being forced by Freedom of Information laws. Public debates sponsored by the government would bring that transparency to the world and the public can decide who is telling the truth. Otherwise scientific discussion is devolving into bouts of intellectual character assassinations and mudslinging. Instead of clarifying the debate and demystifying the issues, advocates like Mann and Gleick are adding to the misinformation and political polarization.

On that same Science Friday, Dr. Mann revealed how readily he would suppress any and all suggestions that natural variability plays any role in climate change. Flatlow opened the telephone lines so listeners could ask Dr. Mann questions. The first caller identified as David described the natural climate change depicted by fluctuating temperatures observed in Greenland's ice cores. I suggest you follow along on Figure 56 and judge how accurately the caller portrayed the data. (I added the numbers for easier reference). David said,

"I'm looking at a graph from the Greenland GISP2 ice core temperature for the last 10,000 years. I'm not disagreeing with the climate change idea. I'm just disagreeing with his facts that we're causing it, because about (1) 3,000 years ago, it was - we lost - started losing about four degrees C and then we had little - in the many dark ages, around (2) 1000 A.D., we had medieval warming that went back up - it looks like about a degree and a half C. And then it came back down in the (3) little ice age to 1905, and then it just started climbing back up again. Looking at the overall graph for the last 10,000 years, we've been in the cool area for the last 152, 150 years, and it's just now starting to climb back up again."

The caller was not highly articulate but was accurately relaying a well established scientific observation. This was an opportunity to educate the public about the natural factors that have contributed to climate change and to discuss what caused those periodic warm spikes. However Dr. Mann simply replied,

"Yeah. Unfortunately, the gentleman has his facts just about all wrong!"

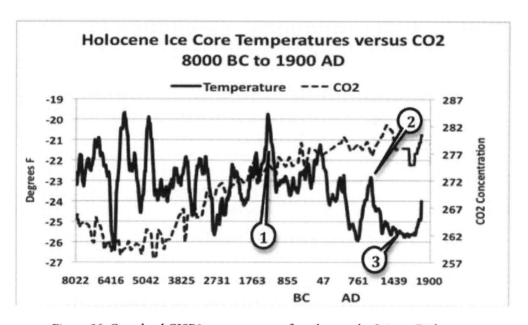

Figure 56. Greenland GISP2 temperatures referred to on the Science Friday.

Mann's treatment of David is an example of how the politics of climate change has defiled the process of communicating science. Ask any climate scientist and they will tell you that the gentleman most definitely did not have his facts wrong. However the GISP2 temperatures are not easily explained by changing levels of CO_2, so Mann just dismissed the caller as wrong. Although the GISP2 temperatures should not be seen as definitively representing global temperatures, that ice core record does show that Greenland and the eastern Arctic are not currently experiencing abnormally high temperatures.

Mann's denial of the credibility of the GISP2 ice core is a tactic he has advocated before. David simply received the same treatment as Harvard's skeptical astrophysicists. In one email in which Dr. Mann and his colleagues discussed how to counter Soon and Baliunas's research, Dr. Mann wrote, "The important thing is to deny that this has any intellectual credibility whatsoever and, if contacted by any media, to dismiss this for the stunt that it is." In another he wrote, "the important thing is to make sure they're loosing the PR battle. That's what the site [Real Climate] is about."[806]

Indeed Mann's RealClimate website further exemplifies the less than honest public relations battle. I have had several polite but skeptical posts deleted by RealClimate's scientists and countless skeptics have been treated similarly. Coincidentally RealClimate was cofounded by Wikipedia's William Connolley who also engaged in climate censorship. Connolley was recently banned from editing Wikipedia's climate change posts because he was deleting all skeptical entries.

Nobody benefits from dismissing legitimate observations. Nobody benefits by embracing intellectual tyranny. The climate debate can not be settled until there is truly a debate, and most Americans have never witnessed an honest face to face debate. The skeptical community has experienced a myriad of underhanded tactics, and unless transparent debates are promoted, most skeptics will believe all climate change policies have been dishonestly forced upon them, leading to a more destructive backlash against legitimate conservation science.

Again I ask President Obama to heed the First Lady's advice. We need to have a greater discussion from a diversity of viewpoints. Deceptive tactics from our leading climate scientists are only dividing the American public and degrading the scientific process. The government needs to sponsor climate debates that are moderated for fairness and honesty. It is always a healing process when all sides feel their concerns have received an honest vetting and will restore trust in the scientific process. If skeptics are wrong then a series of face to face debates should easily expose their misconceptions. Only then can we say the debate has been settled. Promoting a more honest "conversation would do the country good".

Some Future Steps While Waiting for Honest Debate.

"It is not the strongest of the species that survive, nor the most intelligent, but the one most responsive to change. "

Charles Darwin

"It is inconceivable that policymakers will be willing to make billion-and trillion-dollar decisions for adaptation to the projected regional climate change based on models that do not even describe and simulate the processes that are the building blocks of climate variability."[973]

Dr. Jagadish Shukla President, Institute of Global Environment and Society

In the journal Science, a 2013 article "Forecasting Regional Climate Change Flunks Its First Test" asks, "The strengthening greenhouse is warming the world, but what about your backyard, or at least your region? It's hard to say, climate researchers concede."[995] When results from global models were embedded in regional and local models, there was no improvement in their ability to predict regional climate change. I suspect the global model's emphasis on CO_2 as the control knob of climate and the resulting trivialization of landscape and ocean oscillations have largely contributed to these modeling failures. For example regional patterns of rainfall are determined largely by alternating cooling and warming cycles of the ocean's surface temperatures. Models driven by increasing greenhouse gases warm the ocean uniformly. In fact the current cooling trend in the eastern Pacific was considered a very low probability by virtually all global models. These failures are forcing more and more climate scientists to re-evaluate the powerful climate contributions of natural variations and landscape changes.

As we have observed, many regional climates cooled while others warmed. The precautionary principle argues that we must build a more resilient society and a more resilient environment that can adapt to either scenario. Climate change is inevitable and extreme weather is guaranteed whether climate change is wholly natural or driven by rising CO_2. No matter how the global warming debate gets settled, limiting our carbon footprints will never stop tornados or hurricanes, floods or droughts, cold waves or heat waves. It will not restore forests and watersheds, or stop disease transmission. Dealing with those real threats does not require stopping the debate.

As populations increase and cities expand, the likelihood of intersecting the path of a tornado or hurricane increases. We must simply design public places accordingly. Residents of tornado alley usually have less than 15 minutes after a tornado has touched down to seek shelter. All new buildings, especially schools must construct appropriate shelters. Where hurricanes are common we can restore tidal marshes and the dune systems that protect the coast from storm surges.

To date there has been no increase in global droughts or floods.[997] However if history repeats itself, we will experience far worse droughts and floods in the future. Governments must stop encouraging people to build on critical flood plains by subsidizing flood insurance. Wherever there is a loss of flood plains flooding is always amplified downstream. Restoring watersheds enhances the land's ability to store water and lessens local flooding. Improving a watershed's ability to store subsurface water also moderates the impact of droughts.

Droughts and floods are never global, but regional. We can guard against the unpreventable assaults on our food supplies by ensuring a vibrant global economy capable of rapidly transporting food around the world. Although a global transportation system is highly beneficial, it also brings unwanted hitchhikers. As demonstrated by recent amphibian extinctions and the past human extinctions documented by Jared Diamond in *Guns, Germs and Steel* and by Charles Mann in *1491*, the rapid spread of novel disease has devastated humans and wildlife alike. In that regard global warming is irrelevant. The deadliest period of spreading diseases occurred throughout the Little Ice Age. Instead of wasting millions on speculative studies blaming global warming, we need a better understanding of how diseases are transmitted and how that transmission can be limited. Disease transmission is not a matter of global warming but global transportation. Advocates proposals to save wildlife from future climate change via "assisted colonization" will only exacerbate the transmission problem.

Reducing our carbon foot print will not stop bouts of extreme heat waves whether it is in Death Valley or in urban heat islands. But more parks, more greenbelts, and better urban designs that enhance cooling breezes and promote more vegetation will minimize the amplification of natural heat waves that have been so deadly to the elderly and immobile. Organizing a volunteer network to take the aged and immobile out to a cooler park or beach during a heat wave would provide far greater benefits.

More effective agricultural practices and animal husbandry have increased food supplies while allowing more marginal farmlands to return to their wild states. Better food production has lessened the hunting pressures that decimated so many species. By providing an alternative fuel supply, the demonized petroleum industry helped save the whales and walruses and forests. In contrast, the emphasis on biofuels is scraping away more wild lands and reversing the benefits of modern agriculture. No matter what the global models suggest, deforestation is not good for the planet. We should encourage entrepreneurs to seek better energy solutions and support reforestation efforts.

The acknowledged failures of climate models tell us that there is a great need for a better understanding of climate change. Global warming has not caused species to go extinct, so we do not need to rush the implementation of uncertain and potentially damaging solutions. We do not need to embrace the tyrannical call to end any debate. More debate is not preventing us from building a more resilient society or improving our environmental stewardship. We must promote a better understanding of local and regional climate change; it is crucial for making a better world. And if that process is more transparent and more accessible to the public, there are millions of minds from all political persuasions eager to build that better world.

Literature Cited

1. Duffy, P.B., et al., (2006) Interpreting Recent Temperature Trends in California. Eos, Vol. 88, No. 41, 9.
2. Hansen, J. et al., (1988) Global Climate Changes as Forecast by Goddard Institute for Space StudiesThree-Dimensional Model. Journal of Geophysical Research, Vol. 93.
3. Easterling, D.R., et al. (2000) Climate extremes: Observations, modeling, and impacts. Science, 289.
4. Hansen, J. et al., (2006) Global temperature change. PNAS vol. 103 no. 39 14288-14293.
5. Thomas, C.D, et al., (2004) Extinction risk from climate change. Nature , vol. 427.
6. Stone, Brian Jr., (2009) Land Use as Climate Change Mitigation
7. Dai,A., et al. (1999) Effects of Clouds, Soil Moisture, Precipitation, and Water Vapor on Diurnal Temperature Range. Journal of Climate, vol. 12, 2451-2474.
8. Klotzbach, P.J., et al., (2009) An alternative explanation for differential temperature trends at the surface and in the lower troposphere. Journal Of Geophysical Research, Vol. 114
9. McNider , R.T., et al., (2012) Response and Sensitivity of the Nocturnal Boundary Layer Over Land to Added Longwave Radiative Forcing. Journal Of Geophysical Research, Vol. 117
10. Karl, T.R. et al., (1993) Asymmetric Trends of Daily Maximum and Minimum Temperature. Bulletin of the American Meteorological Society, vol. 74
11. Zhang, X. et al., (2000) Temperature and Precipitation Trends in Canada During the 20th Century. ATMOSPHERE-OCEAN 38 (3), 395–429
12. Shen, S., et al., (2009) The twentieth century contiguous US temperature changes indicated by daily data and higher statistical moments. Climatic Change Volume 109, Issue 3-4, pp 287-317.
13. Wilson, and Luckman. (2003) Dendroclimatic reconstruction of maximum summer temperatures from upper treeline sites in Interior British Columbia, Canada. The Holocene 13,6 pp. 851–861
14. Youngblut, D., Luckman, B. (2008) Maximum June–July temperatures in the southwest Yukon over the last 300 years reconstructed from tree rings. Dendrochronologia vol. 25,pp. 153-166.
15. Mildrexler,D.J. et al., (2011) Satellite Finds Highest Land Skin Temperatures on Earth. Bulletin of the American Meteorological Society.
16. K.M.et al. (2003) The Urban Heat island in Winter At Barrow,Alaska. International Journal of Climatology vol. 23: 1889–1905
17. Erella, E., and Williamson, T, (2007) Intra-urban differences in canopy layer air temperature at amid-latitude city. Int. J. Climatol. 27: 1243–1255
18. Goodridge, J., (1996) Comments on Regional Simulations of Greenhouse Warming Including Natural Variability. Bulletin of the American Meteorological Society. Vol.77, p.188-1589
19. Kalnay,E. and Cai M., (2003) Impact of urbanization and land-use change on climate. Nature, Vol 423
20. Balling, R. C., Jr (1998) Impacts of land degradation on historical temperature records from the Sonoran Desert. Climatic Change, 40, 669–681
21. Bonan, G.B.,(2001) Observational evidence for reduction of daily maximum temperature by croplands in the midwest United States, Journal of Climate, 14,

2430-2442.
22. Braganza, K., et al., (2004) Diurnal temperature range as an index of global climate change during the 20th century, Geophysical Research Letters, vol. 31, p. 1-4.
23. Fujbe,F., (2009) Urban warming in Japanese cities and its relation to climate change monitoring. The seventh International Conference on Urban Climate
24. Bohm, R., (1998) Urban Bias in Temperature Time Series – a Case Study for the City of Vienna, Austria, CLIMATIC CHANGE. Volume 38, 113-128.
25. Chemel, C., (2012) Response of London's Urban Heat Island to a Marine Air Intrusion in an Easterly Wind Regime. Boundary-Layer Meteorol (2012) 144:65–81
26. Fall, S., et al., (2011) Analysis of the impacts of station exposure on the U.S. Historical Climatology Network temperatures and temperature trends. Journal Of Geophysical Research, Vol. 116.
27. Stone, D.A., (2003) Factors contributing to diurnal temperature range trends in twentieth and twenty-first century simulations of the CCCma coupled model. Climate Dynamics (2003) 20: 435–445
28. Watts, A., et al. (2012) An area and distance weighted analysis of the impacts of station exposure on the U.S. Historical Climatology Network temperatures and temperature trends. Pre-print discussion paper.
29. McNider, R.T., (2012) Response and sensitivity of the nocturnal boundary layer over land to added longwave radiative forcing. JOURNAL OF GEOPHYSICAL RESEARCH, VOL. 117
30. Przybylak, R. (200) Diurnal Temperature Range in the Arctic and Its Relation To Hemispheric and Arctic Circulation Patterns. International Journal of Climatology 20: 231–253
31. Primack, R.B., (2009) The impact of climate change on cherry trees and other species in Japan. Biological Conservation 142, 1943–1949
32. Neil, K., Effects of urbanization on plant flowering phenology: A review. Urban Ecosystems 9:243–257
33. Briffa, K.R., (1998) Trees tell of past climates: but are they speaking less clearly today? Phil.Trans. R. Soc. Lond. B. 353, 65-73.
34. Rauber, R.M., et al., (2005) Severe & Hazardous Weather: An Introduction to High Impact Meteorolgy, 2nd edition, Kendall/Hunt Pubishing Co.
35. Wang, X., (2003) Comments on "Detection of Undocumented Changepoints: A Revision of the Two-Phase Regression Model". Journal of Climate;Oct2003, Vol. 16 Issue 20, p. 3383-3385
36. National Space Science and Technology Center, http://vortex.nsstc.uah.edu/data/msu/t2lt/uahncdc.lt
37. Chavez,F.P., et al.(2003) From Anchovies to Sardines and Back: Multidecadal Change in the Pacific Ocean. Science 299, 217.
38. Li, H., (2000) Climate Variability in East-Central California during the Past 1000 Years Reflected by High-Resolution Geochemical and Isotopic Records from Owens Lake Sediments. Quaternary Research Volume 54 Pages 189–197
39. Graumlich,L., (1987) Precipitation Variation in the Pacific Northwest (1675-1975) as Reconstructed from Tree Rings. Annals of the Association of American Geographers Vol. 77, p. 19-29.
40. Bonfils,C., et al., (2008) Identification of external influences on temperatures in California, Climatic Change. 87 (Suppl 1):S43–S55
41. Christy, J.R., et al., (2006) Methodology and Results of Calculating Central California Surface Temperature Trends: Evidence of Human-Induced Climate Change? Journal of Climate, vol. 19, p. 548-563.

42. Pielke Sr, R. A., and et al., (2002) The influence of land-use change and landscape dynamics on the climate system: relevance to climate-change policy beyond the radiative effects of greenhouse gases, Phil. Trans. Roy. Soc. Lond, 360, 1-5.
43. Lim,Y-K, et al., (2012) Observational evidence of sensitivity of surface climate changes to land types and urbanization,
44. (Max increase no minimum) Kumar,K.R., et al., (1994) Diurnal asymmetry of surface temperature trends over India. Geophysical Research Letters, Vol. 21, p. 677-680.
45. (decreasing tropical lad precip)Kumar, A., et al., (2004) Differing Trends in the Tropical Surface Temperatures and Precipitation over Land and Oceans, Journal of Climate, vol. 17, p. 653-664.
46. Annamalai, H., et al.,(2005) Response of the Asian summer monsoon to changes in El Niño properties. Q. J. R. Meteorol. Soc., 131, p. 805–831
47. Hall, M., and Fagre, D., (2003) Modeled Climate-Induced Glacier Change in Glacier National Park, 1850–2100, Bioscience, vol. 53, p. 131-140.
48. Moritz, C., et al., (2008) Impact of a Century of Climate Change on Small-Mammal Communities in Yosemite National Park, USA, Science 322, 261.
49. Crimmins, S., et al., (2010) Changes in Climatic Water Balance Drive Downhill Shifts in Plant Species' Optimum Elevations, Science 331 324
50. Zhou,L., et al., (2010) Evidence for a significant urbanization effect on climate in China, PNAS, vol.101, p.9540-9544.
51. Rubidge, E., et al., (2011) The role of climate, habitat, and species co-occurrence as drivers of change in small mammal distributions over the past century. Global Change Biology 17, 696–708
52. Karl, T., et al., (1988), Urbanization: Its Detection and Effect in the United States Climate Record. Journal of Climate, vol. 1, 1099-1123.
53. Peterson,T.C.,   (2003) Assessment of Urban Versus Rural In Situ Surface Temperatures in the Contiguous United States: No Difference Found. Journal of Climate, Vol. 16, 2941-2960.
54. Parker, D., (2006) A Demonstration That Large-Scale Warming Is Not Urban. Journa of Climate, vol. 19, 2882-2896.
55. Quayle, R., et al., (1991) Effects of Recent Thermometer Changes in the Cooperative Station Netwok. Bulletin of the American Meteorological Society, vol. 72, pp.1718-1724
56. Jones, P., et al., (1990) Assessment of urbanization effects in time series of surface temperature over land. Nature, vol. 346, p. 169-172
57. Simmons, J., et al., (2011) False-Positive Psychology: Undisclosed Flexibility in Data Collection and Analysis Allows Presenting Anything as Significant. Psychological Science 1-9
58. Ioannidis, J. P. A., (2006) Why Most Published Research Findings Are False. PLoS Medicine, Volume 2, 696-702
59. Parmesan, C., (1996) Climate and Species Range. Nature, vol. 382, 765-766.
60. Mattoni, R., et al., (1997) The endangered quino checkerspot butterfly, Euphydryas editha quino (Lepidoptera: Nymphalidae). Journal of Research Lepidoptera 34:99–118.
61. Longcore,T., et al., (2003) A Management and Monitoring Plan for Quino Checkerspot Butterfly (Euphydryas editha quino) and its Habitats in San Diego County. A Management and Monitoring Plan for Quino Checkerspot Butterfly.
62. Weiss, S., et al., (1988) Sun, Slope, and Butterflies: Topographic Determinants of Habitat Quality for Euphydryas Editha. Ecology, Vol. 69, pp. 1486-1496
63. Weiss, S., et al., (1987) Growth and dispersal of larvae of the checkerspot, Euphydryas editha. Oikos 50: 161-166
64. McLaughlin, J., et al., (2010) Climate change hastens population extinctions.

Proceedings of the National Academy of Sciences of the United States of America, 99(9), p.6070-6074

65. Ehrlich, P., and Murphy, D. (1987) Conservation Lessons from Long-Term Studies of Checkerspot Butterflies. Conservation Biology, vol. 1, pp. 122-131

66. Ehrlich, P. and Hansk, I., (2004) On the Wings of Checkerspots: A Model System for Population Biology. Oxford University Press

67. Pettion to Emergency List Taylor's (Whulge) Checkerspot Butterfly (Euphydryas editha taylori) as an Endangered Species Under the U.S. Endangered Species Act.

68. Dobkin, D., et al. (1987) Rainfall and the Interaction of Micro-climate with Larval Resources in the Population Dynamics of Checkerspot Butterflies (Euphydryas editha) Inhabiting Serpentine Grassland. Oecologia, Vol. 71, pp. 161-166

69. Seife, C., (2008) Sun in a Bottle: The strange history of fusion and the science of wishful thinking. Viking Press.

70. Wan, H., et al., (2010) Homogenization and Trend Analysis of Canadian Near-Surface Wind Speeds. Journal of Climate, vol. 23, 1209-1225.

71. Limb, R., et al., (2009) Heterogeneity of Thermal Extremes: Driven by Disturbance or Inherent in the Landscape. Environmental Management 43:100–106.

72. Piao, S., et al., (2007) Changes in climate and land use have a larger direct impact than rising CO_2 on global river runoff trends. PNAS, vol. 104, p. 15242–15247.

73. McCabe, G., et al., (2004) Pacific and Atlantic Ocean influences on multidecadal drought frequency in the United States. PNAS, vol. 101, p. 4136–4141

74. Menne. M., (2009) The U.S. Historical Climatology Network Monthly Temperature Data, version 2. The Bulletin for the American Meterological Society. p. 993-1007

75. Pielke, R., et al., (1999) The Influence of Anthropogenic Landscape Changes on Weather in South Florida. The Monthly Weather Review. Vol.127, p. 1663-1973

76. Pielke, R., et al., (2007) An overview of regional land-use and land-cover impacts on rainfall. Tellus, v. 59B, 587–60.

77. Kahl, J., et al., (1993) Absence of evidence for greenhouse warming over the Arctic Ocean in the past 40 years. Nature 361, 335 – 337.

78. Beszczynska-Moller, A., et al., (2011) Synthesis of Exchanges Through the Main Oceanic Gateways to the Arctic Ocean. Oceanography, Vol. 24, 76-93.

79. D'Arrigo, R., et al., (2008) On the 'Divergence Problem' in Northern Forests: A review of the tree-ring evidence and possible causes. Global and Planetary Change, vol. 60, p. 289–305.

80. Wilson, R., and Luckman, B., (2003) Dendroclimatic reconstruction of maximum summer temperatures from upper treeline sites in Interior British Columbia, Canada. The Holocene 13, p. 851–861.

81. Inman, D., and Jenkins, S., (1999) Climate Change and the Episodicity of Sediment Flux of Small California Rivers. The Journal of Geology, , volume 107, p. 251–270.

82. McCabe, G., et al., (2008) Associations of multi-decadal sea-surface temperature variability with US drought. Quaternary International, vol. 188, p. 31–40.

83. Oglesby, R., et al., (2011) The role of the Atlantic Multidecadal Oscillation on medieval drought in North America: Synthesizing results from proxy data and climate models. Global and Planetary Change 84-85 (2012) 56–65

84. Basagic, H., (2008) "Quantifying Twentieth Century Glacier Change in the Sierra Nevada, California". Masters Thesis. Portland State University, OR.

85. Huss, M., et al., (2009) Strong Alpine glacier melt in the 1940s due to enhanced solar radiation. Geophysical Research Letters, vol. 36, p. 1-5.

86. Huss, M. et al., (2010) 100-year mass changes in the Swiss Alps linked to the Atlantic Multidecadal Oscillation. Geophysical Research Letters, vol. 37, p. 1-5.

87. Braganza, K., et al., (2004) Diurnal temperature range as an index of global climate change during the twentieth century. Geophysical Research Letters, vol. 31, L13217.

88. Pileke, R., et al., (2007) Unresolved issues with the assessment of multidecadal global land surface temperature trends. Journal of Geophysical Research, vol. 112, 1-26.

89. USA Today, 8/7/2006, Dr Craig Bohren interview with April Holladay.

90. Pielke, R., and Tisdale, B., (2012) Sea Surface Temperature Trends As A Function Of Latitude Bands. Climate Science website.

91. Lindzen,R. (1990) Some coolness concerning global warming. Bulletin of the American Meteorological Society. vol. 71, p. 288-299.

92. Wikepedia: heat waves

93. Pan, Z., et al, (2004) Altered hydrologic feedback in a warming climate introduces a "warming hole." Geophysical Research Letters, vol. 31, L17109

94. Dole, R., et al., (2011) Was There a Basis for Anticipating the 2010 Russian Heat Wave? Geophysical Research Letters, vol. 38, L06702.

95. Cook, B., et al., (2011) Atmospheric circulation anomalies during two persistent North American droughts: 1932–1939 and 1948–1957. Climate Dynamics, vol. 36, p. 2339–2355.

96. Pielke, R., et al., (2002) The influence of land-use change and landscape dynamics on the climate system: relevance to climate-change policy beyond the radiative effect of greenhouse gases. Phil. Trans. R. Soc. Lond. A, vol. 360, 1705-1719.

97. Kapp, W., (1996) The Firepiston: Ancient Firemaking Machine. Download from internet 2010.

98. Smith, A., (2010) Bodie's Pika: What they have to tell us. Presentation downloaded from ttp://www.tetonscience.org/data/contentfiles/File/downloads/pdf/CRC/CRCPikaP resentations/crc_pika_ppt_Smith.pdf

99. Millar, C., Westfall,R., (2010) Distribution and Climatic Relationships of the American Pika (Ochotona princeps) in the Sierra Nevada and Western Great Basin, U.S.A.; Periglacial Landforms as Refugia in Warming Climates. Arctic, Antarctic, and Alpine Research, vol. 42, pp. 76–88

100. Beever, E., et al., (2003) Patterns of apparent extinction among isolated populations of pikas (Ochotona princeps) in the Great Basin. Journal of Mammalogy, 84(1):37–54

101. Millar, C., (2011) Influence of Domestic Livestock Grazing on American Pika (Ochotona princeps) Haypiling Behavior in the Eastern Sierra Nevada and Great Basin. Western North American Naturalist vol. 71(3), pp. 425–430.

102. Millar, C., Westfall,R., (2010) Distribution and Climatic Relationships of the American Pika (Ochotona princeps) in the Sierra Nevada and Western Great Basin, U.S.A.; Periglacial Landforms as Refugia in Warming Climates. Reply. Arctic, Antarctic, and Alpine Research, vol. 42, pp. 493–496.

103. Center for Biological Diversity, (2007) Endangered Species Act Protection Sought for American Pika : Global Warming Threatens Alpine 'Boulder Bunny'. published on line October 2, 2007.

104. Erb, L., et al., (2011) On the generality of a climate-mediated shift in the distribution of the American pika (Ochotona princeps). Ecology, vol. 92(9), pp. 1730–1735.

105. Beever, E., (2002) Persistence of Pika in two low-elevation National Monument in the western United States. Park Science. vol. 21, p. 23-29.

106. Simpson, W., (2009) American Pikas inhabit low-elevation sites outside the species' previously described bioclimatic envelope. Western North American Naturalist 69(2), p. 243–250.

107. Hafner, D.J. 1993. North American pika (Ochotona princeps) as a Late Quaternary biogeographic indicator species. Quaternary Research 39:373–380.

108. Romm, J., (2010) So long Pika, we hardly knew ya. Climate Progress. Published online on Feb 26, 2010 at 7:50 am.

109. Smith, A., (1974) The Distribution and Dispersal of Pikas: Influences of Behavior and Climate. Ecology, vol. 55, p. 1368-1376.

110. A. Smith, C. Millar, R. Westfall and D. Hik. (2009) North American pikas: population status, thermal environments, and periglacial processes. 2009 Meeting of the American Geophysical Union.

111. Smith, A., (2011) Letter to Dr. Eric Loft, California Department of Fish and Game, regards petiton to list the pika as endangered.

112. Beever, E., et al., (2010) Testing alternative models of climate-mediated extirpations. Ecological Applications, 20(1), p. 164–178.

113. Beever, E., et al., (2011) Contemporary climate change alters the pace and drivers of extinction. Global Change Biology p.1-7.

114. Parmesan, C., (2006) Ecological and Evolutionary Responses to Recent Climate Change. Annu. Rev. Ecol. Evol. Syst., vol.37. p.637-669.

115. Magilligan, F. and Goldstein, P., (2001) El Niño floods and culture change: A late Holocene flood history for the Rio Moquegua, southern Peru. Geology, v. 29 no. 5 p. 431-434.

116. Foster, G., et al., (2010) Comment on "Influence of the Southern Oscillation on tropospheric temperature" by J. D. McLean, C. R. de Freitas, and R. M. Carter. Journal of Geophysical Research, vol. 115, p. 1-4.

117. McLean, J.D., et al., (2009) Influence of the Southern Oscillation on tropospheric temperature. Journal of Geophysical Research, vol. 114, p. 1-4.

118. Torrence, C., and Webster, P. (1998) The annual cycle of persistence in the El Niño/Southern Oscillation. Q.J.R. Meteorological Society, vol. 124, p. 1985-2004.

119. McPhaden, M., et al., (2011) El Niño and its relationship to changing background conditions in the tropical Pacific Ocean. Geophysical Research Letters, vol. 38, p. 1-4.

120. Bond, N., et al., (2006) ENSO'S Effect on Alaska during the Opposite Phases of the Arctic Oscillation. International Journal of Climatology, vol. 26, 1821–1841.

121. Hartmann, B. and Wendler, G., (2006) The Significance of the 1976 Pacific Climate Shift in the Climatology of Alaska. Journal of Climate, vol. 18, p. 4824-4839.

122. Schneider, N. and Cornuelle,B., (2005) The Forcing of the Pacific Decadal Oscillation. Journal of Climate, vol. 18, p. 4352-4375

123. McCabe, G., et al., (2011) Influences of the El Niño Southern Oscillation and the Pacific Decadal Oscillation on the timing of the North American spring. International Journal of Climatology, doi:10.1002/joc.3400.

124. Cayan, D., et al., (2001) Changes in the Onset of Spring in the Western United States. Bulletin of the American Meteorological Society, vol 82, p. 399-415

125. Millar, C., et al., (2004) Response of Subalpine Conifers in the Sierra Nevada, California, U.S.A., to 20th-Century Warming and Decadal Climate Variability. Arctic, Antarctic, and Alpine Research, vol. 36(2), p.181-200.

126. Newman, M., et al., (2003) ENSO-Forced Variability of the Pacific Decadal Oscillation. Journal of Climate, vol 16. p. 3853-3857.

127. Benson, L., et al. (2003) Influence of the Pacific Decadal Oscillation on the climate of the Sierra Nevada, California and Nevada. Quaternary Research, vol. 59, p. 151–159.

128. Alexander, M., (2008) Extratropical Air-Sea Interaction, SST Variability and the Pacific Decadal Oscillation (PDO). in AGU Monograph:Climate Dynamics: Why Does Climate Vary? Chapter 7.

129. D'Arrigo, R., et al., (2001) Tree-ring estimates of Pacific decadal climate variability. Climate Dynamics vol.18, p.219–224.

130. Schoennagel, T., (2005) ENSO and PDO Variability Affect Drought-induced Fire

Occurrence in Rocky Mounain Subalpine Forests. Ecological Applications, vol. 15, pp. 2000-2014.

131.   Goodrich , G., (2004) Modulation of the Winter ENSO Arizona Climate Signal by the Pacific Decadal Oscillation. Journal of the Arizona-Nevada Academy of Science, vol. 36, p. 88-94.

132.   Holbrook, S., et al., (1997) Changes in an Assemblage of Temperate Reef Fishes associated with a Climate Shift. Ecological Applications, vol. 7, pp. 1299-1310.

133.   Parmesan, C. and Yohe, G. (2003) A globally coherent fingerprint of climate change impacts across natural systems. Nature, vol. 142, p.37-42.

134.   Jarvis, E. , et al., (2004) Comparison of Recreational Fish Catch Trends to Environment-species Relationships and Fishery-independent Data in the Southern California Bight, 1980-2000. RECREATIONAL FISH CATCH TRENDS, CalCOFI Rep., Vol. 45.

135.   Peterson, W., and Schwing, F., (2003) A new climate regime in northeast pacific ecosystems. Geophysical Research Letters, vol. 30, doi:10.1029/2003GL017528.

136.   Wikipedia: Peruvian cuisine

137.   Guilyardi E., et al., (2009) Understanding El Niño in Ocean-Atmosphere General Circulation Models:Progress and Challenges. Bulletin for the American Meterological Society

138.   Meehl, G., et al., (2008) A Coupled Air–Sea Response Mechanism to Solar Forcing in the Pacific Region. Journal of Climate, vol. 21 p.2883-2897

139.   van Oldenborgh, G. et al, (2005) El Niño in a changing climate: A multi-model study. Ocean Sci., vol. 1, 81–95.

140.   Eisenman, I., et al., (2005) Westerly Wind Bursts: ENSO's Tail Rather than the Dog? Journal of Climate, vol. 18, 5224-5238.

141.   White, W., et al., (1997) Response of global upper ocean temperature to changing solar irradiance. Journal of Geophysical Research, vol. 102, p. 3255–3266.

142.   Meehl, G.A., et al., (2003) Solar and greenhouse gas forcing and climate response in the 20th century. Journal of Climate, vol. 16, p. 426–444.

143.   van Loon, H. and D. J. Shea, (2000) The global 11-year solar signal in July–August. Geophys. Res. Lett., vol.27, p. 2965–2968.

144.   van Loon, H.,(2004) A decadal solar effect in the tropics in July–August. Journal of Atmospheric and Solar-Terrestrial Physics, vol. 66, p. 1767–1778

145.   Cubasch, U., (1997) Simulation of the influence of solar radiation variations on the global climate with an ocean-atmosphere general circulation model., Climate Dynamics, vol. 13, p. 757-767.

146.   Trenberth, K., (2002) Evolution of El Niño–Southern Oscillation and global atmospheric surface temperatures. Journal of Geophysical Research, vol. 107., 10.1029/2000JD000298, 2002

147.   Sherwood, S. C., et al., (2010) Tropospheric water vapor, convection, and climate, Rev. Geophys., 48, RG2001, doi:10.1029/2009RG000301

148.   Cayan, D., (1996) Interannual climate variability and snowpack in the western United States. Journal of Climate, vol. 9, p.928.

149.   Emile-Geay, J., (2007) El Niño as a mediator of the solar influence on climate. Paleoceanography, vol. 22, PA3210, doi:10.1029/2006PA001304.

150.   Mudelse, M. (2003) No upward trends in the occurrence of extreme floods in central Europe. Nature, vol.425, p. 166-169.

151.   Gedalof, Z., et al., (2002) A multi-century perspective of variability in the Pacific Decadal Oscillation: new insights from tree rings and coral. Geophysical Research Letters, vol. 29, p.1-4.

152.   Written Testimony of Dr. John Overpeck: Hearing on Current Drought Conditions Affecting New Mexico. Committee on Energy and Natural Resources. U.S. Senate,

April 27th, 2011.

153. McCabe, G., (2008) Associations of multi-decadal sea-surface temperature variability with US drought. Quaternary International, vol. 188, p.31–40.

154. Pounds, J.A., et al, (1999) Biological response to climate change on a tropical mountain. Nature, vol. 398, p. 611-615.

155. Crump, M., et al. (1992) Apparent Decline of the Golden Toad: Underground or Extinct? Copeia, vol. 1992, pp. 413-420.

156. Pounds, JA., and Crump, M. (1994) Amphibian Declines and Climate Disturbance: The Case of the Golden Toad and the Harlequin Frog. Conservation Biology, vol. 8, p. 72-85.

157. Pounds. J. A., et al., (1997) Tests of Null Models for Amphibian Declines on a Tropical Mountain. Conservation Biology, vol. 11, p. 1307-1322.

158. Pounds, J.A., et al., (2006) Responding to Amphibian Loss. Science, vol. 314, p.1541.

159. Collins, J. and Crump, M. (2009) Extinction in Our Times: Global Amphibian Decline. Oxford University Press: 2009. 304 pp.

160. Pounds, J.A., Masters, K., (2009)Amphibian mystery misread. Nature, vol. 462, p. 38-39.

161. Pounds, J.A., et al., (2006) Widespread amphibian extinctions from epidemic disease driven by global warming. Nature, vol. 439, p. 161-167.

162. Alford,R.A., (2007) Global warming and amphibian losses. Nature, vol. 447, p. E3-4.

163. Pounds, J.A., and Puschendorf, R. , (2004) Clouded futures. Nature, vol. 427, p. 107-109.

164. Anchukaitis, K. J. and Evans, M., (2010) Tropical cloud forest climate variability and the demise of the Monteverde golden toad. PNAS, vol. 107, p. 5036–5040.

165. Jacobson, S., and Vandenberg, J., (1991) Reproductive Ecology of the Endangered Golden Toad (Bufo periglenes). Journal of Herpetology, vol. 25, p. 321-327.

166. Still, C.J., et al., (1999) Simulating the effects of climate change on tropical montane cloud forests. Nature, vol. 398, p. 608-610.

167. Piotrowski, J. S., et al. (2004) Physiology of Batrachochytrium dendrobatidis, a chytrid pathogen of amphibians. Mycologia, 96(1), 2004, pp. 9-15

168. Johnson, M., et al.,(2003) (Fungicidal effects of chemical disinfectants, UV light, desiccation and heat on the amphibian chytrid Batrachochytrium dendrobatidis. Diseases of Aquatic Organisms, vol. 57, p. 255–260.

169. Skerratt, L., et al., (2007) Spread of Chytridiomycosis Has Caused the Rapid Global Decline and Extinction of Frogs. EcoHealth, DOI: 10.1007/s10393-007-0093-5. Key postulates for this theory have been completely or partially fulfilled. In

170. Kriger, K.M., et al. (2007) Large-scale seasonal variation in the prevalence and severity of chytridiomycosis. Journal of Zoology, vol. 271, p. 352–359.

171. Lips, K., et al. (2008) Riding the Wave: Reconciling the Roles of Disease and Climate Change in Amphibian Declines. PLoS Biology, vol. 6, p. 441-454.

172. Bonaccorso, E. and Guayasamin, J., (2003) Chytridiomycosis as a Possible Cause of Population Declines in Atelopus cruciger (Anura:Bufonidae). Herpetological Review, vol.34, p.331–334.

173. Rohr, J., et al., (2008) Evaluating the links between climate, disease spread and amphibian declines. PNAS, vol. 105, p. 17436–17441.

174. Vredenburg,, V, et al., (2010) Dynamics of an emerging disease drive large-scale amphibian population extinctions. PNAS, vol. 107, p. 9689–9694.

175. Hansen, J., et al. (2006) Global temperature change. PNAS, vol. 103, p. 14288–14293.

176. Ralph, F. and Dettinger, M., (2011) Storms, Floods, and the Science of Atmospheric Rivers. Eos, Vol. 92, p. 265-266.

177. Hansen,J., et al., (1999) GISS analysis of surface temperature change. J. Geophys. Res., 104, 30997-31022, doi:10.1029/1999JD900835.

178. Zhu, Y., and Newell, R. (1998) A Proposed Algorithm for Moisture Fluxes from Atmospheric Rivers. Monthly Weather Review, vol. 126, p. 725-735;

179. Ralph, F. and Dettinger, M. (2012) Historical and National Perspectives on Extreme West Coast Precipitation Associated Atmospheric Rivers during December. Bulletin of the American Meteorological Society, p. 783-790.

180. Stohl, A., et al., (2008) Remote sources of water vapor forming precipitation on the Norwegian west coast at 60°N–a tale of hurricanes and an atmospheric river. Journal of Geophysical Research, vol. 113, D05102, doi:10.1029/2007JD009006.

181. Trenberth, K. and Fasullo, J., (2012) Climate extremes and climate change: The Russian heat wave and other climate extremes of 2010. Journal of Geophysical Research, vol. 117, D17103, doi:10.1029/2012JD018020

182. Kunkel, K., et al., (2006) Can CGCMs Simulate the Twentieth-Century "Warming Hole" in the Central United States? Journal of Climate, vol. 19, p. 4137-4153.

183. Hansen, J., (2012) Game Over for the Climate. Op-ed NY Times, May 9, 2012.

184. Rind, D., et al., (1990) Potential Evapotranspiration and the Likelihood of Future Drought. Journal of Geophysical Research, vol. 95, p. 9983-10,004.

185. Dai, A. and Trenberth, K. (1998) Global Variations in Droughts and Wet Spells:1900-1995. Geophysical Research Letters, vol. 25, p. 3367-3370.

186. Asmerom, Y., et al. (2007) Solar forcing of Holocene climate: New insights from a speleothem record, southwestern United States. Geology, vol.35, p.1-4.

187. St. Jacques, J., et al., (2008) A 900-year pollen-inferred temperature and effective moisture record from varved Lake Mina, west-central Minnesota, USA. Quaternary Scifence Reviews, vol. 27, p. 781–796.

188. Nicault, A., et al., (2008) Mediterranean drought fluctuation during the last 500 years based on tree-ring data. Climate Dynamics, vol. 31, p. 227–245.

189. Buckley, B, et al., (2010) Climate as a contributing factor in the demise of Angkor, Cambodia. PNAS, vol. 107, p. 6748-6752.

190. Stahle, D., et al., (2007) Tree-ring reconstructed megadroughts over North America since A.D. 1300. Climatic Change, vol. 83, p. 133–149.

191. Stine, S. (2004) Extreme and persistent drought in California and Patagonia during medieval time. Nature, vol. 369, p. 546-549.

192. Medina-Elizalde, M. and Rohling, E. (2012) Collapse of Classic Maya Civilization Related to Modest Reduction in Precipitation. Science, vol. 335, p. 956-959.

193. Sinha, A., et al., (2010) A global context for megadroughts in monsoon Asia during the past millennium. Quaternary Science Reviews, 1-16.

194. Cook, E., et al., (2004) Long-Term Aridity Changes in the Western United States. Science 306, 1015-1018.

195. Herweijer,C., et al., (2007) North American Droughts of the Last Millennium from a Gridded Network of Tree-Ring Data. Journal of Climate, vol. 20, p. 1353-1376.

196. Mann, M.E., Park, J., Bradley, R.S., 1995. Global interdecadal and centuryscale climate oscillations during the past five centuries. Nature 378, 266–270.

197. Clement, A., et al., (1996) An Ocean Dynamical Thermostat. Journal of Climate, vol. 9, 2190-2196.

198. Mann, M., et al., (2005) Volcanic and Solar Forcing of the Tropical Pacific over the Past 1000 Years. Journal of Climate, vol.18 , p. 447-456.

199. Trenberth, K., et al., (2002) Evolution of El Niño–Southern Oscillation and global atmospheric surface temperatures. Journal of Geophysical Research, vol. 107, 10.1029/2000JD000298.

200. Oppo. D., et al., (2009) 2,000-year-long temperature and hydrology reconstructions from the Indo-Pacific warm pool. Nature, vol. 460, p.1113-1116.

201.   Trenberth, K., and Hoar, T., (1996) The 1990-1995 El Nifio-Southern Oscillation event: Longest on record. Geophysical Research Letters, vol. 23, p.57-60.

202.   Fleck, J., (2006) Scientist Forecasts 'super El Niño! Albuquerque Journal, April 8, 2006.

203.   Cane, M., (1984) Modeling Sea Level During El Niño. Journal of Physical Oceanography, vol. 14, p. 1864-1874.

204.   Oka, E., and Qiu, B., (2012) Progress of North Pacific mode water research in the past decade. Journal of Oceanography, vol. 68, p.5–20.

205.   McPhaden, M., and Zhang, D., (2003) Slowdown of the meridional overturning circulation in the upper Pacific Ocean. Nature, vol. 415, p. 603-608.

206.   Cook, E., et al., (2007) North American drought: Reconstructions, causes, and consequences. Earth-Science Reviews, vol. 81, p. 93–134.

207.   Schoennagel, T., et al. (2005) ENSO and PDO Variability Affect Drought-induced Fire Occurrence in Rocky Mountain Subalpine Forest. Ecological Applications, vol. 15(6), p. 2000-2014.

208.   Medina-Elizalde, M. and Rohling, E., (2012) Collapse of Classic Maya Civilization Related to Modest Reduction in Precipitation. Science, vol. 335, p. 956-959.

209.   Scarborough, V., et al., (2012) Water and sustainable land use at the ancient tropical city of Tikal, Guatemala. PNAS, vol. 109, p. 12408–12413.

210.   Trenberth, K. (2012) Framing the way to relate climate extremes to climate change. Climatic Change, DOI 10.1007/s10584-012-0441-5.

211.   Scaife, A. A., T. Woollings, J. Knight, G. Martin, and T. Hinton (2010), Atmospheric blocking and mean biases in climate models, J. Clim., 23, 6143–6152, doi:10.1175/2010JCLI3728.1.

212.   Hoerling, M. (2012) "Martin Hoerling on James Hansen's 'game over' thinking." Rebuttal posted to Watts Up With That website August 13, 2012.

213.   Rodionov, S. (2002) Regime Shifts in the Pacific-North American Climate.

214.   Trenberth, K. E., (1990) Recent observed interdecadal climate changes in the Northern Hemisphere. Bulletin of the American Meteorological Society, vol. 71, p. 988-993.

215.   Mehta, V., and Mehta, A., (2004) Natural decadal-multidecadal variability of the Indo-Pacific Warm Pool and its impacts on global climate. CRCES Presentation, www.crces.org/presentations/dmv_ipwp/

216.   Compo, G.P., and P.D. Sardeshmukh, 2009: Oceanic influences on recent continental warming. Climate Dynamics, 32, 333-342 doi: 10.1007/s00382-008-0448-9.

217.   Gillett, N. P., P. A. Stott, and B. D. Santer (2008), Attribution of cyclogenesis region sea surface temperature change to anthropogenic influence, Geophys. Res. Lett., 35, L09707, doi:10.1029/2008GL033670. Hurricane regions, 1999

218.   Yang, X., and T. DelSole (2012), Systematic comparison of ENSO teleconnection patterns between models and observations, J. Clim., 25, 425–446, doi:10.1175/JCLI-D-11-00175.1.

219.   Llu, H., (2012) Atlantic Warm-Pool Variability in the IPCC AR4 CGCM Simulations. Journal of Climate, vol. 25, p. 5612-5628.

220.   Woodhouse, C., and Overpeck, J. (1998) 2000 Years of Drought Variability in the Central United States. Bulletin of the American Meteorological Society, vol. 79, p. 2693-2714.

221.   Fu, C., et al. (1999) Changes in Atmospheric Circulation Over Northern Hemisphere Oceans Associated with the Rapid Warming of the 1920's. International Journal of Climatology, vol. 19, p. 581–606.

222.   Woodhouse, C., et al., (2012) A 1,200-year perspective of 21st century drought in southwestern North America. PNAS,vol. 107, p. 21283–21288.

223.   Pan, A., et al., (2005) Periodic Forcing and ENSO Suppression in the Cane-Zebiak Model. Journal of Oceanography, vol. 61, p.109 to 113

224.   Vecchi, G., et al., (2006) Weakening of tropical Pacific atmospheric circulation due to anthropogenic forcing. Nature vol. 441, doi:10.1038/nature04744

225.   Benson, L., et al., (2002) Holocene multidecadal and multicentennial droughts affecting Northern California and Nevada. Quaternary Science Reviews, vol. 21, p. 659–682.

226.   Karnauskas, K., et al., (2012) A Pacific Centennial Oscillation Predicted by Coupled GCMs. Nature Geoscience , Journal of Climate, vol. 25, p. 5943-5961.

227.   Indermuhle, A., et al., (1998) Holocene carbon-cycle dynamics based on CO2 trapped in ice at Taylor Dome, Antarctica. Nature, vol. 328, p. 121-126.

228.   Cane, M., (2004) The evolution of El Niño, past and future. Earth and Planetary Science Letters, vol. 164, p. 1-10.

229.   Kuper, R.,and Kröpelin, S., (2006) Climate-controlled Holocene occupation of the Sahara: motor of Africa's evolution. Science, vol. 313, p.803-807.

230.   Kröpelin, S., et al, (2008). Climate-driven ecosystem succession in the Sahara: the past 6000 years. Science, vol. 320, p. 765-768.

231.   Cook, E., et al., (2010) Asian Monsoon Failure and Megadrought During the Last Millennium. Science, vol. 328, p. 486-489.

232.   Mehta, V. and Lau, K., (1997) Influence of solar irradiance on the Indian monsoon-ENSO relationship at decadal-multidecadal time scales. Geophysical Research Letters, vol. 24, p. 159-162.

233.   Liu, J., et al., (2009) Centennial Variations of the Global Monsoon Precipitation in the Last Millennium: Results from ECHO-G Model. Journal of Climate, vol. 22, p. 2356-2371

234.   Zhang, P., et al., (2008)A Test of Climate, Sun, and Culture Relationships from an 1810-Year Chinese Cave Record. Science, vol. 322, p. 940-942.

235.   Dai, A., (2012) Increasing drought under global in observations and models. Nature Climate Change, DOI: 10.1038/NCLIMATE1633.

236.   Rajagopalan, B., et al., (1997) Anomalous ENSO Occurrences: An Alternate View, Journal of Climate, vol. 10, p. 3251-2357.

237.   Wunsch, C., (1999) The interpretation of short climate records, with comments on the North Atlantic and Southern Oscillations. Bulleting of the American Meterological Society, vol. 80, p. 245-255.

238.   McGregor, S., et al., (2010) A unified proxy for ENSO and PDO variability since 1650. Climate Past, vol. 6, p. 1–17.

239.   Meehl, G. A., et al. (2012), Monsoon regimes and processes in CCSM4, Part 1: The Asian-Australian monsoon, J. Clim., 25, 2583–2608, doi:10.1175/JCLI-D-11-00184.1.

240.   Haston, L., et al., (1997) Spatial and Temporal Variability of Southern California Precipitation over the Last 400 yr and Relationships to Atmospheric Circulation Patterns. Journal of Climate, vol. 10, p. 1836-1852.

241.   Russell,J.M., et al., (2007) Little Ice Age drought in equatorial Africa: Intertropical Convergence Zone migrations and El Niño–Southern Oscillation variability. Geology, vol. 35. p. 21–24.

242.   Yang, X., and T. DelSole (2012), Systematic comparison of ENSO teleconnection patterns between models and observations, J. Clim., 25, 425–446, doi:10.1175/JCLI-D-11-00175.1.

243.   Hoerling, M. et al., (2006) Detection and Attribution of Twentieth-Century Northern and Southern African Rainfall Change. Joumal of Climate, vol. 19. P. 3989-4008.

244.   Hu, Q., and Feng, S., (2008) Variation of the North American Summer Monsoon Regimes and the Atlantic Multidecadal Oscillation. Journal of Climate, vol. 21, p.

2371-2383.

245. Hu, Z, and Huang, B. (2009) Interferential Impact of ENSO and PDO on Dry and Wet Conditions in the U.S. Great Plains. Journal of Climate, vo. 22, p. 6047-6065.

246. Wake, D., and Vredenburg, V.,(2008) Are we in the midst of the sixth mass extinction? A view from the world of amphibians. PNAS, vol. 105, p. 11466–11473.

247. Bradley, G., et al., (2002) Chytridiomycosis in Native Arizona Frogs. Journal of Wildlife Diseases, vol. 382, p. 206–212.

248. Berger, L., et al. (2004) Effect of season and temperature on mortality in amphibians due to chytridiomycosis. Australian Veterinary Journal, vol. 82, p.31–36

249. Lips, K., (1999) Mass mortality and population declines of anurans at an upland site in western Panama. Conservation Biology, vol. 13, p.117.

250. Lips, K., et al., (2006) Emerging infectious disease and the loss of biodiversity in a neotropical amphibian community. Proceedings of the National Academy of Sciences of the United States of America, vol. 103, p. 3165–3170.

251. Laurance, W., et al., (1996) Epidemic disease and the catastrophic decline of Australian rain forest frogs. Conservation Biology vol. 10, p. 406–413.

252. Polyakov, I., et al., (2010) Arctic Ocean warming contributes to reduced polar ice cap. Journal of Physical. Oceanography, vol. 40, p. 2743–2756. doi: 10.1175/2010JPO4339.1.

253. Ainley, D., et al., (2007) The fate of Antarctic penguins when Earth's tropospheric temperature reaches 2 °C above pre-industrial levels. World Wildlife Fund report, http://assets.panda.org/downloads/wwf_climate_penguins_final_1.pdf.

254. Emperor Penguins March Toward Extinction? ScienceDaily (Jan. 27, 2009), http://www.sciencedaily.com/releases/2009/01/090127090728.htm

255. Jenouvrier, S., et al., (2009) Demographic models and IPCC climate projections predict the decline of an emperor penguin population. Proceedings of the National Academy of Sciences, DOI: 10.1073/pnas.0806638106

256. Brahic, C., (2009) Melting ice could push penguins to extinction. NewScientist, http://www.newscientist.com/article/dn16487-melting-ice-could-push-penguins-to-extinction.html.

257. BBC New, (2009) Emperor penguins face extinction. http://news.bbc.co.uk/2/hi/science/nature/7851276.stm

258. Steinfurth, A., Merlen, G., (2005) Predació'n de gatos salvajes (Felis catus) sobre el pinguino de Galapagos (Spheniscus mendiculus) en Caleta Iguana, Isla Isabela. Report to the Charles Darwin Research Station and Galapagos National Park Service. Charles Darwin Research Station, Puerto Ayora, Isla Santa Cruz, Gala'pagos, p. 1–8.

259. Deem, S., et al., (2010) Exposure to Toxoplasma gondii in Galapagos Penguins (Spheniscus mendiculus) and Flightless Cormorants (Phalacrocorax harrisi) in the Galapagos Islands, Ecuador. Journal of Wildlife Diseases, vol. 46, p. 1005–1011.

260. Jenouvrier, S., et al., (2009) Demographic models and IPCC climate projections predict the decline of an emperor penguin population. Proceedings of the National Academy of Sciences, vol. 106, p. 1844-1847.

261. Barbraud, C., and Weimerskirch, H. (2001) Emperor penguins and climate change. Nature, vol. 411, p.183-186.

262. Fraser, A., et al. (2012) East Antarctic Landfast Sea Ice Distribution and Variability, 2000-08. Journal of Climate, vol. 25, p. 1137-1156.

263. Budd, J., (1962) Population studies in rookeries of the Emperor Penguin Aptenodytes forsteri. Proc. Royal Soc. London 139: 365-388.

264. Kooyman, G.L., et al., (2007) Effects of giant icebergs on two emperor penguin colonies in the Ross Sea, Antarctica. Antarctic Science, vol. 19, p. 31-38.

265. Kirkwood, R., and Robertson, G., (1997) The foraging of female emperor penguins during winter. Ecological Monographs, vol. 67, p. 155–176.

266.   Ainley, D., et al., (2010) Antarctic penguin response to habitat change as Earth's troposphere reaches 2°C above preindustrial levels. Ecological Monographs, vol. 80, p. 49–66.

267.   Emslie, S., et al., (2007) A 45,000 yr record of Adelie penguins and climate change in the Ross Sea, Antarctica. Geology vol.35, p. 61–64.

268.   Massom, R., et al., (1998) The distribution and formative processes of latent-heat polynyas in East Antarctica. Annals of Glaciology, vol. 27, p. 420-426.

269.   Massom, R., et al. (2009) Fast ice distribution in Adelie land, east Antarctica: interannual variability and implications for Emperor penguins Aptenodytes forsteri. Marine Ecology Progress Series, vol. 374, p. 243-257.

270.   Dugger, K., et al., (2006) Effects of Flipper Bands on Foraging Behavior and Survival of Adélie Penguins (Pygoscelisadeliae). The Auk, vol. 123, p. 858-869.

271.   Froget, G., et al., (1998) Is penguin banding harmless? Polar Biology, vol. 20, p. 409-413.

272.   Gauthier-Clerc, M., et al., (2004) Long-term effects of flipper bands on penguins. Proceedings of the Royal Society of London, Series B (Supplement), vol. 271, p. S423-S426.

273.   Petersen, S., et al., (2005) Is flipper banding of penguins a prob- lem? Marine Ornithology, vol. 33, p. 75-79

274.   Fretwell, P., and Trathan, P., (2009) Penguins from space: faecal stains reveal the location of emperor penguin colonies. Global Ecology and Biogeography, vol. 18, p. 543-552.

275.   Jenouvrier,S., et al. (2012) Effects of climate change on an emperor penguin population: analysis of coupled demographic and climate models. Global Change Biology, vol. 18, p. 2756-2770.

276.   Ainley, D., et al., (2010) Antarctic penguin response to habitat change as earths troposphere reaches 2 degrees above preindustrial levels. Ecological Monographs, vol. 80, p. 49-66.

277.   Saraux, C., et al., (2011) Reliability of flipper-banded penguins as indicators of climate change. Nature, 469, 203-206.

278.   Ainley, D., et al., (2005) Decadal-scale changes in the climate and biota of the Pacific sector of the southern ocean, 1950s to the 1990s. Antarctic Science, vol. 17, 171-182.

279.   Ainley, D., et al., (2010) Impacts of cetaceans on the structure of Southern Ocean food webs. Marine Mammal Science, vo. 26, p. 482-498.

280.   Duignan, P., (2001) Diseases of penguins. Surveillance, vol. 28, www.sciquest.org.nz/elibrary/download/47208/Diseases_of_penguins

281.   Thomas, J., et al., (2005) Successful Conservation of a Threatened Maculinea Butterfly. Science, vol. 325, p.80-83.

282.   Thomas, J., and Wardlaw, J., (1992) The capacity of a Myrmica ant nest to support a predacious species of Maculieea butterfly. Oecologia, vol. 91, p.101-109.

283.   Thomas, C. D. and Jones, T. M., (1993) Partial recovery of a Skipper Butterfly (Hesperia comma) from Population Refuges: Lessons for Conservation in a Fragmented Landscape. Journal of Animal Ecology, vol. 62, p. 472-481.

284.   Myxomatosis, Wikipedia, http://en.wikipedia.org/wiki/Myxomatosis

285.   Li, Y., and Carbone, R., (2012) Excitation of Rainfall over the Tropical Western Pacific. Journal of Atmospheric Sciences, vol. 69, p. 2983-2994.

286.   Oka, E., and Qiu, B., (2012) Progress of North Pacific mode water research in the past decade. Journal of Oceanography, vol. 68 p.5–20.

287.   Sea ice data provided by University of Illinois, Polar Research Group, Cryosphere Today, http://arctic.atmos.uiuc.edu/cryosphere/

288.   Barnes, D., et al., (2006) Incursion and excursion of Antarctic biota:past, present

and future. Global Ecology and Biogeography, vol. 15, p. 121–142.

289. Dare,R. and Atkinson, B., (2000) Atmospheric Response to Spatial Variation in Concentrations and size of Polynya in the Southern Ocean Sea-ice zone. Boundary-Layer Meteorology, vol. 94, p. 65–88.

290. Massom, R., et al., (1998) The distribution and formative processes of latent-heat polynyas in East Antarctica. Annals of Glaciology, vol. 27, p. 420-426.

291. Holland, D., (2001)Explaining the Weddell Polynya Large Ocean Eddy Shed at Maud Rise Science, vol. 292., p. 1697-1700.

292. Gordon, A., et al., (2006) A Possible Link between the Weddell Polynya and the Southern Annular Mode. Journal of Climate, vol. 20, p. 2558-2570.

293. Hudson, S., and Brandt, R., (2006) A Look at the Surface-Based Temperature Inversion on the Antarctic Plateau. Journal of Climate, vol. 18, p. 1673-1674.

294. van den Broeke, M., and Lipzig, N. (2003) Response of wintertime Antarctic Temperatures to the Antarctic Oscillation: Results of a Regional Climate Model. Antarctic Research Series, vo. 76, p. 335-347.

295. van den Broeke, M., and Lipzig, N. (2004) Changes in Antarctic temperature, wind and precipitation in response to the Antarctic Oscillation. Annals of Glaciology, vol. 39, p. 119-126.

296. Marshall, G., and King, J., (1998) Southern Hemisphere circulation anomalies associated with extreme Antarctic Peninsula winter temperatures. Geophysical Research Letters, vol. 25, p. 2437–2440.

297. Vaughn, D., et al., (2006) Recent Rapid Regional Climate Warming on the Antarctic Peninsula. Climatic Change, vol. 60, p. 243–274.

298. Connolley, W., (1996) The Antarctica Temperature Inversion. International Journal of Climatology, vol. 16, p. 1333-1342.

299. Massom, R., et al. (2008) West Antarctic Peninsula sea ice in 2005: Extreme ice compaction and ice edge retreat due to strong anomaly with respect to climate. Journal of Geophysical Research , vol. 113, C02S20, doi:10.1029/2007JC004239.

300. Massom, R., et al., (2006), Extreme anomalous atmospheric circulation in the West Antarctic Peninsula region in austral spring and summer 2001/2, and its profound impact on sea ice and biota, Journal of Climate, vol. 19, p. 3544– 3571.

301. Stammerjohn, S., et a., (2008) Trends in Antarctic annual sea ice retreat and advance and their relation to El Niño southern oscillation and southern annular mode variability. Journal of Geophysical Research. Vol. 113, C03S90.doi:10.1029/2007JC004269.

302. Stammerjohn, S., et a., (2008) Sea ice in the western Antarctic Peninsula region: spatiotemporal variability from ecological and climate change perspectives. Deep Sea Research II 55. doi:10.1016/j.dsr2.2008.04.026.

303. Wilson, P., et al., (2001) Adelie penguin population change in the Pacific sector of Antarctica: relation to sea-ice extent and the Antarctic circumpolar current. Mar. Ecol. Progr. Ser. 213, 301e309

304. Smith, R., et al. (1999) Marine ecosystem sensitivity to climate change. BioScience vol. 49, p. 393–404.

305. Turner, J., (2004) Review – The El Niño-Southern Oscillation and Antarctica, International Journal of Climatology, vol. 24, p. 1–31

306. Bertler, N., et al., (2006) Opposing oceanic and atmospheric ENSO influences on the Ross Sea Region, Antarctica. Advances in Geosciences, vol. 6, p. 83–86.

307. Jenouvrier, S., et al., (2006) Sea ice affects the population dynamics of Adelie penguins in Terre Ade´ lie. Polar Biology. doi: 10.1007/s00300-005-0073-6.

308. Wilson, P., et al.,(2001) Adelie penguin population change in the pacific sector of Antarctica: relation to sea-ice extend and the Antarctic circumpolar current. Marine Ecology Progress Series, vol. 213, p. 301-309.

309.   Schofield, O., et al, (2010) How Do Polar Marine Ecosystems Respond to Rapid Climate Change? Science, vol. 328, p. 1520-1523.

310.   Stammerjohn, S., et al., (2011) The influence of winds, sea-surface, temperature and precipitation anomalies on Antarctic regional sea-ice conditions during IPY 2007. Deep-Sea Research II, vol. 58, p. 999–1018.

311.   Wang, M., and Overland, J.E., (2009) A sea ice free summer Arctic within 30 years? Geophysical Research Letters, vol. 36, L07502.

312.   Wilson, K, et al., (1990) The impact of man on Adelie penguins at Cape Hallet, Antarctica. In *Antarctic ecosystems: ecological change and conservation* ed. K. R. Kerry & G. Hempel. Springer, Berlin, pp. 813-90.

313.   Fraser, W. R. and Patterson, D., (1997) Human disturbance and long-term changes in Adelie Penguin populations: a natural experiment at Palmer Station, Antarctic Peninsula. in *Antarctic communities: species, structure, and survival.* Cambridge University Press, Cambridge, U.K.

314.   Bob Dylan

315.   Emmerson, L. and Southwell, C., (2008) Sea Ice Cover and Its Influence on Adélie Penguin Reproductive Performance. Ecology, vol. 89, p. 2096-2102

316.   Emmerson, L. and Southwell, C., (2008) Adelie penguin survival: age structure, temporal variability and environmental influences. Oecologia, vol. 167, p. 951–965.

317.   Trivelpiece, W., and Fraser, W., (1996) The Breeding Biology and Distribution of Adelie Penguins" Adaptations to Environmental Variability. Antarctic Research series, vol. 70, p. 273-285.

318.   Emslie, S.D., et al., (1998) Abandoned penguin colonies and environmental change in the Palmer Station area, Anvers Island, Antarctic Peninsula. Antartic Sci. 10, 257-268.

319.   Emslie, S., Patterson, W., (2007) Abrupt recent shift in δ 13C and δ 15N values in Adélie penguin eggshell in Antarctica. Proc, Natl, Acad, Sci, USA 104:11666–11669.

320.   Marshall, G., et al., (2006) The impact of a changing Southern Hemisphere annular mode on Antarctic Peninsula summer temperatures. J. Climate, 19, p. 5388–5404.

321.   Orr, A., et al., (2008), Characteristics of summer airflow over the Antarctic Peninsula in response to recent strengthening of westerly circumpolar winds, J. Atmos. Sci., 65, 1396–1413.

322.   Marshall, G., et al., 2004: Causes of exceptional circulation changes in the Southern Hemisphere. Geophysical Research Letters, vol. 31, L14205, doi:10.1029/2004GL019952.

323.   Schneider, D., et al., (2006) Antarctic temperatures over the past two centuries from ice cores. Geophysical Research Letters, vol.. 33, L16707, doi:10.1029/2006GL027057

324.   Steig, E., et al., (2009) Warming of the Antarctic ice-sheet surface since the 1957 International Geophysical Year. Nature, vol. 457, doi:10.1038/nature07669.

325.   Schneider, D., and Steig, E., (2008) Ice cores record significant 1940s Antarctic warmth related to tropical climate variability. Proc. Natl Acad. Sci. USA 105, 12154–12158

326.   Chapman, W., and Walsh, J., (2006) A Synthesis of Antarctic Temperatures. Journal of Climate, vol. 20, p. 4096-4117.

327.   O'Donnell, R., et al., 2011. Improved methods for PCA-based reconstructions: case study using the Steig et al. (2009) Antarctic temperature reconstruction. Journal of Climate, 24, 2099-2115.

328.   Gillett, N., et al., (2008) Attribution of polar warming to human influence Nature Geoscience, vol. 1, p. 750 – 754.

329.   Speirs, J., et al., (2012) Regional climate variability driven by foehn winds in the McMurdo Dry Valleys, Antarctica. International Journal of Climatology. DOI:

10.1002/joc.3481.

330. Hofman, E., et al., (1996) Water Mass Distribution and Circulation west of the Antarctic Peninsula and Including Bransfield Strait. Antarctic Research Series. Vol. 70, p. 61-80.

331. Schmidt, K., et al. (2011) Early spawning of Antarctic krill in the Scotia Sea is fuelled by "superfluous" feeding on non-ice associated phytoplankton blooms. Deep-Sea Research II, vol. 59–60, p. 159–172

332. Montes-Hugo, M. et al., 2009. Recent Changes in Phytoplankton Communities Associated with Rapid Regional Climate Change Along the Western Antarctic Peninsula. Science, 323(5920): 1470-1473.

333. Gregg, W. W., and M. E. Conkright (2002), Decadal changes in global ocean chlorophyll. Geophysical Research Letters, vol. 29, 1730, doi:10.1029/2002GL014689.

334. Gregg, W. W., (2005) Recent trends in global ocean chlorophyll. Geophysical Research Letters, vol. 32, L03606, doi:10.1029/2004GL021808.

335. Marrari, M., et al., (2008) Spatial and temporal variability of SeaWiFS chlorophyll a distributions west of the Antarctic Peninsula: Implications for krill production. Deep-Sea Research II, vol. 55, p. 377–392

336. Makarov, R., et al., (1990) Larval ecology and reproduction of Euphausiidae in the Ross Sea (in Russian). Biol. Morya, vol. 3, p. 38–45.

337. Nicol, S. (2006) Krill, Currents, and Sea Ice: Euphausia superba and Its Changing Environment. BioScience, vol. 56, p. 111-117.

338. Atkinson, A., Siegel, V., Pakhomov, E.A., Rothery, P., 2004. Long-term decline in krill stock and increase in salps in the Southern Ocean. Nature 432, 100–103.

339. Atkinson, A., et aal., (2009) A re-appraisal of the total biomass and annual production of Antarctic krill. Deep-Sea Research I, vol. 56, p. 727–740.

340. Trivelpiece, W., et al., (2011) Variability in krill biomass links harvesting and climate warming to penguin population changes in Antarctica. PNAS, vol. 108, p. 7625–7628

341. Reardon,S. (2011) Melting Antarctic Ice Causing Penguins to Starve. Science News. http://news.sciencemag.org/sciencenow/2011/04/melting-antarctic-ice-causing-pe.html

342. Smetacek, V. and Nicol, S., (2005) Polar ocean ecosystems in a changing world. Nature, vol. 437, doi:10.1038/nature04161

343. Fabres, J., et al., (2000) Bransfield Basin fine-grained sediments: late-Holocene sedimentary processes and Antarctic oceanographic conditions. Holocene, vol. 10, p. 703–718

344. Leventer A, et al., (1996) Productivity cycles of 200–300 years in the Antarctic Peninsula region: Understanding linkages among the sun, atmosphere, oceans, sea ice, and biota. Geological Society of America Bulletin 108: 1626–1644.

345. Makarov, R., et al., (1990) Larval ecology and reproduction of Euphausiidae in the Ross Sea (in Russian). Biol. Morya, vol. 3, p. 38–45.

346. Vernet, M., et al., (2008) Primary production within the sea-ice zone west of the Antarctic Peninsula: sea ice, summer mixed layer, and irradiance. Deep Sea Research II 55. doi:10.1016/j.dsr2.2008.05.021.

347. Ainley, D., et al., (2003) Adélie Penguins and Environmental Change. Science, vol. 300, p. 429-430.

348. Thompson, D., and Wallace,J., (2000) Annular modes in the extratropical circulation. Part I: Month-to-month variability. Journal of Climate, vol. 13, p.1000–1016.

349. Prezelin, B., et al., (2000) The linkage between Upper Circumpolar DeepWater (UCDW) and phytoplankton assemblages on the west Antarctic Peninsula continental

shelf. J. Mar. Res., 58, 165–202.

350. Prezelin, B., et al., (2000) The linkage between Upper Circumpolar DeepWater (UCDW) and phytoplankton assemblages on the west Antarctic Peninsula continental shelf. Journal of Marine Research, vol. 58, p. 165–202.

351. Loeb V., et al., (2009) ENSO and variability of the Antarctic Peninsula pelagic marine ecosystem. Antarctic Science, vol. 21, p.135–148

352. Lynch, H., et al., (2012) Spatially integrated assessment reveals widespread changes in penguin populations on the Antarctic Peninsula. Ecology, vol. 93, p. 1367–1377.

353. Branch, T. A. 2009. Humpback abundance south of 60S from three completed sets of IDCR/SOWER circumpolar surveys. Journal of Cetacean Research and Management.

354. The IUCN Red List of Threatened Species. http://www.iucnredlist.org/details/2058/0

355. Trivelpiece, W., et al., (2011) Variability in krill biomass links harvesting and climate warming to penguin population changes in Antarctica. PNAS, vol. 108, p. 7625–7628.

356. Smith, R., (2008) Bellingshausen and western Antarctic Peninsula region: Pigment biomass and sea-ice spatial/temporal distributions and interannual variability. Deep Sea Research II, vol. 55, p.1949-1963.

357. Smith Jr., W., and Comiso, J., (2008) Influence of sea ice on primary production in the Southern Ocean: a satellite perspective. J. Geophys. Res. 113, C05S93. doi:10.1029/2007JC004251.

358. Murphy, J., (2007) Spatial and Temporal Operation of the Scotia Sea Ecosystem: A Review of Large-Scale Links in a Krill Centred Food Web. Philosophical Transactions: Biological Sciences, vol. 362, p.113-148.

359. Ballard G, et al., (2010) Responding to climate change: Adélie penguins confront astronomical and ocean boundaries. Ecology, vol. 91, p.2056-2069.

360. Arrigo, K.R., and van Dijken, G. (2003) Phytoplankton dynamics within 37 Antarctic coastal polynya systems Journal Geophysical Research, vol. 108, doi:10.1029/2002JC001739.

361. Steig, E., et al., (1998) Changes in climate, ocean and ice sheet conditions in the Ross Embayment at 6 ka. Annals of Glaciology, vol. 27, p. 305-310.

362. Shindell,D. et al., (1999) Simulation of recent northern winter climate trends by greenhouse-gas forcing. Nature, vol. 399, p.452-455.

363. Arctic Oscillation 1950-2012, NOAA Nov. 5, 2012. http://www.cpc.ncep.noaa.gov/products/precip/CWlink/daily_ao_index/season.JFM.ao.gif

364. Gore Reports Snow and Ice Across the World Vanishing Quickly, Environment News Service, http://www.ens-newswire.com/ens/dec2009/2009-12-14-02.html

365. Orians, C. (2000) Snowfalls are now just a thing of the past. The Independent. http://www.independent.co.uk/environment/snowfalls-are-now-just-a-thing-of-the-past-724017.html

366. LiveScience.com, (2012) Bering Sea Sees Surprising Record Ice Cover. OurAmazingPlanet Staff, http://news.yahoo.com/bering-sea-sees-surprising-record-ice-cover-185125243.html

367. Hiscock, M., et al., (2003) Primary productivity and its regulation in the Pacific Sector of the Southern Ocean. Deep-Sea Research II, vol. 50, p. 533–558

368. Hurwitz, M., et al., (2011) Response of the Antarctic Stratosphere to Two Types of El Niño Events. Journal of Atmospheric Sciences, vol. 68, p. 812-821.

369. Murphy, J., (2007) Spatial and Temporal Operation of the Scotia Sea Ecosystem: A Review of Large-Scale Links in a Krill Centred Food Web. Philosophical Transactions:

Biological Sciences, vol. 362, p.113-148

370. Meredith, M., et al., (2004) Impact of the 1997/98 ENSO on upper ocean characteristics in Marguerite Bay, western Antarctic Peninsula. *Journal of Geophysical Research* 109, C09013, doi:10.1029/2003JC001784

371. Visbeck, M., et al., (2001) The North Atlantic Oscillation: Past, present, and future. PNAS, vol. 98, p.12876–12877.

372. Furtado, J, et al. (2011) North Pacific decadal variability and climate change in the IPCC AR4 models. J. Climate, 24, 3049–3067.

373. Speirs, J., et al., (2012) Regional climate variability driven by foehn winds in the McMurdo Dry Valleys, Antarctica. International Journal of Climatology. DOI: 10.1002/joc.3481.

374. Schwerdtfeger, W., (1984) Weather and climate of the Antarctic. New York: Elsevier Science.

375. Cryosphere Today, (March 2012) Polar Research Group University of Ilinois, http://arctic.atmos.uiuc.edu/cryosphere/

376. Emslie, S.D., et al., (1998) Abandoned penguin colonies and environmental change in the Palmer Station area, Anvers Island, Antarctic Peninsula. Antartic Science, vol. 10, p. 257-268.

377. Ustrnul, Z., (1992) Influence of Foehn Winds in the Polish Carpathians. Theoretical and Applied Climatology. Vol. 45, p. 43-47.

378. Hall, B., et al., (2010) Reduced ice extent on the western Antarctic Peninsula at 700–970 cal. yr B.P. Geology, vol. 38, p. 635–638; doi: 10.1130/G30932.

379. Delmonte, B., et al., (2005) Ice core evidence for secular variability and 200-year dipolar oscillations in atmospheric circulation over East Antarctica during the Holocene. Climate Dynamics, vol. 24, p. 641–654.

380. Shindell DT, Schmidt GA (2004) Southern hemisphere climate response to ozone changes and greenhouse gas increases. Geophysical Research Letters, vol. 31, doi:10.1029/2004gl020724.

381. Thomas, E., et al. (2008) A doubling in snow accumulation in the western Antarctic Peninsula since 1850. Geophysical Research Letters, vol. 35, L01706, doi:10.1029/2007GL032529.

382. Arel, O., et al., (2006) Sea ice evolution over the 20th and 21st centuries as simulated by current AOGCMs. Ocean Modelling, vol. 12, p. 401–415.

383. Stroeve, J., et al., (2012) Trends in Arctic sea ice extent from CMIP5, CMIP3 and observations. Geophysical Research Letters, vol.. 39, L16502, doi:10.1029/2012GL052676, 2012

384. Pavelsky, T., et al., (2010) Atmospheric inversion strength over polar oceans in winter regulated by sea ice. Climate Dynamics, DOI 10.1007/s00382-010-0756-8

385. Thoma, M., et al., (2008) Modelling Circumpolar Deep Water intrusions on the Amundsen Sea continental shelf, Antarctica. Geophysical Research Letters vol. 35, L18602, doi:10.1029/2008GL034939.

386. Liu, J., et al. 2004: Interpretation of recent Antarctic sea ice variability. Geophysical Research Letters, vol. 31, L02205, doi:10.1029/2003GL018732.

387. Haarangozo, S., et al., (2000) A Search for ENSO Teleconnections in the west Antarctic Peninsula Climate in Austral Winter. International Journal of Climatology, vol. 20, p. 663–679

388. Keys, H., et al., (1998) Continued northward expansion of the Ross Ice Shelf, Antarctica. Annals qf Glaciology, vol. 27. P. 93-98

389. Nicol, S., et al., (2008) Krill (Euphausia superba) abundance and Adelie penguin (Pygoscelis adeliae) breeding performance in the waters off the Bechervaise Island colony, East Antarctica in 2 years with contrasting ecological conditions. Deep-Sea Research II, vol. 55, p. 540-557.

390. Arrigo, K.R., van Dijken, G.L., Bushinsky, S., 2008. Primary production in the Southern Ocean, 1997-2006. Journal Geophysical Research, vol. 113, C08004. doi:10.1029/2007JC004551.

391. Hudson, S., and Brandt, R., A Look at the Surface-Based Temperature Inversion on the Antarctic Plateau. Journal of Climate, vol. 18, 1673-1696

392. Dai, A., et al. (2001) Climates of the Twentieth and Twenty-First Centuries Simulated by the NCAR Climate System Model. Journal of Climate, vol. 14, p. 485-519.

393. Johannessen, O., et al. (2004) Arctic climate change: observed and modeled temperature and sea-ice variability. Tellu, vol. 56A, p. 328–341.

394. Bers, A., et al., (2012) Analysis of trends and sudden changes in long-term environmental data from King George Island (Antarctica): relationships between global climatic oscillations and local system response. Climatic Change, DOI 10.1007/s10584-012-0523-4.

395. Visbeck, M., et al., (2001) The North Atlantic Oscillation: Past, present, and future. PNAS, vol. 98, p. 12876–12877.

396. Baron, C,, & Orombelli, G., (1994) Abandoned penguin colonies as Holocene paleoclimatic indicators in Antarctica. Geology, vol. 22, p.23-26.

397. Cubasch, U., et al., Simulation of the influence of solar radiation variations on the global climate with an ocean-atmosphere general circulation model. Climate Dynamics, vol. 13, p. 757-767.

398. Mayewski, P. A., et al. (2009), State of the Antarctic and Southern Ocean climate system, Rev. Geophys., 47, RG1003, doi:10.1029/2007RG000231

399. Gilett, N., et a., (2008) Attribution of polar warming to human influence. Nature Geoscience, vol. 1, p. 750-754.

400. Crosta, X., et al., (2007)Geochemstry Geophysics Geosystems, vol. 8, Q11009, doi:10.1029/2007GC001718, 2007

401. Shevenell, A. , et al., (2011) Holocene Southern Ocean surface temperature variability west of the Antarctic Peninsula. Nautre, vol. 470, doi:10.1038/nature09751

402. The Guardina, (22 October 2012) Italian scientists convicted for 'false assurances' before earthquake. http://www.guardian.co.uk/world/2012/oct/22/italian-scientists-jailed-earthquake-aquila

403. Mudie, P. (2005) Decadal-scale sea ice changes in the Canadian Arctic and their impacts on humans during the past 4,000 years. Environmental Archaeology, vol. 10, p. 113-126.

404. Mann, M, (2002) The Little Ice Age, volume 1, The Earth system: physical and chemical dimensions of global environmental change, p 504–509, in Encyclopedia of Global Environmental Change.

405. Romm, J. (2012)We're Already Topping Dust Bowl Temperatures — Imagine What'll Happen If We Fail To Stop 10°F Warming. http://thinkprogress.org/climate/2012/07/08/512596/

406. Velarde , E., et al. (2004) Seabird Ecology, El Niño Anomalies, and Prediction of Sardine Fisheries in the Gulf of California. Ecological Applications, vol. 14, p. 607-615

407. Suzuki, D., (March 12, 2012) Deny Deniers their Right to Deny! The Huffington Post. http://www.huffingtonpost.ca/

408. Null, J., (2007) El Niño & La Niña Years: A Consensus List. http://ggweather.com/enso/years.htm

409. Mann, M., et al., (2009) Global signatures and dynamical origins of the little ice age and medieval climate anomaly. Science, vol. 326, p. 1256–60.

410. Chavez,. F., et al., (2011) Marine Primary Production in Relation to Climate Variability and Change. Annual Revie of Marine Science, vol. 3, p. 227–260.

411. JUMBO SQUID (DOSIDICUS GIGAS) INVASIONS IN THE EASTERN PACIFIC OCEAN.

CalCOFI Rep., Vol. 49, 2008

412.   Bengtsson, L., et al., (2004) The Early Twentieth-Century Warming in the Arctic— A Possible Mechanism. Journal of Climate, vol. 445-458.

413.   Clark, W. THE LESSONS OF THE PERUVIAN ANCHOVETA FISHERY. Food and Agriculture Organization of the United Nations (FAO). http://www.calcofi.ucsd.edu/newhome/publications/CalCOFI_Reports/v19/pdfs/Vol_19_Clark.pdf

414.   Mantua,N., et al., (1997) Bulletin of the American Meteorological Society, vol. 78, p. 1069-1106.

415.   Holbrook, S., et al., (1997) Changes in an Assemblage of Temperate Reef Fishes Associated with a Climate Shift. Ecological Applications, vol. 7,p. 1299-1310.

416.   Sagarin, R. et al., (1997) Climate-related Change in an Intertidal Community over Short and Long Time-Scales. Ecological Monographs, vol. 69, p. 465-490

417.   Peterson,W., and Schwing,F., (2003) A new climate regime in northeast pacific ecosystems. Geophysical Research Letters, vol. 30, p. 1896, doi:10.1029/2003GL017528.

418.   Gewin, V., (2010) Dead in the Water. Nature, vol 466, p812-815.

419.   Gutierrez, D., et al. (2009) Rapid reorganization in ocean biogeochemistry off Peru towards the end of the Little Ice Age. Biogeosciences, vol. 6, p.835–848.

420.   Grantham, B., et al. (2004) Upwelling-driven nearshore hypoxia signals ecosystem and oceanographic changes in the northeast Pacific. Nature, vol. 429, p.749-755.

421.   CalCOFI (2008) Jumbo Squid (DOSIDICUS GIGAS) INVASIONS IN THE EASTERN PACIFIC OCEAN. CalCOFI report, vol. 49.

422.   Pierce, S., (2012) Declining Oxygen in the Northeast Pacific. Journal of Physical Oceanography, vol. 42, p. 495-502.

423.   Whitney, F., et al., (2007) Persistently declining oxygen levels in the interior waters of the eastern subarctic Pacific. Progress in Oceanography 75 (2007) 179–199

424.   Weiss, K. (2008) Los Angeles Times May 2, 2008, http://www.latimes.com/news/nationworld/nation/la-na-deadzone2 2008may02,0,1285619.story

425.   Markaida, U, et al., (2004) Age, growth and maturation of jumbo squid Dosidicus gigas (Cephalopoda: Ommastrephidae) from the Gulf of California, Mexico. Fisheries Research, vol. 66, p. 31–47.

426.   Spear, L. & Ainley, D., (1997) Migration Routes of Sooty Shearwaters in the Pacific Ocean. The Condor, vol.101 :205-218.

427.   Keister, J., et al. (2011) Zooplankton species composition is linked to ocean transport in the Northern California Current. Global Change Biology (2011) 17, 2498–2511, doi: 10.1111/j.1365-2486.2010.02383.x

428.   Veit, R., et al., (1996) Ocean warming and long-term change in pelagic bird abundance within the California current system., MARINE ECOLOGY PROGRESS SERIES, vol. 139, p. 11-18.

429.   Baduini, C., et al., (2001) Mass mortality of short-tailed shearwaters in the south-eastern Bering Sea during summer 1997. Fisheries Oceanography, vol. 10, p. 117-130.

430.   KTVU (2007) Giant Squid's California Migration Product Of Warming. http://www.ktvu.com/news/news/giant-squids-california-migration-product-of-warmi/nKxHg/

431.   Coyle, K., et al., (2007)Amphipod prey of gray whales in the northern Bering Sea: Comparison of biomass and distribution between the 1980s and 2002–2003. Deep-Sea Research II, vol. 54,p. 2906–2918.

432. Perry, W., (2012) Blame Hitchcock's Crazed Birds on Toxic Algae. LiveScience, http://www.livescience.com/17713-hitchcock-birds-movie-algae-toxin.html

433. Cayan, D., et al., (2001) Changes in the onset of spring in the western United States. Bull. Amer. Meteor. Soc., vol. 82, p. 399-415.

434. Hartman, B., & Wendler, G., (2005) The Significance of the 1976 Pacific Climate Shift in the Climatology of Alaska. Journal of Climate, vol. 18, p. 4821-4838.

435. Bonsal, B. et al., (2006) Impacts of large-scale teleconnections on freshwater-ice break/freeze-up dates over Canada. Journal of Hydrology, vol. 330, p. 340– 353.

436. Andreoli, R., and Kayano, M., ENSO-Relatd RainfallL Anomalies in South America and Associated Circulation Features During the Warm and Cold Pacific Decadal Oscillation Regimes. Int. J. Climatol. 25: 2017–2030

437. Kayano, M. and Andreoli, R., (2007) Relations of South American summer rainfall interannual variations with the Pacific Decadal Oscillation. International Journal of Climatology, vol. 27, p. 531-540

438. Garcia, S., and Kayano, M., (2007) Climatological aspects of Hadley, Walker and monsoon circulations in two phases of the Pacific Decadal Oscillation. Theor. Appl. Climatology, vol. 91, p.117–127.

439. Dawe, J., and Thompson, L., (2006) PDO-Related Heat and Temperature Budget Changes in a Model of the North Pacific. Journal of Climate, vol. 20, p.2092-2100

440. Kitzberger, T., et al., (2001) Inter-Hemispheric Synchrony of Forest Fires and the El Niño-Southern Oscillation. Global Ecology and Biogeography, vol. 10, p. 315-326.

441. Namdar, R., et al., (2009) Coherence between lake ice cover, local climate and teleconnections (Lake Mendota, Wisconsin). Journal of Hydrology, vol. 374, p. 282– 293

442. Maue, R. N. (2011), Recent historically low global tropical cyclone activity, Geophys. Res. Lett., 38, L14803, doi:10.1029/2011GL047711.

443. Pielke, R., Jr., & Landsea, C., La Niña, El Niño, and Atlantic Hurricane Damages in the United StatesBull. Amer. Meteor. Soc., 80, 2027-2033

444. Enfield, D. & Cid-Serrano, L. (2010) Secular and multidecadal warmings in the North Atlantic and their relationships with major hurricane activity. Int. J. Climatol. 30: 174–184.

445. Rodionov, S., et al. (2007) The Aleutian Low and Winter Climatic Conditions in the Bering Sea. Part I: Classification. Journal of Climate, vol. 18, p. 160-178

446. Shaffer, S., et al., (2006) Migratory shearwaters integrate oceanic resources across the Pacific Ocean in an endless summer. Proceedings of the National Academy of Sciences, vol. 103, p. 12799-12802.

447. Zeidberg, L., et al. (2007) Invasive range expansion by the Humboldt squid, Dosidicus gigas, in the eastern North Pacific. PNAS,, vol. 104, p. 12948–12950.

448. Nigmatulin,C., et al. (2001) A review of the biology of the Jumbo Squid Dosidius gigas (Cephalopoda:Ommastrephidae). Fisheries Research, vol. 54, p. 9-19.

449. Litz, M., et al., (2011) Seasonal Occurences of Humboldt Squid. CalCOFI Rep., vol. 52.

450. Pollack, H., et al., (2005) Surface temperature trends in Russia over the past five centuries reconstructed from borehole temperatures. Journal of Geophysical Research, vol. 108, p. 2180, doi:10.1029/2002JB002154.

451. Giesle. P., and Unruh, C., (2003) Frost Protection for Citrus and Other Subtropicals. University of California, ANR Publication 8100.

452. Cossins, D. (2012) A Decade of Misconduct. The scientist, http://www.the-scientist.com/?articles.list/categoryNo/2625/category/The-Scientist/

453. Hoerling, M., et al., (2010) Regional Precipitation Trends: Distinguishing Natural Variability from Anthropogenic Forcing. Journal of Climate, vol. 23, p. 2131-2147.

454. *Science Watch* Newsletter Interview of Camille Parmesan. (2010)

http://archive.sciencewatch.com/inter/aut/2010/10-mar/10marParm/

455.   Solomon, S., et al. (2010) Contributions of Stratospheric Water Vapor to Decadal Changes in the Rate of Global Warming. Science, vol. 327, 1219-1223.

456.   (2012) Throwing Out the Free Market Playbook: An Interview with Naomi Klein. http://www.thesolutionsjournal.com/node/1053

457.   Hurrell, J. and Deser, C. (2009) North Atlantic climate variability: The role of the North Atlantic Oscillation. Journal of Marine Systems, vo. 78, p. 28–41.

458.   Thomas, J., et al. (1986) Ecology and Declining Status of the Silver-spotted Skipper Butterfly (Hesperia Comma) in Britain. Journal o Applied Ecology. Vol. 23, p. 365-380.

459.   Johansson, P., et al. (2008) From Change Blindness to Choice Blindness. Psychologia, vol. 51, p. 142-155.

460.   Knutti, R. and Hegerl, G., (2008) The equilibrium sensitivity of the Earth's temperature to radiation changes. Nature Geoscience, vol. 1, p. 735-744.

461.   Kiehl, J. and Trenberth, K., (1997)Earth's Annual Global Mean Energy Budget. Bulletin of the American Meteorological Society, vol. 78, p. 197-209.

462.   Pielke Sr, R. et al. (2011), Land use/land cover changes and climate: modeling analysis and observational evidence. Wiley Interdisciplinary Reviews: Climate Change. doi: 10.1002/wcc.144. Published Online: Oct 28 2011

463.   Mildrexler, D., et al. (2011) A global comparison between station air temperatures and MODIS land surface temperatures reveals the cooling role of forests. J. Geophys. Res., 116, G03025, doi:10.1029/2010JG001486.

464.   Mahmood, R., et al, (2010) Impacts of Land Use/Land Cover change on Climate and Future Research Priorities. Bulletin of the American Meteorological Society, p. 37- 47.

465.   Runnalls, K. and Oke, T., (2006) A Technique to Detect Microclimatic Inhomogeneities in Historical Records of Screen-Level Air Temperature. Journal of Climate, vol. 19, p. 959-979

466.   Stone, B., (2009) Land Use As Climate Change Mitigation. *Environ. Sci. Technol, vol. 43,p.* 9052–9056

467.   Mildrexler, D., et al. (2011) J. Geophys. Res., 116, G03025, doi:10.1029/2010JG001486.

468.   Deo, R. (2012) A review and modelling results of the simulated response of deforestation on climate extremes in eastern Australia. Atmospheric Research, vol. 108, p. 19–38.

469.   Costa, M., and Yanagi, S., (2006) Effects of Amazon deforestation on the regional climate-Historical perspective, current and future research. Revista Brasileira de Meteorologia, v.21, p. 200-211.

470.   Bala, G., et al., (2007) Combined Climate and Carbon-Cycle Effects of Large-Scale Deforestation. Proceedings of the National Academy of Sciences of the United States of America, vol. 104, p. 6550-6555.

471.   South, D., et al. (2011) Will afforestation in temperate zones warm the Earth? Journal of Horticulture and Forestry Vol. 3(7), pp. 195-199.

472.   Loughnan, M., ct al. (2012 Mapping Hcat Hcalth Risks in Urban Arcas Intcrnational Journal of Population Research, volume 2012, Article ID 518687, 12 pages doi:10.1155/2012/518687

473.   Vandentorren, S., et al., "Mortality in 13 French cities during the August 2003 heat wave," American Journal of Public Health, vol. 94, no. 9, pp. 1518–1520, 2004

474.   Loughnan, M., et al. (2012 Mapping Heat Health Risks in Urban Areas International Journal of Population Research, volume 2012, Article ID 518687, 12 pages doi:10.1155/2012/518687

475.   Arora, V., & Montenegro, A., (2011) Small temperature benefits provided by realistic   afforestation   efforts.   Nature   Geoscience   4,   514–518   (2011)

doi:10.1038/ngeo1182

476.   Gallo, K., et al. (1996) The Influence of Land Use/Land Cover on Climatological Values of the Diurnal Temperature Range. Journal of Climate, vol. 9, p. 2941-2944.

477.   Steyaert, L., and Knox, R., (2008) Reconstructed historical land cover and biophysical parameters for studies of land-atmosphere interactions within the eastern United States. Journal of Geophysical Research, vol. 113, D02101, doi:10.1029/2006JD008277

478.   Trenberth, K. (2011) Communicating Climate Science and Thoughts on Climategate. "Joint Presidential Session on Communicating Climate Change", January 2011, Seattle Washington.

479.   Woehler, E.J. (1993) *The distribution and abundance of Antarctic and Subantarctic penguins.* Scientific Committee on Antarctic Research, Cambridge.

480.   Fretwell, P., et al.,, (2012) An Emperor Penguin Population Estimate: The First Global, Synoptic Survey of a Species from Space. *PLoS ONE.*

481.   Solomon, S., et al., (2010) Contributions of Stratospheric Water Vapor to Decadal Changes in the Rate of Global Warming. Science, vol. 327, p. 1219-1225.

482.   Rahmstorf, S, (2012) Hot enough for you? New Scientist, vol. 215, Issue 2880.

483.   Xue,Y., et al., (2012) A Comparative Analysis of Upper-Ocean Heat Content Variability from an Ensemble of Operational Ocean Reanalyses. Journal of Climate, vol 25, 6905-6929.

484.   Shimada, K., et al. (2004) Penetration of the 1990s warm temperature anomaly of Atlantic Water in the Canada Basin. Geophys. Res. Lett., 31, L20301, doi:10.1029/2004GL02086.

485.   Polyakov, I., et al. (2010) Arctic Ocean Warming Contributes to Reduced Polar Ice Cap. Journal of Physical Oceanography, vol. 40, p. 2743-2758.

486.   C. Wunsch, 2007. The Past and Future Ocean Circulation from a Contemporary Perspective, in AGU Monograph, 173, A. Schmittner, J. Chiang and S. Hemming, Eds., 53-74.

487.   Meehl, G., (2012) Mechanisms Contributing to the Warming Hole and the Consequent U.S. East–West Differential of Heat Extremes. Journal of Climate, vol. 25, p. 6394-6410.

488.   Johansson, P., et al. (2008) From Change Blindness to Choice Blindness. Psychologia, vol. 51, p. 142-155.

489.   Mares, M., ed. (1999). "Middle East, deserts of". Encyclopedia of deserts. University of Oklahoma Press. p. 362. ISBN 978-0-8061-3146-7.

490.   Sheffield, J., et al., (2012) Little change in global drought over the past 60 years. Nature, vol. 491, p. 435-441.

491.   Lockart, N., et al., (2009) On the recent warming in the Murray-Darling Basin: land surface interactions misunderstood. Geophysical Research Letters, vol 36, L24405

492.   Hirschi, M., et al., (2011) Observational evidence for soil-moisture impact on hot extremes in southeastern Europe. Nature Geoscience, vol. 4, p. 17–21.

493.   Rodysill, J., et a. (2012) A paleolimnological record of rainfall and drought from East Java, Indonesia during the last 1,400 years. Journal of Paleolimnoly,vol.47, p. 25–139.

494.   Mensig, S., et al., (2004) A Holocene pollen record of persistent droughts from Pyramid Lake, Nevada, USA. Quaternary Research, vol. 62. P. 29– 38.

495.   Pederson,G., et al., (2006) Long-Duration Drought Variability and Impacts on Ecosystem Services: A Case Study from Glacier National Park, Montana. . *Earth Interactions,* vol. 10, p.1-28.

496.   Dai, A., (2012) Increasing drought under global warming in observations and models. Nature Climate Change, DOI: 10.1038/NCLIMATE1633

497.   From Ken Burns documentary 'The Dust Bowl' aired on PBS television 2012.

498. Axtell, R., et al. (2002) Population growth and collapse in a multiagent model of the Kayenta Anasazi in Long House Valley. *Proc. Natl. Acad. Sci. USA, vol.* **99**, p. 7275–7279.

499. Woodhouse, C. and Lukas, J. (2006) Multi-century tree-ring reconstructions of Colorado streamflow for water resource planning. Climatic Change, vol. 78, p. 293-315.

500. Dai, A. (2012) The influence of the inter-decadal Pacific oscillation on US precipitation during 1923–2010. Climate Dynamics, DOI 10.1007/s00382-012-1446-5

501. Lips, K., (1998) Decline of a Tropical Montane Amphibian Fauna. Conservation Biology, vol. 12, p. 106-117.

502. Nair, U., et al., (2003) Impact of land use on Costa Rican tropical montane cloud forests: Sensitivity of cumulus cloud field characteristics to lowland deforestation, Journal of Geophysical Research, vol.108, p. 4206, doi:10.1029/2001JD001135.

503. Lawton, R., et al. (2001) Climatic Impact of Tropical Lowland Deforestation on Nearby Montane Cloud Forests. Science, vol. 294, p. 284-288

504. Berger, L., et al. (1998) Chytridiomycosis causes amphibian mortality associated with population declines in the rain forests of Australia and Central America. Proc. Natl. Acad. Sci. USA vol. 95, p. 9031–9036.

505. Hanselmann, R., et al. (2004) Presence of an emerging pathogen of amphibians in introduced bullfrogs Rana catesbeiana in Venezuela. Biological Conservation, vol. 120,p. 115–119.

506. Bellet, G, (2012) Jellyfish population on the rise, perhaps due to global warming and pollution. Postmedia News April 19, 2012

507. Condon, et al., (2012) Recurrent jellyfish blooms are a consequence of global oscillations. www.pnas.org/cgi/doi/10.1073/pnas.1210920110

508. Wendler,G., et al. (2012) The First Decade of the New Century: A Cooling Trend for Most of Alaska. The Open Atmospheric Science Journal, 2012, 6, 111-116

509. Hurrell, J.W., Deser, C., 2010. North Atlantic climate variability: the role of the North Atlantic Oscillation. J. Mar. Syst. 79, 231–244.

510. McKinney, M., et al., (1997) Extinction vulnerability and selectivity: combining ecological and paleontological views. Annual Review of Ecology and Systematics, vol. 28, p. 495–516.

511. Lysne, J., & Deser,C., (2002) Wind-Driven Thermocline Variability in the Pacific: A Model–Data Comparison. Journal of Climate, vol. 15, p. 829-846.

512. Purcell, J., et al. (2007) Anthropogenic causes of jellyfish blooms and their direct consequences for humans: a review. Marine Ecology Progress Series. Vol. 350: 153–174, 2007 doi: 10.3354/meps07093

513. Andreev, A., and Kusakabe, M., (2001) Interdecadal variability in dissolved oxygen in the intermediate water layer of the Western Subarctic Gyre and Kuril Basin (Okhotsk Sea). Geophysical Researcher Letters, vol. 28, p. 2453-2456.

514. King, J.R. (Ed.) 2005. Report of the Study Group on Fisheries and Ecosystem Responses to Recent Regime Shifts. PICES Scientific Report No. 28, 162 p.

515. Keeling,R., et al. (2010) Ocean Deoxygenation in a Warming World. Annual Review Marine Science vol. 2, p.199-229.

516. Perryman,W., et al.(2002) Examination of the Relationship Between Seasonal Ice and Calf Production in the Easstern Pacific Population of Gray Whales. Paper SC/54/BRG4 Presented to the IWC Scientific Committee. http://lsiecosystem.org/wp-content/uploads/2010/07/Gray-Whale-Seasonal-Ice-Calf-ProdIWCBRG4.pdf

517. Saba,V., et al. (2008) Bottom-Up and Climatic Forcing on the Worldwide Population of Leatherback Turtles. Ecology, vol. 89, p. 1414-1427.

518.   Springer, A. et al. (1996)The Bering Sea Green Belt: shelf-edge processes and ecosystem production. Fish. Oceanogr., vol. 5,p.205-223.

519.   Brown, Z. W., and Arrigo, K. R. 2012. Contrasting trends in sea ice and primary production in the Bering Sea and Arctic Ocean. - ICES Journal of Marine Science, 69: 1180-1193.

520.   LeBoeuf, Bet al. (2000) High gray whale mortality and low recruitmentin 1999: potential causes and implications. Journal of Cetacean Research and Management, vol. 2, p. 85-99.

521.   Highsmith, R.C. and Coyle, K.O. 1992. Productivity of Arctic amphipods relative to gray whale energy requirements. *Mar. Ecol. Prog. Ser., vol.* 83, p. 41-50.

522.   Coyle, k., et al. (2007) Amphipod prey of gray whales in the northern Bering Sea: Comparison of biomass and distribution between the 1980s and 2002–2003. Deep-Sea Research II, vol. 54, p. 2906–2918.

523.   Salvadeo, C.,et al.(2011)Review of long term macro-fauna movement by multi-decadal warming trends in the Northeastern Pacific. In: Climate Change— Geophysical   Foundations   and   Ecological   Effects.   In   Technical, /http://www.intechopen.com, Published online.

524.   Kerosky, S., et al., (2012) Bryde's whale seasonal range expansion and increasing presence in the Southern California Bight from 2000 to 2010. Deep-Sea Research I 65 (2012) 125–132

525.   Serreze,M. & Francis, J. (2006) The Arctic Amplification Debate. Climatic Change, vol. 76, p. 241-264.

526.   Robinson, C., et al. (2012) Jumbo squid (Dosidicus gigas) landings in the Gulf of California related toremotely sensed SST and concentrations of chlorophyll a (1998–2012). Fisheries Research, vol. 137,p. 97–103.

527.   Stabeno,P., et al. (2012) A comparison of the physics of the northern and southern shelves of the eastern Bering Sea and some implications for the ecosystem. Deep-Sea Research II, vol. 65-70, p.14–30.

528.   Yall, S. (2013) Heat, Flood or Icy Cold, Extreme Weather Rages Worldwide. NY Times, January 10, 2013

529.   Trenberth, K. (1999) Conceptual Framework for Changes of extremes of the hydrological cycle with climate change. Climatic Change, vol. 42, p.327-339.

530.   Landsea   IPCC   resignation: http://cstpr.colorado.edu/prometheus/archives/science_policy_general/000318chr is_landsea_leaves.html

531.   Hansen, J. et al., (2013) Global Temperature Update Through 2012. http://www.columbia.edu/~jeh1/mailings/2013/20130115_Temperature2012.pdf

532.   Kaser, G., et al. (2012) Is the decline of ice on Kilimanjaro unprecedented in the Holocene?. The   Holocene,   OnlineFirst,   published   on   July   19,   2010   as doi:10.1177/0959683610369498

533.   Walton, M., (2008) Polar Bear resort to cannibalism as Arctic ice shrinks. CNN Tech September 23, 2008.

534.   Parmesan, C., et al. (2011) Overstretching attribution. Nature Climate Change, vol. 1, April 2011

535.   Rigor, I.G. and J.M. Wallace (2004), Variations in the Age of Sea Ice and Summer Sea Ice Extent, Geophys. Res. Lett., v. 31, doi:10.1029/2004GL019492.

536.   Rigor, I.G., J.M. Wallace, and R.L. Colony (2002), Response of Sea Ice to the Arctic Oscillation, J. Climate, v. 15, no. 18, pp. 2648 – 2668.

537.   Kumar, A. et al. (2010) Contribution of sea ice loss to Arctic amplification. Geophysical Research Letters, vol. 37, L21701, doi:10.1029/2010GL045022

538.   Kahl, J., et al., (1993) Absence of evidence for greenhouse warming over the Arctic Ocean in the past 40 years. *Nature, vol.* 361, p. 335-337, doi:10.1038/361335a0

539. Tietsche, S.,et al. (2011) Recovery mechanisms of Arctic summer sea ice. Geophysical Research Letters, vol. 38, L02707, doi:10.1029/2010GL045698.

540. Holloway,G. and Sou, T. (2001) Has Arctic Sea Ice Rapidly Thinned? Journal of Climate, vol. 15, p.1691–1701.

541. Zhang, J (2007) Increasing Antarctic sea ice under warming atmospheric and oceanic conditions. Journal of Climate, vol. 20, p. 2515–2529.

542. Shu, Q., (2012) Sea ice trends in the Antarctic and their relationship to surface air temperature during 1979–2009. Climate Dynamics, vol. 38, p. 2355–2363.

543. Landrum, L., et al. (2012) Antarctic Sea Ice Climatology, Variability, and Late Twentieth-Century Change in CCSM4. *Journal of Climate*, vol. **25**, p. 4817-4838.

544. NASA, (2011) Aquarius: "Salt of the Earth" map. http://www.nasa.gov/mission_pages/aquarius/multimedia/gallery/pia14786.html

545. Liu, J., and Curry, J. (2010)Accelerated warming of the Southern Ocean and its impacts on the hydrological cycle and sea ice. PNAS, vol. 107, p.14987–14992.

546. Woodgate,R., et al. (2006) Interannual changes in the Bering Strait fluxes of volume, heat and freshwater be- tween 1991 and 2004. Geophys. Res. Lett., 33, L15609, doi:10.1029/ 2006GL026931.

547. Holland,P. and Kwok, R. (2012) Wind-driven trends in Antarctic sea-ice drift. Nature Geoscience, ADVANCE ONLINE PUBLICATION. www.nature.com/naturegeoscience m

548. Thompson, D. & Solomon, S. (2002) Interpretation of recent Southern Hemisphere climate change. Science, vol. 296, p. 895–899.

549. Fischetti, M. (2012) Did Climate Change Cause Hurricane Sandy? Scientific American, October 30,2012.

550. Trenberth, K. (2007) Warmer Oceans, Stronger Hurricanes. Scientific American, vol. 297, p44-51.

551. Mehta,V., (1997) Influence of solar irradiance on the Indian monsoon-ENSO relationship at decadal-multidecadal time scales. Geophysical Research Letters, vol. 24, p. 159-162.

552. Heide-Jorgensen, et al.,(2012) Identifying gray whale (Eschrichtius robustus) foraging grounds along the Chukotka Peninsula, Russia, using satellite telemetry. Polar Biology, vol. 35, p. 1035–1045.

553. Gutierrez, M., et al. (2007) Anchovy (Engraulis ringens) and sardine (Sardinops sagax) spatial dynamics and aggregation patterns in the Humboldt Current ecosystem, Peru, from 1983–2003. Fish. Oceanogr., vol 16, p. 155–168

554. Lean,J. and Rind, D., (2008) How natural and anthropogenic influences alter global and regional surface temperatures: 1889 to 2006. Geophysical Research Letters, vol. 35, L18701, doi:10.1029/2008GL034864.

555. Douglas,(2010) Arctic Sea Ice Decline: Projected Changes in Timing and Extent of Sea Ice in the Bering and Chukchi Seas. USGS Open-File Report 2010–1176.

556. Hetzinger, S., et al. (2012) Marine proxy evidence linking decadal North Pacific and Atlantic Climate. Climate Dynamics, vol. 39, p.1447–1455, DOI 10.1007/s00382-011-1229-4.

557. Garlich_Miller, J. et al. (2006) Trends in Age Structure and Productivity of Pacific Walruses. Marine Mammal Science, vol. 22(4), p. 880–896.

558. Bernard, J. (1923) Local Walrus Protection in Northeast Siberia. Journal of Mammalogy, Vol. 4, p. 224-227.

559. Berard, J., (1925) Walrus Protection in Alaska. Journal of Mammalogy, Vol. 6, p. 100-102.

560. Fay, F. (1982) Ecology and Biology of Odobenus rosmarus the Pacific Walrus, divergens. US. Department of the Interior, Fish and Wildlife Service, North American Fauna, No. 74.

561. Kochnev A., (2004) Warming of eastern Arctic and present status of the Pacific walrus (Odobenus rosmarus divergens) population, p.284-288 in: Belkovich V.M., ed. Marine Mammals of the Holarctic. Papers of the Third International Conference. Moscow: Marine Mammal Council, 609 pp.

562. Jay, C., and Hills,S. (2005) Movements of Walruses Radio-tagged in Bristol Bay, Alaska. Arctic, vol. 58, p. 192–202.

563. Garlich_Miller, J. et al. (2011) Status Review of the Pacific Walrus (Odobenus rosmarus divergens). 1U.S. Fish and Wildlife Service, Marine Mammals Management

564. deMarban, A. Walruses lured to their deaths. Anchorage Daily News, May 28th, 2008.

565. Born,E., and Knutsen,L. (1997) Haul-out and diving activity of male Atlantic walruses (Odobenus rosmarus rosmarus) in NE Greenland. J. Zool., Lond. Vol. 243, p.381-396.

566. Cherry, S., et. Al., (2011) Quantifying dietary pathways of proteins and lipids to tissues of a marine predator. Journal of Applied Ecology, vol. 48, p. 373–381.

567. Proceedings of the Twelfth Working Meeting of the IUCN/SSC Polar Bear Specialist Group 3-7 February 1997, Oslo Norway.

568. Derocher,A., et al. (2004) Polar Bears in a Warming Climate. INTEGR. COMP. BIOL., 44:163–176.

569. Regehr, E. et al, (2007) Effects of Earlier Sea Ice Breakup on Survival and Population Size of Polar Bears in Western Hudson Bay. The Journal of Wildlife Management, vol. 71, p. 2673-2683.

570. Lunn, N. et al. (1997) Re-Estimating the Size of the Polar Bear Population in Western Hudson Bay.Arctic, vol. 50, p. 234-240.

571. Hunter, C., et al. (2010) Climate change threatens polar bear populations: a stochastic demographic analysis. Ecology, vol. 91p. 2883–2897.

572. Atkinson, S. (2012) Western Hudson Bay Polar Bear Aerial, 2011. Government of Nunavut, Department of the Interior.

573. Regehr, E.V., Amstrup, S.C., and Stirling, Ian, 2006, Polar bear population status in the southern Beaufort Sea: U.S. Geological Survey Open-File Report 2006-1337, 20 p.

574. Regehr, E., et al. (2010) Survival and breeding of polar bears in the southern Beaufort Sea in relation to sea ice. Journal of Animal Ecology 2010, 79, 117–127

575. Derocher, A. and Stirling I. (1995) Estimation of Polar Bear Population Size and Survival in Western Hudson. The Journal of Wildlife Management, vol. 59, p. 215-221.

576. Stirling, I. and Derocher, A. (1993) Possible Impacts of Climatic Warming on Polar Bears. Arctic, vol. 46, p. 240-245.

577. Vongraven, D and Peacock, E. (2011) Development of a pan-Arctic monitoring plan for polar bears :background paper. Circumpolar Biodiversity Monitoring Programme, CAFF Monitoring Series Report No.1, January 2011.

578. Peacock, E, et al. (2011)Conservation and management of Canada's polar bears (Ursus maritimus) in a changing Arctic. Can. J. Zool. vol. 89, p. 371-386.

579. Arrigo, K. and van Dijken, G. (2004)Geophysical Research Letters, vol. 31, L08304, doi:10.1029/2003GL018978.

580. Miller, G. et al. (2010) Temperature and precipitation history of the Arctic. Quaternary Science Reviews 29 (2010) 1679e1715.

581. Dyke, A., and Savelle, J. (2001) Holocene History of the Bering Sea Bowhead Whale(Balaena mysticetus) in Its Beaufort Sea Summer Grounds off Southwestern Victoria Island, Western Canadian Arctic. Quaternary Research, vol. 55, p.371–379.

582. Dowsley, M. and M. K. Taylor. 2006. Management consultations for the Western Hudson Bay (WH) polar bear population (01-02 December 2005). Government of Nunavut, Department of Environment, Final Wildlife Report: 3, Iqaluit, 55 pp.

583. Dereocher, A. et al. (2013) Rapid ecosystem change and polar bear conservation.

doi: 10.1111/conl.12009

584. Stirling, I and Derocher, A. (2012) Effects of climate warming on polar bears: a review of the evidence. Global Change Biology (2012) 18, 2694–2706, doi: 10.1111/j.1365-2486.2012.02753.x

585. Zeh, J, et al. (1991) Rate of Increase, 1978-1988, of Bowhead Whales, Balena Mysticetus, estimated from ice-based Census Data. Marine Mammal Science, vol. 7, p. 105-122.

586. Stirling, I. and Parkinson, C. (2006) Possible Effects of Climate Warming on Selected Populations of Polar Bears (Ursus maritimus) in the Canadian Arctic. Arctic vol . 59, p. 261-275.

587. Dykstra, P. (2008) Magic Number: a Sketchy "Fact" About Polar Bears Keeps Going...And Going... And Going. Society of Environmental Journalists, August 15, 2008.

588. Stirling, I. et al. (2008) Unusual Predation Attempts of Polar Bears on Ringed Seals in the Southern Beaufort Sea: Possible Significance of Changing Spring Ice Conditions. Arctic, vol 61, p. 14-22.

589. Derocher, A. and Stirling, I. (1992) The population dynamics of polar bears in western Hudson Bay. In: McCullough, D.R., and Barrett, R.H., eds. Wildlife 2001: Populations. London: Elsevier Applied Science. P. 1150–1159.

590. Stirling, I. et al. (1999) Long-term Trends in the Population Ecology of Polar Bears in Western Hudson Bay in Relation to Climatic Change. Arctic vol . 52, p. 294-306.

591. Amstrup, S. et al. (2009) Rebuttal of "Polar Bear Population Forecasts: A Public-Policy Forecasting Audit" Interfaces, Articles in Advance, pp. 1–17, ©2009 INFORMS

592. Amstrup, S. and Durner, G. (1995) Survival rates of radio-collared female polar bears and their dependent young. Canadian Journal of Zoology, vol. 73. P. 1312-1322.

593. Amstrup, S. et al. (2001) Polar Bears in the Beaufort Sea: A 30-YearMark–Recapture Case History. Journal of Agricultural, Biological, and Environmental Statistics, Volume 6, Number 2, Pages 221–234

594. Derocher, A. and Stirling, I (1998) Geographic variation in growth of polar bears (Ursus maritimus). J. Zool., Lond.., vol. 245, p. 65-72.

595. Stirling, I. and Derocher, A. (1990) Factors Affecting the Evolution and Behavioral Ecology of the Modern. Bears: Their Biology and Management, Vol. 8, A Selection of Papers from the Eighth International Conference on Bear Research and Management, Victoria, British Columbia, Canada, February 1989 (1990), pp. 189-204.

596. Wilson, D., (1976) Cranial variation in polar bears. In Bears ± their biology and management: 447±453. Pelton, M. R., Lentfer, J. W. & Folk, G. E. (Eds). Cambridge: IUCN.

597. Lunn, N. and Stenhouse, G. (1985) An observation of possible cannibalism by polar bears (Ursus maritimus). Canadian Journal of Zoology. Vol 63, p. 1516-1517.

598. Monnett, C., and Gleason, J., (2006) Observations of mortality associated with extended open-water swimming by polar bears in the Alaskan Beaufort Sea. Polar Biology, vol. 29, p.681-687.

599. Hunter, C., et al. (2007) Polar Bears in the Southern Beaufort Sea II: Demography and Population Growth in Relation to Sea Ice Conditions. USGS Alaska Science Center, Anchorage, Administrative Report.

600. Regehr, E., et al. (2007) Polar bears in the southern Beaufort Sea I: survival and breeding in relation to sea ice conditions, 2001-2006. USGS Alaska Science Center, Anchorage, Administrative Report.

601. Rode K.,et al. (2010) Reduced body size and cub recruitment in polar bears associated with sea ice decline. Ecological Applications, 20, 768–782.

602. Rode, K. et al. (2007) Polar Bears in the Southern Beaufort Sea III: Stature, Mass, and Cub Recruitment in Relationship to Time and Sea Ice Extent Between 1982 and 2006. USGS Alaska Science Center, Anchorage, Administrative Report.

603.   Derocher, A., and Wiig. (1999) Infanticide and cannibalism of juvenile polar bears (Ursus maritimus) in Svalbard. Arctic 52:307–310

604.   Garner, G., et al. (1990) Seasonal Movements of Adult Female Polar Bears in the Bering and Chukchi Seas. Bears: Their Biology and Management, vol. 8, A Selection of Papers from the Eighth International Conference on Bear Research and Management, Victoria, British Columbia, Canada, February 1989 (1990), pp. 219-226.

605.   Amstrup, S., et al. (2001) Comparing movement patterns of satellite-tagged male and female polar bears. Canadian Journal Of Zoology, vol 79. p. 2147-2160.

606.   Garner, G. et al. (1994) Dispersal Pattersn of Maternal polar bears from the denning concentration on Wrangel Island. Int. Conf. Bear Res. and Manage. vol. 9, p. 401-410.

607.   Amstrup, S.et al., (2006) Recent observations of intraspecific predation and cannibalism among polar bears in the southern Beaufort Sea. Polar Biology, vol. 29, p. 997-1002.

608.   Amstrup, S. C., Stirling, I., and Lentfer, J. W. (1986), "Past and Present Status of Polar Bears in Alaska," Wildlife Society Bulletin, 14, 241–254.

609.   COSEWIC. 2008. COSEWIC assessment and update status report on the polar bear Ursus maritimus in Canada. Committee on the Status of Endangered Wildlife in Canada, Ottawa,

610.   Tyrell, M. (2006) More bears, less bears: Inuit and scientific perceptions of polar bear populations on the west coast of Hudson Bay. Études/Inuit/Studies, vol. 30, p. 191-208.

611.   Wiig, O. (1998) Survival and Reproductive Rates for Polar Bears at Svalbard. Ursus, vol. 10, A Selection of Papers from the Tenth International Conference on Bear Research and Management, Fairbanks, Alaska, July 1995, and Mora, Sweden, September 1995 (1998), p. 25-32.

612.   Peacock E (2009) Davis Strait Polar Bear Population Inventory. Final Report, Government of Nunavut, Department of Environment Report. Government of Nunavut, Igloolik.

613.   Garshelis,D., Peacock, E., Atkinson, S. (2012) Aerial Survey Population Monitoring of Polar Bears in Foxe Basin.

614.   Taylor, M., J. Lee, J. Laake and P. McLoughlin. 2006. Estimating population size of polar bears in Foxe Basin using tetracyclin biomarkers. Government of Nunavut, Department of Environment, Final Wildlife Report. 13 pp.

615. Taylor, M. et al. (2009) Demography and population viability of polar bears in the Gulf of Boothia, Nunavut. Marine Mammal Science, vol. 25, p. 778-796

616.   Taylor, et al. (2008) Mark-Recapture and Stochastic Population Models for Polar Bears of the High Arctic. Arctic, vol. 61, p. 143-152.

617.   Taylor, M. et al. (1985) Observations of Intraspecific Aggression and Cannibalism in Polar Bears (Ursus maritimus). Arctic, vol.38,p.303-309.

618.   Taylor, M. et al. (2005) Demography and Viability of a Hunted Population of Polar Bears. Arctic, vol. 58, p.203-213.

619.   Dowsley, M. and Wenzel, G., (2008) "The Time of the Most Polar Bears": A Co-management Conflict in Nunavut "The Time of the Most Polar Bears": A Co-management Conflict in Nunavut.Arctic, vol 61, p. 177-189.

620.   Booker, C. (2009) Polar Bear expert barred by global warmist. The Telegraph. June 27, 2009.

621.   Hedman, D. (2012) Lethal Control Decisions. 4th Human/ Bear Conflicts Workshop. March 19, 2012. Missoula Montana.

622.   Obbard, M. et al. (2009) Proceedings of the 15th Working Meeting of the IUCN/SSC Polar Bear Specialist Group, 29 June-3 July 2009, Copenhagen, Denmark.

623.   Garrison, E. et al. (2007) Reproductive Ecology and Cub Survival of Florida Black.

The Journal of Wildlife Management, Vol. 71, No. 3 (May, 2007), pp. 720-727

624.   Stirling, I. (2002)Polar Bears and Seals in the Eastern Beaufort Sea and Amundsen Gulf: A Synthesis of Population Trends and Ecological Relationships over Three Decades. Arctic, vol. 55, p. 59-76

625.   Eiler, J. et al. (1989) Reproduction in black bears in the southern Appalachian Mountains. Journal of Wildlife Management, vol. 53, p.353-360.

626.   Kasbohm, J. et al. (1996) Effects of gypsy moth infestation on black bear reproduction and survival. Journal of Wildlife Management, vol. 60, p. 408-416.

627.   Ramsay, M, and Stirling, I. (1988) Reproductive biology and ecology of female polar bears (Ursus maritimus). Journal of Zoology (London) Series A 214:601–634.

628.   LeCount, A. (1987) Causes of Black Bear Cub Mortality: Their Biology and Management, Vol. 7, A Selection of Papers from the Seventh International Conference on Bear Research and Management, Williamsburg, Virginia, USA, and Plitvice Lakes, Yugoslavia, February and March 1986 (1987), pp. 75-82.

629.   Fischbach, ., et al. (2007) Landward and eastward shift of Alaskan polar bear denning associated with recent sea ice changes. Polar Biology, vol. 30, p.1395–1405.

630.   (2007) Nunavut investigates 2 polar bear deaths. CBC News.

631.   McGhee, R. (2007) The Last Imaginary Place: A Human History of the Arctic World. University Of Chicago Press.

632.   Amstrup, S. and Gardner, C. (1994) Polar Bear Maternity Denning in the Beaufort Sea. The Journal of Wildlife Management, vol. 58, p. 1-10.

633.   Nelson, S. (2009) The moment cannibal polar bear eats baby cub. MailONline, Science and Tech. December 8th, 2009.

634.   Rosing-Asvid, A., (2006) The influence of climate variability on polar bear (Ursus maritimus) and ringed seal (Pusa hispida) population dynamics. Can. J. Zool. 84: 357–364

635.   Clark, D. et al. (2008) Polar Bear Conservation in Canada: Defining the Policy Problems. Arctic vol. 61, p. 347– 360.

636.   Miller S, et al. (2006) Demographics and behavior of polar bears feeding on bowhead whale carcasses at Barter and Cross Islands, Alaska. Report by US Fish and Wildlife Service for Minerals Management Service (MMS). OCS Study MMS 2006-14.

637.   Schliebe, S., et al. (2008) Effects of sea ice extent and food availability on spatial and temporal distribution of polar bears during the fall open-water period in the Southern Beaufort Sea. Polar Biology,vol. 31., p. 999–1010.

638.   Derocher, A., and Stirling, I., (1996) Aspects of survival in juvenile polar bears. Canadian Journal of Zoology, vol. 74, p. 1246–1252.

639.   Derocher, A., and Stirling, I., (1998) Offspring size and maternal investment in polar bears (Ursus maritimus). Journal of Zoology (Lond.) vol. 245, p.253–260.

640.   Dyck, M.G. et al., (2007) Polar bears of western Hudson Bay and climate change: Are warming spring air temperatures the "ultimate" survival control factor?, Ecol. Complex. doi:10.1016/j.ecocom.2007.03.002

641.   Durner, G., and Amstrup, S. (1995) Movements of a Polar Bear from Northern Alaska to Northern Greenland. Arctic, vol. 48, p. 338– 341.

642.   Amstrup, S., (2008), A Bayesian network modeling approach to forecasting the 21st century worldwide status of polar bears, in Arctic Sea Ice Decline: Observations, Projections, Mechanisms, and Implications, Geophys. Monogr. Ser., vol. 180, edited by E. T. DeWeaver, C. M. Bitz, and L.-B. Tremblay, pp. 213--268, AGU, Washington, D. C. Mechanisms, and Implications. Geophysical Monograph 180.   American Geophysical Union, Washington DC.

643.   Kattsov, V., et al. (2010) Arctic sea ice change: a grand challenge of climate science. Journal of Glaciology, vol. 56, p. 1115-1121.

644.   Amstrup, S. (2010) Greenhouse gas mitigation can reduce sea-ice loss and increase

polar bear persistence. Nature, vol. 468, p. 955.

645.   Miller,G., et al. (2010) Temperature and precipitation history of the Arctic. Quaternary Science Reviews, vol. 29, p.1679-1715.

646.   Hailer, et al., (2012) Nuclear Genomic Sequences Reveal that Polar Bears Are an Old and Distinct Bear Lineage. Science, vol. 336, p. 344-347.

647.   Shewchuk, D., (2010) Minister of Environment: Polar Bear Not an At-Risk Species. News release May 28, 2010. Nunavut Department of Environment.

648.   Turner, J. (2010) The Melting of Ice in the Arctic Ocean: The Influence of Double-Diffusive Transport of Heat from Below. Journal of Oceanography, vol. 40. P. 249-258.

649.   Woodgate, R., et al. (2010) The 2007 Bering Strait oceanic heat flux and anomalous Arctic sea-ice retreat. Geophysical Research Letters, vol.   37, L01602, doi:10.1029/2009GL041621.

650.   Woodgate, R., et al. (2006) Interannual changes in the Bering Strait fluxes of volume, heat and freshwater between 1991 and 2004. Geophysical Research Letters, vol. 33, L15609, doi:10.1029/2006GL026931

651.   Skagseth, Ø., et al. (2008) Volume and heat transports to the Arctic Ocean via the Norwegian and Barents seas. Pp. 45–64 in Arctic-Subarctic Ocean Fluxes. R.R. Dickson, J. Meincke, and P. Rhines, eds, Springer, Dordrecht.

652.   Schauer, U., et al.(2002) Atlantic water inflow through the Barents and Kara Seas. Deep Sea Research Part I, vol. 49, p.2,281–2,298.

653.   Karcher M., et al. (2005) Arctic Ocean change heralds North Atlantic freshening. Geophysical Research Letters vol. 32, L21606, doi:10.1029/2005GL023861.

654.   Chylek, P. et al. (2012) Greenland ice core evidence for spatial and temporal variability of the Atlantic Multidecadal Oscillation. Geophysical Research Letters, vol. 39, L09705, doi:10.1029/2012GL051241.

655.   Polyakov, I. , et al. (2002), Observationally based assessment of polar amplification of global warming, Geophys. Res. Lett., vol. 29, 1878, doi:10.1029/ 2001GL011111.

656.   Polyakov, I., et al. (2011), Fate of early 2000s Arctic warm water pulse, Bull. Am. Meteorol. Soc., vol. 92, p. 561–566, doi:10.1175/2010BAMS2921.1.

657.   Chylek, P. et al. (2009) Arctic air temperature change amplification and the Atlantic Multidecadal Oscillation. Geophysical Research Letters, vol. 36, L14801 doi:10.1029/2009GL038777

658.   Beszczynska-Moller, A., et al., (2011) Synthesis of Exchanges Through the Main Oceanic Gateways to the Arctic Ocean Oceanography, vol. 24, 76-93.

659.   Tivy, A., et al., (2011) Origins and Levels of Seasonal Forecast Skill for Sea Ice in Hudson Bay Using Canonical Correlation Analysis. Journal of Climate, vol. 24, p. 1378-1397.

660.   Venegas, S. A., and L. A. Mysak, 2000: Is there a dominant timescale of natural climate variability in the Arctic? J. Climate, 13, 3412–3434.

661.   Mysak, L. (1996) The anomalous sea ice extent in Hudson Bay, Baffin Bay and the Labrador Sea during three simultaneous NAO and ENSO episodes. Atmos.–Ocean, 34, 313–343.

662.   Scott, J, et al. (2010)A Step-Change in the Date of Sea-Ice Breakup in Western Hudson Bay. Arrctic, vol. 63, p. 155–164.

663.   Dukhovskoy, D. et al. (2006) Arctic decadal variability from an idealized atmosphere-ice-ocean model: 2. Simulation of decadal oscillations Journal of Geophyiscal Research, vol, 111,, C06029, doi:10.1029/2004JC002820.

664.   Proshutinsky, A. , et al., (2002), The role of the Beaufort Gyre in Arctic climate variability: Seasonal to decadal climate scales, Geophysical Research Letters, 29(23), 2100, doi:10.1029/ 2002GL015847.

665.   Oashi, M. and Tanaka, H. (2010) Data Analysis of Recent Warming Pattern in the Arctic. SOLA, 2010, Vol. 6A, 001–004, doi:10.2151/sola.6A-001

666. Shimada, K. et al. , (2006) Pacific Ocean inflow: Influence on catastrophic reduction of sea ice cover in the Arctic Ocean. Geophysical Research Letters, vol. 33, L08605, doi:10.1029/2005GL025624.

667. Sicre, M., et al. (2008) Decadal variability of sea surface temperatures off North Iceland over the last 2000 yrs Marie-Alexandrine . Earth and Planetary Science Letters 268 (2008) 137-142 DOI :10.1016/j.epsl.2008.01.011

668. Pagano, A. , et al., (2012) Long-distance swimming by polar bears (Ursus maritimus) of the southern Beaufort Sea during years of extensive open water. Canadian Journal of Zoology, vol. 90, p. 663-674.

669. Gough, W. et al. (2004) Trends in Seasonal Sea Ice Duration in Southwestern Hudson Bay. Arctic, vol. 57, p. 299-305.

670. Gough, W. et al. (2004) Interannual variability of Hudson Bay ice thickness. Polar Geography, vol. 28, p. 222– 238

671. Saucier, F. et al. (2004) Modeling the sea ice-ocean seasonal cycle in Hudson Bay, Foxe Basin and Hudson Strait, Canada. Climate Dynamics, vol.23, p.303–326.

672. Vincent-Chambellant, M. (2010) Ecology of ringed seals (Phoca hispida) in western Hudson Bay, Canada. PhD thesis, Department of Biological Sciences, University of Manitoba, Winnipeg.

673. Chambellant, M. et al. (2012) Temporal variations in Hudson Bay ringed seal (Phoca hispida) life-history parameters in relation to environment. Journal of Mammalogy, vol. 93, p.267-281.

674. Frost, K. et al. (2004) Factors Affecting the Observed Densities of Ringed Seals, Phoca hispida, in the Alaskan Beaufort Sea, 1996–99. Arctic, vo. 57. P. 115_128.

675. Kelly, B., et al. (2010) Seasonal home ranges and fidelity to breeding sites among ringed seals. Polar Biology 33:1095–1109.

676. Arrigo, K., et al. (2008) Impact of a shrinking Arctic ice cover on marine primary production. Geophysical Research Letters, vol. 35, L19603, doi:10.1029/2008GL035028

677. Fortier, et al. (2006) Survival of Arctic cod larvae (Boreogadus saida) in relation to sea ice and temperature in the Northeast Water Polynya (Greenland Sea). Canadian Journal of Fisheries and Aquatic Science, vol. 63, p. 1608–1616.

678. Michaud, J., t al. (1996) Feeding success and survivorship of Arctic cod larvae, Boreogadus saida, in the Northeast Water polynya (Greenland Sea). Fisheries Oceanography, vol. 5, p. 120-135.

679. Geoffroy, M. et al. (2011) The aggregation of polar cod (Boreogadus saida) in the deep Atlantic layer of ice-covered Amundsen Gulf (Beaufort Sea) in winter. Polar Biology, vol. 34, p. 1959–1971. DOI 10.1007/s00300-011-1019-9

680. Bouchard, C., et al. (2011) Circum-arctic comparison of the hatching season of polar cod Boreogadus saida: A test of the freshwater winter refuge hypothesis. Progress in Oceanography 90 (2011) 105–116.

681. Kelly, B. et al. (2010) Status Review of the Ringed Seal. NOAA Technical Memorandum NMFS-AFSC-212.

682. Mudie, C. et al. (2005) Decadal-scale sea ice changes in the Canadian Arctic and their impacts on humans during the past 4,000 years. Environmental Archaeology 10, 2005; pp. 113-126.

683. Woollett, J. et al. (2000) Palaeoecological Implications of Archaeological Seal Bone Assemblages: Case Studies from Labrador and Baffin Island. Arctic, vol. 53, p. 3995-413.

684. Funder, S. et al. (2011) A 10,000-Year Record of Arctic Ocean Sea-Ice Variability— View from the Beach. Science vol. 333, p. 747-750

685. Messier, F. et al. (1992) Seasonal activity patterns of female polar bears (Ursus maritimus) in the Canadian Arctic as revealed by satellite telemetry. Journal of

Zoology, London, vol. 226, p. 219-229.

686. Derocher, A. and Stirling, I. (1990) Distribution of polar bears (Ursus maritimus) during the ice-free period in western Hudson Bay. Can J Zool 68:1395–1403

687. Stirling, I., (2005) Reproductive rates of ringed seals and survival of pups in northwestern Hudson Bay, Canada, 1991–2000. Polar Biology, vol. 28, p. 381-387.

688. Thiemann,G. et al. (2011) Individual patterns of prey selection and dietary specialization in an Arctic marine carnivore. Oikos, doi: 10.1111/j.1600-0706.2011.19277.x

689. Iverson, S. J. et al. 2006. Spatial and temporal variation in the diets of polar bears across the Canadian Arctic: indicators of changes in prey populations and environment. – In: Boyd, I. L. et al. (eds), Top predators in marine ecosystems. Cambridge Univ. Press, pp. 98–117.

690. Thiemann, G. W. et al. 2008a. Polar bear diets and arctic marine food webs: insights from fatty acid analysis. Ecol. Monogr. 78: 591–613.

691. Cherry, S. et al. (2011) Quantifying dietary pathways of proteins and lipids to tissues of a marine predator. Journal of Applied Ecology, vol. 48, p. 373-381

692. Bentzen, T., et al. (2007) Variation in winter diet of southern Beaufort Sea polar bears inferred from stable isotope analysis. Canadian Journal of Zoology, vol. 85, p. 596–608

693. Rosing-Avid (2006) The influence of climate variability on polar bear (Ursus maritimus) and ringed seal (Pusa hispida) population dynamics. Canadian Journal of Zoology, vol. 84, p. 357-364.

694. Ovsyanikov N.G., and Menyushina I.E. (2008) Specifics of Polar Bears Surviving an Ice Free Season on Wrangel Island in 2007. Marine Mammals of the Holarctic. Odessa, pp. 407-412.

695. Häggblom, A. (1982)Driftwood in Svalbard as an Indicator of Sea Ice Conditions. Geografiska Annaler. Series A, Physical Geography, vol. 64, p. 81-94

696. Dyke, A., and England, J. (2003) Canada's Most Northerly Postglacial Bowhead Whales (Balaena mysticetus): Holocene Sea-Ice Conditions and Polynya Development. Arcitc, vol. 56, p. 14-20

697. MacDonald, G., et al. (2000) Holocene Treeline History and Climate Change Across Northern Eurasia. Quaternary Research 53, 302–311.

698. Lloyd, A. and Gaumlich,L. (1997) Holocene Dynamics of Treeline Forests in the Sierera Nevada. Ecology, vol. 78, p. 199-1210.

699. Devi,N. et al. (2008) Expanding forests and changing growth forms of Siberian larch at the Polar Urals treeline during the 20th century. Global Change Biology (2008) 14, 1581–1591, doi: 10.1111/j.1365-2486.2008.01583.x

700. (2008) World's Oldest Living Tree -- 9550 Years Old -- Discovered In Sweden. ScienceDaily, April 16, 2008.

701. Kullman, L. (2008) Thermophilic Tree Species Reinvade Subalpine Sweden—Early Responses to Anomalous Late Holocene Climate Warming. Arctic, Antarctic, and Alpine Research, vol. 40, p. 104–110.

702. Esper, J. and Schweingruber, F. (2004) Large-scale treeline changes recorded in Siberia. Geophysical Research Letters, vol. 31, L06202, doi:10.1029/2003GL019178.

703. Millar, C. et al. (2004) Response of Subalpine Conifers in the Sierra Nevada, California, U.S.A., to 20th-Century Warming and Decadal Climate Variability. Arctic, Antarctic, and Alpine Research, vol. 36, p.181-200.

704. Camarero, J., and Guterreez, E., (2004) Pace and Pattern of Recent Treeline Dynamics: Response of Ecotones to Climatictic Variability in the Spanish Pyrenees. Climatic Change, vo. 63, p.181–200.

705. Esper, J. et al. (2012) Variability and extremes of northern Scandinavian summer temperatures over the past two millennia. Global and Planetary Change 88–89

(2012) 1–9.

706. Bond, G., et al. (2001) Persistent Solar Influence on North Atlantic Climate During the Holocene. Science, vol. 294. p. 2130-2136.

707. D'Arrigo, R., et al. (2008) On the 'Divergence Problem' in Northern Forests: A review of the tree-ring evidence and possible causes. Global and Planetary Change, vol. 60, p. 289–305.

708. Briffa, K., et al. (1998) Trees tell of past climates: but are they speaking less clearly today? Phil.Trans. R. Soc. Lond. B, vol. 353, p. 65-73.

709. Mann, M., et al. (1999) Northern Hemisphere temperatures during the past millennium: inferences, uncertainties and limitations. Geophys. Res. Lett., vol.26, p. 759-762.

710. D'Arrigo, R., et al. (2004) Thresholds for warming-induced growth decline at elevational treeline in the Yukon Territory. Glob. Biogeochem. Cycles 18. doi:10.1029/2004GB002249.

711. Esper, J., et al.. (2003) Temperature-sensitive Tien Shan tree ring chronologies show multi-centennial growth trends. Climate Dynamics, vol. 21, p. 699–706.

712. Yadav, R., et al. (2012) Tree ring inferred summer temperature variations over the last millennium in western Himalaya, India. Climate Dynamics, vol.36, p. 1545–1554. DOI 10.1007/s00382-009-0719-0.

713. Buntgen,U. et al. (2008) Testing for tree-ring divergence in the European Alps. Global Change Biology (2008) 14, 2443–2453, doi: 10.1111/j.1365-2486.2008.01640.x

714. Wilson R., et al., (2007) Matter of divergence: tracking recent warming at hemispheric scales using tree-ring data. Journal of Geophysical Research–A, 112, D17103, doi: 10.1029/2006JD008318.

715. Büntgen, U., et al., (2011) European climate variability and human susceptibility over the past 2500 years. Science, vol. 331, p.578–582.

716. Wilson RJS, D'Arrigo R, Buckley B et al. (2007) Matter of divergence: tracking recent warming at hemispheric scales using tree-ring data. Journal of Geophysical Research–A, 112, D17103, doi: 10.1029/2006JD008318.

717. Fischer, E., et al. (2007) Soil Moisture–Atmosphere Interactions during the 2003 European Summer Heat Wave. Journal of Climate, vol. 20, 5081-5100.

718. Buntgen, U., et al., (2012) Causes and Consequences of Past and Projected Scandinavian Summer Temperatures, 500–2100 AD. PLoS ONE 6(9): e25133. doi:10.1371/journal.pone.0025133

719. Fennessy, M. and Kinter, J., (2011) Climatic Feedbacks during the 2003 European Heat Wave. Journal of Climate, vol 24, p.5953-5967.

720. Wilson, R. and Luckman, B. (2003) Dendroclimatic reconstruction of maximum summer temperatures from upper tree-line sites in interior British Columbia, Holocene, vol. 13, p. 853– 863.

721. Youngblut, D., and Luckman, B., (2008) Maximum June–July temperatures in the southwest Yukon region over the last three hundred years reconstructed from tree-rings. Dendrochronologia, vol. 25, p.153–166.

722. Wang, G. et al. (2011) A summer climate regime over Europe modulated by the North Atlantic Oscillation. Hydrol. Earth Syst. Sci., 15, 57–64.

723. Buntgen, U., et al. (2007), Growth/climate response of a multi-species tree-ring network in the western Carpathian Tatra Mountains, Poland and Slovakia, Tree Physiol., 27, 689– 702

724. Mann M., et al (1999) Northern Hemisphere temperatures during the past millennium: Inferences, uncertainties, and limitations. Geophys Res Lett , vol. 26, p. 759-762.

725. Esper, J. et al., 2012, Orbital forcing of tree-ring data. Nature Climate Change,

Online Publication.

726. Wanner, H., et al., (2008) Mid- to Late Holocene climate change: an overview, Quaternary Science Reviews, doi:10.1016/j.quascirev.2008.06.013.

727. Steirou, E., and Koutsoyiannis, D. (2012) Investigation of methods for hydroclimatic data homogenization. Geophysical Research Abstracts, vol. 14, EGU2012-956-1.

728. MacDonald, G., and Case, R. (2005) Variations in the Pacific Decadal Oscillation over the past millennium. Geophysical Research Letters, vol. 32, L08703, doi:10.1029/2005GL022478.

729. Cook, E. et al., (2003), Dendroclimatic signals in long tree-ring chronologies from the Himalayas of Nepal, Int. Journal of Climatology, vol. 23, p. 707–732.

730. Wilson, R., and Luckman, B., (2002) Tree-ring reconstruction of maximum and minimum temperatures and the diurnal temperature range in British Columbia, Canada, Dendrochronologia, vol. 20, p. 1 –12.

731. Cook, E., et al. (2002) Evidence for a 'Medieval Warm Period' in a 1,100 year tree-ring reconstruction of past austral summer temperatures in New Zealand. Geophysical Research Letters, vol. 29, NO. 14, 1667, 10.1029/2001GL014580.

732. Payette, S. (2007), Contrasted dynamics of northern Labrador tree lines caused by climate change and migrational lag, Ecology, vol. 88, p. 770– 780.

733. Chylek, P., et al. (2006) Greenland warming of 1920–1930 and 1995–2005. Geophysical Research Letters, vol. 33, L11707, doi:10.1029/2006GL026510.

734. Naurzbaev, M., et al. (2002) Summer temperatures in eastern Taimyr inferred from a 2427-year late-Holocene tree-ring chronology and earlier floating series. Holocene, vol. 12, p. 727–736.

735. Briffa, K., et al. (1998) Reduced sensitivity of recent tree-growth to temperature at high northern latitudes. Naature, vol. 391. P. 678-682.

736. Mann,M. et al., (2009) NH temperature reconstruction, Science, vol. 326, p.1256-1260. doi:10.1126/science.1177303, downloaded from KMNI Explorer.

737. Bennike,O., (2004) Holocene sea-ice variations in Greenland: onshore evidence. The Holocene, vol. 14, p. 607–613.

738. Easterling, D., et al. (2000) Observed climate variability and change of relevance to the biosphere. Journal of Geophysical Research, vol. 105, p. 101-120.

739. Smith, S., et al. (2004) A 300 year record of environmental change from Lake Tuborg, Ellesmere Island, Nunavut, Canada. Journal of Paleolimnology, vol 32, p.137–148.

740. Southward, A. et al. (1995) Seventy Years' Observations of changes in Distribution and Abundance of Zooplankton and intertidal Organisms in the Western English Channel in relation to Rising Sea Temperature. J. Thermal Biology. vol. 20, p. 127-155.

741. Hakkinen ,S, and Rhines, P., (2009) Shifting surface currents in the northern North Atlantic Ocean. Journal of Geophysical Research, vol. 114, C04005, doi:10.1029/2008JC004883.

742. The Extended Ellet Line (2013) The Rockall Trough Hydrogrpahic Time Series. http://www.noc.soton.ac.uk/obe/PROJECTS/EEL/latestresults.php n

743. Mayewski, P. et al. (2004) Holocene climate variability. Quaternary Research, vol. 62, p. 243– 255.

744. Hansen, J. and Sato, M. (2011) Paleoclimate Implications for Human-Made Climate Change. http://arxiv.org/vc/arxiv/papers/1105/1105.0968v2.pdf

745. Romm, J. (2011) Must-read Hansen and Sato paper: We are at a climate tipping point that, once crossed, enables multi-meter sea level rise this century. Think Progress/Climate Progress. January 20, 2011.

746. Horton, B. et al., (2007) Reconstructing Holocene Sea-level Change for the Central

Great Barrier Reef (Australia) Using Subtidal Foraminifera. Journal of Foraminiferal Research, v. 37, no. 4, p. 47-63.

747. Watson, P. (2011) Is there evidence yet of acceleration in mean sea level rise around mainland Australia? Journal of Coastal Research, vol.27(2), p. 368–377.

748. Lessan, G. and MAsselink, G. (2007) Evidence of a Mid-Holocene Sea Level Highstand from the Sedimentary Record of a Macrotidal Barrier and Paleoestuary System in Northwestern Australia. Journal of Coastal Research 22(11), p. 100-112.

749. Dickinson, W. ()Impact of Mid-Holocene Hydro-Isostatic Highstand in Regional Sea Level on Habitability ofIslands in Pacific Oceania . Journal of Coastal Research, vol. 19, p. 489-502.

750. Morhange, C. and Pirazzoli ,P. (2005) Mid-Holocene emergence of southern Tunisian coasts. Marine Geology, vol. 220, p.205–213

751. Hantemirov, R. and Shiyatov, S., (2002) A continuous multimillennial ring-width chronology in Yamal, northwestern Siberia. The Holocene, vol. 12, p. 717–726.

752. Cook, E., (2002) A multi-millennial palaeoclimatic resource from *Lagarostrobos colensoi* tree-rings at Oroko Swamp, New Zealand. Global and Planetary Change, vol. 33, p. 209–220.

753. Buntgen, U. et al. (2006) Summer Temperature Variations in the European Alps, A.D. 755–2004. Journal of Cllimate, vol. 19, p. 5606-5624.

754. Oppo, D., et al, (2009) 2,000-year-long temperature and hydrology reconstructions from the Indo-Pacific warm pool. Nature, vol. 460, doi:10.1038/nature08233.

755. Ljungqvist, F., et al. (2012) Northern Hemisphere temperature patterns in the last 12 centuries. Climate Past, vol. 8, p. 227–249.

756. Sachs, P. (2007) Cooling of Northwest Atlantic slope waters during the Holocene. Geophysical Research Letters, vol 34, p.L03609.

757. Sachs, J. (2007) Cooling of Northwest Atlantic slope waters during the Holocene. Geophysical Research Letters, vol. 34, L03609, doi:10.1029/2006GL028495.

758. ABQjournal (2006) Scientist Forecasts 'super El Niño'. April 8, 2006. http://www.abqjournal.com/news/metro/449795metro04-08-06.htm

759. Wannamaker,A. et al. (2008) Coupled North Atlantic slope water forcing on Gulf of Maine temperatures over the past millennium. Clim Dyn (2008) 31:183–194 DOI 10.1007/s00382-007-0344-8

760. Smithers. S., et al. (2006) Fringing and Nearshore Coral Reefs of the Great Barrier Reef: Episodic Holocene Development and Future Prospects. Journal of Coastal Research, vol. 22, p. 175-187.

761. Koshkarova, V. and Koshkarov, A. (2004) REGIONAL SIGNATURES OF CHANGING LANDSCAPE AND CLIMATE OF NORTHERN CENTRAL SIBERIA IN THE HOLOCENE. Russian Geology and Geophysics, vol. 45, p. 717-729.

762. Gagan, et al. (1998) Temperature and Surface-Ocean Water Balance of the Mid-Holocene Tropical Western Pacific. Science, vol. 279, p. 1014-1018.

763. Ciais, P. et al. (1992) Evidence for an early Holocene climatic optimum in the Antarctic deep ice-core record. Climate Dynamics, vol 6. p. 169 177.

764. Briffa, K. et al. (2008) Trends in recent temperature and radial tree growth spanning 2000 years across northwest Eurasia. Phil. Trans. R. Soc. B (2008) 363, p. 2271–2284, doi:10.1098/rstb.2007.2199.

765. Tornqvist, T. et al. (2004) Deciphering Holocene sea-level history on the U.S. Gulf Coast: A high-resolution record from the Mississippi Delta. GSA Bulletin; July/August 2004; v. 116; no. 7/8; p. 1026–1039; doi: 10.1130/B2525478.1

766. Blum, M., et al., (2002) Middle Holocene sea-level and evolution of the Gulf of Mexico coast (USA): Journal of Coastal Research, Special Issue, v. 36, p. 65–80.

767. Bauer, E., et al., (2003) Assessing climate forcings of the Earth system for the past millennium. Geophysical Research Letters, vol. 30, doi:10.1029/2002GL016639.

768. Jones, P. and Mann, M. (2004) CLIMATE OVER PAST MILLENNIA. Rev. Geophys., 42, RG2002, doi:10.1029/2003RG000143.

769. Yu, S., (2003) Centennial-scale cycles in middle Holocene sea level along the southeastern Swedish Baltic coast. GSA Bulletin, vol. 115, p. 1404–1409.

770. Briffa, K. and Osborn, T. (1999) Seeing the Wood from the Trees. Science, vol. 284, p. 926-927.

771. Feng, X. and Epstein, S. (1994) Climatic implications of an 8000-Year Hydrogen Isotope Time Series f r0m Bristlecone Pine Trees, Science, vol. 265.

772. Masson-Delmotte, V., et al. (2004) Past temperature reconstructions from deep ice cores: relevance for future climate change. Clim. Past Discuss., vo,2, p. 399–448.

773. Masson-Delmotte, V., et al. (2005) Holocene climatic changes in Greenland: Different deuterium excess signals at Greenland Ice Core Project (GRIP) and NorthGRIP. Journal of Geophysical Research, vol. 110, D14102, doi:10.1029/2004JD005575

774. Marchal, O., et al. (2002), Apparent long-term cooling of the sea surface in the northeast Atlantic and Mediterranean during the Holocene, Quat. Sci. Rev., 21, 455–483.

775. Masson-Delmotte, V., et al. (2004) Common millennial-scale varability of Antarctic and Southern Ocean temperatures during the past 5000 years reconstructed from the EPICA Dome C ice core. The Holocene, vol. 14, p. 145-151.

776. Cohen,A and Tyson, P. (1995) Sea-surface temperature fluctuations during the Holocene off the south coast of Africa: implications for terrestrial climate and rainfall. Holocene, vol. 5, p. 304-312.

777. Patterson, R.T., et al. (2011) Dinoflagellate cyst-based reconstructions of mid to late Holocene winter sea-surface temperature and productivity from an anoxic fjord in the NE Pacific Ocean. Quaternary International, vol. 235, p.13-25.

778. Sundqvist, H., et al. (2010) Climate change between the mid and late Holocene in northern high latitudes – Part 1: Survey of temperature and precipitation proxy data. Climate Past, vol. 6, p.591-608.

779. Birks, C, J, A, and Koc. N. (2002)A high-resolution diatom record of late-Quaternary sea-surface temperatures and Oceanographic conditions from the eastern Norwegian Sea, Boreas, vol.31, p.323-344.

780. Jansen, E., et al. (2008) The early to mid-Holocene thermal optimum in the North Atlantic, in: Natural Climate Variability and Global Warming - A Holocene Perspective, edited by: Battarbee, R. W. and Binney, H. A., Wiley-Blackwell, Chichester, 123-137.

781. Renssen,H. et al. (2005) Simulating the Holocene climate evolution at northern high latitudes using a coupled atmosphere-sea ice-ocean-vegetation model. Climate Dynamics, vol. 24, p. 23-43.

782. Ilyashuk, E. et al., (2005) Holocene climatic and environmental changes inferred from midge records (Diptera: Chironomidae, Chaoboridae, Ceratopogonidae) at Lake Berkut, southern Kola Peninsula, Russia. The Holocene vol. 15, p. 897- 914.

783. Jiang, D. (2012) Considerable Model–Data Mismatch in Temperature over China during the Mid-Holocene: Results of PMIP Simulations. Journal of Climate, volume 25, p. 4135-4155.

784. Venegas, S. and Mysak, L. (1999) Is There a Dominant Timescale of Natural Climate Variability in the Arctic? Journal of Climate, vol. 13, p. 3412-3435.

785. Renssen,H., et al. (2006) Coupled climate model simulation of Holocene cooling events: oceanic feedback amplifies solar forcing. Clim. Past, vol. 2, p. 79–90.

786. Shen, C. et al. (2006) A Pacific Decadal Oscillation record since 1470 AD reconstructed from proxy data of summer rainfall over eastern China. Geophysical research Letters, vol. 33, doi:10.1029/2005GL024804.

787. Holzhauser, H. et al. (2005) Glacier and lake-level variations in west-central Europe over the last 3500 years. The Holoccene, vol. 15, p. 789-803.

788. Ferguson, S. et al. (2005) Climate change and ringed seal (Phoca hispida) recruitment in western Hudson Bay. Marine Mammal Science 21:121–135.

789. Kukla, G. and Gavin, J. (2005) Did glacials start with global warming? Quaternary Science Reviews, vol. 24, p. 1547–1557.

790. Robson, J., et al. (2012) Causes of the Rapid Warming of the North Atlantic Ocean in the Mid-1990s. Journal of Climate, vol. 25, p. 4116_4136.

791. Lucas, Z., and Daoust, P. (2002) Large increases of harp seals (Phoca groenlandica) and hooded seals (Cystophora cristata) on Sable Island, Nova Scotia, since 1995. Polar Biology, vol 2, p. 562–568.

792. Sjare, B., and Stenson, G. B. (2010) Changes in the reproductive parameters of female harp seals (Pagophilus groenlandicus) in the Northwest Atlantic. – ICES Journal of Marine Science, vol. 67, p. 304–315.

793. Langehaug, H. et al. (2012) Arctic/Atlantic Exchanges via the Subpolar Gyre. Journal of Climate, vol. 25, p. 2421-2441.

794. Thornalley, D., et al. (2009) Holocene oscillations in temperature and salinity of the surface subpolar North Atlantic. Nature, vo. 457, p. 711-714.

795. Moros, M, et al. (2012) Reconstruction of the late-Holocene changes in the Sub-Arctic Front position at the Reykjanes Ridge, north Atlantic. The Holocene, vol. 22, p. 877-886.

796. Zeeberg, J. and Forman, S. (2001) Changes in glacier extent on north Novaya Zemlya in the twentieth century. The Holocene, vol 11, p. 161–175.

797. Buntgen, U. et al, (2008) Long-term summer temperature variations in the Pyrenees. Climate Dynamics, vol. 31, p. 615-631.

798. Soon, W. and Legates, D., (2013) Solar irradiance modulation of Equator-to-Pole (Arctic) temperature gradients: Empirical evidence for climate variation on multi-decadal timescales. Journal of Atmospheric and Solar-Terrestrial Physics, vol. 93, p. 45–56.

799. Jiang, D. et al. (2012) Considerable Model–Data Mismatch in Temperature over China during the Mid-Holocene: Results of PMIP Simulations. Journal of Climate, vol. 25, p. 4135-4155.

800. Hinkel, K. et al. (2003) The Urban Heat Island in Winter at barrow Alaska. Int. J. Climatol. Vol. 23, p. 1889–1905.

801. Montford, A. (2010) The Hockey Stick Illusion: Climategate and the Corruption of Science (Independent Minds).

802. Mann, M. (2012) The Hockey Stick and the Climate Wars: Dispatches from the Front Lines.

803. Drinkwaer, K. (2006) The regime shift of the 1920s and 1930s in the North Atlantic. Progress in Oceanography vol. 68, p.134–151.

804. Skinner,W., et al. (1998) Prediction of reproductive success and failure in lesser geese based on early season climatic variables. Global Change Biology, vol. 4, p. 3-16.

805. Scott, J, and Marshall, G., (2010) A Step-Change in the Date of Sea-Ice Breakup in Western Hudson Bay. Arctic, vol. 63, p. 155-164.

806. Nelson, T., (2011) Climategate 2 FOIA 2011 Searchable Database, http://foia2011.org/index.php?id=4

807. Gardelle, J, et al. (2012) Slight mass gain of Karakoram glaciers in the early twenty-first century. Nature Geoscience, www.nature.com/naturegeoscience.

808. Cogley, J. et al. (2010) Tracking the Source of Glacier Misinformation. Science, vol. 327, pp. 522-522.

809. Kobashi, T., et al. (2011) High variability of Greenland surface temperature over the past 4000 years estimated from trapped air in an ice core. Geophysical Research

Letters, vol. 38, L21501, doi:10.1029/2011GL049444.

810. Christiansen, B., and Ljunqvist, (2012) The extra-tropical Northern Hemisphere temperature in the last two millennia: reconstructions of low-frequency variability. Clim. Past, vol. 8, p. 765-786.

811. Weng, H., (2012) Impacts of Multi-Scale Solar Activity on Climate. Part I: Atmospheric Circulation Patterns and Climate Extremes. Advances in Atmospheric Sciences, vol. 29, p. 867–886.

812. Croci-Maspoli, M., et al. (2012) Atmospheric blocking: space-time links to the NAO and PNA. Climate Dynamics, vol. 29, p.713–725. DOI 10.1007/s00382-007-0259-4

813. Hinton, T. et al., (2009) The influence of tropical sea surface temperatures and precipitation on north Pacific atmospheric blocking. Clim Dynamics, vol. 33, p. 549–563. DOI 10.1007/s00382-009-0542-7.

814. Barriopedro , D. et al., (2008) Solar modulation of Northern Hemisphere winter blocking. Journal of Geophysical Research, vol.113, D14118, doi:10.1029/2008JD009789.

815. Woolings, T., (2011) Ocean Effects of Blocking. Science, vol. 334, p. 612-613.

816. Häkkinen, S., et al. (2011) Atmospheric Blocking and Atlantic. Multidecadal Ocean Variability. Science, vol. 334, p. 655-659.

817. Lockwood, M., et al., (2011) Are cold winters in Europe associated with low solar activity? Environmental Research Letters, vol. 5, 024001 (7pp).

818. Taylor, M. and Dowsley, M., (2008) Demographic and Ecological Perspective on the status of the Polar Bears. Science and Public Policy Institute. March 2008.

819. Regehr, E. et al., (2007) Effects of Earlier Sea Ice Breakup on Survival and Population Size of Polar Bears in Western Hudson Bay. Journal of Wildllife Management, vol 71, p. 2673-2683.

820. Dowsley, M. and Taylor, M. (2006) Management Consultations for the Western Hudson Bay (WH) Polar Bear Population (01-02 December 2005). Final Wildlife Report , No. 3.

821. Venegas, S. et al. (1999) Is There a Dominant Timescale of Natural Climate Variability in the Arctic? Journal of Climate, vol. 13, p. 3412-3435.

822. Christiansen, B. and Ljungqvist,L. (2012) The extra-tropical Northern Hemisphere temperature in the last two millennia: reconstructions of low-frequency variability Climate of the Past, vol. 8, p. 765–786.

823. Nesje, A., and Dahl, S. (2003) The 'Little Ice Age' – only temperature? The Holocene, vol. 13, p. 139-145.

824. Rasmussen, L., et al. (2010) 'Little Ice Age' precipitation in Jotunheimen, southern Norway. The Holocene, vol. 20. DOI: 10.1177/0959683610369510.

825. Kokfelt,U. and Muscheler, R., (2012) Solar forcing of climate during the last millennium recorded in lake sediments from northern Sweden. The Holocene, vol 23, p. 447-452.

826. Haigh, J., (2003) The effects of solar variability on the Earth's climate. Philosophical Transactions of the Royal Society in London A, vol. 361, p. 95–111.

827. Kaser, G. et al. (2004) Modern Glacier Retreat on Kilimanjaro as evidence of climate change: Observatons and Facts. International Journal of Climatology, vol. 24, p.329–339.

828. Molg, T. et al. (2004) Solar-radiation-maintained glacier recession on Kilimanjaro drawn from combined ice-radiation geometry modeling. Journal of Geophysical Research. vol. 108, doi:10.1029/2003JD003546.

829. Pepin, N. et al. (2010) The montane circulation on Kilimanjaro, Tanzania and its relevance for the summit ice fields: Comparison of surface mountain climate with equivalent reanalysis parameters. Global and Planetary Change, vol. 74, p.61–75.

830. Winkler, S. and Matthews,J. (2010) Holocene glacier chronologies: Are'high-

resolution' global and inter-hemispheric comparisons possible? The Holocene, vol. 20, p. 1137-1147.

831. Nesje, A. and Matthews,J. (2011) The Briksdalsbre Event: A winter precipitation-induced decadal-scale glacial advance in southern Norway in the ad 1990s and its implications. The Holocene, vol. 22, p. 249-261.

832. Nesje, A., et al. (2001) Holocene glacier fluctuations of Flatebreen and winter-precipitation changes in the Jostedalsbreen region, western Norway, based on glaciolacustrine sediment records: The Holocene, vol. 11, p. 267-280, doi:10.1191/095968301669980885

833. Nesje, A., et al. (2007) Norwegian mountain glaciers in the past, present and future. Global and Planetary Change, vol. 60, p. 10–27.

834. Basagic, H. (2008) Quantifying twentieth Century Glacier Change in the Sierra Nevada California. Master of Science in Geography, Portland State University.

835. Howat, I., et al. (2007) A precipitation-dominated, mid-latitude glacier system: Mount Shasta, California. Climate Dynamics, vol.28, p. 85-98.

836. Lillquist, K. and Walker, K. (2006) Historical Glacier and Climate Fluctuations at Mount Hood, Oregon. Arctic, Antarctic, and Alpine Research, vol. 38, p. 399-412.

837. Nicolussi, K. et al. (2005) Holocene tree-line variability in the Kauner Valley, Central Eastern Alps, indicated by dendrochronological analysis of living trees and subfossil logs: Veget Hist Archaeobot, vol. 14, p. 221–234, doi:10.1007/s00334-005-0013-y.

838. Tahir, A. , et al. (2011) Snow cover dynamics and hydrological regime of the Hunza River Basin, Karakoram Range, Nothern Pakistan. Hydrol. Earth Syst. Sci., vol. 15, p. 2275-2290.

839. Fowler, H. & Archer, D.(2006). Conflicting signals of climatic change in the Upper Indus Basin. Journal of Climate, vol.19, p. 4276-4293.

840. Garcıa-Herrera, R. & Barriopedro, D. (2006) Northern Hemisphere snow cover and atmospheric blocking variability. Journal of Geophysical Research , vol. 111, D21104, doi:10.1029/2005JD006975. f

841. Trouet, V. & Taylor, A. (2010) Multi-century variability in the Pacific North American circulation pattern reconstructed from tree rings. Climate Dynamics, vol. 35, p. 953-963.

842. Cheung, H., et al., (2013) Revisiting the Climatology of Atmospheric Blocking in the Northern Hemisphere. Advances in Atmospheric Sceincese, vol. 30, p. 397-410.

843. Meehl, G. et al. (2009) Amplifying the Pacific Climate System Response to a Small 11-Year Solar Cycle Forcing. Science, vol. 325, p. 1114-1119.

844. Gershunov, A., et al. , (2009) The Great 2006 Heat Wave over California and Nevada: Signal of an Increasing Trend. Journal of Climate, vol. 22, p. 6181-6205.

845. Sillmann, J. et al., (2011) Extreme Cold Winter Temperatures in Europe under the Influence of North Atlantic Atmospheric Blocking. Journal of Climate, vol. 24, p. 5899-5915.

846. Croci-Maspoli, M. (2005) A Climatological Investigation of Atmospheric Blocking - Dynamically-based Statistical Analyses. Ph.D. thesis, ETH Zu ̈rich, Institute for Atmospheric and Climate Science. Dissertation Nr. 16151.

847. White, W. & Liu, Z., (2008) Resonant excitation of the quasi-decadal oscillation by the 11-year signal in the Sun's irradiance. Journal of Geophysical Research, vol. 113, C01002, doi:10.1029/2006JC004057.

848. Goehring, B., et al. (2011) The Rhone Glacier was smaller than today for most of the Holocene. Geology, vol. 39, p. 679-682.

849. Porter, S. (2000) Onset of Neoglaciation in the Southern Hemisphere. Journal of Quaternary Science, vol. 15, p. 395–408.

850. Thompson L, et al. (2002) Kilimanjaro ice core records: Evidence of Holocene

climate change in tropical Africa. Science, vol. 298, p.589–593.

851.   Yang, W., et al. (2011) Summertime surface energy budget and ablation modeling in the ablation zone of a maritime Tibetan glacier. Journal of Geophysical Research, vol. 116, D14116, doi:10.1029/2010JD015183.

852.   Fujita, K. (2008) Effect of precipitation seasonality on climatic sensitivity of glacier mass balance. Earth and Planetary Science Letters, vol. 276, p.14–19.

853.   Rupper, S. and Roe, G. (2008) Glacier Changes and Regional Climate: A Mass and Energy Balance Approach. Journal of Climate, vol. 21, p. 5384-5401.

854.   Ummenhofer , C. et al. (2012) Links between Indo-Pacific climate variability and drought in the Monsoon Asia Drought Atlas. Climate Dynamics, DOI 10.1007/s00382-012-1458-1.

855.   Kaser, G., et al. (2006) Mass balance of glaciers and ice caps: Consensus estimates for 1961–2004. Geophysical Research Letters, vol. 33, L19501, doi:10.1029/2006GL027511

856.   Straeno, F., et al. (2012) Characteristics of ocean waters reaching Greenland's glaciers. Annals of Glaciology, vol. 53, doi: 10.3189/2012AoG60A059.

857.   Motyka, R., et al. (2010) Submarine melting of the 1985 Jakobshavn Isbræ floating tongue and the triggering of the current retreat. Journal of Geophysical Research, vol. 116, F01007, doi:10.1029/2009JF001632.

858.   Howat, I., and Eddy, A., (2011) Multi-decadal retreat of Greenland's marine-terminating glaciers. Journal of Glaciology, Vol. 57, p. 38-396.

859.   Seff, P. and Seef, N. (1996) Our Fascinating Earth. Contemporary Books (April 1996).

860.   Bevan, S., et al. (2012) Glacier dynamics over the last quarter of a century at Helheim, Kangerdlugssuaq and 14 other major Greenland outlet glaciers. The Cryosphere, vol. 6, p. 923–937.

861.   Murray, T., et al., (2010) Ocean regulation hypothesis for glacier dynamics in southeast Greenland and implications for ice sheet mass changes. Journal of Geophysical Research, vol. 115, F03026, doi:10.1029/2009JF001522.

862.   Young, N., et al., (2011) Response of Jakobshavn Isbræ, Greenland, to Holocene climate Change. Geology, vol. 39, p. 131-134.

863.   Csatho, B., et al., (2008) Intermittent thinning of Jakobshavn Isbræ, West Greenland, since the Little Ice Age. Journal of Glaciology, vol. 54, p. 131-145.

864.   Steig, E., et al., (2008) Tropical forcing of Circumpolar Deep Water Inflow and outlet glacier thinning in the Amundsen Sea Embayment, West Antarctica. Annals of Glaciology vol. (53)60, doi: 10.3189/2012AoG60A110.

865.   Jacobs,S., et al., (2011) Stronger ocean circulation and increased melting under Pine Island Glacier ice shelf. Nature Geosci., 4(8), 519–523.

866.   Cullen N., et al., (2006) Kilimanjaro: Recent areal extent from satellite data and new interpretation of observed 20th century retreat rates. Geophysical Research Letters, vol. 33, L16502, doi:10.1029/2006GL0227084.

867.   Vincent C, et al., (2005) Solving the paradox of the end of the Little Ice Age in the Alps. Geophysical Research Letters, vol. 32, L09706, doi:10.1029/2005GL022552.

868.   Yang, B., et al. (2009) A 622-year regional temperature history of southeast Tibet derived from tree rings. The Holocene, vol. 20, p. 181–190.

869.   You, Q., et al., (2012) Variability of temperature in the Tibetan Plateau based on homogenized surface stations and reanalysis data. Int. J. Climatology, DOI: 10.1002/joc.3512.

870.   Sisson, T., et al. (2011) Whole-edifice ice volume change A.D. 1970 to 2007/2008 at Mount Rainier, Washington, based on LiDAR surveying. Geology, vol. 39; p. 639–642; doi:10.1130/G31902.1.

871.   Stuman, A., and Wanner, H., (2001) A Comparative Review of the Weather and

Climate of the Southern Alps of New Zealand and the European Alps. Mountain Research and Development Vol 21 No 4 Nov 2001: 359–369.

872. The Desertification Crisis. Savory Institute. http://www.savoryinstitute.com/desertification/

873. Lundquist, J. and Cayan, D. (2007) Surface temperature patterns in complex terrain: Daily variations and long-term change in the central Sierra Nevada, California. Journal of Geophysical Research, vol. 112, D11124, doi:10.1029/2006JD007561.

874. Seager, R. et al. (2008) Drought in the Southeastern United States: Causes, Variability over the Last Millennium, and the Potential for Future Hydroclimate Change. Journal of Climate, vol. 22, p. 5021-5047.

875. Poyry, J., et al. (2009) Relative contributions of local and regional factors to species richness and total density of butterflies and moths in semi-natural grasslands. Oecologia, vol. 160, p.577–587.

876. Parmesan, C., et al. (2000) Impacts of Extreme Weather and Climate on Terrestrial Biota. Bulletin of the American Meteorological Society, vol. 81, 443-451.

877. Thomas, C.D, et al., (2000) Ecological and evolutionary processes at expanding range margins. Nature, vol. 411, p. 577-581.

878. Thomas, C.D. et al. (1996) Catastrophic extinction of population sources in a butterfly metapopulation. American Naturalist, vol. 148, p. 957–975.

879. Singer, M., and C. D. Thomas (1996) Evolutionary responses of a butterfly metapopulation to human and climate-caused environmental variation. American Naturalist, vol. 148, p. S9–S39.

880. Alfred Adler, Austrian psychiatrist.

881. N. Nicholls et al., (1996) in Climate Change 1995: The Science of Climate Change [Intergovernmental Panel on Climate Change (IPCC), Cambridge Univ. Press, Cambridge, p. 133.

882. Read, W.G., et al., (2004) Dehydration in the tropical tropopause layer:Implications from the UARS Microwave Limb Sounder. Journal of Geophysical Research, vol. 109, D06110, doi:10.1029/2003JD004056

883. Sirocko, F., et al., (2012) Solar influence on winter severity in central Europe. Geophysical Research Letters, vol. 39, DOI: 10.1029/2012GL052412.

884. Renwick, J., and Wallace, J., (1996) Relationships between North Pacific Wintertime Blocking, El Niño, and the PNA pattern. Monthly Weather Review, vol. 124, p. 2071-2077.

885. Wiedenmann, J., et al., (2002) The climatology of blocking anticyclones for the Northern and Southern Hemispheres: Block intensity as a diagnostic. Journal of Climate, vol. 15, p. 3459–3473.

886. Climate Change 2007 - The Physical Science Basis Contribution of Working Group I to the Fourth Assessment Report of the IPCC (ISBN 978 0521 88009-1

887. Kukla, G., et al., (1995) Comparison of observed seasonal temperature maxima, minima and diurnal range in North America with simulations from three global climate models. Atmosphedc Research, vol. 37, p. 267-275.

888. LaDochy , S., et al. (2007) Recent California climate variability: spatial and temporal patterns in temperature trends. Climate Research, vol. 33 , p. 159–169.

889. Deubreuil, V., et al. (2012) Impact of land-cover change in the Southern Amazonia climate: a case study for the region of Alta Floresta, Mato Grosso, Brazil. Environmental Monitoring Assessment, vol. 184, p. 877–891.

890. Williams, C. and Kniveton, D., (2011) Atmosphere-land surface interactions and their influence on extreme rainfall and potential abrupt climate change over southern Africa. Climatic Change, DOI 10.1007/s10584-011-0266-7

891. Cordero, E., et al., (2011) The identification of distinct patterns in California

temperature trends. Climate Change, DOI 10.1007/s10584-011-0023-y.

892. Nicholson, S. (2013) The West African Sahel: A Review of Recent Studies on the Rainfall Regime and Its Interannual Variability. ISRN Meteorology Vol, 2013, Article ID 453521.

893. Easterling, D., et al. (2000) Observed Variability and Trends in Extreme Climate Events: A Brief Review. Bulletin of the American Meteorological Society, vol. 81, p. 417-425.

894. Rauthe, M., et al. (2004) A Model Intercomparison Study of Climate Change-Signals in Extratropical Circulation. International Journal of Climatology. Vol. 24, p.643-662.

895. Center for Biological Diversity (2010) Climate Scientists, Biologists and Groups Representing Millions of Americans Ask Obama to Follow Science in Determining Polar Bears' Fate.

896. Steionhoff, D., et al. (2012) Dynamics of the Foehn Mechanism in the McMurdo Dry Valleys of Antarctica from Polar WRF. Quarterly Journal of the Royal Meteorological Society.

897. Normilie, D. (2012) A New Record For Retractions? ScienceInsider, AAAS, online July 2, 2012.

898. Vonder Haar,T., et al., (2012) Weather and Climate Analyses Using the New NVAP-Measures Global Water Vapor Dataset. Weather and climate analyses using improved global water vapor observations. Geophysical Research Letters, 39, L15802, doi:10.1029/2012GL052094.

899. Trenberth, K, et al., (2005) Trends and variability in column-integrated atmospheric water vapor. Climate Dynamics, vol. 24, p. 741-758

900. Mogensen, I. (2009) Dangaard-Oeschger Cycles. Encyclopedia of Paleoclimatology and Ancient Environments. Encyclopedia of Earth Sciences Series. Springer Verlag.

901. Thomas, J., et al (2011) Evidence based conservation of butterflies. J. Insect Cons., vol. 15, p. 241-258.

902. King, J. (2010) Analysis of a rapid sea ice retreat event in the Bellingshausen Sea, Journal Geophysical Research, vol. 115, C12030, doi:10.1029/2010JC006101.

903. Wolf, S. (2010) Obama Administration Denies American Pika Endangerd Species Act Protection. Center for Biological Diversity, February 4, 2010.

904. Hoerling, M., et al. (2013) An Interpretation of the Origins of the 2012 Central Great Plains Drought. Assessment Report, NOAA Drought Task Force, March 2013.

905. Borenstein, S., (2013) Report: Global warming didn't cause big US drought. Yahoo News. April 12, 2013.

906. Cosens, S.et al., (1997) The distribution and numbers of bowhead whales, Balaena mysticetus, in northern Foxe Basin in 1994. Canadian Field-Naturalist, vol. 111, p.381–388.

907. Steinhoff, D., (2012) Dynamics of the Foehn Mechanism in the McMurdo Dry Valleys of Antarctica from Polar WRF. Q. J. R. Meteorol. Soc DOI:10.1002/qj.2038

908. Gonzales-Trueba, J., et al. (2008) 'Little Ice Age' glaciation and current glaciers in the Iberian Peninsula. The Holocene, vol. 18, p. 551–568.

909. Balmaseda, M., et al., (2013) Distinctive climate signals in reanalysis of global ocean heat content. Geophysical Research Letters, DOI: 10.1002/grl.50382

910. Than, K., (2006) Global Warming Weakens Pacific Trade Winds. Long-term effect could disrupt food chain. LIveScience, NBC News. http://www.nbcnews.com/id/12612965/#.UX2v047R5-8

911. Wolf, S., (2009) Climate Change Threatens Penguins. ActionBioscience, http://www.actionbioscience.org/environment/wolf.html

912. Center for Biological Diversity (2006) Petition to List 12 Penguin Species Under the Endangered Species Act.

913. Thomas, T. (1986) L'effctif des oiseauxnicheurs de l'archipel de Pointe Geologie

(Terre Adelie) et son evolution au cours des trente denriers annees. L'Oiseau RFO vol. 56, p. 321-330.

914. Micol, T. and P. Jouventin. 2001. Long-term population trends in seven Antarctic seabirds at Point Geologie, Terre Adelie: Human impact compared with environmental change. Polar Biology 24: 175-185.

915. Kunkel, K., et al. (2009) Trends in Twentieth-Century U.S. Extreme Snowfall Seasons. Journal of Climate, vol 22, p. 6204-6217.

916. Houston, T. and Changnon, S. (2009) Characteristics of the top ten snowstorms at First-Order Stations in the U.S. Natural Hazards, vol. 48, p. 101-113.

917. Seager, R., et al. (2010) Northern Hemisphere winter snow anomalies: ENSO, NAO and the winter of 2009/10. GeophysicalResearch Letters, vol. 37, L14703, doi:10.1029/2010GL043830

918. Changnon,S. et al. (2006) Temporal and Spatial Characteristics of Snowstorms in the Contiguous United States. Journal of Applied Meteorology and Climatology, vol. 45, p. 1141-1157.

919. Wunsch, C. (2002) What Is the Thermohaline Circulation? Science, vol. 298, p. 1179-1180.

920. Hanawa,k. and Sugimoto, s., (2004)"Re-emergnce" area of winter sea surface temperature anomalies in the world's oceans. Geophysical Research Letters, vol. 31, L10303, doi:10.1029/2004GL019904, 2004

921. Liu, Z., Huang, B. (2000) Cause of tropical Pacific warming trend, Geophysical Research Letters, vol. 27(13), p. 1935-1938.

922. Diolaiuti, G., et al. (2011) Glacier retreat and climate change: Documenting the last 50 years of Alpine glacier history from area and geometry changes of Dosde Piazzi glaciers (Lombardy Alps, Italy). Progress in Physical Geography, vol. 35(2), p. 161–182.

923. Hodgson, D., and Bentley, M. (2012) Lake highstands in the Pensacola Mountains and Shackleton Range 4300–2250 cal. yr BP: Evidence of a warm climate anomaly in the interior of Antarctica. The Holocene, vol. 23, p. 388-397.

924. Crespin, E., et al. (2009) The 15th century Arctic warming in coupled model simulations with data assimilation. Climate of the Past, vol. 5, p. 389–401.

925. Smedsrud, L. et al. (2011) Recent wind driven high sea ice export in the Fram Strait contributes to Arctic sea ice decline. The Cryosphere Discuss., vol. 5, p. 1311–1334.

926. Doran, P., et al (2008) Hydrologic response to extreme warm and cold summers in the McMurdo Dry Valleys, East Antarctica. Antarctic Science, vol. 20 (5), p. 499–509.

927. MacDonald, G. (2007) Severe and sustained drought in southern California and the West:Present conditions and insights from the past on causes and impacts. Quaternary International 173–174 (2007) 87–100.

928. Kennett, D.J., Kennett, J.P., 2000. Competitive and cooperative responses to climatic instability in Southern California. American Antiquity, vol. 65, p. 379–395.

929. Shu, Q. et al. (2012) Sea Ice Trends in the Antarctic and their relationship to surface temperature during 1979-2009. Climate Dynamics, vol. 38, p. 2355-2363.

930. Trenberth, K. et al. (2011) Opinion: The damaging impact of Roy Spencer's science. http://wwwp.dailyclimate.org/tdc-newsroom/2011/09/spencer-faulty-science

931. Revkin, A. (2012) Peter Gleick Admits to Deception in Obtaining Heartland Climate Files. NY Times, Dot Earth, http://dotearth.blogs.nytimes.com/2012/02/20/peter-gleick-admits-to-deception-in-obtaining-heartland-climate-files/

932. The Canadian Press (2011) Scientists find herd of 'lost' caribou in Saskatchewan. http://www.ctvnews.ca/scientists-find-herd-of-lost-caribou-in-saskatchewan-1.728755

933. Schmidt, G. (2011) Lunchtime seminar on polar bears and Martha Stewart.

http://www.youtube.com/watch?v=fhi0II5Py2A

934.   Bard, E., et al. (2000) Solar irradiance during the last 1200 years based on cosmogenic nuclides. Tellus, vol. 52B, p. 985–992.

935.   Feulner, G. and Rahmstorf, S. (2010) On the effect of a new grand minimum of solar activity on the future climate on Earth. Geophysical Research Letters, vol. 37, doi:10.1029/2010GL042710.

936.   Easterling, D., et alo. (1997) Maximum and Minimum Temperature Trends for the Globe. Science. Science, vo. 277, p. 364-367.

937.   Lindzen, R., (2012) Global Warming: How to approach the science. February 22, 2012 seminar for England's House of Commons Committee.

938.   Appell, D. (2013) Whither Global Warming? Has It Slowed Dpwn? The Yale Forum on   Climate   Change   and   the   Media. http://www.yaleclimatemediaforum.org/2013/05/wither-global-warming-has-it-slowed-down/

939.   Schiermeier, Q., (2013) Climate models fail to 'predict' US droughts. Nature, vol. 496, p. 284.

940.   Abdussamatov, H., (2012) Bicentennial Decrease of the Total Solar Irradiance Leads to Unbalanced Thermal Budget of the Earth and the Little Ice Age. Applied Physics Research, vol. 4, p. 178-185.

941.   Dole, R. and Gordon, N. (1983) Persistent Anomalies of the Extratropical Northern Hemisphere Wintertome Circulation: Geographical Distribution and Regional Persistence Characteristics. Monthly Weather Review, vol. 111, p. 1567-1587.

942.   Schreiner, B. (2013) Mrs. Obama: Seek out those with different beliefs. Associated Press, May 11, 2013.

943.   Bertrand Russell, "A History of Western Philosophy", Simon & Schuster, 1972.

944.   Trenberth, K. and Hoar,T (1997) El Niño and climate change. Geophysical Research Letters, vol.. 24, p. 3057-3060.

945.   Trenberth, K. (2008) The Impact of Climate Change and Variability on Heavy Precipitation, Floods and Droughts. In the Encyclopedia of Hydrological Sciences.

946.   Monaghan, A. et al., (2008). Recent variability and trends of Antarctic near-surface temperature. J. Geophysical Research Letters, vol. 113, D04105 (2008)

947.   Greene, C.and Monger, B. (2012) An Arctic wild card in the weather. Oceanography, vol. 25, p.7–9, http://dx.doi.org/10.5670/oceanog.2012.58.

948.   Kerr, R. (2000) A North Atlantic Climate Pacemaker for the Centuries. Science, vol. 288, p. 1984-1985.

949.   Galielo, G, (1638) Discourses and Mathematical Demonstrations Relating to Two New Sciences

950.   Galielo, G, (1632) Dialogue Concerning the Two Chief World Systems: Ptolemaic and Copernican

951.   Marshall, C., et al. (2004) The impact of anthropogenic land-cover change on the Florida peninsula sea breezes and warm sensible weather. Mon. Weather Review., vo. 132, p.28–52.

952.   Wickham, T., et al. (2012) Comparison of cropland and forest surface temperatures across the conterminous United States. Agricultural and Forest Meteorology, vol. 166-167, p.137– 143.

953.   Swanson, K., (2013) Emerging selection bias in large-scale climate change simulations. Geophysical research Letters, doi: 10.1002/grl.50562

954.   Ramankutty, N.,(2006) Feedbacks between agriculture and climate: an illustration of potential unintended consequences of human land use activities. Global Planet. Change vol 54, p.76–93.

955.   Ramankutty, N.,(2006) Feedbacks between agriculture and climate: an illustration of potential unintended consequences of human land use activities. Global Planet.

Change vol 54, p.76–93.

956.   John P. Gagan, Alan Gerard, and John Gordon (December 2010) "A historical and statistical comparison of "Tornado Alley" to "Dixie Alley", " National Weather Digest, vol. 34, no. 2, pages 146-155; see especially page 146.

957.   Biello, D. (2013) What Role Does Climate Change Play in Tornadoes? Scientific American, May21, 2013

958.   Prof. Dan Shechtman 2011 Nobel Prize Chemistry Interview with ATS. YouTube.

959.   McGowan, C. (2007) Biofuel Could Eat Brazil's Savannas & Deforest the Amazon. Huffington Post. Spet. 14, 2007.

960.   Guidelines for Writing a Scientific Paper.
http://www.sci.sdsu.edu/~smaloy/MicrobialGenetics/topics/scientific-writing.pdf

961.   Gutting, G. (2011) On Experts and Global Warming. New York Times, July 12, 2011.

962.   Romm, J. (2013) Yes, ClimateChange is Worsening US Drought-NOAA report Needlessly Confuses the Issue. Climate Progress, April 12, 2013.

963.   South, D. (2011) Will afforestation in temperate zones warm the Earth? Journal of Horticulture and Forestry Vol. 3, p. 95-199.

964.   Yang, X., et al. (2011) Observed surface warming induced by urbanization in east China. Journal of Geophysical Research, vol. 116, D14113, doi:10.1029/2010JD015452

965.   Pielke, R. (2004) Assessing "Global Warming" with Surface Heat Content. Eos, vol. 85, 210-211

966.   Christy, J. , et al. (2009) Surface Temperature Variations in East Africa and Possible Causes. Journal of Climate, vol. 22, p. 3342-3358.

967.   Lean, J. and Rind, D. (2009) How will Earth's surface temperature change in future decades?. Geophysical ResearchLetters, vol. 36, L15708, doi:10.1029/2009GL038932

968.   Thorne, P., et al. (2005) Uncertainties in Climate Trends,: Lessons from Upper-Air Temperature Records. Bulletin of the American Meteorological Society. October 2005, 1437-1442

969.   Curry, J. (2011) Reasoning about climate uncertainty. Climatic Change, vol. 108, p. 723-732

970.   Pope,J. (2013) Quantifying uncertainty in climate science. Weather, vol. 68, p. 69

971.   Maslin, M.(2012) Uncertainty: Climate models at their limit? Nature, vol. 486, p.183–184

972.   Mahlstein, I. and Knutti, R. (2011) Ocean Heat Transport as a Cause for Model Uncertainty in Projected Arctic Warming. Journal of Climate, vol. 24, p. 1451-1462

973.   Shukla, J (2008) email:Future of the IPCC. 13 Feb 2008 .

974.   Hodson, D. et al, (2013) Identifying uncertainties in Arctic climate change projections. Climate Dynamic. Vol. 40, p. 2849–2865. DOI 10.1007/s00382-012-1512-z

975.   Buser, C. et al (2010) Biases and Uncertainty in Climate Projections. Scandinavian Journal of Statistics, vol. 37:, p.179–199.

976.   Pielke, R. (2012) Regional Climate Downscaling: What's the Point? EOS, vol. 93, p. 52-53.

977.   van der Ent, R. J, et al. (2010), Origin and fate of atmospheric moisture over continents, Water Resource Research, vol. 46, W09525, doi:10.1029/2010WR009127.

978.   Pielke, R. (2009) Short Circuiting The Scientific Process – A Serious Problem In The Climate Science Community.Pielke Research Group: News and Commentary, June 4, 2009.

979.   Hudson, P. (2009) Wht Happened to Global Warming. BBC News, October 9, 2009.
http://news.bbc.co.uk/2/hi/8299079.stm

980. Revkin, A. (2009) A climate scientist who engages Skeptics. Dot Earth, New York Times Novemeber 27, 2009.

981. Butler, D. (2003) Heatwave underlines climate-model failures. Nature, vol. 424, p. 867

982. Mann, M. (2010) Get the anti-science bent out of politics. Washington Post, Friday October 8, 2010.

983. Gianotti, R., et al. (2011). "Assessment of the Regional Climate Model Version 3 over the Maritime Continent Using Different Cumulus Parameterization and Land Surface Schemes." Journal of Climate, vol. 25, p.638–656.

984. Mann, M. (2012) Besieged by Climate Deniers, A Scientist Decides to Fight Back. Environment 360. April 12, 2012.

985. Overland, J. and Stabno, P. (2004) Is the Climate of the Bering Sea Warming and Affecting the Ecosystem? Eos, vol. 85.

986. Paul Valdes, 2011: Built for stability. Nature Geoscience Volume: 4, Pages: 414–416 DOI: doi:10.1038/ngeo1200 Published online26 June 2011

987. Curry, J. (2012) What can we learn from climate models? Part II, Posted to Climate Etc. March 1, 2012.

988. Zorita, E. (2009) Why I think that Michael Mann, Phil Jones and Stefan Rahmstorf should be barred from the IPCC process. Posted to Roger Pielke Jr.'s Blog, November 28, 2009

989. Soon, W. et al. (2003) Reconstructing Climatic and Environmental Changes of the Past 1000 Years: A Reappraisal. Energy & Environment

990. Soon, W. and Baiunas, (2003) Proxy climatic and environmental changes of the past 1000 years. Climate Research, vol. 23, p. 89–110.

991. The 14 USHCN stations were Bartlesville, Buffalo, Cherokee, Claremore, Enid, Guthrie, Jefferson, Meeker, Miami, Mutual, Okeene, Paul's Valley, Pawhuska, and Perry.

992. Mann, M. *(2008) Dire Predictions: Understanding Global Warming. DK Publishing Inc.*

993. Dai, A. (2012) The influence of the inter-decadal Pacific oscillation on US precipitation during 1923–2010. Climate Dynamics,DOI 10.1007/s00382-012-1446-5

994. Ronald Coase, https://en.wikipedia.org/wiki/Ronald_Coase

995. Kerr, R. (2013) Forecasting Regional Climate Change Flunks Its First Test. Science, vol. 339, p.638.

996. Sanchez-Lorenzo, A., et al. (2013) "Global and diffuse solar radiation in Spain: Building a homogeneous dataset and assessing their trends". Global and Planetary Change, vol. 100, p. 343–352.

997. Stampf, O. and Traufetter , G. (2013) Spiegel International, http://www.spiegel.de/international/world/interview-hans-von-storch-on-problems-with-climate-change-models-a-906721.html

998. Holzhauser, H., et al. (2005) Glacier and lake-level variations in west-central Europe over the last 3500 years. The Holocene, vol. 15, p. 789-801.

999. Liu, J., et al. (2012) Changes in the strength and width of the Hadley circulation since 1871. Climates of the Past Discussions, vol. 8, p. 695-713.

Made in the USA
Middletown, DE
15 October 2022